SURVEILLANCE IN AMERICA

SURVEILLANCE IN AMERICA

Critical Analysis of the FBI, 1920 to the Present

Ivan Greenberg

LEXINGTON BOOKS
Lanham • Boulder • New York • Toronto • Plymouth, UK

Published by Lexington Books
A wholly owned subsidiary of The Rowman & Littlefield Publishing Group, Inc.
4501 Forbes Boulevard, Suite 200, Lanham, Maryland 20706
www.rowman.com

10 Thornbury Road, Plymouth PL6 7PP, United Kingdom

British Library Cataloguing in Publication Information Available

Library of Congress Cataloging-in-Publication Data

The hardback edition of this book was previously cataloged by the Library of
Congress as follows:

Greenberg, Ivan, 1962-
  Surveillance in America : critical analysis of the FBI, 1920 to the present /
Ivan Greenberg.
      p. cm.
  Includes bibliographical references and index.
  1. United States. Federal Bureau of Investigation—History. 2. Subversive
activities—United States—History. 3. Criminal investigations—United
States—History. I. Title.
  HV8144.F43G743 2012
  363.250973—dc23

                                                      2012010397

ISBN: 978-0-7391-7247-6 (cloth : alk. paper)
ISBN: 978-0-7391-8971-9 (pbk. : alk. paper)
ISBN: 978-0-7391-7248-3 (electronic)

∞™ The paper used in this publication meets the minimum requirements of
American National Standard for Information Sciences—Permanence of Paper
for Printed Library Materials, ANSI/NISO Z39.48-1992.

Printed in the United States of America

To critics of government abuse of power, who risk a lot by asserting their voices.

Contents

Acknowledgments

I began writing this book as my previous study, *The Dangers of Dissent*, was in press. It took less time to write the second book than the first. Conversant in the historical literature, and skilled at obtaining FBI files under the Freedom of Information Act, I wrote the essays here without many obstacles in writing and research. Other obstacles were overcome with determination and perseverance. Several people read the work at different stages and made perceptive comments. Michael Ravnitzky read the manuscript and pointed me to some important spy documents he helped obtain and has put online. Dolores Greenberg, my mother and a historian, read several chapters and lent an ear as I discussed ideas for the study. The artist Dean Haspiel did the cover. This is the second cover he has done for me and I appreciate his vision interpreting the subject matter. At Lexington Books, a special thanks to my editor, Erin Walpole, who has remained very supportive.

Introduction

In 1953, the American government learned that some offices of U.S. diplomats in the Soviet bloc had been bugged with electronic listening devices. This revelation was not completely a surprise. Since 1940, the Federal Bureau of Investigation (FBI) had also bugged several foreign embassies in Washington, DC. As a result of the surveillance against U.S. diplomats, the Radio-Electrical Section of the FBI for the first time obtained the necessary technological capability to detect secret listening devices. The bureau began to conduct regular sweeps of its offices, as well as those at the White House and in Congress, as a precautionary counterintelligence measure.[1] The technology was rather primitive. It could take at least two days to fully sweep one room and was not fail-proof, as one official reported:

> As previously pointed out by me, the "room search" approach will not as a practical matter insure 100 percent against the presence of microphones since it is entirely possible to conceal microphones in such a way that they cannot be detected with present day equipment without substantial damage to wall surfaces, and, of course, the destruction of wall surfaces is not a practical approach.[2]

Special attention was directed to secure the office of the FBI director. We have this technical account of the first check of J. Edgar Hoover's work quarters.

> Accordingly, beginning on 4-6-53 and on such occasions thereafter as the Director's office space was available during the normal work day, listening tests were conducted to determine whether any radio beams could be detected as activating sources for listening devices. You will recall that the limitation to the normal work day arises from the fact that such activating radio beams would not be expected to be in operation after hours.

Moreover, the sweep included an "exhaustive search of all wall, ceiling, and floor space in the Director's immediate offices. No clandestine listening devices of any kind were found." Indeed, in early 1953 the FBI reported that no known bugs had been planted within the nation by foreign intelligence agencies.[3]

The FBI's attention also turned to detecting the potential wiretapping of its telephones. Hoover acknowledged in a memo: "Since it appears to be open season for wire tapping, I think regular checks should be made of office and home phones of Ex-Conf. [Executives Conference] & a Sac [Special Agent in Charge] & a Sac of Wash. Field. [Washington Field Office]"[4] The office and home phones of 13 top FBI officials immediately were inspected and no wiretaps ("resonant listening devices") were discovered. Hoover instructed subordinates to supervise these checks monthly. However, the inspections should not be predictable so a potential enemy could successfully adapt and adjust. "That the times of these checks be staggered in such a way that no definite pattern can be established on a recheck of the facilities."[5]

U.S. government leaders never before conducted regular anti-spying sweeps of their offices. Anxiety about surveillance now reached the inner circles of power. With the McCarthy-era Red Scare at its height, fear of surveillance could generate paranoia. While institutional leaders feared monitoring by overseas nation states, Americans began to fear surveillance at the hands of their own government. There was good reason for such fear.

The FBI engaged in massive domestic surveillance of Americans during the 20th century.

Surveillance in America builds on my previous book, *The Dangers of Dissent* (2010), which studied FBI conduct since 1965 through a prism of political policing. It continues a historical exploration of the FBI's attack on political speech and social action. I address surveillance as it is used by government for political purposes and as it is experienced by subjects. In recent years, the new field of surveillance studies explores many other dimensions, but it is well to remember, as David Lyon suggests, that "surveillance is always hinged to some specific purpose" and "usually involves relations of power in which watchers are privileged."[6] With the aid of government spy files, we can view the activity of top FBI officials as they develop surveillance practices and maneuver to implement them. In this sense, the book is an expose: It makes visible what previously was hidden. A critical scholarly gaze is cast on official power, which for years trampled on the rights of innocent people.

Several chapters engage questions about government power and the production and distribution of information, and more broadly, of culture. This includes efforts to manipulate the media and to impose a "terrorism" framework as the legal basis of domestic security investigations. Almost all the subjects of FBI watch considered here—political radicals, trade unionists, immigrants, African Americans, organizers of the unemployed, anti-war protestors, journalists, and American historians—were defined as enemies and viewed as contributing nothing to society. Their experiences under surveillance are explored from 1920 to the present using primary research materials obtained under the Freedom of Information Act (FOIA). I cite material from 59 declassified FBI files. These documents, despite some limitations due to official redactions, can serve as an extraordinary source for illuminating government misconduct.

The G-men depicted in these pages are not heroes but rather are closer to villains who abused power to fight change in society. The bureau was not a renegade agency or a "rogue elephant" functioning without support from the leaders of the two-party system. The federal government under both Republican and Democratic control fought political formations that challenged its supremacy. But, critically, much of this surveillance was done secretly, beyond the knowledge of the general population which did not have the opportunity to express approval or disapproval of political spying. In a democracy, is it possible for popular democratic governance of surveillance systems? Who gets to define the nature of political threats? The working definitions developed by J. Edgar Hoover (and his successors as director) were based on very narrow political views. During the Cold War, the FBI directed efforts to contain a broad range of political expression, not just groups and individuals associated with Communism. After the Cold War, the federal role to limit political expression continued under the banner of fighting terrorism. Generally, the creation of a "culture of insecurity" helped limit what was considered acceptable and possible in the society.[7] While a small segment of the public engaged in alternative politics, the rest of the populace seemed to be influenced negatively by scare tactics that shuttered popular dialogue and deliberation.[8]

Over the last decade, the rapid expansion of the national surveillance state has threatened civil liberties in ways never before anticipated. The administrations of George W. Bush and Barack Obama, with congressional backing, sanctioned broad spying on Americans using advanced technology which intruded on privacy in deleterious ways. How did it get this bad? Historical study can help frame an understanding of how the U.S. over time transformed into its current condition. I focus on the FBI because while it is not the sole entity comprising the surveillance state, it is the oldest and most important agency to patrol the domestic political sphere. My critical analysis of the FBI over more than 90 years challenges many popular perceptions about the relationship between dissent and the state in the U.S. For example, was speech and protest "protected" by the Constitution if government, through the FBI, extensively surveilled it? How free were Americans to criticize and assemble in opposition to their government? Is the state a repressive social actor that discriminated against people who espoused unpopular views?

Answers to these questions can be framed after rigorous study of FBI practices. It is my contention that relatively little political expression outside the mainstream of American politics truly was protected. Americans who challenged their leaders often faced sanctions. The American state actively fought movements for social change employing methods that are not permissible under the law and find no support in the American constitution. The state worked outside the "rule of law." For some people, who are conditioned to accept whatever their rulers say and do, these conclusions will appear shocking. But for many others these conclusions merely will confirm their existing beliefs. My contribution is to ground these conclusions with historical evidence gathered through extensive research in recently declassified spy files. These government documents demonstrate in new ways not only the nature of surveillance but also that its scope has been far greater than most people recognize. To be sure, at different times the government faced select internal threats, but how it defined these threats and responded to them remains a subject of intense debate. Massive domestic surveillance only can undermine the functioning of a robust democracy.

The Beginning of Political Spying

In 1908, the U.S. Department of Justice established the Bureau of Investigation (renamed the Federal Bureau of Investigation in 1935). President Theodore Roosevelt hoped the new bureau would enforce the law against powerful corporate interests and work to end political corruption in government. In its initial formation, the BOI spent most of its time on interstate commerce crimes as well as "moral" crimes such as prostitution.[9] While this new federal detective force was conceived as Progressive reform, it changed its focus with the outbreak of World War I (WWI) in Europe in 1914 and the success of the Bolshevik Revolution in 1917. These two events brought loyalty, political ideology, and security issues to the forefront, and the bureau began to view itself as the chief protector against crimes directed at the United States.

As a result of WWI, the FBI began to investigate the loyalty of recent immigrants, especially those from the Axis Power nations (Germany and Austria-Hungry) and their sympathizers (Ireland). The Woodrow Wilson administration feared enemy recruitment for espionage and sabotage within America's immigrant communities. Moreover, once the U.S. entered the European conflict Congress passed the Espionage Act (1917) and Sedition Act (1918) criminalizing anti-war speech and resulting in more than 2,000 convictions. The emerging Red Scare also received congressional sanction with passage of the Immigration Act (1918) authorizing the deportation of immigrants ("aliens") who were members of anarchist or other revolutionary groups. By 1919, FBI files listed about 80,000 people or groups as threats. More than 6,000 radicals were arrested during the notorious Palmer Raids; 556 people were deported.[10]

The focus on national security "government protection," instead of government corruption, constituted a major shift. And, instead of investigating corporate antitrust crimes, the bureau began to act against working-class movements and labor unions, such as the Industrial Workers of the World (IWW). A wave of political violence in 1919 (led by anarchists) prompted the Justice Department to consolidate its spying activities into a special Radical Division headed by the young J. Edgar Hoover, which functioned as an interdivisional task force within the bureau.[11] Hoover, thus, came to head the government's anti-radical campaign, a responsibility he assumed until his death in 1972. Hoover changed the name of the Radical Division to the General Intelligence Division (GID) in 1920 to conceal its political ideology. The designation "general intelligence" suggested neutrality—spying without bias. Fighting radicals no longer was official state policy.

Spying became a permanent condition rather than merely periodic. Record keeping, as well as disruptive "counter-intelligence" tactics, focused not only on American communists and anarchists but also extended over time to many other radicals as well as liberals. It seems rather obvious, though as yet not fully appreciated, that the emergence of political intelligence monitoring occurred within the context of the rise of the American industrial economy. Scholars have suggested several other motives to explain why the FBI turned its attention to containing radicalism: anxiety and insecurity about social mobility; nativism and ethnocentrism; and popular obsession with irrational conspiracy theories. It is argued that government Red Scares were a response to calm public hysteria rather than a creation largely of the government itself to advance a conservative political agenda. I adopt a different view by extending the interpretation of Regin Schmidt, who sees the origins of the political intelligence system as part of the centralization of power in the federal government. He believes "the role of the state was to support, stabilize and defend the emerging corporate order against 'irresponsible' competition, economic waste and inefficiency as well as social unrest and threats to the status quo." He refers to the bureau's conduct after 1919 as "part of the federalization of social control in the form of political surveillance."[12]

During the early 1920s, surveillance focused on many groups with special attention to organizing by the working class. As historian Richard Gid Powers writes, "During the [Warren] Harding Administration the bureau became even more aggressive in working against labor in its struggles with capital, and it regularly engaged in red-smearing to brand the labor disturbances of the early 1920s as communist-inspired."[13] By 1923, an estimated 450,000 people were included in spy files. Although an official list of subjects of investigation does not exist in the public domain, the net was cast wide with a bias against the Left and minority groups, especially African Americans.[14]

In 1924, the Justice Department "reformed" the FBI to reduce political spying. Attorney General Harlan Stone, a critic of the Palmer Raids, instructed Hoover, who just had been named head of the bureau, that the BOI should "not be concerned with political or other opinions of individuals. It is concerned only with their conduct and then only with such conduct as is forbidden by the laws of the United States."[15] However, this change was not written into formal guidelines and did not involve congressional action. While the bureau scaled back some anti-labor and anti-radical surveillance, the government still engaged in control of social movements. As Athan G. Theoharis concludes in *The FBI and American Democracy* (2004): "Bureau agents continued to monitor radical activists and organizations but disguised their sources reporting that the information that they had collected had been volunteered by patriotic citizens or provided by 'confidential informants.'"[16] Progressive historians are correct to minimize the degree of FBI reform during the 1920s and early 1930s. Powers describes the contours of this historiographical debate:

> Was Hoover telling the truth? Did he really end the Bureau's intelligence gathering on radical groups and individuals? Later historians, incensed at Hoover's repressive campaigns against radicals during the Cold War and Vietnam eras and his sorry record on civil rights, have poured [sic] over the files of the Bureau during the twenties, looking for evidence that Hoover disobeyed [Attorney General] Stone's edicts, secretly continuing to gather information on radicals. They have been able to find some instances, triumphantly trumpeted as proof that the Bureau was forever and always bent on political repression, in the twenties as well as later. But while the Bureau did, in a handful of cases, gather information on individuals not under any investigation for federal offenses, it was always when ordered to do so by the White House.[17]

It seems irrelevant whether the impetus for spying derived from the White House or the FBI. In either case, the American government still engaged in policing to contain movements for social change.

In 1936, Hoover urged President Franklin D. Roosevelt to authorize new political intelligence gathering on subversive threats, especially organizations associated with Fascism, Communism, and organized labor. Investigations should identify threats in key areas such as industry, governmental affairs, the armed forces, and educational institutions. Theoharis refers to the New Deal's initiation of a "new intelligence paradigm" that transformed the FBI into a proactive "intelligence agency that would seek to acquire advance information" on noncriminal threats.[18] While

Roosevelt initiated historic social programs helping to establish a safety net for the "forgotten man" and the "one-third of a nation" suffering distress, his FBI aggressively monitored collective organizing by this segment of the population. Roosevelt and Hoover apparently formed a "close partnership" and Roosevelt expressed "unwavering support" for the bureau.[19]

Why a liberal president supported the expansion of FBI spying is not entirely clear. Generally, American presidents seemed to develop uneven relationships with Hoover. On the one hand, intimidation played a factor: Hoover secretly collected information on presidents and other leaders in the executive branch and many feared to challenge his power, let alone fire him. During the New Deal, for example, the FBI started intelligence files on leading liberals such as Labor Secretary Frances Perkins and First Lady Eleanor Roosevelt.[20] But apart from intimidation, modern presidents supported many of the goals of FBI policing in order to reduce the power and influence of radicals even though presidents may have been unaware of the excessive methods employed by the bureau to achieve these ends.

The expansion of surveillance during the Second New Deal proved lasting, leading by World War II to the use of wiretaps, break-ins, and mail-opening. Electronic surveillance often required break-ins to plant listening devices. In 1940, the FBI began to wiretap the German, Japanese, Italian, and Soviet embassies. But the targets were not limited to foreign entities on U.S. soil. "The shift in FBI wiretapping from national defense to political surveillance began within a year after Franklin Roosevelt issued his secret wiretapping directive in May 1940," notes Theoharis. While Roosevelt had required prior review and approval of all wiretaps by the attorney general, the FBI did not follow this process in political surveillance cases.[21] (The FBI's Electronic Surveillance Card file, an index of wiretaps and bugs carried out under Hoover, contains at least 13,500 entries.[22])

The FBI's expansion included the development in 1939 of plans for the indefinite detention of thousands of "subversives" during a national emergency. FBI officials assembled the so-called Custodial Detention List without outside supervision. During World War II, the agency's size also grew: The number of special agents tripled from 1,596 in 1941 to 4,886 in 1944. They undertook extensive loyalty investigations of German Americans and Italian Americans.[23] A special program named RACON focused on the wartime loyalty of African Americans.[24] Additionally, in 1940 the FBI initiated the large Plant Informant Program to surveil labor and radical activities in the industrial work sector. Surveillance conducted in conjunction with thousands of American Legion members focused as well on draft evasion. Historian James T. Sparrow writes, "Without the mass surveillance of everyday life instilled by government to safeguard morale, the job of policing draft compliance would have been far more difficult."[25] Bureau eyes (and ears) also turned to the Hollywood motion-picture industry to identify communist influence. In 1942, the establishment of the program named COMPIC, which lasted until 1956, formed an integral part of broader bureau efforts to combat left-wing influence on public opinion and culture.[26]

As the nation faced the postwar period, the FBI broadened its autonomy by conducting intelligence operations no one else in government knew existed. The bureau's supremacy in the areas of both domestic law enforcement and national security became evident with the revival of a public Red Scare during the early Cold War years. While the FBI played a leading role in promoting the Scare, it, of course, was not the only government actor: Members of Congress (such as Senator Joseph McCarthy of Wisconsin and Representative Richard Nixon of California), as well as officials at all levels of government, touted the grave danger posed by the Red Menace. The FBI fed information to the House UnAmerican Activities Committee (HUAC) during the late 1940s and throughout the early 1950s, although it sometimes set conditions for its cooperation. In this sense, it became complicit in the domestic blacklist against alleged communists. Loyalty investigations of federal employees also occupied its time. As one indication of its large surveillance and intelligence-gathering capacity, in 1950 the FBI prepared about 6,500 index cards daily from their reports on liberal and radical political activity.[27]

Since the mid-1940s, the FBI began collecting intelligence on the sexual orientation and affairs of elected leaders and other prominent citizens. Hoover kept a secret file in his office on these matters, and members of Congress, cabinet officers, and even presidents and their families were subject to this type of snooping. Information on "immoral conduct" (homosexuality, adultery, prostitution) systematically was assembled as derogatory intelligence to be used for political gain. For example, Hoover used as leverage (intimidation) reports about Presidents Dwight D. Eisenhower's and John F. Kennedy's personal sexual conduct.[28] The likelihood that Hoover himself was gay, or at least shunned sexual intimacy with women for most of his life, as recently explored in Clint Eastwood's movie, *J. Edgar* (2011), suggested that the FBI's sexual surveillance was as much a personal matter for the director as having any usefulness for protecting the nation against internal threats.[29]

The depth of the Red Scare was reflected in the Attorney General's official list of "subversive" organizations, based on FBI investigations, which included 254 separate groups during the early 1950s. The list compiled by HUAC referenced 624 groups.[30] The number of people investigated during the 1950s may have reached nearly half a million even though FBI sources indicated CP membership was limited to about 24,000 in 1953.[31] When the U.S. Supreme court seemed certain to strike down the Smith Act (1940), which had resulted in the arrest and imprisonment of leading communists, the FBI in 1956 initiated the infamous COINTELPRO (Counter Intelligence Program). Theoharis describes the Program as marking "a major departure in the FBI's role, the abandonment of a law enforcement mission for a course of political containment and the willful reliance on more aggressive tactics in part for the purpose of influencing public opinion."[32] Indeed, near the end of the 1950s the bureau's Red Scare propaganda machine proceeded as if the threat was enormous, although officials privately acknowledged that popular support for domestic communism rapidly had declined. In 1958, an internal Inspection Division Report located only 8,150 CP members:

> Communist Party (CP) membership declined past fiscal year from 11,504 to 8,150. Case load decline not due to lessening

security threat but to factionalism in Party causing withdrawal from active membership, less active participation in organizations and front groups, tenor of recent court decisions, rising tide of public apathy and complacency, legislation, propaganda, etc.[33]

When the McCarthy-era Red Scare ended, the FBI's secret political surveillance continued in full form joined by city police "red squads" which engaged in political intelligence gathering.[34] In 1961, Hoover told Congress: "Some 200 known or suspected communist front and communist-infiltrated organizations are now under investigation by the FBI. Many of these fronts are national in scope with chapters in various cities."[35] As social movements grew during the 1960s, the bureau responded by expanding COINTELPRO to address "racial matters" (black power and black civil rights); white hate groups (such as the Ku Klux Klan); Trotskyite Socialists; and the New Left protest movement. By 1967, the Internal Security Division at the Justice Department received about 150 reports and memoranda daily from the FBI on "organizations and individuals engaged in agitational activity."[36] Between 1960 and 1974, FBI Headquarters developed more than 500,000 domestic intelligence files, which were augmented by files started in local field offices. By the mid-1970s, the FBI held about six million dossiers on Americans. The government feared radical social change and employed secret methods to curtail it. COINTELPRO ran more than 2,300 disruptive operations.[37]

Two related "scares" emerged in American politics by the late 1960s: a New Left Scare and a Black Power Scare. These scares, while no longer focused on communism, engendered illegal FBI spying and lasted, more or less, until the resignation of President Richard Nixon in 1974. Government records reveal a large volume of illegal surveillance practices in two areas—wiretaps and break-ins conducted without warrants—directed against activists associated with Students for a Democratic Society (SDS) and the Black Panther Party (BPP). In contrast to the 1950s, the FBI now feared the beginnings of a radical revolution. In their view, domestic Communism had formed a subversive force but never posed a popular threat to legal and political authorities. The protest movements of the 1960s (and early 1970s) challenged government authority and societal stability in ways the nation had not experienced since the Civil War. I discuss this view more fully in chapter 4 by looking at the speeches of FBI Directors L. Patrick Gray III and Clarence M. Kelley. Both spoke at length about how the nation faced a formidable revolutionary challenge.

This sentiment was also expressed at the local level. For example, an FBI memo from June 3, 1968, expressed concern about a "revolution" in Syracuse, NY. The FBI cited three sources to warn headquarters that "members of SDS are in the process of attempting to obtain and stockpile arms and explosives, primarily for the purpose of starting what they refer to as 'revolution' at Syracuse, NY, during the summer of 1968. This revolution is supposed to be timed to take place on the occasion of a race riot which the organization is allegedly attempting to bring about during the summer. Informant could furnish no timetable."[38]

In this environment, the FBI placed warrantless wiretaps against both SDS and the BPP with the knowledge of the U.S. Justice Department. In a long memo, DOJ officials provided a "summary of the content of the electronic surveillance" conducted at the national office of SDS in Chicago during the last seven months of 1969. This time period was critical in SDS history as the organization began to split into factions with the Weathermen as the dominant force.

> The logs reveal the names, addresses and phone numbers of a great many members and contacts of the Weathermen. They also reveal the time and dates of meetings, activities, demonstrations and speeches plus they give one an insight into the internal structure and policy of the organization. . . . Most of the conversations recorded in the NO [national office] deal with day to day affairs. The NO does a great deal of printing for the BPP, the Young Lords, and various other groups and people. The SDS is also constantly raising bail money, money for everyday expenses and money for projected trips from various sources who are set out in the logs. Some prominent names and organizations are mentioned as sources.[39]

BPP leaders Bobby Rush, Bobby Seale, and David Hilliard were overheard on the SDS wiretaps. The FBI also monitored the telephones at BPP headquarters in Oakland and Berkeley, California, and in Chicago and New York City. The FBI worried about alliances between SDS and the Panthers. On the SDS phones, "The conversation to and from the Black Panther offices deal mainly with SDS printing up materials for the BP's."[40] Of equal interest to the government were calls to SDS from draft resisters and soldiers in the military. The FBI began to worry about SDS influence in high schools. "The SDS is not only attempting to organize the workers and colleges but also the high schools. Quite a number of calls are received from high school students and teachers regarding either the setting up of chapters or the obtaining of information or speakers. One of the National Staff is delegated the high school area specifically."[41]

SDS suspected the FBI tapped their phones but did not try to conceal their activities. "Many calls indicate that the parties either know or assume that their phones are tapped. Even so, the NO continues to furnish names, addresses, plans, and internal information over the phones. They make no effort to disguise their policy."[42]

The volume of political intelligence gathered on SDS/ Weathermen and the BPP was enormous. It is impossible at this stage in research to ascertain the total size of FBI files on each group and its members. We do know that by 1974 FBI files on the Weather Underground Organization totaled about 90,000 pages.[43] Other groups associated with the New Left also amassed large files. Recently, the FBI estimated they held about 20,000 pages on the activities of the Yippies (Youth International Party) in New York City.[44] However, the files on the Panthers were significantly larger. Again, we have data for New York City, where the FBI gathered about 300,000 pages on the BPP.[45] How does this compare to the size of the files on the Old Left? First, there was a major difference in duration. Surveillance of SDS/Weathermen and the Panthers did not exceed more than a single decade, while surveillance of the CP and the Socialist Workers Party (SWP) lasted for many decades. The FBI's CP files were estimated to be as large as 26 million pages.[46] The intelligence on the Socialist Workers Party totaled at least 8 million pages.[47]

During the mid-1970s, a second attempt to "reform" the FBI took place to limit spying in politics. The U.S. Senate Church Committee hearings in 1975 and 1976 on abuse of power by the intelligence community exposed years of misconduct. Critics of FBI surveillance, such as Senator Walter Mondale (D-MN), helped lift the veil of secrecy on political policing practices. (See Textbox 1.) For the first time, the Justice Department imposed guidelines on the FBI (the Levi Guidelines) to specify their spying authority. Under President Jimmy Carter, significant reform took place and the number of investigations dropped precipitously. The FBI was instructed to investigate political groups only if they engaged in violent acts. The FBI would investigate "terrorism"—not "subversion"—a change with enormous implications.

Textbox 1

On November 19, 1975, Senator Walter Mondale (D-MN) made the following critical comments about the FBI during hearings of the U.S. Senate Select Committee to Study Governmental Operations with Respect to Intelligence Activities (Church Committee).

Yesterday, this committee heard some of the most disturbing testimony that can be imagined in a free society. We heard evidence that for decades the institutions designed to enforce the laws and Constitution of our country have been engaging in conduct that violates the law and the Constitution. We heard that the FBI, which is part of the Department of Justice, took justice into its own hands by seeking to punish those with unpopular ideas. We learned that the chief law enforcement agency in the Federal Government decided that it did not need laws to investigate and suppress the peaceful and constitutional activities of those whom it disapproved.

We heard testimony that the FBI, to protect the country against those it believed had totalitarian political views, employed the tactics of totalitarian societies against American citizens. We heard that the FBI attempted to destroy one of our greatest leaders in the field of civil rights and then replace him with one of the FBI's choosing.

From the evidence the committee has obtained, it is clear that the FBI for decades has conducted surveillance over the personal and political activities of millions of Americans. Evidently, no meeting was too small, no group too insignificant to escape their attention. It did not seem to matter whether the politics of these Americans were legal or radical or whether the participants were well known or obscure. It did not matter whether the information was intimate and personal. The FBI created indexes, more commonly called enemy lists, of thousands of Americans and targeted many of the Americans on these lists for special harassment. Hundreds of thousands of Americans were victims of this surveillance program. Most of this was done in secret. Much of it was kept from Congress and the Justice Department and all of it from the American people. No one outside the FBI has ever had an opportunity to know and appreciate the full extent of the domestic surveillance program that was then being conducted.

However, FBI reform again did not prove lasting. In fact, when former California Governor Ronald Reagan defeated Carter in the 1980 election, FBI policies and procedures began to change. Reagan revived aggressive FBI spying within the new terrorism framework for investigations. Rather than limit investigations to political acts of violence, the FBI also considered violent speech by groups or individuals sufficient to activate surveillance. As in the past, political spying became fairly routine. While the full scope of this surveillance has not yet been exposed, enough evidence of such monitoring has surfaced to conclude that under Reagan the reform of the bureau had been undone. In a major change, the bureau began to label peaceful dissidents as "terrorists" to undermine their legitimacy and to scare the public about progressive organizing.[48]

Ironically, the legal framework used to justify surveillance expanded vastly in the post-COINTELPRO period. Much of what previously was done outside the law now had been legalized. That is, the FBI sought surveillance warrants from federal judges; such requests *never* were turned down. Since the 1990s, successive presidents (Bush, Clinton, Bush, Obama) expanded FBI power retaining the distorted terrorist paradigm to conduct political policing. Well before 9/11, the FBI criminalized many forms of dissent. For example, under President Bill Clinton the FBI experienced one of its greatest expansions in budgetary and personnel terms, and the number of terrorist investigation increased dramatically. The Terror Scare after 9/11, officially known as the "war on terror," did not involve fear of political revolution. In fact, it largely did not involve fear of U.S. social movements, at least in official rhetoric. The primary enemy became Islamic radicalism rooted overseas but with homegrown adherents. Still, a broad range of legal and peaceful protest came under scrutiny, as I discuss in chapter 6. This included antiwar and anti-globalization protesters, demonstrators at the Democratic and Republican national conventions, as well as what some are calling a new "Green Scare": government efforts to suppress the environmental and animal rights movements by labeling them "eco-terrorists."

Literature Review

The history of the FBI is constantly changing. To an extent, this is true of all historical topics. As the old truism goes, "Every generation writes its own history." Revisionists are always at work digging in the archives and producing new scholarship with new interpretations. As a result, there is a "new" social history and a "new" political or economic or military history. But when we consider the FBI, the process of change in historical knowledge is greater than for most other topics. Why? The FBI holds several billion pages of primary source documents and the ongoing availability of new elements of this information as a result of Freedom of Information Act (FOIA) requests and declassification requires constant revision of what we know. The sheer scope of the records held by the FBI is mind-boggling. In 2003, the bureau admitted possessing some 4.5 billion pages of material.[49] By 2006, only about 6 million pages had been released

under the FOIA. Let's make the point again: 6 million pages declassified out of 4.5 billion. At the same time, the routine destruction of FBI files remained a serious problem. In 2009, the FBI
director told Congress that the bureau held only about 2 billion
pages of paper records.[50] So what happened to about 2.5 billion
pages between 2003 and 2009?

The FOIA is not the only means for FBI record declassification. Old records voluntarily are transferred to the National Archives if they are deemed to have historical value. By 2011, the
FBI had sent the Archives about 35 million pages of material.[51]
However, much of this material remains unavailable for public
use. As Michael Ravnitzky, who has used the FOIA for more
than 20 years to obtain FBI files, notes: "Ironically, FBI files sent
to the National Archives are frequently less available for public
inspection. NARA keeps secret the subjects or titles of FBI files
transferred from the FBI to NARA."[52]

The primary source material to write the history of the FBI still
largely is hidden from view. A few years ago, Theoharis, the dean
of FBI scholars, noted the FBI's resistance to openness—he called
it a "culture of secrecy"—probably made it impossible for a comprehensive FBI history ever to be written.[53] That may be so. But,
in recent years important FBI records are being requested under
the FOIA by individuals and public interest organizations. New
dimensions of FBI activity are being exposed for the first time. In
sum, the historical literature on the FBI is a work in progress.

Unfortunately, not many scholars write in this field. Only
seven writers—Theoharis, Powers, Claire A. Culleton, Kenneth O'Reilly, James Kirkpatrick Davis, and co-authors Ward
Churchill and Jim Vander Wall—have published more than a
single book on the bureau.[54] That does not mean that writers
who compose only one book do not produce excellent work.
Recent quality scholarship by Regin Schmidt, David H. Price,
Steve Rosswurm, and David Cunningham has enhanced our
understanding of the Hoover era.[55] Overall, the study of the
post-Hoover period generally remains beyond focus. In his most
recent book, *Abuse of Power* (2011), Theoharis reexamines the
Hoover era with an eye toward the post-9/11 present. Since the
mid-1970s, he has worked extensively with FBI records: hun-

dreds of thousands of pages obtained under the FOIA. He believes current FBI practices ignore the lessons of the past. "As in the case of the FBI's World War Two and cold war investigations of suspected subversives, the FBI's post-9/11 counterterrorist investigations resulted in very few prosecutions." Secrecy and lack of accountability have not served the FBI's interest in capturing either spies or terrorists. Theoharis concludes by noting: "[T]he seamy side of cold war surveillance and secrecy policy has been ignored—that ambitious, if sincerely motivated, presidents and intelligence agency officials, if granted broad discretion to monitor suspected terrorists, would once again abuse that power and promote a culture of lawlessness."[56]

The *Journal of American History* published a roundtable discussion on the history of terrorism in the U.S. shortly before the 10th anniversary of 9/11. Beverly Gage, author of a recent book on political violence during the First Red Scare (1919-1920), noted that U.S. historians rarely address the history of counterterrorism policy or official definitions of it. "Despite the decades-old call to 'bring the state back in,' perhaps the dissident rebel holds still greater allure as a subject of study than the elite policy actor."[57] Meanwhile, Ann Larabee, editor of the *Journal for the Study of Radicalism*, noted the dearth of scholarly attention to the role of government informers in fomenting conflict and mayhem. "The drive to establish the political consistency of terrorist groups—to maintain a vision of their pure intention—has led scholars to overlook the state's role in providing inspiration and tools for violence. The *agents provocateur* demonstrates the close linkage between terrorist ensembles and state power."[58]

I have tried to offer insight into both these topics. In a recent article in *Radical History Review* ("The FBI and the Making of the Terrorist Threat"), I addressed how the American government came to view peaceful and legal activity as "terrorism" over a 40-year period beginning in the early 1970s. The FBI no longer categorized radical political activity as "subversion," as in the past, but began to associate it with violence. At first, this change was embraced primarily by the executive branch via the FBI, but then spread over time throughout the other coordinate branches of the government. Thus, the 9/11 attacks did not create the terrorist threat but certainly elevated it in the minds of both poli-cymakers and the general population.[59] Second, the role of the undercover informer was a major topic in *The Dangers of Dissent*. Their officially sanctioned behavior formed a major determinant of the degree of danger dissidents faced when they spoke in politics or participated in organized action. The informer again appears throughout this current study in different capacities be-cause until very recently the government viewed them as more effective and efficient than other forms of spying.

The Good Citizen Informs

Before providing an overview of the book's chapters, it is useful to discuss in more detail the role of informers because the state's surveillance system depended on their labor to provide an in-side view of oppositional political activity. There are two main types of FBI surveillance—human (HUMINT) and electronic (ELSUR)—and until the 21st century people constituted the sin-gle greatest intelligence resource. Informers attended meetings, gathered literature and other internal documents within groups, engaged in social relations taking notes on subjects, and even be-came political leaders. The informant corps included convicted felons who worked for the FBI to reduce their criminal charges. Moreover, people agreed to inform because of monetary incen-tives, personal animosities, or political allegiances.[60]

In 1975, the FBI admitted deploying about 50,000 informers in security cases during the prior twenty years. Scholars believe the number may be significantly higher.[61] The bureau used in-formants in the vast majority of COINTELPRO investigations, while using electronic surveillance much less often. Monitoring phone calls or conversations via bugs required many hours of la-bor and specialized equipment and was not as useful. Informers were able to report on face-to-face conversations and sometimes took photographs of people and protests. Personal interactions could serve as an informal method of interrogation when inform-ers asked subjects scripted questions prepared by their handlers. Informers inside the homes or offices of a subject could report on the surroundings: pictures on walls and personal tastes. Such intimate details could be used in designing counter-intelligence operations. Informers also gathered information in a subject's network of relations.

During the early Cold War the FBI began to issue special research monographs—about 200 between 1947 and 1960—to advance surveillance knowledge within its ranks. In "Stool Pigeon or Loyal Citizen?" (1952), agents were instructed how to overcome popular objections about snitching both within communist circles and among the broader American populace. In order to recruit informers, agents should stress it was loyal, patriotic service. "To stool pigeon [for your nation] is a good thing; it is to return good with good, kindness with kindness, life with life. It is gratitude. . . . Communists are guilty of gross distortion when they describe it in any other way." This monograph served as internal, motivational propaganda.[62] In a second edition, the FBI noted: "It is the consensus of all Agents that the 'stool pigeon' objection is one of the most difficult, if not the most difficult objection, to overcome in the development of a security informant."[63]

In "Pretexts and Cover Techniques" (1956), the FBI detailed ruses both informers and undercover agents could use to pursue investigative objectives. Pretexts helped operatives conceal the true purpose of inquiry. "Like an actor, the Agent should know his role," the FBI wrote. The undercover operative should pay attention to small details as they assumed fictional identities. "If an Agent is pretending to be a fisherman, the pretext should be carried out during the fishing season with the proper clothes and fishing equipment. If using the pretext of being an insurance salesman, the Agent should carry an insurance manual with the necessary rate charts and policy data." Research about subjects of investigation may be required. "Pretexts which tie in with subjects' activities or interest have a greater chance of succeeding. The use of a dialect or expressions familiar to subjects is helpful in some cases."[64]

In "Unusual Investigative Techniques" (1961), the FBI leadership once again reminded its personnel about context when assuming undercover identities. "[D]isguise designed to blend into an environment in order to conduct a discreet surveillance" included "clothing and objects to visually assist in carrying out the disguise." Yet even with such ruses, operatives encountered difficulties. In the FBI's view, American citizens fell for their traps more easily than recent immigrants, who might hold suspicious attitudes toward outsiders to their enclaves. "Experience has demonstrated that frequently it is difficult to obtain any information in large city neighborhoods which contain a preponderance of recent immigrants or first-generation Americans." [65]

It was not always the number of informants deployed that mattered but their particular placement and access. In 1947, the FBI leadership met in a special Executives Conference[66] and discussed infiltration of the CP in New York City. An official recommendation suggested "buying" a top Party official.

> One informant highly placed in the Party in New York would be of far more real value to the Bureau than all the other informants combined. We don't need more informants; we need *good* informants who can give us real quality. From a purely dollars and cents standpoint, considering that we are spending approaching $5,000,000 per year on Communist investigations, it would represent a profitable investment to pay a member of the Communist "inner circle" $1,000,000 a year to give us the inside picture which we only partially get now from any source by scratching around the periphery. While such a payment to an informant is, of course, absurd, I do think we should start thinking in terms of $25,000 or $50,000 or even more with a view to "buying" a top Party functionary.[67]

The FBI not only infiltrated political groups by recruiting from within the existing membership. They also worked from the outside by enrolling their own people as members. These "human assets" gathered information and participated in organizational activity to influence the content of speech and protest.[68] In some cases, they worked to inhibit political activity by creating divisions within or between groups. Informers engaged in crimes or other disreputable acts to discredit subjects creating an unfavorable public image of protest activity. In its most extreme form, informers advocated political violence and acted in militant and radical ways to entrap activists. This behavior stood outside the rule of law. Americans do not expect that government operatives secretly promote a particular set of politics and work to curtail political activity with which it disagrees. There is no place in constitutional culture for government political harassment. Yet, the state engaged in this type of behavior for decades and tried to hide their conduct from the public.[69]

Informers sometimes made surveillance conspicuous or overt, a disruptive technique to generate paranoia. A subject's awareness of surveillance might result in their limiting activism. An agent reported in 1970 about the New Left: "Informant has also indicated that the majority of the SMC group [Student Mobilization Committee] is paranoid concerning the police informants and suspects everyone at USC [University of South Carolina] of being an informant. Informant stated that he believes this attitude has kept the majority of students from becoming involved in dissident activities."[70] In Chicago, the bureau's aggressive pursuit of Weathermen fugitives in 1971 did not always result in finding subjects but the spread of paranoia hurt New Left organizing. An agent noted: "[I]ncreasing paranoia among the underground—This is serving to disrupt their organization and creating distrust of their support apparatus. This is preventing their taking any effective steps to organize a following."[71]

The use of informers within groups could be manipulated according to the "snitch-jacketing" technique. The FBI tried to create the false impression that particular activists worked for them in order to undermine the subjects in their groups. In 1968, the FBI office in Newark, NJ, recommended this strategy to neutralize the New Left:

> Certain key leaders must be chosen to become the object of a counterintelligence plot to identify them as government informants. It appears that this is the only thing that could cause some of these individuals concern. . . . Attacking their morals, disrespect for the law, or patriotic disdain will not impress their followers, as it would normally to other groups, so it must be by attacking them through their own principles and

beliefs. Accuse them of selling out to "imperialistic monopoly capitalism."[72]

As one example of this method, the FBI forged documents and sent an anonymous mailing to convince the peers of a New Left leader that he worked for Army Intelligence. The FBI had obtained the subject's personal diary and the FBI Laboratory received permission to forge entries. Specifically, they added several phone numbers to government agencies to suggest secret government spying. "These entries were phone numbers at Army and Secret Service, which when called would identify the agency. Other notations in the diary indicate that [text redacted] has been furnishing information to these agencies. He thus would be branded as an informant." The FBI mailed the altered diary to his peers at the Progressive Labor Party headquarters in New York City along with "an anonymous note indicating that more than one person has knowledge of the diary's existence."[73] The goal, at a minimum, was to get this leader kicked out of the Party. In some cases, "snitches got stitches"—that is, activists sought physical revenge against people thought to be spying on them for intelligence agencies.

Before the late 1970s, there were few checks on FBI conduct. Agents did not need legal warrants then (or now) to deploy informers. They could direct them to break the law by supplying illegal drugs to subjects or by deliberately provoking police during demonstrations to cause arrests. The only restraint was the FBI leadership's subjective judgment about avoiding adverse public exposure.

The FBI rigidly maintained secrecy about the identities of all informers. Informers usually functioned on a "need to know" basis and were unaware of the identity of others working alongside them for the bureau. In a few cases during inter-organizational conflict, informers in one group unwittingly attacked informers in another group resulting in several known deaths.[74] The names of informers were redacted, as well as contextual material that might hint at their identity, when FBI records were declassified. This censorship was sanctioned under the law and most federal judges during FOIA litigation protected the informer system even when records were fifty years old.

The FBI rarely released statistics about its use of informers. However, newly declassified internal FBI reports from the 1960s indicate that the vast majority of political informers were not focused on the communist threat, despite the privileged rhetoric of the Cold War. There were many other targets. In 1962, less than one-quarter of all political informants were targeting the CP and the number decreased as the decade progressed.[75] In 1965, the FBI's Inspection Division, headed by W. Mark Felt, described the diverse use of informers against the Klan, Martin Luther King, Jr., W.E.B. DuBois Clubs, Nation of Islam, and the American Nazi Party.

> Division must continue and intensify penetration of Klan-hate groups, ensure prompt reporting and timely dissemination of pertinent data. Considerable data re moral degeneracy and subversive associates of Martin Luther King, Jr., developed, given timely dissemination to White House, Attorney General, and interested agencies. Counterintelligence actions attained some success in disrupting efforts of communist youth W. E. B. DuBois Clubs and Ad Hoc Operation has developed numerous domestic and foreign Chinese contacts, including known intelligence sources. Division must plan and execute vigorous, imaginative counterintelligence action against such new targets as Nation of Islam and American Nazi Party.[76]

By 1968, the FBI deployed only 318 informants targeting the CP—less than 15 percent of its total political informant corps.[77] By contrast the number of "racial" informants (see below) totaled 1,146 and increased by more than 600 percent over five years.

1964—177
1965—313
1966—440
1967—574
1968—1,146[78]

The race issue had come to dominate the FBI's thinking, especially the impact of the "long hot summers" of rioting during the prior three years and the expanding black power movement. Moreover, the Reverend King remained a problem. The FBI wrote about his call for economic justice, in addition to racial equality, and organization of a Poor People's March for later that year.[79] Felt indicated in his 1968 Inspection Report:

> Potentially explosive racial situation exists with activities of militant and violence-prone leaders such as Stokely Carmichael attempting to unite Negro civil rights groups into a Black United Front, and Martin Luther King planning massive civil disobedience demonstration in April, 1968. Marked increase in racial informants from 574 to 1,146 or 98%. Need for additional informants strongly stressed.[80]

As a new initiative, the FBI opened the massive Ghetto Informant Program establishing "listening posts" in African American communities. By 1972, the Program enlisted the aid of about 7,500 employees of stores, bars, and restaurants to spy on people. Political policing had extended into the realm of daily commercial transactions.[81] In later years, the FBI also recruited employees of commercial establishments, although information on this recruitment largely remains secret. We do know that under both Bush and Obama the FBI used the listening post technique in Muslim and Arab-American communities. It seems highly likely that listening posts are put in place elsewhere independent of specific investigations.

How easy was it for the FBI to recruit new informers? Data from the 1960s suggested overall it proved very difficult when they approached radicals. The vast majority refused to work for the bureau. The Inspection Division reported that during the first 8 months of 1962 the FBI interviewed "1,587 subversives" and developed only "118 security informants, potential informants and sources of information."[82] In sum, only about seven percent of recruits agreed to spy on their peers. Two years later, the FBI interviewed more than twice that number of people. The Inspection Division found: "Since last [yearly] inspection, 3,829 individuals interviewed which resulted in obtaining informants, potential informants, and sources totaling 319."[83] Again, recruitment was not very successful—about eight percent joined FBI ranks. The resistance to snitching occurred because many people apparently felt it was a dishonorable act. It was undemocratic behavior. Many radicals held strong political views and proved unwilling to switch their allegiances.

No comparable data on the use of informers is publicly available for any period before or after the 1960s. A recent estimate is that about 15,000 informers currently work for the bureau.[84] We can speculate that in recent years the FBI found ways to increase its success rate in recruiting radicals through intimidation and coercion. It may dig up dirt on individuals (such as illicit drug use) and threaten to prosecute. It may adopt authoritarian tactics and threaten a blacklist if a person decides not to inform. Immigrants face particular issues: The FBI may pressure them to inform or face deportation. Conversely, the bureau may promise aid in getting a "green card" if immigrants agree to work for them. It appeared Arab Americans faced the issue of coercion more than other groups. According to Skakeel Syed, a leader of the Islamic Shura Council of Southern California which represents 68 mosques, the FBI has told Muslim immigrants: "We will make your problems vanish if you cooperate. . . . For some individuals who have refused recruitment, there is startling evidence that the FBI has actually retaliated against them."[85] The *Orange County Register* newspaper observed in an editorial: "Muslims are afraid to talk about politics or civil liberties issues within their mosques or even among their friends because of fear that it will draw attention from undercover agents . . . .there should not be a presumption of guilt among an entire community."[86]

Power and Secrecy

Reconstructing the history of the FBI's massive surveillance on Americans is not an easy task because for many years a wall of secrecy protected surveillance practices from public disclosure.[87] This wall was maintained by employing several methods specifically to conceal agency records: segregating them; posing obstacles in the declassification process; and destroying them on a mass basis. For example, in order to limit knowledge of sensitive or illegal methods, files containing information on "highly confidential sources" or "highly confidential techniques" were kept segregated outside the FBI Central Records System. These files were stored in a special area in FBI's Headquarters known as Room 6527 or the "confidential file room." Segregating them helped to ensure "restricted handling and selective routing." Room 6527 was kept locked requiring the permission of top FBI officials to access. When Hoover established it in 1948, he noted: "No doubt [text redacted] types will find something sinister in such a set up." By 1964, Room 6527 contained in excess of 5,000 files in 79 file cabinets.[88]

Many of the records in Room 6527 were labeled "Do Not File" to conceal them from inside and outside investigators, including Justice Department officials. This included what came to be known as "June Mail." Some June Mail comprised relatively innocuous and insignificant material such as letters and personal notes from the Director's friends and colleagues. However, a large portion of June Mail covered material which revealed human or electronic investigative techniques.[89]

In 2011, the FBI declassified descriptions of some Room 6527 files. In 1955, a large file, "Ultrasonic Listening Devices (Radio Frequency Microphones)," contained all known information on this technological capability as well as "countermeasures being taken to protect against microphones of this category" by enemies.[90] A 1961 memo noted surveillance practices in a program titled the "Gus Survey" regarding the U.S. mail and Soviet agents. "[I]ncoming mail arriving in certain postal zones is examined in an attempt to locate mail destined for Soviet illegal agents. From past experience it is known that Soviet illegal agent mail is usually included in a white envelope, with a typed, double spaced name and address and no return address. The addresses are complete and Lincoln stamps are used." [91] In 1967, an index file on all U.S. persons under FBI electronic surveillance also was stored in Room 6527.[92]

Two weeks after the assassination of the Reverend King in 1968, the FBI worried that disruptive techniques used in its Black Nationalist investigations might be made public. In order to limit knowledge of its dirty tricks, the files were put away for safekeeping in Room 6527. Official G.C. Moore wrote a memo to William C. Sullivan, who oversaw the entire COINTELPRO activities, noting that the Black Nationalist file included material on "a variety of techniques, many of which are highly confidential. Thus the sensitive nature of this material indicates it should be available on a restricted basis. Access to this file should be cleared with the Section Chief of the Racial Intelligence Section."[93] Was assassination an FBI counterintelligence technique? No evidence yet found in FBI files established this fact, but the revelation of other acts of sabotage against the civil rights movement might inflame public sentiment as the nation reckoned with the King killing.

During the early 1970s, the FBI increasingly relied on its own agents to go undercover to infiltrate the new social movements. In order to protect agent identities, their files received special secrecy protection.[94] The utmost secrecy also surrounded the files on confidential informants to protect their identities. These files were identified by number rather than by name and stored in the confidential file room.[95] Room 6527 also housed records on top government leaders. For example, after Gerald R. Ford assumed the presidency in 1974, his large FBI file was transferred to this location. Information in his file revealed that as a congressman, Ford secretly informed for the FBI about the inner workings of the Warren Commission. We also know that Hoover's Official and Confidential Files, as well as files relating to Director Kelley, were stored in Room 6527.[96]

Segregating records was not always sufficient to conceal documentation of illegal practices. Records could be removed from the bureau and placed in other government offices. As one example, during 1969 through 1971 the FBI placed wiretaps on 17 individuals, including five journalists, to uncover leaks by members of the National Security Council. Assistant Director Sullivan, who ran the op, secretly moved these "extremely sensitive" records to the White House in order to conceal knowledge of the wiretap operation.[97]

Hiding FBI files from the public, as opposed to their own personnel, formed another aspect of the wall of secrecy. With the passage of the FOIA in 1966, the FBI lobbied to prevent the Act's application to its records. Initially, they succeeded. However, in 1974 Congress amended the FOIA and subjected FBI records to the provisions of the Act. The political environment had changed after the death of Hoover and the eruption of the Watergate scandal. Although the FBI and the Justice Department convinced President Ford to veto the changes to the FOIA, Congress overwhelmingly overrode the veto.[98]

The FBI's arguments against the FOIA were specious. It said the Act "would distort the purpose of agencies such as the FBI, imposing on them the added burden of serving as a research source for every writer, busybody, or curious person." Moreover, the FBI feared a flood of new litigation—the prospect of "an endless number of suits by individuals who disagree with the investigative agencies' decisions on whether or not to release some information." Any potential bottom-up challenge to the informer system must be opposed. "[I]t will be apparent [the FBI] no longer can assure them [informers] their identities and the information they furnish in confidence for law enforcement purposes will not some day be disclosed to the subject."[99] This argument misread the changes in the law, which gave the FBI wide latitude to redact records to protect their sources.

As a result of the 1974 FOIA amendments, for the first time the public could ask to review security files on individuals, groups, and organizations. Americans made about 10,000 record requests with the bureau in 1975 and thereafter the number of requests increased to a peak of about 24,000 in the year 2000.[100] The process of breaking down the wall of secrecy, however flawed, remains critical to democratic praxis.

Destroying records became the most obvious method to protect the wall of secrecy. The FBI worked under the presumption that records routinely were to be destroyed unless they received special designation for saving. In recent years, the FBI retained records if they were related to litigation or were deemed to have "historical value." Many other files initially were saved for five to ten years but if no FOIA request is made of them they subsequently may be destroyed.[101] Overall, the weak criteria for record retention enabled the bureau to destroy hundreds of thousands of record pages each year.

A less obvious method to restrict openness is to pose obstacles in the declassification process. This applies to record requests, when the FOIA office at the FBI deliberately chooses to release partial files, instead of complete ones, content to let the requestor pursue administrative appeals or litigation. Many requestors do not have the time or resources to pursue either option. In litigation, the FBI may deceive the court to conceal material it does not want to make public. In a recent example involving Islamic organizations in California, the FBI lied to the court to hide surveillance only to be rebuffed by a federal judge. "The government's representations were then, and remain today, blatantly false. . . . The Government asserts that it had to mislead the Court regarding the Government's response to Plaintiff's FOIA request to avoid compromising national security. . . . The Government cannot, under any circumstances, affirmatively mislead the Court."[102] Too often the bureau did not believe in checks and balances in cases of national security. It is a rare court that will locate such deception and choose publicly to challenge FBI power.

In another case involving spying on Muslim Americans in Southern California (*Fazaga v. FBI*), the Justice Department invoked the "states' secrets" privilege to quash an important civil rights lawsuit. Several plaintiffs, represented by the American Civil Liberties Union, charged the FBI unjustly spied on Arab American mosques and groups using an informer, Craig Monteilh, who led discussions on violent jihad, planted listening devices, and collected phone numbers and email addresses. Monteilh, a convicted felon, spent 15 months in 2006 and 2007 pursuing "Operation Flex" and acted in such an extreme and radical manner that several Muslim Americans called the FBI to alert them about a possible terrorist. Attorney General Eric Holder insisted the court dismiss the case. If allowed to proceed, he said "disclosures would reveal to subjects who are involved in or are planning to undertake terrorist activities what the FBI knows and does not know about their plans and the threat they pose to national security."[103]

In the 21st century, the FBI also concealed information by storing it in secret locations within its computer systems. The bureau established segregated computer drives—named the I-drive and the S-drive—that contained numerous raw investigatory records situated beyond the scope of FOIA requests and hidden from federal judges and prosecutors. When the computer drives were first identified in 2004, the FBI responded by establishing additional secret ones unknown to outsiders.[104] Is illegal or unconstitutional behavior recorded in this latest version of the "Do Not File" system?

My experience requesting FBI records under the FOIA is mixed. I obtained 25 separate files for this book. Some files were released without much contention, although doubts remain they are the full record of what the FBI holds. However, I also faced obvious agency obfuscation. As one example, the FBI resisted releasing their file on the *Rational Observer*—a college newspaper distributed at American University in Washington, DC, during the late 1960s. The FBI wrote, published, and circulated the newspaper as a form of opinion management to fight student radicalism. I discovered the paper's existence after reading a reference to it in a federal civil rights lawsuit, *Hobson v. Wilson*. I hoped to get the FBI file to use in chapter 2 ("Manipulating the Media"). After I filed a records request, the FBI told me they could find no material on the subject and asked if I could provide additional information. I wrote a second letter and enclosed the portion of the *Hobson* court opinion that referenced the newspaper.

> I have attached copies of parts of two legal opinions in the *Hobson* case. I circled the material relevant to my request. I hope this additional information helps you find these records. If not, I plan to appeal to the Director, Office of Information Policy, U. S. Department of Justice.[105]

Next, I received a letter from the FBI indicating that the file (100-HQ-153356) already had been transferred to the National

Archives for permanent retention. The FBI suggested I request it directly from the Archives.

However, the Archives told me the FBI had not transferred this file to them. The file was still in the FBI's possession. The Archives wrote: "[Y]ou were informed by the FBI's FOIA/PA branch that the above case file had been transferred to the National Archives. This is incorrect. The FBI is in the process of transferring file Classification 100 (Domestic Security); as of this date our holdings of this file classification ends with case file 100-HQ-34099. We do not know when the above case file will be transferred to our custody. Until that time, any FOIA requests for this file are the responsibility of the FBI."[106] At that point, I decided to let the matter pass without further contestation.

Chapter Overview

I offer a critical view of the FBI in *Surveillance in America* by demonstrating that politically biased "security" investigations sought to limit the range of legitimate political expression in society. Whose security really was at stake? The FBI's overreach early on in its history is explored in chapter 1 by focusing on surveillance of the American working class between 1920 and 1945. My "class analysis" frames government efforts to contain worker movements, suggesting the bureau not only opposed groups which organized for workplace rights or challenged the supremacy of management. Surveillance also was directed against groups and individuals questioning the legitimacy of capitalism. The FBI viewed the working class—especially the large immigrant component—as "dangerous" and potentially subversive in a society with an immense, growing industrial economy. In large labor disputes, the FBI almost always took the side of management.

This chapter highlights the persistence of the Red Scare against labor during the 1920s. Spying in the case of Italian American anarchists Nicola Sacco and Bartolomeo Vanzetti occurred as the legal proceeding became a cause célèbre on the Left between 1920 and 1927. When their execution seemed certain in

1927, the FBI sent a special directive to field offices to ascertain the level of radical activities and the likelihood of violence in response to the killings. Although very little disturbance occurred, the FBI's investigation of radicalism in connection with the case reveals extensive surveillance. Existing scholarship also fails to appreciate that wholesale spying occurred during the Great Depression against organized working-class movements represented by the Bonus Army or Expeditionary Force (BEF), the Workers Alliance of America (WAA), and the Committee for Industrial Organization (CIO). In 1940, the FBI initiated surveillance in the factory workplace through the extensive Plant Informant Program and in working-class communities through the American Legion Contact Program in order to monitor loyalty and radical political activity.

Chapter 2 studies media manipulation from the 1940s to the present. The bureau's media policy had three basic dimensions. First, the FBI tried to advance positive portrayals of itself. The leadership cared deeply about its public reception in order to generate support for FBI actions. In addition, agents supplied information to dozens of friendly contacts in the mainstream media to discredit liberals and radicals. By working in the area of opinion management, the FBI hoped to fight the growth of radical movements by reducing their popular appeal. Lastly, it carried on surveillance and counterintelligence operations against alternative and radical media, which included suppressive efforts to limit circulation and defund newspapers.

After the Cold War, the bureau embraced more open media access that, ironically, led to a higher level of misleading. The FBI spread false information about peaceful political activity, which they categorized as "terrorism," naming particular groups to vilify and demonize. Yet, the rise of new media—particularly on the Internet—increased the range of critical discourse on FBI conduct.

American university and college teachers also faced hostile surveillance. While scholars wield the pen in different ways than reporters by engaging more complex theoretical considerations, attacks on writers in any form limited the free expression of ideas. Chapter 3 ("Threatening Historians") adds to a growing literature on FBI surveillance of academic life. Campus spying became commonplace during the Cold War. Teachers who stood against McCarthyism and the anti-communist crusade were considered suspect. Association with anti-war protest, the civil rights movement, or Left organizations could lead to monitoring. Ellen Schrecker and others have written about universities and the Red Scare.[107] Recently, scholars focus on particular disciplines: David H. Price studied surveillance of anthropologists;[108] Mike Forrest Keen detailed surveillance of sociologists.[109] I obtained FBI files on leading American historians (Herbert G. Gutman, John Hope Franklin, Howard Zinn, C. Vann Woodward, Henry Steele Commager, Richard Hofstadter, Warren Susman, and William Appleman Williams). These individuals were not on the fringe of the profession but integral to the writing of the past in new ways. Why the FBI collected intelligence on them, and the differential treatment afforded liberals and radicals, sheds new light on the troubled relationship between higher education and the surveillance state.

Chapter 4 analyzes FBI language use in the public speeches of Directors L. Patrick Gray III and Clarence M. Kelley during the 1970s. I obtained copies of their speeches as a result of FOIA litigation (*Greenberg v. FBI*). I read them as a form of political communication focusing on content as well as style to delineate FBI ideology—their attitude toward radicals; understanding of the Constitution and civil liberties; grievances and complaints; and views about containing social movements and opponents of the status quo. Generally, studying the language of government officials is a new subject of inquiry.[110] An analysis involving FBI leaders, who presided over a relatively secret organization, provides an original contribution. For example, they used the term "peace officer" to describe themselves and belittled critics and radicals as "misfits." They repeatedly asserted FBI policing was non-political, and made claims their secret operatives worked under the "rule of law." They associated the New Left with terrorism conflating differences between peaceful and violent resistance.

The issue of media manipulation is revisited in chapter 5 focusing on the Watergate scandal of the early 1970s and the bureau's covert relationship with print journalists. My discussion of official W. Mark Felt's service as Deep Throat is based on a close reading of his FBI file. It is not widely known that Felt worked with several other top FBI officials to leak material to the *Washington Post*. A secret "faction" led by Felt played a critical role in forcing President Nixon from office and by doing so created a Constitutional crisis. I view the work of Felt and his collaborators as an example of official abuse of power. Moreover, important questions remain about FBI conduct and how it impacted the 1972 presidential election. It appeared no one at the FBI wanted to expose Nixon's crimes before the election fearful that his progressive Democratic opponent, Senator George McGovern, might secure a victory. McGovern was a public FBI critic. Thus, the Felt faction helped determine how the Watergate scandal unfolded with political considerations in mind.

The final chapter, "Surveillance Society Policing," addresses the period since the early 1990s. Political spying persisted despite the end of the Cold War. New technologies made surveillance more intrusive than in the past. Electronic monitoring and informational data mining replaced the informer as the most important intelligence sources. I consider the issue of "surveillance as harassment" and look at the erosion of privacy. Moreover, in the new era of globalization FBI activity has become part of neo-liberal state efforts to contain critics of the status quo. While the bureau rarely stated it functioned to promote open markets and the flow of capital, by policing dissent it helped stifle critics of capitalist globalization. Again, the FBI labeled protestors as terrorists when they organized against the World Bank, the International Monetary Fund, or the World Trade Organization. When the Occupy Wall Street movement spread across urban America in Fall 2011, many activists worried about not only about city police spying but also FBI surveillance.[111]

Chapter 6 also considers the impact of the Millennium on protest and repression. As an event, of course, the Millennium largely was formless and amorphous. But the social construction of "what might happen" included a high level of Y2K fear exploited by the government. After January 1, 2000, arrived without terrorism, some Arab Americans felt relieved but still noticed the high level of suspicion cast on them.[112] The Millennium was not an Islamist event. The popular meaning of the year 2000 varied and could lead to disparate non-Christian responses. Its worldwide focus may have generated a high level of resentment within radical Islam. The strike against America on September 11 can be reframed as a Millennial plot.

The 9/11 attacks prompted transformation of the American intelligence community. While the Bush Administration proved a disaster for civil liberties, Obama has not reined in the FBI, making only symbolic changes. He longer used the term "war on terror" and shed the overblown and exaggerated discourse associated with it. Obama eventually abolished the vague, five-tiered color-coded terror warning system put in place in the aftermath of 9/11.[113] These efforts have reduced, in all likelihood, the level of popular anxiety about enemy violence. However, not much has changed in terms of structure and motive for investigating political activity. Obama has not put an end to the practice of political policing. Indeed, in some ways he permitted the expansion of FBI spying capabilities. A consensus has emerged within the civil liberties community that his administration extended Bush-era counterterror and surveillance policies, rather than pushing them back.[114]

The post-9/11 FBI investigative paradigm of "preempt, prevent, and disrupt" encapsulated the problem. The idea of "preempt" meant to take action ahead of the organization of dissident activity. It actively sought to fight social movements to reduce their opportunity to form and develop. Meanwhile, "prevent" referred to police efforts to curtail protest and controversial political expression. The meaning of "disrupt" included harassment and threats against anyone who disobeyed—that is, managed to circumvent the preempt and prevent methods. Disruption is the clearest, most unambiguous form of official repression. The new paradigm was akin to the "broken windows," zero tolerance police approach to crime. In official ideology, the FBI said the zero tolerance was for "threats," but how they defined a threat was riddled with bias. Almost all street demonstrations were interpreted as threats. Most forms of anti-capitalist politics were defined as threats even when democratic and nonviolent.

Zero tolerance political policing depended on the collaboration of many third parties. These third parties—whether bank officials, college administrators, communications carriers, or medical authorities—were compelled by law to participate in state surveillance. The FBI imposed gag orders and provided promises of confidentiality. For example, the government continued to conceal which big telecom companies provided the phone records of millions of Americans under the Terrorist Surveillance Program's dragnet system. In 2011, the FBI claimed:

> [D]isclosure of the identities of electronic communication service providers would cause substantial harm to their competitive position. Specifically, these businesses would be substantially harmed if their customers knew that they were furnishing information to the FBI. The stigma of working with the FBI would cause customers to cancel the companies' services and file civil actions to prevent further disclosure of subscriber information.[115]

The FBI also believed the telecom companies might initiate litigation to refuse cooperation.

> [G]iven that these companies would pay a high price if it were known that they were providing information about their customers to the FBI, it is likely that companies, though lacking grounds to do so, would nevertheless avail themselves of legal options to resist cooperation . . . if their confidentiality could not otherwise be assured. It is only with the understanding of complete confidentiality that full cooperation of such sources can be enlisted.[116]

Where is America headed with regard to surveillance and attacks on civil liberties? How much has the society degenerated so criticizing the government can bring surveillance, harassment, or even (false) arrest? In March 2010, the FBI office that handles Freedom of Information requests—the Records Information Dissemination Section (RIDS)—published a startling short article in its monthly internal newsletter deploying humor to depict encroaching police state conduct. The article was titled: "On the Lighter Side! 'Bureau Controls.'" (See Textbox 2) While seemingly of little importance, the piece can be viewed as representative of a mind-set dangerous to democracy. The point of

---

Textbox 2

In March 2010, the article below ("On the Lighter Side! 'FBI Controls'") appeared in an internal FBI newsletter, *RIDS FOIA BUZZ*. It was distributed by the Records Information Dissemination Section (RIDS), which handles FOIA requests made to the FBI, and illustrates an anti-democratic attitude.

A guy named Bob is traveling by Amtrak with two strangers sitting by him. He is trying to sleep, but those guys were speaking loudly for a long time heavily criticizing George Bush, the war in Iraq, corruption, etc. So Bob, in an attempt to force these guys to stop talking and let him sleep, tells them as a joke that there is a new total control system developed by the FBI that spies upon all citizens, and there are lots of listening devices everywhere, so that anyone criticizing the gov't. would be severely punished. This didn't have any effect on those guys; moreover they just laughed and carried on and on, saying even more rude jokes about Bush and the gov't. Finally, close to 3 am, Bob goes to the restroom, and runs into the conductor. Bob ask [sic] the conductor to bring him some water and sleeping pills at exactly 3 am. He goes back to his place and says loudly into the base of his seat, so that the talkative guys could hear him, "If the FBI director can hear me, could you please bring me a glass of water and some sleeping pills at 3 a.m. because there are some idiots here who are speaking too loudly about some political issues and won't let me sleep." The guys continue talking. Exactly at 3:00 am, the conductor comes and gives the water and sleeping pills. The guys are shocked and finally stop talking. Bob is happy and falls asleep. When Bob awakes the guys are no where to be found. Out of curiosity he asks the conductor about them. The conductor replies that some people in black suits stopped the train and arrested those guys. Bob asks why he wasn't arrested. The conductor said he doesn't have a clue but one of the guys in the black suit said the FBI director liked Bob's joke!

the article was that very little "control" over FBI activity existed in the field of domestic security. The author mocked the lack of accountability. Uncontrolled. It mattered that the story occurred on an Amtrak train owned by the federal government. If they bug and tap, it was their prerogative. There were arrests for political speech. This was no laughing matter. There were political prisoners in the United States. There also was an "op"—a trick involving the train conductor and the construction of a "coincidence" to unnerve an opponent. The goal became inhibiting political speech—an effort to get two people to stop talking, suppressing discourse.

In this article, the subjects of criticism were Bush and the war in Iraq. Thus, the state did not permit dissenting views on these topics. Men in black suits appeared at the speech crime scene to take away the First Amendments extremists. Indeed, total information control was facilitated by secret electronic eyes and ears. Moreover, law and order was subject to the whims of the director, who dispensed punishment based on his likes and dislikes. There was nothing "light" about the lack of bureau controls.

Surveillance in America concludes with a short postscript looking at the much anticipated 10th anniversary of the September 11 attacks. After ten years, there seemed to be some fatigue about living in a constant state of emergency, which the "war on terror" tried to impose. Yet, there was little prospect that the development of the surveillance society would be halted in the near future, let alone reversed. As an engaged scholar-activist, I hope this book helps to build a movement that questions the utility of massive government spying and embraces the tradition of civil liberties and a democratic public sphere where everyone can freely talk, write, and argue the world. Today, democracy is at risk. Americans must resist the entreaties of authoritarian entities which seek to undermine democratic society by shouting "terrorism" in the town square. Soon after 9/11, the American Civil Liberties Union noted: "It doesn't require some apocalyptic vision of American democracy being replaced by a dictatorship to worry about a surveillance state . . . All that is required is the continued construction of new surveillance technologies and the simultaneous erosion of privacy protections."[117]

Notes

1. W. A. Branigan to O. A. Ezwell, "Security of the Offices of the Domestic Intelligence Division," March 10, 1953; I. W. Conrad to Mr. Harbo, "Security of Bureau Offices," March 18, 1953. These memos are from a declassified FBI file, "Security of Telephone Services, 1952-1995" (hereafter STS file).

2. Conrad to Mr. Harbo, "Security of Bureau Offices."

3. I. W. Conrad to Mr. Harbo, "Security Check of Director's Office," June 16, 1953; Conrad to Mr. Harbo, "Security of Bureau Offices." STS FBI file.

4. SAC WFO to Director, "Senate Subcommittee Investigating Crime in the District of Columbia Information Concerning," April 19, 1952, STS FBI file.

5. Executives Conference to Director, "Security Survey, Telephones of Members of Executives Conference," May 7, 1952, STS FBI file.

6. David Lyon, *Surveillance Studies: An Overview* (Malden, MA: Polity Press, 2007), 15.

7. Several recent studies focus on the politics and culture of insecurity. See, for example, Craig Campbell and Fredrik Logevall, *America's Cold War: The Politics of Insecurity* (Cambridge, MA: Harvard University Press, 2009); Torin Monahan, *Surveillance in the Time of Insecurity* (New Brunswick, NJ: Rutgers University Press, 2010); Wolfgang Sutzl and Geoff Cox, eds., *Creating Insecurity: Art and Culture in the Age of Security* (Brooklyn, NY: Autonomedia, 2009).

8. Surprisingly, recent studies of the American Left devote very little attention to the role of the FBI in monitoring and suppressing dissent. See, for example, Michael Kazin, *American Dreamers: How the Left Changed a Nation* (New York: Alfred A. Knopf, 2011); Maurice Isserman and Michael Kazin, *America Divided: The Civil War of the 1960s* (New York: Oxford University Press, 2000).

9. Richard Gid Powers, *Broken: The Troubled Past and Uncertain Future of the FBI* (New York: Simon and Schuster, 2004), 60-61.

10. Athan G. Theoharis, *The FBI and American Democracy: A Brief Critical History* (Lawrence: University Press of Kansas, 2004), 17-28.

11. Powers, *Broken*, 109-110.

12. For a detailed discussion of the historiography, see Regin Schmidt, *Red Scare: The FBI and the Origins of Anticommunism, 1919-1943* (Copenhagen: Museum Tusculanum Press, 2000), 10-20. (Quote on p. 20.)

13. Powers, *Broken*, 124.

14. Theoharis, *The FBI and American Democracy*, 2

15. Powers, *Broken*, 130-131.

16. Theoharis, *The FBI and American Democracy*, 36.

17. Powers, *Broken*, 131

18. Theoharis, *The FBI and American Democracy*, 2-3.

19. Powers, *Broken*, 175.

20. Kirstin Downey, *The Woman Behind the New Deal: The Life and Legacy of Frances Perkins* (New York: Anchor Books, 2010), 277; Allida Black, *Casting Her Own Shadow: Eleanor Roosevelt and the Shaping of Postwar Liberalism* (New York: Columbia University Press, 1996), 151-176.

21. Athan G. Theoharis, *Abuse of Power: How Cold War Surveillance and Secrecy Policy Shaped the Response to 9/11* (Philadelphia: Temple University Press, 2011), 27, 45-46.

22. Athan G. Theoharis, "The FBI and Dissent in the United States," in C. E. S. Franks, ed., *Dissent and the State* (Toronto: Oxford University Press, 1989), 95.

23. Powers, *Broken*, 187; Nancy C. Carnevale, "'No Italian Spoken for the Duration of the War': Language, Italian-American Identity, and Cultural Pluralism in the World War II Years," *Journal of American Ethnic History* 22 (Spring, 2003): 3-33; Stephen Fox, *Fear Itself: Inside the FBI Roundup of German Americans during World War II* (New York: iUniverse, 2007).

24. Robert A. Hill, ed., *The FBI's RACON: Racial Conditions in the United States during World War II* (Boston: Northeastern University Press, 1995); Patrick S. Washburn, *A Question of Sedition: The Federal Government's Investigation of the Black Press during World War II* (New York: Oxford University Press, 1986).

25. James T. Sparrow, *Warfare State: World War Two Americans and the Age of Big Government* (New York: Oxford University Press, 2011), 208.

26. Theoharis, *The FBI and American Democracy*, 59-64; John Sbardellati, "Brassbound G-Men and Celluloid Reds: The FBI's Search for Communist Propaganda in Wartime Hollywood," *Film History: An International Journal* 20 (2008): 412-436.

27. Gerald K. Haines and David A. Langbart, *Unlocking the Files of the FBI: A Guide to its Records and Classification System* (Wilmington, DE: Scholarly Resources, 1993), 222.

28. Theoharis, *The FBI and American Democracy*, 96-104.

29. See also Claire Bond Potter, "Queer Hoover: Sex, Lies, and Political History," *Journal of the History of Sexuality* 15 (July 2006): 355-381.

30. Robert Justin Goldstein, *American Blacklist: The Attorney General's List of Subversive Organizations* (Lawrence: University of Kansas, 2008), 92, 181; Griffen Fariello, *Red Scare: Memories of the American Inquisition* (New York: Avon Books, 1995), 36. For an overview of FBI activity during the 1950s, see Ellen Schrecker, *Many are the Crimes: McCarthyism in America* (Boston: Little Brown and Company, 1998), 203-239.

31. The FBI closely tracked Communist Party membership. FBI monograph, "Membership of the Communist Party USA, 1919-1954," May 1955, iii.

32. Theoharis, *The FBI and American Democracy*, 121.

33. H. L. Edwards to Mr. Mohr, "Domestic Intelligence Division Inspection," Nov. 11, 1958, 2, Alan Belmont FBI file. Thanks to Ernie Lazar for providing copies of this file, as well as the files of FBI officials William C. Sullivan and Donald E. Moore.

34. Frank J. Donner, *Protectors of Privilege: Red Squads and Police Repression in Urban America* (Berkeley: University of California Press, 1990), 1, 2, 39-43, 57, 143.

35. Quoted in Julia Brown, *I Testify: My Years as an Undercover Agent for the FBI* (Boston: Western Islands, 1966), 131.

36. U.S. Senate Church Committee, *Intelligence Activities and the Rights of Americans, Final Report of the Select Committee to Study Governmental Operations*, Vol. 2, 1976, 254.

37. William W. Keller, *The Liberals and J. Edgar Hoover: Rise and Fall of a Domestic Intelligence State* (Princeton: Princeton University Press, 1989), 157; W. G. Campbell to Mr. Callahan, "Request for Public Source and Statistical Type Information by Former Acting Associate Director W. Mark Felt," Aug. 15, 1973, W. Mark Felt FBI file; "Ex-Hoover Aide Says White House Meddled with FBI," *Courier Post*, Oct. 11, 1973.

38. SAC Albany to Director, "Counterintelligence Program, Internal Security, Disruption of the New Left," June 3, 1968, 8, New Left FBI file.

39. John Waltz to Carl W. Belcher, "National Office of the SDS, Chicago, Illinois," March 17, 1970, 1, 4, Clarence M. Kelley FBI file.

40. Ibid, 2, 4- 5.

41. Ibid., 3-4.

42. Ibid., 5.

43. Francis J. Martin to Paul V. Daly, *United States v. Felt*, June 8, 1979, L. Patrick Gray III FBI file.

44. The New York FBI file on the Youth International Party (Yippies) is identified as 100-NY-162260. Phil Lapsley to Ivan Greenberg, email, June 6, 2011.

45. "Interview with Dhoruba Bin Wahad," *Shadow* 36 (June-Aug. 1995):1.

46. John J. Abt with Michael Myerson, *Advocate and Activist: Memoirs of an American Communist Lawyer* (Urbana: University of Illinois Press, 1993), 282-283.

47. Robert Justin Goldstein, "The FBI and American Politics Textbooks," *PS: Political Science and Politics* 18 (Spring 1985): 238.

48. Ivan Greenberg, "Reagan Revives FBI Spying," in Kimberly Moffitt and Duncan Campbell, eds., *The 1980s: A Critical and Transitional Decade* (Lanham: Lexington Books, 2010), 43-63.

49. "Putting Records to Work," *Federal Computer Week*, June 21, 2001, www.fcw.com/Articles/2004/06/21/Putting-records-to-work.aspx?sc_lang+en&Page=2.

50. Ronald Weich to Senator Patrick J. Leahy, Sept. 15, 2009, 9, www.fas.org/irp/congress/2009_hr/fbi-qfr.pdf.

51. National Archives and Record Administration, "Records of the Federal Bureau of Investigation," www.archives.gov/research/guide-fed-records/index-numeric/001-to-100.html#RG065 (accessed Aug. 30, 2011).

52. Michael Ravnitzky to Ivan Greenberg, email, Sept 13, 2011.

53. Theoharis, *The FBI and American Democracy*, 180.

54. Theoharis, *Abuse of Power*; Theoharis, *The FBI and American Democracy*; Theoharis, ed., *A Culture of Secrecy: The Government Versus the People's Right to Know* (Lawrence: University of Kansas Press, 1998); Theoharis, ed., *From the Secret Files of J. Edgar Hoover* (Chicago: Ivan R. Dee, 1991); Theoharis, *Spying on Americans: Political Surveillance from Hoover to the Huston Plan* (Philadelphia: Temple University Press, 1978); Theoharis, ed., *Beyond the Hiss Case: The FBI, Congress, and the Cold War* (Philadelphia: Temple University Press, 1982); Theoharis, ed., *The FBI: A Comprehensive Reference Guide* (Phoenix: Oryx Press, 1999); Theoharis and John Stuart Cox, *The Boss: J. Edgar Hoover and the American Inquisition* (Philadelphia: Temple University Press, 1988); Powers, *Broken*; Powers, *Secrecy and Power: The Life of J. Edgar Hoover* (New York: The Free Press, 1987); Powers, *G-Men: Hoover's FBI in American Popular Culture* (Carbondale: Southern Illinois University Press, 1983); Claire A. Culleton, *Joyce and the G-Men: J. Edgar Hoover's Manipulation of Modernism* (New York: Palgrave Macmillan, 2004); Culleton and Karen Leick, eds., *Modernism on File: Modern Writers, Artists, and the FBI, 1920-1950* (New York: Palgrave Macmillan, 2008); Kenneth, O'Reilly, *Hoover and the Un-Americans: The FBI, HUAC, and the Red Menace* (Philadelphia: Temple University Press, 1983); O'Reilly, *"Racial Matters": The FBI's*

Secret File on Black America, 1960-1972 (New York: The Free Press, 1989); James Kirkpatrick Davis, *Assault on the Left: The FBI and the Sixties Antiwar Movement* (Westport: Greenwood Press, 1997): Davis, *Spying on Americans: The FBI's Domestic Counterintelligence Program* (New York: Praeger, 1999); Ward Churchill, and Jim Vander Wall, *The COINTEL-PRO Papers: Documents From the FBI's Secret War Against Dissent in the United States* (Boston: South End Press, 1990); Churchill and Vander Wall, *Agents of Repression: The FBI's Secret Wars Against the Black Panther Party and the American Indian Movement* (Boston: South End Press, 1988).

55. Schmidt, *Red Scare*; David H. Price, *Threatening Anthropology: McCarthyism and the FBI's Surveillance of Activist Anthropologists* (Durham: Duke University Press, 2004); Steve Rosswurm, *The FBI and the Catholic Church, 1935-1962* (Amherst: University of Massachusetts, 2009); David Cunningham, *There's Something Happening Here: The New Left, the Klan and FBI Counterintelligence* (Berkeley: University of California Press, 2004). See also Douglas M. Charles, *J. Edgar Hoover and the Anti-Interventionists: FBI Political Surveillance and the Rise of the Domestic Security State, 1939-1945* (Columbus: Ohio State University Press, 2007); Raymond J. Batvinis, *The Origins of FBI Counterintelligence* (Lawrence: University of Kansas Press, 2007).

56. Theoharis, *Abuse of Power*, ix, 153, 165.

57. Beverly Gage, "Terrorism and the American Experience: A State of the Field," *Journal of American History* 98 (June 2011): 85.

58. Ann Larabee, "Why Historians Should Exercise Caution When Using the Word 'Terrorism,'" *Journal of American History* 98 (June 2011): 109.

59. For a succinct statement of this argument, see my article: "The FBI and the Making of the Terrorist Threat," *Radical History Review* 111 (Fall 2011): 35-50.

60. Studies of informers include Gary T. Marx, *Undercover: Police Surveillance in America* (Berkeley: University of California Press, 1988); Daniel J. Leab, *I Was a Communist for the FBI: The Unhappy Life and Times of Matt Cvetic* (University Park, PA: Pennsylvania State University Press, 2000).

61. David Garrow, "FBI Political Harassment and FBI Historiography: Analyzing Informants and Measuring Their Effects." *The Public Historian* 4 (Fall 1988): 5-18.

62. FBI monograph, "Stool Pigeon or Loyal Citizen?" 1952, 1, 3. The FBI encouraged the public to become informers by providing heroic public confessions by its own undercover operatives. Cynthia

Hendershot, *Anti-Communism and Popular Culture in Mid-Century America* (Jefferson, NC: McFarland and Co., 2003), 108-120.

63. Upon its declassification in 2008, a total of 95 of 97 pages of the second edition were redacted. The FBI found successful recruitment efforts varied by age. The young more easily could be manipulated than those older. "A person who is middle aged with wide experience (some of which may relate to different phases of law enforcement) is a much more different task than overcoming the same objection coming from a young man out of college and with limited experience and no knowledge at all of law enforcement work." "Stool Pigeon or Loyal Citizen?" 2nd edition June 1955, i, iii, 1-2.

64. FBI monograph, "Pretexts and Cover Techniques," May 1956, ix, 5.

65. FBI monograph, "Unusual Investigative Techniques," August 1961, ii, v, 3.

66. The Executives Conference consisted of about 10 top FBI officials, who planned policy and strategies.

67. FBI Executives Conference report, "Redirections of Communist Investigations," March 10, 1947, 12, Executives Conference FBI file.

68. In the left-wing Socialist Workers Party, which embraced Marxism in the tradition of Leon Trotsky, more than 50 informers held posts between 1960 and 1976. Meanwhile, in 1964 the FBI began to target the Ku Klux Klan at the urging of the Johnson administration and 87 informers served as KKK officials within two years. Ivan Greenberg, *The Dangers of Dissent: The FBI and Civil Liberties since 1965* (Lanham: Lexington Books, 2010), 256; W. M. Felt to Mr. Tolson, "Inspection – Domestic Intelligence Division," June 1, 1966, William C. Sullivan FBI file.

69. Most discussions of American Constitutional culture ignore the role of government political harassment.

70. SAC Columbia to Director, "COINTELPRO – New Left, IS," Dec. 12, 1970, 2, New Left FBI file.

71. SAC Chicago to Director, "COINTELPRO – New Left," March 3, 1971, New Left FBI file.

72. SAC Newark to Director, "Counterintelligence Program, Internal Security, Disruption of the New Left," May 27, 1968, New Left FB I file.

73. SAC Los Angeles to Director, "COINTELPRO -- New Left," Aug. 31, 1970, New Left FBI file.

74. Scot Brown, *Fighting For Us: Maulana Karenga, The US Organization and Black Cultural Nationalism* (New York: NYU Press, 2003), 107-131.

75. The FBI's CP informant corps of 423 people totaled about 7 percent of the Party's membership of 5,260. J. F. Malone, "Inspection – Domestic Intelligence Division," Dec. 29, 1961, 4, Donald E. Moore FBI file.

76. W. M. Felt to Mr. Tolson, "Inspection – Domestic Intelligence Division," May 20, 1965, William C. Sullivan FBI file.

77. Ibid, Dec. 11, 1962; March 6, 1968.

78. Ibid., July, 31, 1964.

79. See, for example, Gerald D. McKnight, *The Last Crusade: Martin Luther King, Jr., the FBI, and the Poor People's Campaign* (New York: Basic Books, 1998).

80. W. M. Felt to Mr. Tolson, "Inspection – Domestic Intelligence Division," March 6, 1968, Sullivan FBI file.

81. Greenberg, *The Dangers of Dissent*, 77.

82. W. M. Felt to Mr. Tolson, "Inspection – Domestic Intelligence Division," Dec. 11, 1962, Sullivan FBI file.

83. Ibid., July 31, 1964.

84. Trevor Aaronson, "The Informants" *Mother Jones*, September/October, 2011, 32.

85. Quoted in Congressional Research Service, "American Jihadist Terrorism: Combating a Complex Threat," Dec. 7, 2010, 56-57, www.fas.org/sgp/crs/terror/R41416.pdf.

86. "FBI Creates Climate of Fear," *Orange County Register*, March 22, 2009.

87. Two different views of FBI secrecy are presented in the historical literature. Richard Gid Powers titles his book on Hoover's life *Secrecy and Power* and views the FBI's secret files and secret leadership as beneficent and beneficial to the nation. It did not pose a threat to democracy or individual freedom but made the director a "hero" to Americans who believed "Hoover's secret power was all that stood between them and sinister forces that aimed to destroy their way of life." According to this view, there were few other ways for the FBI to be effective during the Cold War. Fighting internal threats during wartime required a minimum of transparency and visibility. Of course, all large bureaucracies rely on secrecy to maintain efficiency, but the FBI's efforts fundamentally were designed to impose a conservative agenda. In contrast to Powers, Athan G. Theoharis also titles an article in the *Political Science Quarterly* "Secrecy and Power" and edited a book, *A Culture of Secrecy*, which views FBI secrecy as a method to maintain illegitimate power. Deliberate acts of concealment hurt democratic society and prevented contemporaries and later researchers from discerning

the policies undertaken by their government. Americans did not give "consent" to FBI actions because they largely were unaware of the bureau's surveillance and counterintelligence operations. Powers, *Secrecy and Power,* 2; Theoharis, "Secrecy and Power: Unanticipated Problems in Researching FBI Files," *Political Science Quarterly* 119 (Summer 2004): 271-290; Theoharis, ed., *A Culture of Secrecy.*

88. J. H. Gale to Mr. Tolson, "Security of Criminal Intelligence Information," Oct. 20, 1964, 1, 9. This memo is contained in the FBI file known as "Confidential Files Maintained in Room 6527" (hereafter referred to as the CFR file).

89. June Mail dates to 1950. An official described its history: "This system arose out of the threats of a defense attorney in the trial of Judy Coplon that he would subpoena anybody and everybody including messengers and file clerks who might be in any way aware of certain surveillance techniques that he believed had been utilized by the FBI in investigating this case. In other words, the basis for the special handling of so-called 'June' mail was intended not to hide the contents of but only to limit the knowledge of the techniques utilized to the least number of employees possible." Ibid., 8-9.

90. R. J. Lamphere to W. A. Branigan, "Ultrasonic Listening Device," April 8, 1955, CFR file.

91. Mr. W. A. Branigan to Mr. W.C. Sullivan, "Gus Survey Espionage –R," Oct. 16, 1961, CFR file.

92. T. J. McAndres to Mr. Gale, "Department of Justice Requests for Electronic Surveillance Checks," Jan. 30, 1967, CFR file.

93. G. C. Moore to W. C. Sullivan, "Counterintelligence Program Black Nationalist-Hate Groups Racial Intelligence," April 17, 1968, CFR file.

94. R. L. Shackleford to Mr. E. S. Miller, "Revolutionary Activities– Violence IS" Aug. 16, 1972, CFR file.

95. FBI Records Management Division, "Addendum," April 18, 1983, Employee Suggestion FBI file.

96. J. J. McDermott to Mr. Jenkins, "Gerald Rudolph Ford, Jr.," May 3, 1976; J. R. Hogan to Mr. Bassett, "Gerald Rudolph Ford Special Inquiry," March 3, 1979, Ford FBI file.

97. Besides Sullivan, only Hoover knew about these bugs but the director had not authorized the record removal. On Nov. 12, 1971, Hoover wrote a special memorandum to W. Mark Felt outlining the fate of the records. Sullivan had just resigned his post at the FBI, pushed out because he opposed Hoover on key issues. Hoover told Felt: "[T]he Sensitive Files which W. C. Sullivan had, without my authority, turned

over to Assistant Attorney General Mardian had not been destroyed but had been sent to [text redacted] at the White House to be kept there. The Attorney General stated this was done in view of the fact that should any Congressional inquiry be made and subpoena issued to the Department of Justice or the FBI, we would not have such files in our custody and the White House under Executive privilege would be in a position to refuse availability to the files." Ironically, the memo between Hoover and Felt, as well as several others related to Sullivan's disposal of the records, were segregated in the confidential file room. John Edgar Hoover, "Memorandum for Mr. Felt," Nov. 12, 1971; Mark Felt, "Memorandum for Mr. Tolson," Oct. 31, 1971, Felt FBI file.

98. There was broad support in the legal community to apply FBI records to the law. The Chairman of the Administrative Law Division of the American Bar Association affirmed that "with passage of time,… when the [FBI] investigation is all over and the purpose and point of it has expired, it would no longer be an interference with enforcement proceedings and there ought to be disclosure." Quoted in *NLRB v. Robbins Tire and Rubber Co.*, 437 U.S. 214 (1978).

99. S. 1142, 93rd Congress 1973, xviii; National Security Archive, "Veto 30 Years Ago Set Freedom of Information Norms," Nov. 23, 2004 http://www.gwu.edu/~nsarchiv/NSAEBB/NSAEBB142/index.htm (accessed Nov. 30, 2010).

100. Greenberg, *The Dangers of Dissent*, 221.

101. [Text redacted] to Assistant Director, Administrative Services Division, Feb. 23, 1987, Employee Suggestion FBI file.

102. "District Court Finds FBI Lied to Court," *Access Reports*, May 4, 2001, 1.

103. Josh Gerstein, "Obama Administration Asserts State Secrets Privilege to Dismiss Muslims' Suit," Politico, Aug. 1, 2011, www.politico.com/blogs/joshgerstein/0811/Obama_admin_asserts_state_secrets_privilege_to_dismiss_Muslims_suit.html; Hamed Aleaziz, "Want to Sue the FBI for Spying on Your Mosque? Sorry, that's Secret," *Mother Jones*, Aug. 8, 2011.

104. Center for Public Integrity, "Judge Orders FBI to Cough Up Information about a Previously Secret Computer Drive," June 2, 2011, http://www.iwatchnews.org/2011/06/02/4790/judge-orders-fbi-cough-information-about-previously-secret-computer-drive.

105. Ivan Greenberg to David M. Hardy, Jan. 13, 2011.

106. Martha Wagner Murphy to Ivan Greenberg, March 1, 2011.

107. Ellen Schrecker, *No Ivory Tower: McCarthyism and the Universities* (New York: Oxford University Press, 1986); Noam Chomsky et

al., *The Cold War and the University: Toward an Intellectual History of the Postwar Years* (New York: New Press, 1997); Christopher Simpson, ed., *Universities and Empire: Money and Politics in the Social Sciences During the Cold War* (New York: New Press, 1998); Philip Zwerling, ed., *The CIA On Campus: Essays on Academic Freedom and the National Security State* (Jefferson, NC: McFarland, 2011).

108. Price, *Threatening Anthropology*; Price, *Weaponizing Anthropology: Social Science in the Service of the Militarized State* (Oakland: AK Press, 2011).

109. Mike Forrest Keen, *Stalking the Sociological Imagination: J. Edgar Hoover's Surveillance of American Sociology* (Westport: Greenwood Press, 1999).

110. A recent work is Ernst Andrews, ed., *Legacies of Totalitarian Language in the Discourse Culture of the Post-Totalitarian Era* (Lanham: Lexington Books, 2011).

111. Several media and protest groups filed FOIA requests with the FBI to uncover FBI spying on the Occupy Wall Street movement. To date, not much relevant material has been declassified. Juan Cole, "Police Crackdown on OWS Coordinated among Mayors, FBI, DHS," Common Dreams.org, Nov. 16, 2011, www.commondreams.org/view/2011/11/16-3; Jason Leopold, "FBI Claims It Does Not Have Any Documents on Occupy Wall Street," Truthout, Nov. 22, 2011, www.truth-out.org/fbi-headquarters-says-it-does-not-have-any-documents-occupy-wall-street/1321994542.

112. A writer noted in the *Arab American News*: "Everyone escaped unscathed from the impending stigma of the Y2K bug except Arabs and Muslims in general. The last two weeks of the past year witnessed a reincarnation of the ugly ghost of biased media coverage targeted against us. For quite some time now we thought that we'd really made some inroads towards eradicating the ignorance and paranoia projected by the American media towards Islam and Arabs in particular. It was disappointing to see how wrong we were." Neal Abunab, "Y2K Bug Bites Arabs, Muslims in America: Media Wrongly Projected the Threat of `Muslim Terrorism' Synonymously Connected with the Threat of Y2K," *Arab American News*, Jan. 14, 2000.

113. "Color-Coded Terror Warnings to be Gone by April 27," *Washington Post*, Jan. 27, 2011.

114. See, for example, Emily Berman, "Domestic Intelligence: New Powers, New Rules," Brennan Center for Justice, New York University Law School, Jan 18, 2011, 1-2, http://www.brennancenter.org/content/resource/domestic_intelligence_new_powers_new_risks/; Bill

Quigley, "Twenty Examples of the Obama Administration's Assault on Domestic Civil Liberties," Common Dreams.org., Dec. 1, 2011, www.commondreams.org/view/2011/12/01-7.

115. Quoted in ACLU, "FBI: If We Told You, You Might Sue," May 10, 2011, http://www.freerepublic.com/focus/f-news/2719616/posts.

116. Quoted in ACLU: "If We Told You...(Part II)," May 11, 2011, http://www.aclu.org/blog/national-security/fbi-if-we-told-you-part-ii.

117. Quoted in Nat Hentoff, *The War on the Bill of Rights and the Gathering Resistance* (New York: Steven Stories Press, 2003), 30.

1

A Class Analysis
of Early FBI Spying

In 1963, the historian Herbert G. Gutman called for enhanced study of the American working class beyond the traditional focus on trade unions to understand the experiences of wage-earners as a social class.[1] In 1985, the sociologist Theda Skocpol urged scholars to "bring the state back in," viewing it as an institution and a social actor.[2] Both Gutman and Skocpol influenced a large number of scholars. But few have combined the two calls by studying state surveillance of the working class. Between approximately 1920 and 1945 class conflict in America reached significant proportions and the bureau did not sit passively on the sidelines. Rather, it deployed substantial resources to track and curtail worker organizing. The bureau defined as an "enemy" a broad range of working-class movements in order to aid management to assert its supremacy on the shop floor. As America became a leading imperial power, it worried about domestic dissent that might pose obstacles to unfettered industrial growth, especially organizing from below against capitalist development.

The scholarly neglect of surveillance of the working class is not by accident. Until recently, the basic archival material necessary to write this history was unavailable to researchers. For example, I refer to eight declassified FBI files in this chapter. At the time that Gutman as well as Skocpol wrote, these files still were stored secretly away at FBI Headquarters. Their subsequent liberation allows us to view the subject matter.

We learn that the FBI sided with bosses during large labor strikes viewing work stoppages as a threat to the smooth running of industry. The FBI also tracked protests outside the workplace by wage earners and the unemployed unconcerned about their legitimate grievances. As part of the bureau's law enforcement mandate to prevent "disorder" at almost any cost, it investigated working-class organizations that articulated a vision of a better world. All labor philosophies that challenged capitalism were equated with subversion. Radical trade unions—whether socialist, communist, anarchist, or a combination of these ideologies—emerged as top targets of government spying.

J. Edgar Hoover held a secret plan to identify as many radicals as he could. Historian Richard Polenberg writes: "The project dearest to Hoover's heart was the development of a master file of left-wing organizations and individuals, a file as comprehensive as he could make it. By 1919 more than half the Bureau of Investigation's field force was covering radical activities, and every agent's report, sent from anywhere in the country, was summarized and 'carded alphabetically in the radical index.'" Hoover boasted about the new intelligence system. "At a moment's notice a card upon an individual, organization, or a general society existing in any part of the country can be obtained and a brief resume found on the card requested."[3]

The FBI targeted the Industrial Workers of the World (IWW), founded in 1905 by Eugene Debs and Big Bill Haywood. The IWW embraced anarcho-syndicalism, a radical philosophy to transform the capitalist system through direct action such as strikes. The bureau targeted its leaders and rank and file. Historian Richard Gid Powers calls the FBI's anti-IWW efforts: "[T]he Bureau's most ambitious and consequential wartime operation," which resulted in the "destruction of the largest radical labor union in the nation's history." The bureau conducted raids in 24 cities arresting hundreds of IWW members; more than a hundred were convicted under the Espionage Act.[4] During World War I and the First Red Scare the bureau targeted not only the militant labor movement but also antiwar socialists and the new communist parties. During the large strike wave of 1919, the bureau assumed main two functions: track the strikes for the government and investigate radicals who participated in them.[5]

The experience of Irish American radical James Larkin illustrates the FBI's containment efforts. Scholar Claire A. Culleton, who obtained his 490-page FBI file, describes both his success at union and political organizing and the state's repressive response to neutralize him. Larkin left for America in 1913 after organizing thousands of Irish workers. In America, he organized a half-dozen worker groups into unions and gave political speeches in many cities to large working-class gatherings. Arrested in 1919 during a Red Scare raid in New York, he spent several years in prison before Governor Al Smith pardoned him in 1923. Yet, as Culleton notes, "Hoover had made James Larkin's arrest and conviction a Justice Department priority, and as Larkin's FBI file shows, Hoover would not desist until he saw the radical deported to Ireland." Indeed, soon after his release from prison, the government forced his deportation. Culleton suggests the case "remains symptomatic of Hoover's growing distrust of alien radicals, his mounting hysteria in the face of the burgeoning immigrant and alien populations in America's cities, his increasing frustration over their involvement in the labor movement, and his anxiety over the rise of unionization among the American workforce."[6]

During most big events involving workers and the labor movement during the 1920s and 1930s, the FBI conducted surveillance and built dossiers. One of the best examples concerns the Railroad Shopmen's Strike of 1922, when employees of railroad maintenance and repair shops started a nationwide work stoppage to protest a wage cut. The Attorney General asked the bureau to investigate the workers and to help arrest them for lawlessness. The FBI later acknowledged, "It was the policy of the [Harding Administration] . . . to call the Bureau of Investigation, whenever there were national strikes affecting key industries, to keep Government officials fully informed of the activities surrounding the strikes and to report on any acts of violence arising in connection therewith." Bureau agents were deputized as armed marshals to help contain the disturbance. "During the course of this strike," the FBI said, "the activities of over 2,000 individuals involved in the strike were investigated, resulting in the arrest of more than 1,200 for violations of Federal Court injunctions."[7]

In a time of labor strife, the FBI also focused on allies of workers by spying on the Women's Trade Union League (WTUL). It is unclear when the FBI first began tracking the WTUL. Several memos from 1921 and 1922 show their investigation for "radical activities." For example, the New York office collected the proletarian writings of Violet Pike and the League's Education Committee. Pike's so-called "radical pamphlet" entitled, "New World Lessons for Old World Peoples," consisting of eight poems and four very brief short stories, is included the WTUL's FBI file. The poem, "Factory Laws," detailed a labor program.

> We do not want to work more than eight hours a day.
> We do not want children to work.
> We want all workers to get enough to live on.
> We want a benefit for every worker who is hurt.
> We want pensions for old people.
> Some day soon we working women will make our own laws.
> We will make good laws for the workers.[8]

While the WTUL was affiliated with the American Federation of Labor (AFL), not all of the Federation's leaders supported them. In 1922, an official from the National Metal Trades Association provided the FBI with internal WTUL documents.[9]

By 1925, European immigrants and their children made up a large segment of the urban working class. The FBI tracked immigrant communities through its foreign-language press by reading about 500 ethnic newspapers.[10] Hoover assumed those of "foreign extraction" were likely to be dangerous or disloyal. Their American-born children often were included in this "foreign equals dangerous" paradigm.

Spying on Black Radicals

The FBI closely watched black labor radicals. The American Negro Labor Congress (ANLC) met in Chicago for six days in late

October 1925. The ANLC advocated the end of segregated "Jim Crow" unions in the AFL. The exclusion of African Americans in the labor federation, with only a few exceptions, posed a major obstacle to their economic advancement. The ANLC did not argue for the creation of a rival all-black labor movement. Its goals were more narrowly constructed despite the influence of communists among its ranks. At the meeting, black workers wanted to speak for themselves about challenging both management and a white-dominated organized labor movement.

The FBI file on the ANLC is 87 pages. The Chicago FBI office described the inquiry as part of its surveillance of "Radical Negro Communist Activity." Three key words here were reason for surveillance. *Radical*: Despite the reform of the FBI, radical activities continued to be monitored. *Negro*: The bureau viewed most efforts by African Americans to organize protest as subversive. *Communist*: Hoover believed black Americans protested only when communist agitators prodded them into action. Moreover, black communists were doubly dangerous as outsiders who demanded justice along both race and class lines.

According to the FBI, about 600 African Americans and 30 whites attended the Congress. On the opening night, journalist Andrew Torrence "welcomed the delegates to the congress on behalf of the negro press of Chicago. N. S. Taylor, a local negro attorney and Garveyite who ran as alderman of the 3rd ward about a year ago, welcomed the delegates on behalf of the legal profession." There were appeals for class-conscious black workers to unite. The bureau quoted the speech of Lovett Fort-Whiteman, national organizer of the Congress. Notably, the class language did not include references to socialism or revolution. Fort-Whiteman told the delegates: "The aim of the congress is to mobilize and coordinate into a fight-machine the most enlightened and militant and class conscious workers of the Negro race in the struggle for the abolition of lynching, Jim Crowism, industrial discrimination, political disfranchisement, and segregation of the race." He attacked AFL President William Green, a bureau ally. Fort-Whiteman said: "We demand that the American Federation of Labor tear down the barriers that segregate us from the white workers and keep us out of the white unions. We colored workers will, through this congress, correct the mistakes of our white brothers, who have been foolishly misled by the wrong kind of leaders...The natural enemies of the Negro are the boss, the landlord, and the capitalist."[11]

An undercover FBI agent described the political pictures on the walls in "guilt by association" manner. He suggested a "colored" radicalism of liberation coexisted with communist ideas. "The hall is decorated with pictures of leaders of revolutions among colored peoples in different lands, such as Saklatvala of India, Sun Yat-sen of China, Abd-al Krim of Morocco, Toussaint L'Overture of Haiti, and Nat Turner and Denmark Vesey, who led slave uprisings in the South during the Civil War days. Over the platform is a large picture of a Negro laborer and farmer greeting each other under the Communist symbols of crossed hammer and sickle."[12] Of course, the hammer and sickle symbol was taboo, associated with an enemy. Whenever the FBI noticed communist symbols in a public meeting, they assumed the whole space was organized against the government.

We do not know if the FBI limited their surveillance to this one conference without spin-off probes of those in attendance. The FBI file contained the names of almost 50 people gathered from internal conference documents. The Chicago office believed the Congress had "value as a propaganda device for Communism among the Negro masses."[13] Yet, black support for communism was probably less than white support relative to their percentage of the American population. For example, when the Communist Party membership reached a pre-WWII high of about 70,000 in 1939, scholars estimate that no more than 4,000 African Americans had joined their ranks. The total black population at this time was about 13 million.[14]

The FBI in this period exhibited a deep race problem. As the nation's top law enforcement agency, its failure to protect black crime victims set a precedent local police often followed. For example, the FBI refused to stop the extra-legal practice of lynching before the 1960s. Even the liberal Democratic President Franklin D. Roosevelt refused to support anti-lynching efforts during the 1930s in part because of opposition by Director Hoover. The director long equated civil rights activism with disloyalty to the nation. He wanted African Americans to remain second-class citizens and subjected many of their leaders and organizations to extra-legal "dirty tricks," including false prosecutions.[15]

When black leaders urged "self-defense," such as fighting back against white rioters, the government labeled it "negro subversion," a radicalism it sought to monitor and suppress. By the mid-1920s, investigations focused on many black leaders and organizations: A. Philip Randolph and the *Messenger*; Marcus Garvey and the United Negro Improvement Association; the National Association for the Advancement of Colored People (NAACP); and the African Blood Brotherhood. The bureau investigated institutions critical of Jim Crow segregation, especially black-owned newspapers such as the *Chicago Defender*, *Negro World*, the *Crusader*, and *Crisis*. Agents interviewed editors, conducted secret surveillance of some journalists, filed regular reports on the content of articles, and added subscriber lists to their intelligence files. Hoover discussed in memos to agents that the press incited "the negro elements of the country to riot and to the committing of outrages of all sorts."[16]

Sacco and Vanzetti

The murder trial of Italian American anarchists Nicola Sacco and Bartolomeo Vanzetti generated a large FBI file (2,189 pages) spanning the years 1921 to 1927. The legal proceeding became a major cause for liberals and the Left leading to marches and protests in favor of Sacco and Vanzetti's innocence. This political agitation drew the attention of the FBI, especially the unusual unity of communists, socialists, and liberals with anarchists. Of additional concern to the government, the case brought together labor and literary activists associated with the modernist movement in the arts. Culleton notes: "The [FBI] files of many modern writers contain paperwork outlining their involvement in agitating for the release and pardon of the men."[17] Although the 1920s Left was weak compared to the Progressive era, the FBI believed any opposition posed a threat and attempted to track groups and individuals which supported these radicals.

The bureau deployed undercover informers, including jailhouse snitches, worked with city police to monitor suspects, and spied on defense lawyers in the case. In 1927, the FBI opened a special nationwide probe to ascertain the state of "radical activities" in connection with the pending execution of the defendants. Hoover ordered field offices to evaluate potential threats: Would the execution provoke any type of radical uprising?

The persecution of Sacco/Vanzetti—most scholars think they were innocent—symbolized the government's attack on immigrants, labor, and the Left. The legal defense believed there was a conspiracy by the government to frame the two radicals because the Justice Department, via the FBI, already had investigated Sacco and Vanzetti before their arrest. Hoover raised this important issue with the New York and Boston FBI offices and found conflicting internal views. In Boston, special agent John A. Dowd reported that the two anarchists were not known to the local field office. "[T]he Boston office, which caused a number of arrests of alien Communists in January of 1920, was not conducting any so-called drive on Italian anarchists in the Spring of 1920 or at any time of the arrest of the two defendants." Dowd claimed the FBI's intelligence on Sacco/Vanzetti was gathered only after their arrest. However, he provided contradictory information by acknowledging that "a small card bearing the name Bartolomeo Vanzetti which was found long after the arrest of this defendant in a lot of rubbish in the office and is presumed to have been a card taken in at some sort of anarchist raid back in 1918, presumably at the arrest of Iugli Galleani although there is nothing on the card to indicate its source."[18] So it appears Vanzetti was known to the FBI prior to 1920. A second Boston agent, Fred J. Weyand, completed an affidavit for the defense.

> Sometime before the arrest of Sacco and Vanzetti on May 5, 1920—just how long before I do not remember—the names of both of them had got in the files of the Department of Justice as radicals to be watched. . . . Both of these men were listed in the files as followers or associates of an educated Italian editor named Galleani. . . . The suspicion entertained by the Department of Justice against Sacco and Vanzetti was that they had

violated the Selective Service Act, and also that they were anarchists or held radical opinions of some sort or other.[19]

In one of the first known cases, the FBI infiltrated the political defense committee which formed to support the defendants.
Weyand acknowledged, "We also assigned a certain 'undercover' man, as we called them, to win the confidence of the
Sacco-Vanzetti [Defense] Committee, and to become one of the
collectors [of funds]. This man used to report the proceedings
of the Committee to the Department agents in Boston and has
said to me that he was in the habit of taking as much money
collected for his own use as he saw fit."[20] Such infiltration was
unethical and challenged the integrity of the legal proceedings.
A third agent, Lawrence Letherman, who headed the Boston office, confirmed surveillance of the Defense Committee. "Before,
during and after the trial, the Department of Justice had a number of men assigned to watch the activities of the Sacco-Vanzetti
Defense Committee. No evidence warranting prosecution of
anybody was obtained by these men." There may have been
more than one mole inside the Committee. "They were all 'undercover' men, and one or two of them obtained employment by
the Committee in some capacity or other."[21]

The FBI also gathered the names of several dozen Italian
American anarchists in Massachusetts associated with the Defense Committee. "Many, if not practically all of the foregoing
have been the subjects of reports to this Bureau in the past."[22]

At the original trial, agents sat in the courtroom conducting
surveillance with the goal of "picking up any information in
regard to the radical activities of Sacco and Vanzetti or of any of
their friends." Again, the FBI tried to identify "any radicals from
out of this district who might be present."[23]

The case revealed other surveillance tactics. A jailhouse
snitch tried to get close to the defendants as they sat in the Dead-
ham prison. On Oct. 18, 1920, a Boston agent outlined the FBI's
plans. "The only thing that suggests itself is an Italian attempt to
'rope' Vanzetti. It would be an easy matter to place someone in
Vanzetti's cell." Instead, an informant was placed in an adjacent
cell. "He was instructed carefully that he was not to approach

Mr. Sacco, nor was he under any circumstances to refer to anarchist activities, but was to let the man approach him." This intelligence exercise failed. Sacco told the "informant that he was innocent of the crime with which he was charged."[24]

Hoover tried to monitor the class sentiment expressed by Sacco-Vanzetti supporters. Labor organizers told their audiences the case proved that workers suffered injustices under capitalism. Some of these appeals were radical by advocating the "emancipation" of the working class. The FBI retained in their file a political leaflet ("Sacco and Vanzetti Must Not Die") calling for a mass demonstration for June 5, 1926. The leaflet reads:

> The Massachusetts State Supreme Court has refused a new trial to Nicola Sacco and Bartolomeo Vanzetti.
> THEY ARE NOW SLATED FOR IMMEDIATE EXECUTION!
> They are guilty of one crime only. DEVOTION AND LOYALITY TO THE WORKING CLASS.
> A few days ago they wrote:
> "We are and will remain to the death for the emancipation of the workers; for the elimination of every form of oppression, exploitation and injustice."
> ONLY THE REVOLUTIONARY WORKERS—THE PEOPLE—CAN GIVE US LIFE AND FREEDOM.
> ATTEND THE MASS DEMONSTRATION!
> SACCO AND VANZETTI MUST NOT DIE![25]

In 1927, FBI monitoring intensified in anticipation of the executions. After announcement of the final sentencing, the FBI monitored a large protest at Union Square in Manhattan. "[A]bout 8,000 or more persons were present in demonstration against the execution of Sacco and Vanzetti, handbills in several languages were distributed in the crowd, samples of same are attached to the Washington Copies of this report, some of which advocate a GENERAL STRIKE, as a means of preventing said execution." The New York office noted a future meeting to surveil. "Another meeting is to be held on April 28th, at which it will be decided whether or not the protest strike will be a half day or longer, a tentative date for the strike being set for June 5, 1927."[26]

During the two weeks prior to Sacco and Vanzetti's death, Hoover received reports from around the nation about whether to expect a disturbance. The FBI file is inconsistent in this area. There are field office reports from the cities of Butte, Omaha, New Orleans, Reno, Washington, Chicago, Mobile, Denver, San Francisco, and Oakland, California. Why these cities and not New York and Boston? If Butte was urged by Hoover to watch out for a radical uprising, many other cities also must have gotten the order from the director. In all likelihood, these other local reports were not preserved for historical purposes. However, available documents reveal the discourse of political policing.

In Butte, an agent reported that radical protest was not anticipated because attendance at meetings was very small. "[T]here is not much doing and everything seems quiet in and around Butte and Anaconda, where I was yesterday. If anything further should develop, I shall at once advise you."[27] In New Orleans, the FBI relied on local police, who "had not heard of any contemplated action or demonstration, but they would instruct their forces to keep a diligent lookout and listen for any remarks that would lead to incite trouble or indicate violence, and if any was heard of, proper action would be taken by them and the Bureau advised." In Mobile, Alabama, the police chief "already advised his entire force to be on lookout for radical demonstrations and listen for any remarks that may be made in sympathy with SUBJECTS."[28]

FBI reports from Iowa indicated a low level of political activity. "It was learned that no trouble whatever was expected in the State of Iowa; that there were only three places where anything would likely happen at all, one being Mystic, one Centerville, both mining towns, and the other Sioux City, which was formerly headquarters for the I.W.W. organizations which, however, appears to have melted away." After canvassing law enforcement in Nebraska, the FBI office concluded: "There was no thought there would be any trouble in the State of Nebraska and if any at all, it would be, in all probability Omaha, but it was not thought that even this would occur." In Omaha, the FBI conducted a major review of radical activities by consulting with the Police Department, Post Master, Acting Custodian of the

Federal Building, Post Office Inspector, Secret Service Agents, Special Agents of the Railroads, United States Attorney's Office, Marshal's Office, and assorted informants. An agent attended two meetings organized by the International Defense League. "These meetings were attended by approximately four hundred people, nothing of violence was advocated."[29]

In San Francisco, radical activity surprisingly was not viewed as a threat. Once again, city police shared political dossiers with the bureau. "From the information furnished by the San Francisco Police officials," an FBI agent found, "it appears that the Radical Organizations here are very inactive, that the attendance of their meetings is very small, and that the local authorities do not anticipate any violence or any demonstrations in this city." They contacted Naval Intelligence which reported "the Radical Societies in this District are not very well organized and have been very inactive." [30] The FBI office noted one radical meeting attended by about 400 people featuring speaker Anita Whitney. "A number of RADICAL LEADERS attended this meeting," including J.A. McDonald, of the San Francisco Labor College. "Mr. McDonald received the heartiest response from the audience when he shouted, 'We are not here to talk of bombing but of teaching.'"[31] The San Francisco FBI office canvassed its informants and tried to explain the absence of radical activity.

> That local radicals are without a capable leader, therefore, there is little danger of a concerted out-break of violence. That there exists the possibility of violence by individuals, but such action is improbable, and the danger from this source lies [sic] chiefly from ITALIANS. Informants state they have found no evidence of contemplated violence. . . . Informants will keep in touch with the situation and will report all material developments.[32]

An agent contacted the police department in nearby Oakland and attended several protest meetings undercover. "It is believed that this Office has been able to fully carry out the instructions in the Director's telegram," the field office reported. "The situation in this District may briefly be summarized as being very quiet, that the Radicals are apparently few in number and lack organization and leadership. It is believed that there will be no acts of violence or demonstrations here."[33]

No disturbances were anticipated in Reno, Nevada, but the city police chief "would instruct all of the police officers to keep in close touch with the matter, and any suspicious characters who appeared in Reno would be immediately investigated; that he at this time was making a general clean-up in getting rid of all undesirables, and for that reason he felt that it would be almost impossible for any one to be in or around Reno for any length of time without the police knowing who they were and what their business was."[34] This is the language of social control. Meanwhile, in St. Louis the FBI engaged in ethnic profiling attending meetings at the Italian Fraternal Hall. "Any disturbances which can be traced to this [Sacco and Vanzetti] will be immediately reported. No disturbances have been traced to them to date, and the meetings held have been without incident."[35]

The FBI's description of radicals can be analyzed for language use. How information is communicated in FBI reports and memos provides linguistic evidence of political policing and expressions of official deviance. For example, all uppercase letters highlight both specific individuals as well as categories that denote individuals in political capacities. All uppercase letters were used for the words Sacco, Vanzetti, General Strike, Communists, Radical Leaders, Subjects, and Italians. On a psychological level, all uppercase letters can indicate heightened emotional expression or even emotional instability. Here, it was the opposite of language with the intent to conceal. The uppercase words stand out in the text identifying for the reader an urgent political problem and threat. The responsible parties constituted the Other, who must be isolated and contained.[36]

Sacco and Vanzetti were electrocuted on Aug. 23, 1927. Only one known violent disturbance immediately occurred apart from clashes with police during demonstrations in Boston. In Cleveland, Ohio, a bombing took place at the Franciscan Monastery of St. Joseph's Church "apparently with dynamite, shortly after the execution of these parties." No one was injured in the explosion. "There have been no indications of other disturbances or anarchistic activities."[37] By mid-September, many local FBI offices closed their special investigations in the case. Overall, the FBI did not believe "radical activities" posed a serious threat in 1927. This situation would soon change. Spying in politics rose to new levels as the Left increased in popularity during the early years of the Great Depression.

The Bonus Army under Surveillance

The economic crisis ushered in by the 1929 stock market crash devastated working-class communities. By 1932, the national unemployment rate reached about 25 percent. Several thousand banks had closed and depositors lost their savings. Tens of thousands of people faced eviction from their homes. Under President Herbert Hoover (1929-1932), the federal government responded sluggishly to address the crisis. The depth of the hard times undermined popular confidence in the free market and the capitalist system. Data on social mobility indicate little upward movement during the 1930s—one of the only decades in U.S. history in which Americans hit a wall in terms of advancement. Rampant discrimination in the labor market against blacks, women, and some European immigrants and their children added to the sense of insecurity. Only during the second New Deal (1935-1939) had life began to change with better labor standards and wages.[38]

During the early years of the Great Depression, a movement of the poor and the unemployed took to the streets in many cities out of desperation to find sources of sustenance and relief. One reflection of this crisis was the mob looting of food, which became a nationwide phenomenon. Many newspapers did not report this food resistance out of fear of encouraging the practice. People also marched in political protests. The American Communist Party (CP) declared March 6, 1930, to be International Unemployment Day and rallies took place in most major cities; workers clashed with police who tried to disperse crowds with tear gas. In addition to food and jobs, the issue of shelter maintenance emerged as a priority leading to rent riots. Groups of residents resisted eviction using force; they were not always

successful, but the challenge to authorities (landlords and police) was not lost on political leaders. Social action also took
place as people descended on local government relief offices to
demand greater compensation. In 1932, more than 560 "relief
insurgency" protests were held at city government offices. [39]

In this environment of economic crisis, in June 1932 U.S.
army veterans, as well as other low-income Americans, formed
the Bonus Expeditionary Force (BEF) or "Bonus Army." This
working-class grouping marched on Washington, DC, to make
demands of the federal government. They wanted Congress to
grant a special "soldier's bonus" or monetary award for service
during World War I. After Congress adjourned without providing relief, many marchers remained in the city living in encamp-
ments. On July 28, conflict erupted with the police, who shot
two Bonus marchers "causing the entire mob to become hostile
and riotous," according to the FBI. The Herbert Hoover administration looked askance at the protestors. As Attorney General
William D. Mitchell reported: "[I]t is intolerable that organized
bodies of men having a grievance or demand upon the Government should be allowed to encamp in the city and attempt to live
off the community like soldiers billeted in an enemy country.
Attempts by such groups to intimidate or coerce Congress into
granting their demand hurts rather that helps their cause, and
can only end as this one did, in riot and disorder." [40]

Predictably, FBI and Military Intelligence spied on the Bonus
Army. The historical literature generally ignores this dimension
of the conflict. Lucy G. Barber in *Marching on Washington* (2002)
notes only that President Hoover met in early August with the
FBI director, as well as other government officials, ordering
them "to secure evidence to prove that the Bonus marchers were
under the control of Communists." [41] Paul Dickson and Thomas
B. Allen in *The Bonus Army* (2004) ignore state suppression other
than to note: "J. Edgar Hoover treated the Bonus Army march
as a milestone in his career-long search for Communists. . . .
Hoover's 1932 relationship with the Army's Military Intelligence
Division (MID) continued into the prewar years." [42] Athan G.
Theoharis refers to the state response in a minor way. "In 1932,
Bureau agents also infiltrated the so-called Bonus March. . . .

Bureau agents sought information that the beleaguered president, up for reelection, could use to discredit the marchers as criminals or Communists."[43]

The surveillance went much deeper than these accounts suggest. Initially, President Hoover ordered the Justice Department to conduct an investigation into the July 28 riots. Thereafter, the FBI tracked the BEF providing regular updates to the attorney general. The bureau conducted background checks on 362 protestors, some of whom had been arrested by police in a different incident for disorderly conduct, parading without a permit, assault with a dangerous weapon, trespass on private property, and soliciting alms. Of these 362 people, the police had fingerprints on 51. The FBI found that about one-third had a prior arrest and lacked World War I military service. In other words, they were not entitled to a bonus award. In the FBI's view, these riff-raff and ne'er-do-wells had no legitimate grievances.

The FBI started a second listing consisting of about 4,700 BEF demonstrators. These individuals had signed special papers seeking short-term government loans while in Washington for the protest; the government had promised them a small sum of money if they left the city and returned home. The bureau conducted background checks revealing that 23 percent (1,069 people) had been arrested before. The greatest offenses were for larceny theft (167 people), disorderly conduct and vagrancy (107 people), and drunkenness (98 people). These categories of crime were committed disproportionately by the poor and working class. A very small hard-core criminal element existed among the marchers—only 26 people had more than three prior convictions.[44]

The BEF developed into a social movement consisting of an unusual underclass alliance of veterans, the unemployed, and farmers. Additional marches were planned for the fall and winter of 1932. The FBI director alerted local offices to gather intelligence about these plans. Hoover demanded advance notice if working Americans mobilized in the nation's capitol. The communist issue continued to dominate the director's thinking. He privately discussed the threat of revolution. Hoover wrote to an assistant attorney general:

> We see the Communist Party slowly but surely capitalizing
> upon the unrest and dissatisfaction which has been devel-
> oped by the constant agitation of subversive agencies in this
> country. Communism is accomplishing its objective of unit-
> ing the classes which have become radicalized by constant
> propaganda and turned toward revolutionary channels. The
> converging of these three major class groups [veterans, unem-
> ployed, farmers] upon Washington within a period of a week
> has indeed a major significance and out of it may develop
> almost anything. [45]

Working-class unity posed a threat. Without solid evidence,
Hoover assumed the march constituted a communist conspiracy. He envisioned "gunmen and thugs" resisting the authorities and predicted "almost any form of violence." Hoover,
trained as a lawyer, assumed the role of crude political scientist. He talked about a "mass movement invasion of the Nation's capital [sic]."

> That the Communists are planning on creating trouble is
> evidenced by the careful plans that have been laid with the
> greatest of skill and thought. This includes the massing of vet-
> erans, which will include gunmen and thugs under the guise
> of veterans, to provide a defense group to oppose any action
> on the part of the federal authorities to regulate and check
> the activities of the reds when they reach Washington. This
> will mark a decided advance in the Communist movement
> in the United States and once again the Press will contribute
> thousand of lines of free advertising to the Communist move-
> ment. Basing conclusions upon the ever increasing boldness of
> the Communist's groups, almost any form of violence may be
> anticipated in connection with this combined mass movement
> invasion of the Nation's capital [sic] from December 3rd to
> December 11th, 1932. [46]

How did you start a revolution in the United States? Hoover
heard of one plot in New York City, which he detailed for the
Justice Department. "[T]here is an alleged plot of one Hadley of
New York City to organize a revolution against the Government
of the United States, through enlisting members of the Bonus

Expeditionary Force, and the ultimate seizure of the various Government arsenals."[47]

The narrative was more complicated. On Oct. 27, 1932, the former treasurer of the BEF visited the FBI field office in Manhattan. FBI agent L. E. Kingman reported that the BEF leader had been contacted by an individual named Duke Hadley, who might contribute funds to the BEF. Instead, Hadley suggested a wild plan for violent revolution.

> Hadley outlined a plan for a revolution against the government of the United States and stated that he was anxious to interest the members of the B.E.F. in his plan and that if they would be interested he had definite plans for the seizing of government arsenals and that he could also get members of the Army and Navy to lay down their arms and refuse to support the United States against the revolutionists, and that by means of his plan it could be possible to seize the entire government structure. Hadley claimed to have connections in Washington with senators and congressmen, and other government officials, and claimed he knew "the inside stuff" of how the government is operated by the officials.[48]

The story got thicker with hints of government infiltration. The FBI director reported that the BEF leader "stated that for a time he was of the opinion that Hadley might have been an undercover agent of some sort working for the government, and had outlined these revolutionary plans merely for the purpose of ascertaining if the members of the B.E.F. were already engaged in revolutionary activities." This view was very plausible. In the history of political policing, undercover government agents have been known to advocate violence to illicit information to entrap activists.[49] Hadley might have been an operative of Military Intelligence.

In Fall 1932, Hoover and local agents communicated about their surveillance of working-class groups intent on returning to Washington. Again, FBI language use in memos by the director illustrates several points. Hoover framed working-class organizers as the enemy using the terms "troublemaker" and "agitator" along with communist. He referred to subjects as "one" John

Doe, etc. This made the person an object of suspicion separate from the rest of us. In several cases, Hoover noted local leaders had visited the Soviet Union, which de facto signified sympathy for the Soviets.

Only a political police organization adopts the troublemaker/ agitator view of social protest. Study the local protest leaders, looking for criminal records. The G-men and their surrogates wrote down automobile license plate numbers to aid background research. Informers attended political meetings. The FBI viewed itself at war with street protestors. They talked in military terms about containing "columns" of demonstrators worried about an "invasion."

The Bonus Army FBI file contains no discussion of the demands of protestors, and why they undertook long travel to voice their grievances. There is very little understanding of the Depression conditions, which prompted thousands of people to march to improve their lives. The FBI held the narrow and distorted view that most forms of dissent must be inspired by communists. Blame all troubles on a "dangerous" UnAmerican entity without an understanding of its appeal in working-class life.

By October 1932, FBI agents and other operatives put a variety of working-class organizations under surveillance and researched some of their leaders. For example, intelligence suggested that Vernon Butler, Michigan State Commander of the BEF, was a communist. An agent interviewed BEF members in Detroit and learned that Butler was not popular. "[I]t is claimed by the majority that he is a strong sympathizer of local communists and has been accused of turning foodstuffs over to such organizations rather than to the B.E.F. for whom it was originally secured . . . I have learned that Butler is still hanging out in the cellar of an old building located on the corner of John R. and Elizabeth St., Detroit, where it is stated that he occasionally secures food and other supplies, allegedly for the B.E.F."[50]

Other local BEF leaders also were under surveillance. On Oct. 12, 1932, Hoover wrote a memorandum in an attempt to prosecute Hoke Smith from Pennsylvania. In Uniontown, the city police found an outstanding warrant for child abandonment. "It is understood that Smith was one of the alleged leaders of the Bonus Expeditionary Force, a number of the members of which organization are at present in a camp called Fort Necessity, near Uniontown, Pennsylvania." Hoover recommended the arrest of Smith *after* the camp disbanded in order not to provoke the protestors. In Charlotte, North Carolina, the FBI paid special attention to Bernie B. Sprouse—leader of the North and South Carolina contingents of the BEF—but found he no longer was an activist. They referred to other agitation. "The reports [from informers] indicate that there are two or three ex-servicemen in Charlotte, whose names are unknown, who are endeavoring to start a Bonus March, but have apparently made no progress to date."[51]

In mid-October, surveillance of the National Unemployed Council uncovered plans for a national Hunger March on Washington planned for early December 1932. A long Hoover memorandum, "Marches on Washington," discussed the participation of about "3,000 official delegates from forty-eight states." The march would originate in "eight remote cities, the columns to merge as they approached Washington." The Unemployed Council "was to be in full charge of all arrangements . . . and the Workers International Relief was to share the responsibility."[52] Again, the FBI worried about Communist infiltration.

Of equal concern, veterans planned a second rally in Washington to join the Hunger March. The veterans and the unemployed delegates would present shared demands. This coalition also included the Farmers National Relief Convention. The FBI viewed the leader of the Farmers, Lem Harris, in Red Scare terms. "Reports state that Harris is a young Harvard graduate, who was formerly a correspondent for the Moscow Daily News in Russia." Hoover traced the roots of the Farmers Convention to communist organizing in Sioux City, Iowa, and St. Louis, Missouri. How large a march should the FBI expect? The FBI exaggerated its size by quoting an organizer who "was confident that there would be representatives in Washington of at least one million members and sympathizers" and the "Washington Bonus Marchers would be 100,000 strong."[53]

In 1932, political protests focusing on the nation's capitol were a relatively new phenomenon, although precedents existed like Coxey's Army in the 1890s and female suffrage advocates during the Progressive era.

The FBI infiltrated a meeting of the Workers Ex-Service-men's League and became alarmed when some members asked the group's leader, William Guest, "if guns and ammunition would be available" for the march because "they did not like to fight with bare hands and brickbats." The FBI noted, "Guest did not respond to these queries." A background check on Guest found that "he is an ex-convict and on parole from a fifteen-year sentence for murder in Mobile, Alabama, and was arrested on the morning of October 12, 1932 on suspicion of highway robbery, being released for lack of evidence." The FBI believed "functionaries of the Communist Party" directed the Workers Ex-Servicemen's League.[54]

Particular "troublemakers" were under watch. The Radical Squad of the New York City Police Department identified "Larry McQuestion and George A. McQueen, alias George Queen, who were actively engaged with the Maritime Workers Industrial Union." The two activists, along with several other individuals, organized "plans for the housing and parking of the hunger strikers. The New York City Police Department suggested that all precautions should be taken with McQuestion because of the fact that he was known to carry a gun at times and was a great troublemaker."[55]

In Detroit, the FBI noted that children from the Youth Pioneers Organization might travel to Washington and a "notorious Communist," John T. Pace, "will evidently take the leading part." The intelligence on Pace indicated he was "recently arrested at Lincoln Park on a charge of assault. The Police at Lincoln Park, Michigan, while referring to John Pace, stated that they had received information that he has in his possession a considerable amount of dynamite. The reliability of this information is unknown, and efforts are being made to verify it." Why cite it if it was not verified?[56]

The FBI feared the idea of the "rank and file": Workers who occupied the bottom tiers of the economy; the untold millions who might rise up and demand a voice in the democracy. A political circular in Cleveland, Ohio, entitled "Rank and File

Veterans March to Washington," indicated that this formation planned to arrive on the opening day of the congressional
session on December 5. One sentence in the circular alarmed
Hoover. "This time we will have fighting leadership that won't
sell us out." Of course, Hoover did not care if veterans needed
government help. Rather, the social control dimension—contain all disturbances—negated consideration of the merits of
a protest movement. Hoover listed the itinerary of eight protest "columns," including stops in 22 cities along the route to
Washington. Did FBI agents investigate the working class in
each of these 22 cities? The Bonus March FBI file is not clear
on this point. But reports from the midwest, the south, and the
far west were sent to FBI headquarters, in addition to coverage
of worker activism on the east coast. The intelligence could be
very detailed. "[A]n agitator claims that 3,000 are to assemble at
Chattanooga on Nov. 29, 1932" but "only three automobiles had
been tendered for transportation by local people." The bureau
also tracked the number of children participating in the protest,
as well as the number of "colored" activists.[57]

They also heard of plans for future protests. "One Dirk
DeJonge and Louis Olsen are said to be known in Portland,
Oregon as Communist leaders and agitators. They are reported
to be advocating a further hunger march on Washington after
the outcome of the present efforts. Information, the reliability of
which is unknown, is to the effect that these leaders are claiming that there will be some 30,000 to 50,000 who will assemble
in Washington."[58]

As the December 5 Hunger March approached, Hoover
wrote several memos a week to the attorney general reporting
on mini-marches in several cities. Field reports noted license
plate numbers of cars and trucks transporting protestors as well
as, again, the presence of communists. Hoover discussed the
Cincinnati leader Leo (Polly) Starke, "one of the most dangerous
communists in the United States, with a police record in several
states." In Colorado Springs, Colorado, the FBI focused on a
troublemaker named John Sallak, "who was arrested at Colorado Springs August 17, 1932, for violation of the Prohibition
Law." In Chicago, the FBI formulated a "list of the functionaries

said to be connected with the Communist Party and charged with the coordination of local Communist activities for the Hunger March." Sixteen names were mentioned, which survived the censor's hand in the declassified file.[59] In Oklahoma City, the FBI discussed a communist organizer named J. I. Whidden. "He was arrested October 15, 1930, on a charge of rioting, it appearing that at the time of his arrest he was a leader of a mob of unemployed which stormed grocery stores and raided them for food. The picture of this man has also been obtained and will be forwarded." In Youngstown, Ohio, the FBI identified a man known as A. B. Lewis, who had run on the communist ticket for Sheriff. "Reports indicate that he has been to Russia and is a troublesome agitator. He expects to be in Washington for the hunger march."[60]

The FBI noted some workers were arrested along the way to Washington. "There were a number of arrests at Youngstown for inflammatory speeches." In Chattanooga, Tennessee, 47 people were charged with crimes. "The leaders of this contingent are William McCuston and James Smith, a Negro." In Philadelphia, 96 marchers were under surveillance, including 39 "colored" protestors and "practically all of the [white] marchers are of foreign birth or extraction." During a rally in Minneapolis, Minnesota, a riot broke out. "A number of speeches were made and a crowd of about fifteen hundred proceeded to the City Hall and Courthouse, where they were met by police officers. A riot was started which resulted in eighteen being arrested. Several policemen were injured and some automobiles damaged. The names of the persons jailed are as follows: [18 names follow]."[61]

The Bonus Army and Hunger Marches were a success. When President Franklin D. Roosevelt took office in January 1933, he immediately responded with a "hundred days" of legislation and government action to help ease the plight of the poor and working class. These protests undoubtedly helped push FDR and the New Deal into action.

Hoover kept the Bonus March file open for several years. FBI agents reported to headquarters whenever they heard rumors about new marches. On March 16, 1934, Hoover referred to "an anonymous communication received in this Division, advising

that one Mike Thomas is now in New York endeavoring to recruit a new Bonus Army."[62] Hoover worried the unemployed
might march in early January 1935 led by the National Unemployed League.[63] Later that year an informant "mingling with
people loafing in Union Square, New York City" also heard
plans for a march on Washington. The informant talked about
guns, so Hoover notified both the New York City police and the
Secret Service. "[M]any of the marchers are armed with pistols
and that there are two armored trucks at Hornell, New York,
which are loaded with machine guns. These trucks, it was stated,
will leave for Washington to participate in the bonus demonstration."[64] No march of this kind ever took place. Unfortunately, the
local reports in the Bonus March FBI file were destroyed so the
file consists only of the director's correspondence.

Spying on the Workers Alliance of America

During the early Depression, working-class radicals helped organize tens of thousands of the unemployed in American cities
to demand relief and jobs, and to prevent evictions from their
homes. Street protests helped shape the feeling of class tension
during these unprecedented "hard times." Sometimes the unemployed were met with police violence.[65] Communists were
active in the Unemployed Councils. Socialists participated in the
Workers Unemployed League. The two organizations largely
remained separate because communists and socialists refused
to work together, fragmented by ideological, political disagreements. However, in 1935 unity became possible after the CP endorsed the "popular front" to join with others on the Left. As the
communist position changed, almost immediately unemployed
groups throughout the nation merged into a new organization,
the Workers Alliance of America (WAA) led by David Lasser
and Herbert Benjamin. The WAA claimed to represent the interests of the jobless as well as relief workers employed by the government's Works Progress Administration (WPA). By 1938, the
WAA claimed 800,000 members in about 1,400 chapters. They
adopted the slogan of the resurgent labor movement—the "right

to organize"—and led walk-outs and strikes. They wanted the federal government to treat WPA workers as employees, not "relief workers" or "paupers."[66]

The FBI opened a file on the WAA within a year of the group's founding and eventually collected more than 10,000 pages.[67] The WAA posed three threats: It represented poor working Americans and the government feared the disenfranchised, especially when it had a large component of young workers.[68] They also tracked the WAA because of its radical leaders. Lasser identified as a socialist; Benjamin as a communist. Lastly, the WAA agitated for public sector unionism, which was not yet well established at the time. According to the FBI, the idea that socialists and communists were trying to influence federal workers was intolerable. As one example of the FBI's surveillance, in June 1936 the WAA won a WPA strike in Detroit gaining increased benefits for men on relief. An FBI informant tracking the Alliance reported they consisted of "remnants of the Communist Unemployed Councils" and noted organizing success in nearby Hamtramck with headquarters at the Russian Communist Club.[69] By 1939, the WAA became a victim of congressional witch-hunts when communists were banned from federal relief programs.[70]

The CIO and the FBI

"Organize the unorganized" proclaimed the reinvigorated labor movement after the founding in 1935 of the Committee for Industrial Organization (CIO). The new CIO enrolled about 4 million workers between 1936 and 1940, breaking down many old barriers in the workforce along race, skill, and gender lines. The CIO pressed for union recognition, higher wages, vacations with pay, and enhanced workplace control. Nearly 500,000 workers engaged in about 400 "sit-down" strikes between September 1936 and June 1937. This popular strike movement threatened the status quo as wage-earners occupied sites of production to demand changes in their work lives. Conservatives were shocked and outraged. *Life* magazine reported these strikes were the "Nation's No. 1 problem." But the sit-down to a great extent gained mass appeal as a method of expressing grievances. The mainstream press around the nation reported on sit-down actions outside the workplace led by such disparate actors as children, widows, beer drinkers, and sports teams.[71]

For the FBI, the new working-class unity signaled danger. It meant not only that Communists and their allies were advancing their cause. But big business would have to share a greater part of their wealth with their employees, an idea that conservatives found reprehensible. The FBI initiated surveillance against workers in three dimensions of their lives. They planted informers inside the CIO, inside factories, as well as in local communities to monitor working-class development.

On Aug. 24, 1936, President Roosevelt met with Director Hoover to discuss domestic subversive activities. Hoover told the president that communists sought to gain control of several CIO unions: the United Mine Workers Union, the International Longshoremen's Union, and the Newspaper Guild. "By doing so they would be able at any time to paralyze the country."[72] Two weeks later Hoover, with Roosevelt's backing, reinvigorated political policing by ordering each FBI office to monitor important industries—maritime, steel, coal, clothing, newspapers, and governmental affairs. He also demanded local surveillance of political activity in the armed services and educational institutions as well as coverage of the "general activities of Communist and Affiliated Organizations, Fascist, Anti-Fascist movements, and activities in Organized Labor organizations."[73] The call to spy on the union movement had been issued despite the New Deal's embrace of worker rights. The National Industrial Recovery Act (1933) and the Wagner Act (1935) had established collective bargaining; the Social Security Act (1935) provided for old age pensions and unemployment insurance; the Fair Labor and Standards Act (1938) established the minimum wage and the 40-hour work week for the first time. Labor leaders were known to tell wage-earners: "The President wants you to join a union."[74] Yet, the president's FBI watched these developments very closely, worried about the influence of radicals.

CIO President John L. Lewis correctly perceived that the FBI put him under surveillance. Saul Alinsky recounts the following exchange between Lewis and Roosevelt in 1940:

> Lewis asked the President, "If you want the CIO's support, what assurances can you give the CIO?" Roosevelt did not appreciate the labor leader's attitude. Lewis recalls, "The President became irritated and snapped at me. 'Well, what do you mean, haven't I always been friendly to the CIO?'"

> Lewis answered, "Well, Mr. President, if you are a friend of labor, why is the FBI tapping all my phones, both my home and my office, and why do they have instructions to follow me about?"

> The President said, "That's not true!" Lewis pressed the point. "I say it is true!" The President said, "That's a damn lie." Lewis recalls, "I got up, looked down at him and said, 'Nobody can call John L. Lewis a liar and least of all Franklin Delano Roosevelt!'"

> "Then I started walking out and got my hat and coat. Just as I got to the door, the President called out, 'Come back, John, I want to talk to you.' I walked back and I said, 'My phones are tapped, and they are, and everything I said is true, and whatever I said I know because I can prove it by [Attorney General] Frank Murphy, who told me so and who knows about it because he has seen your orders to the FBI to do so."[75]

Lewis, who contemplated a run for president, opposed Roosevelt in the 1940 election by supporting Republican candidate Wendell Willkie. After Roosevelt won reelection, Lewis resigned as head of the CIO. In all likelihood, the FBI's wiretapping helped precipitate Lewis' split with both FDR and the CIO.

The FBI investigated Lewis from 1937 through 1941 generating a 2,815-page file.[76] The government's attack on labor also included radical longshoremen's leader Harry Bridges. Lewis had appointed Bridges, president of the ILWU on the San Francisco waterfront, the Western Regional Director of the CIO. In 1936,

Bridges first faced deportation hearings. The FBI hotly pursued him, although it is unclear when the investigation began. His declassified FBI file reportedly contains no material before 1940.[77] How many other prominent labor leaders were under put surveillance? We know the FBI tracked the CIO's top lawyer, Lee Pressman, who had communist ties. The FBI also assembled files on Sidney Hillman, president of the Amalgamated Clothing Workers Union (ACWU), and Walter Reuther of the United Auto Workers.[78] The surveillance extended to Frances Perkins, the Secretary of Labor in President Roosevelt's cabinet, who became a friend of the labor movement.[79]

FBI spying again focused on leaders of the Women's Trade Union League. WTUL became one of the most active women's groups in Washington and the bureau referred to its "definitely Communistic leanings." WTUL leader Margaret V. Buffum, who worked for the U.S. Department of Labor, was "very Communistic and one of the more active members of this league." An FBI source reported Buffum "came from New York City with some other Jews of Communistic leanings and that she was one of the more prominent figures in their recent meeting at the Y.M.C.A."[80] Meanwhile, the bureau also collected intelligence on Elizabeth Christian, the WTUL secretary-treasurer, even though she "did not have Communist leanings and does not have a Communistic background." She was a dupe, who "became involved in the activities of the league and chartered the club innocently prior to her having had an opportunity to become aware of the real purpose and intent of the other members."[81]

By 1940, the FBI developed a national program to illegally open mail, plant bugs in homes and offices, and conduct break-ins. The targets included at least four CIO unions: the National Maritime Union; the United Auto Workers; the United Electrical, Radio and Machine Workers; and the United Mine Workers. In a major move, the FBI wiretapped the headquarters of the CIO Industrial Union Council, a leadership group consisting of members from many of the new unions.[82]

The CIO investigations continued through and after World War II. In order to convince President Harry Truman to act against CIO communists, FBI officials sent numerous memos to the White House with reports of communist activity in the meatpacking, telephone, railroad, and retail industries.[83] In 1947, the FBI leadership met in its Executives Conference and reaffirmed their investigations of seven CIO unions. The new targets included the United Public Workers; the Transport Workers Union; National Union of Marine Cooks and Stewards; International Longshoremen's and Warehousemen's Union; CIO Maritime Committee; and the American Communications Association. A wide array of techniques were used in the surveillance: informants, technical and microphone surveillance, trash covers, and collecting literature.[84]

Scholars have not often studied surveillance in local working-class communities. But we know that in Baltimore the CIO organized in the steel industry and the FBI took the side of big management. By 1940, the CIO's Steel Workers Organizing Committee (SWOC) tried to sign up workers at the large Bethlehem Steel and Glenn Martin factories, which were dependent on defense contracts. Historian Kenneth D. Durr notes that at Bethlehem the company resorted to repressive measures to keep the CIO out. "The company used Pinkerton agents, armed 'special police,' and even local law enforcement officers against SWOC. Even the FBI cooperated, planting an agent in a Highlandtown row house to monitor a SWOC organizer's activities."[85]

Anticommunism became a leading issue in the Congress led by Representative Martin Dies of Texas. Beginning in 1938, Dies Committee hearings targeted the CIO. Among the witnesses was John Frey, head of the AFL's Metal Trades Department, who charged that 238 communists served as CIO organizers. Frey called the CIO's sit-down strikes a "Communist training camp."[86] The Red-baiting in Congress led to the passage of the Smith Act (1940), which outlawed speech that advocated the violent overthrow of the government. The Act was designed to criminalize the speech of the American Communist Party and resulted in prosecutions against more than 100 of its leaders over the next decade.[87]

In 1939 and 1940 a massive expansion of FBI spying took place with much of it focused on workers in industry and in their neighborhoods. Three new FBI initiatives began: the

American Legion Contact Program; the Custodial Detention List; and the Plant Informant Program. The upsurge in spying was tied to the looming war in Europe. Although the U.S. was not yet engaged militarily, the domestic defense industry had begun to gear up for wartime arms production. Of course, how the FBI interpreted threats was politically biased against workers, particularly immigrants and their children. Indeed, the foreign-born were considered "foreign"—that is, outsiders whose loyalties could not be trusted. The urban working class in 1940 was predominantly first- and second-generation immigrants with the young, adult second generation forming the backbone of organized worker movements.[88]

Moreover, the FBI privileged the threat posed by workers because of the preceding decade-long upsurge in bottom-up organizing. This key period of FBI expansion occurred in reaction to the enhanced presence of the American working class. In sum, the FBI developed a battle plan to curtail the rise of militant working-class movements.

The bureau recruited tens of thousands of new informers, planting them across industrial America. The FBI did not need congressional approval to hire new informers, as opposed to other new employees such as agents. The FBI already increased its personnel at a very rapid rate at this time—about a 600 percent increase occurred between 1936 and 1945.[89] Thus, the rapid expansion of investigative activity directed against labor and other subversive entities had never been greater.

Surveillance extended into local communities. Under the American Legion Contact Program, the FBI recruited more than 40,000 war veterans between 1940 and 1945 to serve as informers. The FBI directed them to monitor radicals and immigrants—"groups or settlements of persons of foreign extraction or possible un-American sympathies." The informers identified "the leaders of these groups, the locations of their meeting places, the identities and scope of operation of their social clubs, societies, language schools, etc." The call to surveil the social life of ethnic groups reflected deeply held nativist views. The FBI also wanted to know "whether persons are sent into communities to spread propaganda, to raise funds for various purposes, or for the purpose of agitating such foreign extraction groups."[90] The task of spying was not too difficult to accomplish since the Legion already had "posts" or headquarters in many small towns and big cities from which to coordinate their counter-subversive activities. More than 11,000 Legion posts reported suspicious activity to the FBI.[91] This included looking out for draft evaders. During the war, the FBI pursued 445,649 cases of draft evasion and convicted 11,320 men.[92]

The potential for fascist sympathies among Italian Americans and German Americans was investigated, but the hunt for disloyalty and subversion extended to anyone with radical politics. The problem of "fronts" always posed a problem from a civil liberties perspective. That is, if a communist was active in a group, such as a CIO trade union, the FBI often assumed the group as a whole served as a cover for CP activity. CIO chief John L. Lewis initially had welcomed communist participation in the labor movement to help it organize and grow. Thus, Lewis and the FBI had very different visions of the role of communists, and the FBI became determined to surveil any organization in which communists played a role.

Moreover, the task to surveil Italian Americans and German Americans was not easily accomplished. Several million Italian Americans resided in the nation. The number of German Americans, a long settled group, was even larger. These ethnic groups established their own enclaves upon initial settlement in the U.S. but by 1940 many had moved out of them into other areas. Working-class neighborhoods could be multiethnic in composition, that is, people of many different backgrounds lived on the same block or even within the same building.

American Legion members were chosen to conduct surveillance because these ex-military men usually were super patriotic and unlikely to question FBI orders. Veterans had been trained to kill the enemy. Reconnaissance on the domestic front would be an extension of their prior service to the nation. The Legion easily became integrated into the right-wing, anti-communist network.

The Legion also aided the preventative Custodian Detention Program to identify politically dangerous people in time of a national emergency. The plan initially focused on communists as well as Italian Americans and German Americans. FBI agents used five surveillance methods to generate a special list consisting of several thousand people. They reviewed subscription lists of communist, Italian, and German newspapers published in the U.S.; consulted membership lists of communist and fascist groups; infiltrated the meetings of these groups; collected intelligence from public rallies and demonstrations; and, lastly, relied on other confidential reports. The Detention Plan, while unilaterally established by Hoover, soon won sanction from the attorney general and the U.S. Justice Department.[93]

The bureau's Plant Informant Program (1940-1969) added another layer of spying in industry. Informants were sent into factories in the defense sector to secretly monitor employee politics. By mid-1942, these labor spies numbered nearly 21,000 employed in about 4,000 plants.[94] They focused on activists in labor organizations and strike activities. Although I only cover the period roughly up to 1945 in this chapter, the Plant Informant Program in its entirety needs further study. During the Korean War, for example, it expanded dramatically. By the end of 1951, some 52,791 informants patrolled industry for the FBI.[95] The FBI file on the Program totals 2,564 pages.[96]

By 1940, segments of the organized Left criticized FBI spying. The National Lawyers Guild (NLG), founded in 1937, began to contest the practice of "political policing" and called for Hoover's removal. The NLG, an alternative to the American Bar Association which excluded blacks and Jews, also assisted the emerging CIO by providing legal advice. Lee Pressman, a NLG member, testified in 1940 before the U.S. House Judiciary Committee against FBI wiretapping. The FBI also investigated Maurice Sugar, general counsel of the UAW and a leading labor lawyer in Detroit.[97] Ernie Goodman, a Sugar law partner active in both the NLG and the UAW, received national notoriety for opposing the bureau. In 1940, he successfully gained the release of Americans prosecuted for recruiting volunteers to fight for the Loyalists in the Spanish Civil War. Goodman, himself a subject of FBI surveillance, publicly denounced the role of the FBI in violating the civil liberties of his clients. In Washington, Hoover took note of these comments and retaliated against Goodman by providing derogatory material to journalist Walter Winchell, who published a column about efforts to hinder FBI investigations. The controversy led Senator George Norris of Nebraska, the aging Progressive reformer, to met with Goodman and warn in a congressional speech that "the time will soon arrive when there will be a spy behind every stump and a detective in every closet in the land."[98]

In August 1940, the small Trotskyite faction of the Left organized in the Socialist Workers Party (SWP) identified the FBI as strike breakers and union busters. Carl O'Shea wrote in the *Fourth International*: "[T]he defense program backed by Roosevelt and Willkie is being used as an excuse to direct all sorts of repressive measures against organized labor—such as the use of the Federal Bureau of Investigation against unions and strikers." O'Shea noted the leadership of the American Federation of Labor (AFL) embraced the FBI and its president, William Green, gave the main address before the graduating class at the FBI academy. In several strikes, the FBI took the side of management. "It was Green's friends of the FBI who functioned as agents provocateur and stool pigeons among the Minneapolis WPA strikers; who worked for a whole year to frame leaders of drivers' unions in the Middle West; who were sent into the New York drivers' strike and the Kearny strike; and who used thuggery and third-degree methods against members of the Mine, Mill, and Smelter Workers Union. It is the FBI men who have a standing order to bust EVERY important strike today."[99]

The latter statement was an exaggeration. New research in FBI files is still needed to document the scope of FBI spying across industrial America. However, it does seem certain that between World War I and the end of World War II the FBI devoted considerable resources to contain organizing from the bottom up.

Notes

1. Herbert G. Gutman, "The Workers' Search for Power: Labor in the Gilded Age," reprinted in Gutman and Ira Berlin, eds., *Power and*

Culture: Essays on the American Working Class (New York: The New Press, 1987), 70-92.

2. Theda Skocpol, "Bringing the State Back In: Strategies of Analysis in Current Research," in Peter B. Evans, Dietrich Rueschemeyer, and Skocpol, eds., *Bringing the State Back In* (New York: Cambridge University Press, 1985), 3-43.

3. Richard Polenberg, *Fighting Faiths: The Abrams Case, the Supreme Court and Free Speech* (New York: Viking, 1987), 165.

4. Richard Gid Powers, *Broken: The Troubled Past and Uncertain Future of the FBI* (New York: Simon and Schuster, 2004), 91; Melvyn Dubofsky, *"We Shall Be All": A History of the Industrial Workers of the World* (New York: Quadrangle, 1969), 233, 250.

5. Regin Schmidt, *Red Scare: The FBI and the Origins of Anticommunism, 1919-1943* (Copenhagen: Museum Tusculanum Press, 2000), 212.

6. Claire A. Culleton, *Joyce and the G-Men: J. Edgar Hoover's Manipulation of Modernism* (New York: Palgrave Macmillan, 2004), 123, 138-139.

7. FBI Monograph, "Smear Campaign Against the FBI: The Nation," April 1959, 125-126; Schmidt, *Red Scare*, 78, 332-333.

8. Edward J. Brennan to Director, "'New World Lessons for Old World Peoples' – Radical Pamphlets," Dec. 12, 1921, Women's Trade Union League (WTUL) FBI file.

9. Edward J. Brennan to Director, "Women's Trade Union League, Radical Activities," March 10, 1922, WTUL FBI file.

10. Athan G. Theoharis, *The FBI and American Democracy: A Brief Critical History* (Lawrence: University of Kansas Press, 2004), 24-25.

11. Chicago FBI office, "American Negro Labor Congress, Radical Negro Communist Activity," Nov. 25, 1925, 1-2, American Negro Labor Congress (ANLC) FBI file.

12. Ibid., 4.

13. Ibid.

14. FBI monograph, "Membership of the Communist Party USA, 1919-1954," May 1955, iii; T. H. Watkins, *The Hungry Years: A Narrative History of the Great Depression in America* (New York; Henry Holt, 1999), 364.

15. Ivan Greenberg, "Federal Bureau of Investigation," in Nikki Brown and Barry Stentiford, eds., *The Jim Crow Encyclopedia* (Westport: Greenwood Press, 2009), 294-298.

16. Ibid.

17. Culleton, *Joyce and the G-Men*, 142, 200n3.

18. Boston SAC John A. Dowd to FBI Director, July 8, 1926, Sacco-Vanzetti FBI file.

19. Affidavit of Fred J. Weyand, July 17, 1926, 2, Sacco-Vanzetti FBI file.

20. Ibid., 3.

21. Affidavit of Lawrence Letherman, July 8, 1926, Sacco-Vanzetti FBI file.

22. Washington, D.C., FBI office, "Memorandum for the Director," July 21, 1926, Sacco-Vanzetti FBI file.

23. Affidavit of Fred J. Weyand; Dowd to FBI Director, Sacco-Vanzetti FBI file.

24. Boston SAC John A. Dowd to FBI Director, July 17, 1926, Sacco-Vanzetti FBI file.

25. Leaflet, "Sacco and Vanzetti Must Not Die," n.d., Sacco-Vanzetti FBI file.

26. New York FBI office, "Sacco-Vanzetti Protest Meeting," April 20, 1927, Sacco-Vanzetti FBI file.

27. SAC D. H. Dickson to FBI Director, Aug. 15, 1927, Sacco-Vanzetti FBI file.

28. FBI New Orleans field office, "Nicola Sacco and Bartolomeo Vanzetti," Aug. 16, 1927, Sacco-Vanzetti FBI file.

29. FBI Field office Omaha, "Radical Activities in Connection with Case of Sacco and Vanzetti," Aug. 15, 1927, Sacco-Vanzetti FBI file.

30. San Francisco FBI report, "N. Sacco, B. Vanzetti," Aug. 15, 1927, Sacco-Vanzetti FBI file.

31. Ibid.

32. The FBI also wrote: "Informants advanced the interesting theory that the automobile has much to do with this lagging interest. As most of the workers now own automobiles, they spend their spare time riding with their families. Thus occupied and interested, they have neither the opportunity, desire nor inclination to engage in radical work or listen to agitators." This observation seems misleading because the American car culture broadly reached the working class only after World War II. San Francisco FBI report, "Niccolla [sic] Sacco, Bartholomeo Vanzetti," Aug. 13, 1927, Sacco-Vanzetti FBI file.

33. San Francisco FBI report, "N. Sacco, B. Vanzetti," Aug. 15, 1927, Sacco-Vanzetti FBI file.

34. San Francisco FBI office, "N. Sacco, B. Vanzetti," Aug. 16, 1927, Sacco-Vanzetti FBI file.

35. St. Louis FBI field report, "Nicole [sic] Sacco and Bartolomeo Vanzetti," Aug. 16, 1927, Sacco-Vanzetti FBI file.

36. I've read thousands of pages of FBI memos and reports and the discourse in the Sacco-Vanzetti case is unusual. In most instances, FBI writers only use all capitals to identify the subjects of investigation.

37. Columbus, Ohio, FBI field report, "Sacco-Vanzetti," Aug. 23, 1927, Sacco-Vanzetti FBI file.

38. One of the best surveys of the thirties is Robert S. McElvaine, *The Great Depression: America, 1929-1941* (New York: Times Books, 1984).

39. Frances Fox Piven and Richard A. Cloward, *Poor People's Movements: How They Succeed, How They Fail* (New York: Vintage, 1979), 49-59; Irving Bernstein, *The Lean Years: A History of the American Worker, 1920-1933* (New York: Houghton Mifflin, 1970), 421-423.

40. Attorney General's Report, Sept. 9, 1932. The FBI holds a 232-page file on the Bonus Army, which covers the years 1932 to 1935.

41. Lucy G. Barber, *Marching on Washington: The Forging of an American Political Tradition* (Berkeley: University of California Press, 2002), 103.

42. Paul Dickson and Thomas B. Allen, *The Bonus Army: An American Epic* (New York: Walker and Co., 2004), 293-294.

43. Theoharis, *The FBI and American Democracy*, 36.

44. J. E. Hoover, "Memorandum for Assistant Attorney General Dodds," Sept. 7, 1932, Bonus Army FBI file.

45. J. E. Hoover, "Memorandum for Assistant Attorney General Dodds," Nov. 8, 1932, Bonus Army FBI file.

46. Ibid.

47. Ibid.

48. Ibid.; NY SAC J.E.P. Dunn to FBI Director, Nov. 2, 1932; SAC L. E. Kingman, "Memorandum For Special Agent in Charge J. E. P. Dunn," Oct. 28, 1932. Bonus Army FBI file.

49. Kingman, "Memorandum for Special Agent in Charge J. E. P. Dunn."

50. William Larson to FBI Director, Sept. 28, 1932, Bonus Army FBI file.

51. FBI Director, "Memorandum for Assistant Attorney General Dodds," Oct. 12, 1932. Bonus Army FBI file.

52. J. E. Hoover, "Marches on Washington and Demonstrations Scheduled for the Opening of Congress," Nov. 21, 1932, Bonus Army FBI file.

53. J. E. Hoover, "Memorandum for the Attorney General Dodds," Nov. 8, 1932, Bonus Army FBI file.

54. Hoover, "Marches on Washington and Demonstrations Scheduled for the Opening of Congress,"

55. Ibid.

56. Ibid.

57. Ibid

58. Ibid.

59. The subversives who helped to build America were: Mrs. Ashley; Nick Barta; Ethel Peran; Nick Blattner; Leslie Burt; Adolph Davis;

John Hecker; H.L.A. Holeman; Nelis Kjar; Carl Lochner; Morris Nelson; Herbert Newton; Steve Rubicki; Alex Spencer; Otto Wangerin; and John Williamson. J.E. Hoover, "Memorandum for the Attorney General," Nov. 26, 1932, Bonus Army FBI file.

60. Ibid.; J. E. Hoover, "Memorandum for Attorney General Dodds," Nov. 30, 1932, Bonus Army FBI file.

61. J. E. Hoover, "Memorandum for Attorney General," Dec. 2, 1932, Bonus Army FBI file.

62. J. Edgar Hoover to Assistant Attorney General, March 16, 1934, Bonus Army FBI file.

63. J. Edgar Hoover to Assistant Attorney General, Nov. 29, 1934, Bonus Army FBI file.

64. J. Edgar Hoover to Assistant Attorney General, May 31, 1935, Bonus Army FBI file.

65. McElvaine, The Great Depression, 75; Marilyn S. Johnson, Street Justice: A History of Police Violence in New York City (Boston: Beacon Press, 2004), 157-164.

66. Chad Alan Goldberg, Citizens and Paupers: Relief, Rights, and Race from the Freedmen's Bureau to Workfare (Chicago: University of Chicago Press, 2007), 106-122.

67. Prof. Eric Davin won release of the WAA FBI file in litigation under the Freedom of Information Act and donated the records to the labor archives at the University of Pittsburgh.

68. See, for example, Randall G. Shelden, Controlling the Dangerous Classes: A History of Criminal Justice in America (Boston: Allyn and Bacon, 2007).

69. James J. Lorence, Organizing the Unemployed: Community and Union Activists in the Industrial Heartland (Albany: SUNY Press, 1996), 127, 130.

70. Robert Justin Goldstein, American Blacklist: The Attorney General's List of Subversive Organizations (Lawrence: University of Kansas Press, 2008), 14.

71. Ivan Greenberg, "At the Center: Sit-Down Strikes by U.S. Women, 1937," paper presented at the 22nd Annual Conference of the Western Association of Women Historians, Asilomar, CA, June 2, 1991.

72. Theoharis, The FBI and American Democracy, 45.

73. Ibid., 46.

74. Lawrence Richards, Union-Free America: Workers and Antiunion Culture (Urbana: University of Illinois Press, 2008), 91.

75. Saul Alinsky, John L. Lewis: An Unauthorized Biography (New York: Vintage Books, 1970), 187; Melvyn Dubofsky and Warren R. Van

Tine, *John L. Lewis: A Biography* (Urbana: University of Illinois Press, 1986), 256-257.

76. John L. Lewis FBI file, www.vault.fbi.gov/John%20L.%20Lewis (accessed Sept. 8, 2011).

77. Robert W. Cherney, "Anticommunist Networks and Labor: The Pacific Coast in the 1930s," in Shelton Stromquist, ed., *Labor's Cold War: Local Politics in a Global Context* (Urbana: University of Illinois Press, 2008), 39.

78. Gilbert J. Gall, *Pursuing Justice: Lee Pressman, the New Deal and the CIO* (Albany: SUNY Press, 1999), 118; Nelson Lichtenstein, *Walter Reuther: The Most Dangerous Man in Detroit* (New York: Basic Books, 1995), 45, 166-167.

79. Kirstin Downey, *The Woman Behind the New Deal: The Life and Legacy of Frances Perkins* (New York: Anchor Books, 2010), 277.

80. SAC Guy Hottel to Director, "Women's Trade Union League, Internal Security," Jan. 23, 1941, WTUL FBI file.

81. Ibid.

82. Theoharis, *The FBI and American Democracy*, 58.

83. Athan G. Theoharis, *Abuse of Power: How Cold War Surveillance and Secrecy Policy Shaped the Response to 9/11* (Philadelphia: Temple University Press, 2011), 176 n33.

84. FBI Executives Conference report, "Redirection of Communist Investigations," March 10, 1947, 5, FBI Executives Conference FBI file; Theoharis, *Abuse of Power*, 46.

85. Kenneth D. Durr, *Behind the Backlash: White Working-Class Politics in Baltimore, 1940-1980* (University of North Carolina Press, 2003), 19.

86. Ted Morgan, *Reds: McCarthyism in Twentieth-Century America* (New York: Random House, 2004), 189-190.

87. Victor Rabinowitz, *Unrepentant Leftist: A Lawyer's Memoir* (Urbana: University of Illinois Press, 1996), 101-102.

88. Robert H. Zieger, *The CIO, 1935-1955* (Chapel Hill: University of North Carolina Press, 1995),111-120.

89. Theoharis, *Abuse of Power*, 6-7.

90. Theoharis, *The FBI and American Democracy*, 53.

91. Charles H. McCormick, *The Nest of Vipers: McCarthyism and Higher Education in the Mundel Affair, 1951-52* (Urbana: University of Illinois Press, 1989), 43.

92. James T. Sparrow, *Warfare State: World War Two Americans and the Age of Big Government* (New York: Oxford University Press, 2011), 208.

93. Theoharis, *Abuse of Power*, 9-12.

94. Powers, *Broken*, 188.

95. Benjamin O. Fordham, *Building the Cold War Consensus: The Political Economy of U.S. National Security Policy, 1945-1951* (Ann Arbor: University of Michigan Press, 1998), 171.

96. David M. Hardy to Ivan Greenberg, January 10, 2012 (in author's possession).

97. Gall, *Pursuing Justice*, 118-119; Christopher H. Johnson, *Maurice Sugar: Law, Labor and the Left in Detroit, 1912-1950* (Detroit: Wayne State University Press, 1988), 245-246, 320; Goldstein, *American Blacklist*, 243-244.

98. Steve Babson, Dave Riddle, and David Elsila, *The Color of Law: Ernie Goodman, Detroit, and the Struggle for Labor and Civil Rights* (Michigan: Wayne State University Press, 2010), 78-79.

99. Carl O'Shea, "'National Defense' Hits Labor," *Fourth International* 1 (August 1940). The SWP also discussed "FBI-Gestapo attacks" in St. Paul-Minneapolis, after SWP leaders were elected to head a local CIO union of truck drivers. Local 544 of the United Construction Workers Organizing Committee consisted of about 4,000 workers. The Justice Department targeted Local 544 leaders bringing indictments for "seditious conspiracy." "The FBI-Gestapo Attack on the Socialist Workers Party," *Fourth International* 2 (July 1941).

2

Manipulating the Media

After World War II, the FBI conducted a major campaign to surveil and influence the media to help shape the communication of political ideas in American society. Working in the area of "opinion management," the bureau recognized the critical role that print, radio, film, and television played in the construction of political culture, especially the definition of threats and enemies. The FBI tried to influence—not control—the media through both covert and overt methods. While the United States long engaged in self-celebration that it possessed a "free press," which served as much as an adversary as an ally of the government, it is not well known that during the Cold War the FBI engaged in substantial manipulation. This manipulation focused especially on the popular depiction of political groups and social movements forming a neglected element of what sociologist David Cunningham calls the "patterning of repression": How authorities allocate resources to fight political challenges.[1]

FBI media policy advanced three related goals. First, the FBI worked to promote a positive portrayal of itself. The bureau viewed this form of manipulation as "educational." In 1956, the FBI's Mass Media Program formalized these efforts during the fight against communism. Shaping its public image had consequences: It could increase FBI power within the government, curtail congressional oversight, and help to build a popular consensus around its Red Scare campaigns. The Crime Records Division managed public relations issues, produced educational material, and ghost-wrote articles and books under Hoover's name. The Division worked on movies, radio, and television programs. As one example, the long-running radio crime drama *This is Your FBI* (1945 to 1963) aired with bureau approval. The FBI closely supervised the production of the television show, *The F.B.I.,* between 1965 and 1974, as well as the movies *Walk East on Beacon!* (1952) and *The FBI Story* (1959).[2]

In this period, J. Edgar Hoover rarely gave interviews or held news conferences. He almost never spoke in public in unscripted ways except when he appeared each year before congressional committees. Hoover limited public expression to prepared speeches and newspaper articles. Frank J. Donner in *The Age of Surveillance* compiled a list of about 280 Hoover speeches and articles between 1940 and 1972.[3] This closed media policy extended down the chain of command: FBI agents almost never appeared in news forums without authorization. Rules governed what they could say in public. A 1946 memo reaffirmed the policy: "Special Agents in Charge should make no references to Communism in the body of a speech but in response to questions should indicate the bureau's position by quoting the Director's speeches."[4] A carefully orchestrated speech program helped FBI messaging. For example, in 1961 Hoover's subordinates gave 186 public addresses.[5]

A second media strategy tried to "discredit" liberals and radicals for political reasons. In 1976, the U.S. Senate Church Committee documented FBI actions to "influence the public's perception of persons and organizations by disseminating derogatory information to the press, whether anonymously or through 'friendly' news contacts."[6] The bureau promoted negative mass media representations of dissident activity to limit their public appeal thereby reducing mobilization. Moreover, discrediting a subject helped the government justify the violation of their civil liberties.[7]

The bureau did not compel news organizations to publish particular articles. But their carefully chosen media contacts voluntarily printed material at their request. The secret flow of information from the bureau to journalists included not only fact-based material collected from public sources and secret surveillance. The flow included fabricated, false material to sabotage subjects. Most of the bureau's media relationships were kept secret as "press friends" concealed their cooperation agreeing "that the Bureau's interest in these matters is to be kept in the strictest confidence."[8] In addition, the bureau leadership publicly denied all covert media contact to protect its reputation embracing Hoover's "Number One Rule": Do not embarrass the bureau.[9]

The third goal consisted of direct attacks against alternative and radical media to limit their influence. Surveillance operations gathered intelligence on individuals and their media organizations. The bureau studied articles to identify new suspects and to understand their "subversive" or dangerous ideas. Writers and editors sometimes were monitored, and the FBI put subscriber lists into their files. Counterintelligence "dirty tricks" operations included efforts to force publications to fold.

Overall, I reference 70 journalists and writers subject to monitoring during the Cold War. (See Appendix A.) This includes both brief surveillance contexts as well as spying that lasted over several decades. The bureau also infiltrated a large number of both mainstream and radical publications. In other instances, the FBI refused to cooperate with reporters critical of the bureau or its director and targeted some for hostile surveillance. Lastly, in a few known cases agents posed as reporters to collect intelligence and published their own newspapers under false cover to frame issues in their favor.

In 1975, a top FBI official faced tough questioning about Cold War media manipulation while testifying before the Church Committee. Deputy associate director James B. Adams responded to questions by senator Walter D. Huddleston of Kentucky with obfuscation and deception. Adams covered up bureau misconduct, uncertain what the senators knew. He refused to offer any new details to enlighten them. Misleading congressional testimony by FBI officials was not new, but in this instance it could be challenged effectively because the Committee had been granted rare access to study FBI files.

Senator Huddleston: Do you have knowledge of a number of instances in which the Bureau carrying out COINTELPRO activities utilized the existing press in order to attempt to discredit some individual?

Mr. Adams: I don't have an idea of the number, but I don't think there were very many.

Mr. Huddleston: Do you have a list on the instances in which the Bureau attempted to discredit other publications?

Mr. Adams: No, I don't

Mr. Huddleston: Do you know that they did occur?

Mr. Adams: I can ask. I get, "No," so far as my knowledge in that regard.

Senator Huddleston: As far as knowledge.

Mr. Adams: That means knowledge of what we have come up with in our current review, I would assume.

Senator Huddleston: It seems to me that is an area in which we are particularly troubled and rightly should be. If there is any right that is specifically called for in our Constitution, and has been upheld and reaffirmed in court decision after court decision, it is the right to publish in this country. The first amendment speaks not only of freedom of speech, but also freedom of the press. And it seems that we have a pattern here of the chief law enforcement agency of the country attempting to suppress that very right.

Mr. Adams: I haven't seen—I think any effort to manipulate the press of this country. I just don't see any possibility in that regard, and I don't see the logic of anyone even attempting such.

Senator Huddleston: But it did happen.

Mr. Adams: It may have happened in –

Senator Huddleston: In a rather extensive field.

Mr. Adams: I disagree with that rather extensive field. I just don't know the extent that you are talking about.

Senator Huddleston: We are talking about the cases where –

Mr. Adams: Are you lumping in cases where we disseminated public source information? Are you lumping in a case where we may have gone to a –

Senator Huddleston: I think disseminating public source information is somewhat different than furnishing a TV commentator with derogatory information about a specific individual, who has been targeted as one that apparently the Bureau thinks is dangerous or that his ideas ought to be suppressed.

Mr. Adams: Is that manipulating the press, though? Here you have a situation where an individual is going around the country advocating off-the-pig or kill-the-police or something like that. And a newspaperman was furnished, say, some background information on him which would have been in the area of public source material which he could use in an article. Are we really, if the information is true? The final decision, it would seem to me, would be in the newspaperman as to whether he would use any such information.

I think if we concealed our motives from the newspaperman, or furnished false information, which I think we did in one anonymous letter or something that I saw in all of this, I would say that was improper.

Senator Huddleston: Or –

Mr. Adams: I think newsmen have sources, I think –

Senator Huddleston: Or convincing a cartoonist, for instance, to draw a derogatory cartoon about a college professor who certainly did not constitute a threat to the violent overthrow of the Government.

Mr. Adams: If anyone accuses of having any great success in trying to influence the press, I think that their objectivity stands very high.

Senator Huddleston: I think the point is not whether there was success or not, there was an effort made. I'm glad to hear you acknowledge now that is almost an impossibility. But more than that it seems to me that at the beginning when these type of techniques were used, it seemed to indicate a lack of confidence, or faith in the American people to believe that they could not hear ideas that might be contrary to their own without being seriously damaged. One of the great freedoms we have is the freedom of hearing other ideas, whether we agree with them or not. I think this is an area that we are concerned with and one technique which I hope is being discontinued and one that will be, by the time these hearings end, and by the time proper legislation is drawn.

Mr. Adams: Well, I think you can be assured that any techniques in that area died with COINTELPRO in 1971.[10]

Journalists as Friends and Enemies

In 1950, President Harry Truman publicly appealed to media organizations to join a "Campaign of Truth" to fight Soviet propaganda and defeat communism. Most mainstream editors and reporters supported this nationalistic reference frame practicing Cold War journalism under the banner of "objectivity" or "straight reporting." This form of objectivity rarely permitted reporters to challenge the pronouncements of government officials, rejected radical politics, and included loyalty oaths and blacklisting. For example, the Hearst newspapers were notorious for witch-hunts.[11] Between 1952 and 1957, more than 100 journalists were compelled to testify before congressional security committees about alleged communist associations. Many had been investigated by the FBI.[12] *New York Times* reporter James Aronson, who later helped edit the *National Guardian* newspaper, described the atmosphere in the newsroom: "A censorship so subtle that it was invisible affected everyone on the staff. The 'approach' (it was never a vulgar 'line') was made clear in casual conversations, in the editing of copy for 'clarity,' and in the deletion of any forthright interpretation as 'emotionalism.'"[13]

The number of journalists on the bureau's "friendly" press list is unknown. On a national level, at least several hundred may have collaborated. In 1965, the bureau reported that at least 28 journalists in New Haven, Connecticut, were reliable sources. In Chicago, the number reached 25, including contacts at leading newspapers, and television and radio stations.[14] We know the FBI successfully recruited sources inside many popular magazines (*Life*, *Time*, *Reader's Digest*, *Colliers*, *Fortune*, *Newsweek*, *Business Week*, *U.S. News and World Report*, and *Look*). *Reader's Digest* and *Look*, which published several dozen Hoover articles, were granted special access to FBI reports.[15]

Efforts to recruit working journalists included African-American Earl Caldwell of the *New York Times*. During the early 1970s, he rejected an offer by the FBI to inform on black power groups.[16] By contrast, the prominent civil rights photojournalist Ernest C. Withers agreed to work for the FBI as a paid informer as he circulated within the highest levels of black activism to photograph key figures like Martin Luther King, Jr. While Withers' photography is recognized as a unique visual source for documenting the past, it seems pertinent to ask how his collaboration influenced his vision as a photographer. How was the focus of his lens shaped, if at all, by police employment? Withers reported on both people and protests and his photographs helped the FBI identify new activists to investigate. He even acted as a spy during King's funeral in Atlanta by providing intelligence on the ongoing Memphis sanitation strike. In Memphis, he helped the FBI surveil and crush the Invaders, a Black Panther-styled organization.[17]

The popular radio commentator Paul Harvey worked in concert with the FBI for about 20 years (1952-1972). According to his 1,400-plus-page FBI file, he sent radio scripts to Hoover for comment and approval. The FBI helped him with research and suggested changes in his presentations. In 1957, assistant director Louis Nichols told Harvey: "For a number of years, you have been kind enough to send me your daily copy." Hoover lauded praise on the radio commentator. "All of us at the FBI count it as a great honor to have you as one of our closest friends." After one of Harvey's broadcasts in May 1958, Hoover told him, "You were never in better form." And Harvey returned the compliment. "From some future pinnacle, if the Republic has survived, history will record that it was largely due to your vigilance."[18] Harvey, whose broadcasts reached millions of people, held strong anti-communist views and concealed his ties to the bureau.

Other prominent journalists also secretly worked with the state. Conservative commentator Pat Buchanan admitted he passed on FBI smears as an editorial writer for the St. Louis *Globe-Democrat* in the early 1960s.[19] His open admission was unusual. In most cases, the only way to uncover such ties is by obtaining declassified FBI files. The file on Jesse Helms, who worked as a broadcast executive before serving in the U.S. Senate, depicts him as a trusted "contact." A September 1971 FBI memo noted that Helms "is a great admirer of the Director and the FBI and for a long period of time has been a staunch defender of the Director and his policies." For example, in editorials broadcast on his station, WRAL-TV, Helms echoed Hoover's views and tried to discredit Martin Luther King, Jr. and the civil rights movement by claiming communist influence. The FBI also noted Helms "is most cooperative and has offered the facilities of his station to assist the FBI in any time."[20]

Newspaper and radio commentator Walter Winchell also became a close friend for more than 30 years. The FBI describes his 3,900-plus-page file by noting: "The famous newspaper columnist discussed FBI cases with Director Hoover and publicized FBI accomplishments."[21] He often boosted the reputations of top FBI officials. In a broadcast in January 1954, Winchell said: "G-Man J. Edgar Hoover is quietly being groomed by some Texans for the 1956 Presidential nomination in the event Mr. Eisenhower rejects a second term."[22] He announced in another instance: "J. Edgar Hoover—'Look' magazine next Tuesday has a very wonderful article about three of your top men, Tolson, Nichols and Ladd." FBI officials had helped the author prepare the article.[23]

The FBI provided Winchell with classified information, which could be used in Red-baiting. During a radio program on Jan. 31, 1954, Winchell said: "The Civil Rights Congress, a notorious Red front, will promote a march on Washington February 28 demanding the repeal of the McCarran Act." A few days earlier this information appeared in the FBI's secret Weekly Intelligence Summary.[24] Winchell's Red-baiting and scare tactics sometimes went beyond FBI intelligence, which left the bureau wondering about his sources. On Feb. 14, 1954, Winchell said on air: "To the President of the United States—Former Communist newspaper people have a plant in the White House." This statement prompted an FBI official to comment in an internal memo: "The significance of this statement is not known. Winchell may be dramatizing the fact that Tass, the official Soviet news agency, has an accredited correspondent in Washington who regularly attends White House press conferences; or he may be referring to the *Daily Worker* correspondent in Washington."[25]

Hoover had a direct line to CBS president William S. Paley, who was placed on the director's Special Correspondents list. People on this list were considered friends and the director sometimes did favors for them. According to author Curt Gentry, "Almost every former SAC could, if so inclined, cite criminal charges which were dropped, or never pursued, because they involved persons known to be on the director's Special Correspondents list." NBC president David Sarnoff also made the list.[26]

The FBI kept tabs on at least several dozen prominent reporters at the request of the White House and also independently of it. President Lyndon B. Johnson, for example, sought intelligence on at least seven journalists, including David Brinkley of NBC, Peter Arnett of the Associated Press, and columnist Joseph Kraft.[27] The FBI file on CBS news journalist Eric Sevareid dates from the 1950s finding alleged communist ties.[28] Sevareid's CBS colleague Charles Kuralt came under FBI scrutiny when he served as the news bureau's Latin America chief during the early 1960s.[29] The FBI focused attention on David Halberstam while a *New York Times* correspondent in Poland during the mid-1960s. In 1968, the FBI noted "that articles written in the past, including those written about the Vietnamese War, had been critical of the U.S. participation in that conflict." Agents later debated whether they should interview Halberstam, but for what purpose was unclear.[30] Other journalists with FBI files include Haywood Broun, Walter Lippmann, Edward R. Murrow, Walter Cronkite, Harrison Salisbury, Peter Lisagor, and Ben Gilbert. Historian Athan G. Theoharis, who has studied FBI files related to electronic wiretapping, found the names of several journalists in these records: Ingra Arvad, I. F. Stone, Philip Jaffe, Kate Mitchell, Mark Gayn, Leonard Lyons, William Beecher, Marvin Kalb, Hanson Baldwin, Hedrick Smith, and Lloyd Norman.[31]

When Edward R. Murrow, the iconic CBS broadcaster, challenged conservative Red-baiting and McCarthyism during the early 1950s, the FBI investigated his political views and associations. At first, the bureau found nothing objectionable. An FBI official told Hoover: "Our files contain no information to the effect that Edward R. Murrow is a member of the group in CBS believed to be communistically inclined or a fellow traveler." However, by the mid-1950s Hoover had come to view Murrow as an opponent and collected material that impugned his integrity and loyalty. When FBI officials assembled a list of 100 "prominent molders of public opinion" and researched their backgrounds, Murrow was one of 40 people found to have "pertinent factors in their backgrounds . . . which could be influencing such slanted views." Hoover directed FBI officials to have no contact with Murrow throughout the 1950s.[32] But the distance that separated Hoover and Murrow would be shortened when Murrow officially disseminated government propaganda as head of the U.S. Information Agency under President John F. Kennedy.[33]

Whether the FBI's interest in Cronkite was friendly or antagonistic remains unknown because most of his file was destroyed before it could be declassified. The routine destruction of records continues to pose a significant obstacle to researchers. I requested Cronkite's file after his death and the FOIA office at the FBI initially indicated "no records," an assertion they made to several other requestors.[34] However, after I filed an appeal with the Office of Information at the U.S. Justice Department, the FBI released several dozen pages which do not indicate how they viewed the "most trusted man in America."

The bureau targeted several investigative reporters for aggressive surveillance because they exposed corrupt government conduct thereby situating themselves outside Cold War journalism. I. F. Stone, Joseph Alsop, Jack Anderson, and Daniel Schorr amassed large FBI files and became subjects of counterintelligence operations. The bureau assembled a 5,000-plus-page file on Stone, a harsh Hoover critic, spanning more than 45 years. The bureau bugged his phone, went through his trash, opened his mail, and monitored the content of his writing and public speeches. They also interfered in his network of relations by interviewing family, friends, and work peers. During the 1950s, the FBI placed Stone on the Security Index—the successor to the Custodial Detention List. In the event of a national emergency, he would be detained indefinitely. The FBI also sent advisories overseas regarding his travels. The tracking continued until his death in 1972.[35]

The FBI's interest in Alsop, a Republican, was much more limited. In 1957, the bureau learned Alsop was gay and disseminated this information throughout the government to isolate and slander the reporter, whose articles had angered the Eisenhower administration. In 1959, Attorney General William Rogers contacted the FBI to get a full report on Alsop's sexual orientation after the reporter published a series of articles suggesting Eisenhower's fiscal conservatism contributed to a "missile gap" with the Soviet Union. Officials expressed the intention of informing Alsop's publisher of his deviant ways and hoped the information would reach the broader public.[36] During the mid-1960s, the FBI again circulated the Alsop file. After learning of Alsop's sexual orientation, President Johnson limited contact with the reporter.[37]

President Richard Nixon's antipathy toward the press was unmatched in modern presidential history. He railed against the elite media establishment and urged the FBI to dig up dirt on journalists. In 1970, the FBI investigated the Washington press corps looking to uncover any "homosexuals." In a 1970 memo,

Hoover indicated that H.R. Haldeman, Assistant to the President, called him on behalf of Nixon. "He stated that the President wanted him to ask, and he would imagine I would have it pretty much at hand so there would be no specific investigation, for a run down on the homosexuals known and suspected in the Washington press corps. I said I thought we have some of that material."[38]

In 1971, Nixon placed CBS correspondent Daniel Schorr on his "enemies list." The FBI started a full investigation as retaliation after Schorr broadcast an unfavorable analysis of a presidential speech. The inquiry began as a background check, with interviews of at least 25 people, and escalated into a full investigation when knowledge of the inquiry leaked to the press. The FBI's conduct formed part of an impeachment charge against Nixon. As Schorr wrote in the November 1974 issue of the *Columbia Journalism Review*:

> Maybe a name check was what the former President wanted. What he got was a full investigation, frantically aborted, then covered up with a bogus explanation. What he also got was one more item in the impeachment litany.
>
> It was Item 65 in the Statement of Information on surveillance activities. It was Paragraph E in the Summary of Information on Illegal Intelligence Gathering. Finally, in the Judiciary Committee's reports to the House of Representatives it was one of the instances of abuse of presidential powers listed in Article II.[39]

Schorr reflected on the "chilling" impact of the FBI's inquiry, which "complicated" his relationship with his employer and many news sources. "I had to worry about being projected into an undesirable role of administration adversary. . . . He [Nixon] forced me to submit to a thousand jokes about whether my FBI 'shadow' was still with me, and whether it was safe to talk on the telephone."[40]

Nixon also placed syndicated *Washington Post* columnist Jack Anderson on his enemies list. Anderson, who won a Pulitzer Prize in 1972 and was published in nearly a thousand newspapers, exposed many of the Nixon administration's most embarrassing early scandals. Nixon assigned his dirty tricks "plumbers" to stop leaks to him. In one conversation, White House operatives E. Howard Hunt and G. Gordon Liddy plotted to assassinate the reporter.[41] The bureau also pursued separate anti-Anderson efforts. As early as 1951, Hoover wrote: "This fellow Anderson and his ilk have minds that are lower than regurgitated filth of vultures." His file includes copies of his writings, notes of his movements based on surveillance, and FBI efforts to identify government sources used in his "Washington Merry-Go-Round" column.

The bureau repeatedly claimed Anderson got his facts wrong. In one instance, Hoover scribbled comments on a copy of his column: "This is the greatest conglomeration of vicious lies that this jackal has ever put forth." The column had stated accurately that FBI agents researched and ghost-wrote three Hoover books.[42] The FBI grudge persisted after Anderson's death in 2006. When the reporter's papers awaited cataloging by George Washington University, the bureau made the unprecedented (and unsuccessful) demand to search them to remove classified government material.[43]

Several presidents asked the FBI to spy on journalists to locate press leaks from inside the government. Finding leaks was a high priority for Nixon, who had the FBI illegally wiretap five media representatives, as well as 12 other people, during 1969 through 1971 to expose unauthorized press contacts by members of his National Security Council. The FBI also followed columnist Joseph Kraft and conducted a break-in to plant a bug in his home.[44] Nixon asked the FBI to submit an intelligence report on James B. Reston of the *New York Times*, whose file dates from the early 1950s.[45]

An equally severe attack on journalistic independence occurred when FBI agents posed as news reporters with fake press credentials. In a case documented by the Church Committee, one of the major television networks at the 1964 Democratic National Convention gave press credentials to the bureau. It allowed the FBI "to insert an agent as a bogus newsman into legitimate discussions of political persons and protest groups and acquire information concerning their plans, pretending to be a reporter and in fact acquiring it for the purposes of the bureau and transmission to higher authority."[46] In another instance, an agent posed as a reporter for the *Herald Tribune* to attend a 1966 news conference sponsored by *Ramparts*, a progressive Catholic lay magazine, opposing U. S. military intervention in Vietnam.[47]

A case study of the FBI's relationship to a single newspaper—the *St. Louis Post-Dispatch*, founded by Joseph Pulitzer—shows both friendly and antagonistic attitudes. Recently, the newspaper obtained about 1,200 pages of its FBI file dating from the 1930s. It reported: "The bureau alternately schmoozed and browbeat the Post-Dispatch reporters, editors and owners in an effort to influence news stories and opinions. And the records reveal Hoover's hair-trigger sensitivity to criticism from an editorial page whose support for the bureau waxed and waned."[48] Before 1940, relations mostly proved positive. "Hoover's agents provided information and arranged interviews for some of the paper's legendary reporters." However, after the newspaper ran a critical editorial calling Hoover the "publicity-mad chief" for arresting 12 people in Milwaukee and Detroit for recruiting volunteers to fight in the Spanish Civil War, FBI agents privately began to Red-bait the newspaper. One agent told Hoover that a "very reliable" informer reported the Communist Party had "friendly contacts employed by the Post-Dispatch." In an effort to mend ties with the bureau, the newspaper cooperated in 1942 to smash a Nazi spy ring and "submitted the stories to the FBI in advance of publication, where agents had spiked one and edited others. . . . Over the next several years, the bureau would continue to shape and edit stories by several of the paper's reporters." As the Red Scare intensified during the late 1940s, Joseph Pulitzer, Jr., who had succeeded his father as publisher, offered to provide the names of his employees to the FBI to screen for CP membership.[49]

However, in 1953 relations again turned sour. FBI Headquarters removed the newspaper from its mailing list and cut off most other forms of access, including interviews, after a *Post-Dispatch* editorial criticized FBI conduct in a criminal kidnapping case. The FBI paid close attention to the politics of editorial policy. When the newspaper began printing the rival *Globe-Democrat* in 1959, FBI Headquarters told local agents to "keep the bureau advised as to any deviations in the editorial policy of the Globe-Democrat to see if it is being influenced by the previously unfriendly attitudes of the Post-Dispatch." Relations during the 1960s remained strained and before Hoover's death in 1972 he compared the newspaper to the *Washington Post* and the *New York Times*—"classic examples of the worst in newspaper reporting."[50]

Critics of the FBI

Hoover's conception of free speech did not tolerate criticism of the FBI. Public expression that challenged the supremacy of political policing should be monitored and, if possible, sabotaged. The "free press" was not free enough to question the validity of the government's domestic intelligence system without facing retaliation. A chief example of intolerance of press criticism is the FBI's treatment of the *Nation*. The magazine's FBI file totals about 2,000 pages with the largest portion covering the late 1950s when the bureau believed it faced growing opposition to its spying practices. The *Nation* directly challenged FBI power when it devoted the October 18, 1958, issue to a single article on the FBI by Fred J. Cook. The bureau viewed the article as "vicious" and "destructive" and began to track Cook, interviewing his friends and family and opening his mail. (See Textbox 2.1) Hoover wrote in a memo, "I think we should discreetly get a line on this man and his background and associations for current article just didn't 'bloom'—it is planned literary garbage barrage against FBI by a dedicated [Alger] Hiss apologist." The FBI also identified *Nation* editor Carey McWilliams as someone "long publicly identified with the activities of a number of subversive organizations."[51]

The bureau investigated *Nation* contributors and leaked negative information about the magazine to members of Congress and friendly press sources to undermine its reputation.[52] In 1959, the bureau produced a 180-page research monograph, "Smear

Textbox 2.1

On Oct. 18, 1958, the *Nation* magazine published a special issue devoted to FBI misconduct authored by Fred J. Cook. In response, the FBI issued a special internal research monograph entitled, "The Smear Campaign Against the FBI, *The Nation*" (1959), which is excerpted below.

Conclusions

1. The article in The Nation is the articulate expression of the current smear campaign against the FBI.
2. It serves to identify the issues on which the current smear efforts are based.
3. Chief among these issues is the fantastic charge that the FBI is a police-state organization.
4. Concealed behind specious attempts to pin the police-state label on the FBI is to be found a deliberate effort to drive the FBI out of the internal security field.
5. The Nation article and other current smears represent, in reality, a concerted attack on the internal security of the country, the FBI being only an intermediary target in the campaign.
6. The strategy of the smear campaign is now transparently revealed. With the FBI discredited and disposed of, communist and other subversive operations would be able to flourish with relative impunity.
7. The article is a compilation of lies, factual inaccuracies, half-truths, innuendos, misrepresentations, and distortions, blended with views which strikingly parallel the Communist Party line.
8. The phase of the smear campaign represents a manifesto for intensified attacks against the Bureau which can be expected in the future.

Campaign Against the FBI," which focused exclusively on the magazine. The FBI feared that the views of the *Nation* might become popular, prompting congressional action to restrict its investigations. Cook had written that FBI critics run "the risk of being considered an enemy of the nation." The FBI seemed to affirm this view when it wrote: "Cook's article represents a manifesto for intensified attacks against the Bureau which can be expected in the future." Only Communists (and their allies) wanted to limit FBI power. "The strategy of the smear campaign is now transparently revealed. With the FBI discredited and disposed of, communists and other subversive operatives would be able to flourish with relative impunity."[53]

Historian Henry Steele Commager often wrote for the popular press critical of FBI power and the Red Scare. His file (457 pages) covers more than 20 years. In 1947, the FBI opened an investigation after Commager's article in *Harper's* magazine ("Who is Loyal in the U.S.?") attacked emerging McCarthyism. Commager's defense of liberalism and criticism of the director led top officials, such as assistant director William C. Sullivan, to view him as "a too vocal, bombastic and misinformed liberal or 'fellow traveler.'"[54] The FBI questioned his loyalty after an article he wrote for the *Nation* was distributed by the Communist Party to attract members. When Commager argued in the *New York Times* that the CP had a constitutional right to exist, the FBI noted that he "was making Communistic addresses and remarks which appeared to be harmful and not to the best interests of the Government of the United States."[55] In another article, Commager denounced loyalty tests ("Where Government May Not Trespass"), prompting a comparison to the left-wing National Lawyers Guild. The bureau continued to condemn him for how others used his work: Commager "has long been considered a 'darling' of the Communist Party." The bureau expressed anti-intellectual sentiment: "Commager's article illustrates that the real danger to *needed* Governmental authority is from the pseudo-intellectual realm."[56] By the early 1960s, the FBI placed Commager on its "Do Not Contact" list. They would have no dealings with him because "he has been a long-time critic of the FBI."[57]

New York Post columnist and editor James Wechsler challenged Hoover's leadership and defended FBI critics. Wechsler began his career working for liberal-Left publications: the *Nation* during the late 1930s; and the newspaper *PM* during the early 1940s. While at *PM*, the FBI placed him on the Custodial Detention List and Hoover described him (and his wife, Nancy) as "radicals and leftists of the most dangerous type."[58] At the *Post* during the 1950s and 1960s, Wechsler criticized the FBI in three key areas. He viewed the infiltration of the CP as counter-productive. He criticized the bureau's failure to protect black civil rights workers in the South. In this regard, he proposed stripping the FBI of its jurisdiction for civil rights enforcement. Lastly, Wechsler wrote against FBI surveillance of student activism at the University of California, Berkeley.[59] Wechsler's FBI file grew to about 530 pages with critical notes about his journalism.[60]

In 1962, a *Post* article featured historian Howard Zinn, who had authored a report critical of the FBI's civil rights enforcement in Albany, Georgia. A memo in Zinn's FBI file says his views were "slanted and biased" but "expected from an individual of Zinn's background." The FBI identified Zinn as a former communist. In response to the *Post* article, Hoover directed agents to discredit Zinn by spreading information about his CP associations and sympathy for Cuba. "Suggest our friends on Georgia papers be alerted." An FBI official also wrote: "Zinn should not be dignified by contact by this Bureau."[61] After an article appeared in the *Boston Globe* in 1964 again quoting Zinn, an FBI official noted: "This is the second time the 'Boston Globe' has published distorted articles concerning the FBI . . . the Crime Records Division [should] attempt to set the record straight through other friendly news sources in the Boston area." Hoover approved this recommendation with a short note—"yes and promptly."[62]

The FBI demonized media criticism even in the form of satire. The director called *Washington Post* columnist Art Buchwald a "sick comic" and directed agents to monitor his writing. As an example of Buchwald's satire, in 1964 he suggested that President Johnson was unable to fire Hoover as director because the lawman actually did not exist. "What happened was that in 1925 the Reader's Digest was printing an article on the newly formed Federal Bureau of Investigation and as they do with many pieces they signed it with a nom de plume," Buchwald wrote. "They got the word Hoover from the vacuum cleaner—to give the idea of a clean-up. Edgar was the name of one of the publisher's nephews, and J. stood for jail."[63] An interview with Buchwald in *Playboy* magazine elicited a long FBI memo about the writer's subversive Cold War humor. "Buchwald previously had come to the Bureau's attention in connection with his writings." The FBI noted:

> [He] spoke of FBI informers in the Communist Party and the possibility that "someday soon J. Edgar Hoover will be elected Chairman of the American Communist Party."[64] Buchwald also commented that "you're allowed to make fun of the FBI because they have such a good sense of humor. They never get upset when you make fun of them. You may get a call from two FBI Agents the morning after the column appears, at 3 o'clock in the morning, but it always is a friendly call. It is the one organization in Washington that doesn't mind being laughed at."[65]

In a separate file, the FBI monitored *Playboy* for carrying on "a campaign of snide innuendoes against the FBI and at times was outright critical of the Bureau and the Director."[66]

The editorial cartoonist Herbert Block came under scrutiny for creating "derogatory" depictions of the FBI and HUAC. In a 1950 cartoon, Block coined the term McCarthyism. In 1954, he won a Pulitzer Prize and became the leading newspaper cartoonist to challenge the domestic Red Scare. Throughout the 1950s, the FBI compiled a dossier on him.[67] They reviewed his book, *Herblock Special for the Day* (1958), a collection of more than 400 cartoons that appeared in the *Washington Post* and *Times-Herald,* and highlighted the anti-HUAC and anti-FBI sentiment. "Herblock attacks Congressional investigative committees," the reviewer said. "He also is critical of the FBI. His comments are a rehash of well-known canards about the Bureau."[68]

Oliver Harrington, who created cartoons for the black press, was hounded by the government. Overall, surveillance of black media after World War II needs further study. Harrington began his career drawing for the *Amsterdam News* in New York City and later worked for the *Pittsburgh Courier,* the *People's Voice,* and the *Freedom* newspaper founded by singer Paul Robeson. His work addressed such topics as lynching and white supremacy and the FBI started an investigation in 1950, and questioned him, while he taught art at the left-wing Jefferson School in Manhattan. Within two years, he had left the nation for Paris to avoid the witch-hunt.[69]

The bureau's hypersensitivity to criticism led them to search their files in 1962 for information on Donald Myers, a history professor at UCLA, after he criticized the FBI in a book review. The book in question was *Rebel in Paradise: A Biography of Emma Goldman* by Richard Drinnon. The review angered the FBI because "Meyer makes derogatory references to the Director."[70] Of course, the subject of the book was not a bureau ally. Emma Goldman had been targeted by the FBI, leading to a prison term and eventually deportation. In addition, Drinnon, a history professor at the University of California at Berkeley, was viewed as an opponent with "numerous references" in bureau files. Meyer's review appeared in *Frontiers* magazine, which the FBI investigated during the mid-1950s.[71]

When radicals published articles against FBI spying, officials responded in vicious personal terms. Paul Jacobs, an associate of the Institute for Policy Studies, wrote a piece in the August 1973 issue of *Ramparts* magazine highlighting FBI abuse of power in its use of informers for spying. Top official G. C. Moore informed Edward S. Miller, chief of the Intelligence Division:

> It appears the entire article is just one more case of sniping at the FBI in particular and law enforcement in general as well as an attempt to further embarrass the [Nixon] administration over the Watergate incident. There are no new charges or allegations made which have not been set forth at some time in the past by disgruntled and self-motivated people who are attempting to spread their individual malignancy into society in general.[72]

The FBI infiltrated writers' organizations (American Newspaper Guild, Radio Writers Guild, and American Authors League) and focused surveillance on a broad segment of allegedly "anti-American" book authors: E. B. White, Sinclair Lewis, John Steinbeck, Upton Sinclair, Carl Sandburg, Theodore Dreiser, John Dos Passos, Pearl S. Buck, Dorothy Parker, H. L.

Mencken, Edmund Wilson, John Kenneth Galbraith, Nat Hentoff, Norman Mailer, Irving Howe, Betty Friedan, and Studs Terkel.[73] The bureau developed a file on Barney Rosset, founding editor of Grove Press, who fought censorship battles during the 1950s and 1960s.[74] The FBI also placed informants in the publishing world. The best known case involved Henry Holt and Company. As Claire A. Culleton notes, for several decades Hoover reviewed manuscripts and the firm sought "his explicit approval on authors and his advanced sanction on works and topics under consideration by the press." Once the FBI approved a book for production, it obtained advance copies of page proofs and played a central role in designing Holt's advertising and marketing campaigns.[75]

The FBI's Book Review File

In 1959, the bureau established a special "Book Review File" in which personnel summarized the content of particular volumes published on such topics as domestic security, communism, espionage, and crime. While my request for this large 5,614-page file has not yet been processed by the FBI's FOIA office, a researcher who has obtained this file shared several hundred pages indicating that books critical of the FBI received special notice. According to assistant director William Sullivan: "Central Research Section will continue to recommend for review books critical of the Director or the Bureau which have not been reviewed or considered for review." Overall, about 50 books were reviewed each year.[76]

While many of the books evaluated by the FBI already had been reviewed in the mainstream press, several were obtained in advance of publication. For example, Benjamin Ginzburg's *Rededication to Freedom* (1959) published by Simon and Schuster was obtained by an informer, Irving Ferman, who served as a leader of the American Civil Liberties Union in Washington, DC. As the FBI's Clyde Tolson, a close confidant of Hoover, wrote on March 12, 1959: "Irving Ferman has given me an advance copy of captioned work. He states there is criticism of the Bureau and the Director in this book."[77] By providing an advance copy to Tolson, Ferman betrayed his ACLU connections.

The FBI viewed Ginzburg as a suspicious character who echoed the critical views expressed by Fred Cook in the *Nation*. Ginzburg, who was born in Russia, earned degrees from Columbia University and Harvard and worked for the U.S. Senate Subcommittee on Constitutional Rights during the mid-1950s. FBI investigations had determined he was a "progressive," a "left-winger," and an "evolutionary, as opposed to revolutionary, Marxist." Surprisingly, he passed federal loyalty probes.[78]

The official review of *Rededication to Freedom* totals five pages and reads as a simplistic summary to demonize the author. "Ginsburg's book shows a complete lack of awareness of the menace of communism," the reviewer observed, referring to "Ginzburg's complete naivete on this question." The author's blunt criticisms of FBI practices were enumerated. "By tapping telephones, conducting 'promiscuous' surveillance, and compiling 'dossiers,' the FBI has become 'a law until itself.'" Ginzburg held the heretical view that "The FBI is likely to 'fabricate' evidence."[79]

Wade Thompson's satirical *Egghead's Guide to America* (1962) included a chapter on the FBI. Although the official review noted the book was "intended to be humorous," the FBI did not appreciate references to Hoover as promoting "national hysteria" about communism and the identification of the bureau as a "secret police." The reviewer contrasted a "responsible" and "clear-thinking" mentality with the author's "trash" and "nonconformity." Thompson, a college professor, was dismissively grouped together with other FBI critics. "His treatment of the Director and the FBI is merely a rehash of the trash which has been previously issued from Fred Cook, John Crosby and Murray Kempton. . . . His writing, his wild theories and penchant for nonconformity point up his true character and fuzzy thinking, all of which should be easily recognizable by the clear-thinking, responsible reader."[80]

In 1965, the FBI planned to reprimand Cornell professor Douglas Dowd, an editor of *Step by Step* (1965), which recounted the efforts of 50 Cornell students who volunteered to promote voting rights for African Americans in Fayette County, Tennessee. In the book, the Cornell students criticized the FBI for failing to protect black rights. The FBI feared the book might serve as a "handbook for future civil rights workers." The review of *Step by Step* includes background material on Dowd, who taught economics. "Bufiles reflect that Dowd, who is 45, has been associated with cited and leftist groups dating to 1949." The FBI was so angry at Dowd that apparently it sent an agent to talk to him to retract his work.

> No single author is responsible for the material [in the book] but it is apparent that the scope and emphasis of the book was dictated by Douglas Dowd. It is believed Dowd should be contacted by SAC, Albany, to straighten him out with regard to the misstatements and distortions about the FBI which appear in this book. In view of Dowd's ultraliberalism and his position on the Cornell faculty, this contact should be handled with tact and diplomacy in order to preclude Dowd from charging us with harassment or interference with academic freedom. This should be a straightforward presentation of the facts, accompanied by a request that Dowd retract the critical statements in the book.[81]

The FBI also reviewed the books of its own assets. Morris L. Ernst, a leader of the ACLU in Washington, DC, informed for the bureau.[82] When he co-authored a book, *Privacy: The Right to Be Let Alone* (1962), he sent a complimentary copy to Hoover. The official review found no references to the FBI and the book "is of no direct interest to the Bureau's work." It is hardly surprising the topic of privacy did not engage surveillance workers. "We have no criticism of the book," the reviewer noted, "although we admittedly are not sufficiently expert in those aspects of the right to privacy discussed here to reach an informed conclusion."[83] While no mention is made of Ernst's informer status, in other reviews the issue of secret ties to the FBI were acknowledged.[84]

C. Eric Lincoln, an expert in African-American studies who published more than 20 books, began his career collaborating with the bureau. This shocking revelation is contained in the official review of his first book, *The Black Muslims in America* (1961). A section of the review titled "Background on Author" is partly redacted so the full details of his FBI work are not disclosed. But, it is revealed that in August 1958, Lincoln advised the Atlanta office of the FBI of plans to research the Nation of Islam as part of his doctoral dissertation. In that meeting, the FBI reported, "He was impressed at this time with the necessity of not mentioning his previous relationship with the Bureau or the FBI's interest in the NOI." Lincoln got close to the NOI leadership interviewing Elijah Muhammad, Malcolm X, and others. He attended NOI meetings in several cities. Before his book appeared in 1961, he told the FBI he "feared for his personal safety when certain NOI officials read the book." At the time, 35 FBI field offices conducted NOI investigations, according to the official review. Lincoln was careful to conceal his ties. The official review noted: "The book makes a dozen references to the FBI, none of which contain information alluding to the author's former relationship with the Bureau or which could be interpreted as showing the author was anymore aware of the Bureau's interest in the NOI than anyone else who reads newspapers."[85]

Almost every official review, regardless of topic, noted any reference to the FBI. The bureau noted if they were "derogatory." That was the standard to judge if a book was friendly or antagonistic to FBI interests. For example, the review of Nathan Glazer's *The Social Basis of American Communism* (1961), indicated: "References to Director are not derogatory . . . Author Nathan Glazer not investigated by Bureau but several references in Bufiles."[86] Meanwhile, a positive review of Theodore Draper's *American Communism and Soviet Russia* said there were "no references in this volume to the Director or the FBI."[87] By contrast, editorial writer Alan Barth in *The Price of Liberty* (1961) makes "numerous derogatory references to the FBI and/or the Director." Each one is detailed in the review. Reference to Barth's two previous books, *The Loyalty of Free Men* (1951) and *Government by Investigation* (1955), established that he "has long been critical of the Bureau."[88]

Efforts at opinion management even included monitoring works of fiction. In the case of Herman Wouk's *Youngblood Hawke*

(1962), a critical depiction of the FBI led to a counterintelligence action. One subplot in the novel concerned a Marxist character compelled to testify before a congressional security committee. The character expressed negative views of the FBI and HUAC. A defensive and intolerant bureau reviewer observed the subplot "was totally unnecessary. . . . It adds nothing to the main theme of the story and references to the FBI are indeed uncalled for." The FBI reached out to a contact at the Washington *Evening-Star* to "tactfully . . . counteract the critical part of the book." The *Star* then published a review of Wouk's book by staff writer Jeremiah O'Leary, who followed the bureau's advice that "the attack against the FBI was unwarranted."[89] O'Leary later served as a press secretary in the Reagan administration.

A second satirical work of fiction aroused the FBI's wrath. After publication of *Little Brother is Watching* (1962) by Walter E. Dillon, which mocked government security investigations, the FBI placed the author on its "Do Not Contact" list.[90] A similar designation was applied to Rex Stout after he published a mystery novel, *The Doorbell Rang* (1965), as part of his Nero Wolfe series. In the novel, detective Wolfe is hired to stop FBI wiretapping, physical surveillance, and harassment of a woman who donated thousands of copies of a book critical of the bureau. The FBI's reviewer called it a "vicious book" which depicted "the FBI in the worst possible light." Advance galley proofs of the book had been provided to the bureau by Nat Goldstein, a "confidential source" at the *New York Times*. The official reviewer did not anticipate much success for Stout's work. The intelligence on Stout, 79 years old, indicated he held progressive politics.

> The plot of this book is weak and it will probably have only limited public acceptance despite Stout's use of the FBI in an apparent bid for sensationalism to improve sales. The false and distorted picture of the FBI which Stout sets forth is an obvious reflection of his leftist leanings as indicated in our files. It is believed that Stout should be placed on the list of persons not to be contacted and that a letter should be sent to all SACs advising of the forthcoming release of this book in order that any inquiries concerning the book can be answered.[91]

According to Herbert Mitgang, the FBI devoted about 100 pages of Stout's FBI file to the novel.[92]

Boston Globe reporter Joseph F. Dinneen wrote two crime novels in which the FBI appeared unfavorably in the narrative. The bureau was alerted to the second book, *The Alternative Case* (1960), by contact Miriam Ottenberg of the Washington *Evening Star*, who "intimated that the FBI had tortured witnesses" in the fiction. The FBI reviewer evaluated Dinneen's relationship to the bureau. "Dinneen was bitter towards the Bureau for a period, but by letter dated 2-9-54, the SAC at Boston advised that he had paid a visit to the 'Boston Globe', and while there, he was introduced to Dinneen. Dinneen advised that he wanted the Bureau to know that he held no malice toward the FBI."[93]

After official review, the FBI sometimes engaged in counterintelligence against book authors. The FBI's Sullivan, who oversaw COINTELPRO, testified in 1975: "Anyone who wrote a book or was writing a book or we knew was going to be critical of Mr. Hoover and the FBI, we made efforts right then and there to find out anything that we could to use against them"[94] A separate FBI file labeled "Magazine Subscriptions" adds further evidence of the bureau's prosecutorial reading habits. All articles and books written by subjects of investigation were acquired so they could "be used as evidence in subsequent legal proceedings."[95] In this regard, Sullivan recommended the acquisition and review of historian Herbert Aptheker's edited volume, *Disarmament and the American Economy* (1960), as well as *Dare We Be Free?*(1961). Both books were placed in the library at FBI Headquarters for reference.[96] In another instance, the FBI reviewed *Cuba: Anatomy of a Revolution* (1961) by Leo Huberman and Paul Sweezy. "We have main files on Huberman and Sweezy," the reviewer noted. "Both are in the Reserve Index . . . both are avowed socialists." The book, published by Monthly Review Press, was also shelved in the FBI library.[97]

Four books critical of the FBI prompted direct efforts at suppression. In the case of Max Lowenthal's *The Federal Bureau of Investigation* (1950), Hoover obtained an advance copy and tried to plant anti-Lowenthal editorials in newspapers. In an effort at censorship, agents discouraged booksellers from stocking the work.[98] In order to counter the book's impact, the FBI distributed a reprint of a *Reader's Digest* article, "Why I No Longer Fear the FBI," by Morris Ernst. Representatives from HUAC visited Lowenthal's publisher, William Sloan, and subpoenaed the author to appear before the Committee.[99]

Hoover obtained an advance copy of Fred Cook's *The FBI Nobody Knows* (1964) and helped delay publication for several years. Cook's book built on his *Nation* article and the FBI believed the negative depiction of Hoover's relationship with others in government posed a challenge to its organizational integrity. The FBI told its agents:

> Cook claims that official Washington is intimidated by Mr. Hoover, citing a situation in which the publisher of the "New York Post" had found that "some of the most distinguished figures in the Hill simply will not be quoted on the subject of Hoover." In addition, Cook, through quotes from unnamed liberal Congressman who express fear of Mr. Hoover, attempts to make Mr. Hoover responsible for an atmosphere of conformity. It can be said that the unnamed Congressmen seem to be feeble carriers of the liberal tradition if they are afraid to express their views.[100]

In 1962, former FBI agent William Turner discussed on a radio program that he was preparing a memoir about his experiences at the bureau. FBI officials then asked their sources at several publishing houses—Random House, Henry Holt, and Harpers—if anyone knew of the project. None had heard of it. However, when Turner began sending the manuscript to publishers several months later, a copy made its way to Hoover, who directed agents to write a chapter-by-chapter rebuttal to discourage publication. It took seven years before the work, *Hoover's FBI: The Man and the Myth,* was published in 1970 by Sherborne Press. The FBI then went after the author, as Curt Gentry notes. "Not only was Turner subjected to a vicious campaign of personal vilification and harassment; his editor would be labeled a pornographer, the FBI resurrected a 1965 indictment for allegedly publishing obscene books, neglecting to mention, when it spread the tale, that the charges had been dismissed."[101]

The FBI tried to suppress Peter Matthiessen's *In the Spirit of Crazy Horse* (1983), which offered a sympathetic history of the American Indian Movement (AIM). The book focused on the FBI's role in the flawed prosecution of AIM leader Leonard Peltier, which Matthiessen compared to the Sacco and Vanzetti case of the 1920s. Matthiessen hoped his book "might become an organizing tool in his [Peltier] fight for justice," while the FBI sought to limit the book's circulation. Within a year of publication, an FBI special agent cited in the book filed a $25 million libel suit against Matthiessen and his publisher, Viking Press. Although the FBI lost the case after eight years of litigation, the lawsuit substantially delayed paperback and foreign editions.[102] In the Peltier case, two FBI agents had been killed in the line of duty and the bureau's pursuit of justice included legal misconduct.

Media Smears

In order to influence public opinion, the FBI organized media campaigns to discredit radicals. The Church committee critically referred to "media manipulation" as abuse of power by the bureau. That journalists participated in this manipulation process demonstrates the enormous power wielded by the FBI within the society. From a historical perspective, a state-controlled media never developed in the U.S., but the influence of the American intelligence community on news organizations undermined the integrity of independent and objective reporting.

These efforts to discredit subjects focused primarily on the communist, socialist, black power, and civil rights movements. As one example, the FBI prepared a news item for "a cooperative news media source" dosed with sarcasm to mock a CP leader's consumption habits. "Comrades of the self-proclaimed leader of the American working class should not allow this example of [the leader's] prosperity to discourage their continued contributions to Party coffers."[103] In another case, the bureau acted against a couple identified with the Community Party movement by preparing a news release on the drug arrest of their son. They distributed it to "news media contacts and sources on Capitol Hill."[104]

The smears often included Red-baiting, as the Church committee noted. The FBI tried to "influence public opinion by using news media sources to discredit dissident groups by linking them to the Communist Party." In an operation directed against the United Farm Workers union (UFW), FBI agents told their media contacts that a CP leader marched in an UFW picket line. During a civil rights employment campaign directed at several northern California newspapers, the FBI intervened by "confidentially" informing newspaper friends that communists participated in the organizing.[105] In the Pentagon Papers case in 1971, the FBI's covert contact with the media attempted to discredit Leonard Boudin, attorney for whistleblower Daniel Ellsberg, by telling a Washington news bureau of Boudin's alleged "sympathy" and legal services for "communist causes."[106]

The FBI used friendly media to damage the reputations of black protest leaders and groups during 27 separate COINTELPRO operations. The bureau's negative representations varied according to the context. Subjects were depicted as militant and aggressive; criminal and violent; and, conversely, cowardly. Whatever image the bureau believed effectively would undermine social action. Several efforts focused on Martin Luther King, Jr. In one plan, the FBI contacted southern newspapers claiming King preferred to stay in white-owned hotels in the South.[107] Agents distributed a story to five newspapers charging that a King associate, Jack O'Dell, had communist ties.[108] In 1968, Headquarters pressured a "cooperative national news media source" to publish an article "designed to curtail success of Martin Luther King's fund raising" for the Poor People's March on Washington, D.C. The source falsely reported that "an embarrassment of riches has befallen King . . . and King doesn't need the money." The Miami office followed orders "to furnish data concerning money wasted by the Poor People's Campaign" to a friendly news reporter. "The Bureau must not be revealed as the source."[109] In Cleveland, the FBI took photographs of demonstrators and furnished them to reporters accompanied by a provocative note: "These show the militant, aggressive appearance of the participants and might be of interest to a cooperative news source."[110] Miami agents helped produce a television program and by "editing comments of these extremists . . . brought out that they were in favor of violent revolution without explaining why. But he also brought out that they, personally, would be afraid to lead a violent revolution, making them appear to be cowards."[111]

In 1961, the *New York Daily News* cooperated with the FBI to publicize the criminal record of a black Socialist Workers Party candidate.[112] In Boston, the field office discussed strategies to spread derogatory information about the Nation of Islam. "[T]he NOI predilection for violence, preaching of race hatred, and hypocrisy, should be exposed. Material furnished [text redacted] should be either public source or known to enough people as to protect your sources. Insure the Bureau's interest in this matter is completely protected."[113]

During the 1960s, information dissemination to the news media also sought to discredit the New Left movement. In several cities, the FBI focused on Students for a Democratic Society (SDS). In Chicago, an FBI agent contacted a major newspaper to place an article "greatly [to] encourage factional antagonisms during the SDS Convention."[114] In Ithaca, New York, SDS factionalism at Cornell University weakened the organization and the local field office "prepared material concerning this factionalism so that this material can be furnished on a selective and discreet basis to press contacts."[115] Hoover approved a plan in an unnamed city "to get cooperative news media to cover closed meetings of Students for a Democratic Society (SDS) and other New Left groups" with the aim of "disrupting them."[116] Another local FBI office sought retaliation against an activist who had been "active in showing films on the Black Panthers and police in action at various universities during student rioting" by providing a media contact with "background information and any arrest record" on the individual in order to "have a detrimental effect on activities."[117]

Headquarters hoped to cause "embarrassment" to the movement by providing lifestyle information "depicting the scurrilous and depraved nature of many of the characters, activities, habits and living conditions."[118] It circulated photographs to depict living conditions as "a shambles with lewd, obscene and revolutionary slogans displayed on the walls." Headquarters wrote: "As this publicity will be derogatory in nature and might serve to neutralize the group, it is being approved."[119] Another technique involved mailing bogus letters to media organizations. A letter to *Life* magazine "call[ed] attention to the unsavory character" of an underground magazine editor associated with the Youth International Party (Yippies). The fictitious letter contained violent overtones: "The cuckoo editor of an unimportant smutty little rag" should be "left in the sewers."[120]

In a well-known case, the FBI contacted a Hollywood newspaper columnist to libel actress Jane Fonda. The bureau claimed she chanted slogans, accompanied by members of the Black Panther Party, calling for President Nixon's death.[121] Fonda was investigated in 1971 and 1972. The FBI consulted friendly journalists to help gather intelligence. Rick Perlstein writes:

> They tapped their network of friendly media propagandists, like the future Senator Jesse Helms, then a TV editorialist, who supplied an invented quotation that still circulates as part of the Fonda cult's liturgy. Supposedly asked—it isn't clear where or by whom—how far America should go to the left, she said, according to Helms: "If everyone knew what it meant, we would all be on our knees praying that we would, as soon as possible, be able to live under . . . a Communist structure."[122]

Another strategy urged journalists to undervalue protest militancy on college campuses. "[C]ooperative press contacts should be encouraged to emphasize that the disruptive elements constitute a minority of the students and do not represent the conviction of the majority."[123] The FBI asked a Washington, DC, reporter from the Scripts-Howard News Service to write a "special visual feature story" to aid the capture of Weather Underground fugitives.[124] An unnamed syndicated columnist was recruited to create divisions between white and black radicals by distributing a newspaper column written by the bureau. The article, "The Widening Rift," said Black Panthers tried to "exhort" money from SDS and "white liberals." An agent noted the counterintelligence goals:

> Assuming that the "expose" is written and picked up by one of the wire services, it would serve the purpose of alerting Black militant groups in other cities of the possibility of milking white liberals in their community. . . . The resulting bickering, resentment and mistrust could be fomented by sources with the hope that the New Left and the Blacks become so ineffective they will be spending all of their time and energy defending themselves.[125]

Surveillance of Radical Media

The surveillance of alternative and radical media served several purposes. It generated intelligence on writers, editors, advertisers, and subscribers, as well as providing scheduling information on demonstrations, lectures, and meetings. In addition, the bureau educated themselves about "subversive" political ideas based on articles in these publications. By the early 1970s, the FBI had collected about 32,000 different radical publications and referred to "periodicals which are useful to our supervisory staff in staying abreast of current developments in the new left, racial or nationality fields but which have little or no permanent value, such as the 'AFL-CIO News,' or 'Dissent.'"[126] As a reader, the FBI adopted a narrow disciplinary attitude. They rejected the idea of pluralism, which valued multiple viewpoints. Radicals had nothing to contribute to society, and their media formed a dangerous communication vehicle contributing to disorder.

The scope of this surveillance only recently has become clear. Again, declassification of spy files sheds new light on monitoring and containment. Under the Freedom of Information Act, I obtained a list of 61 publications monitored by the FBI office in New York City during the mid-1960s. (See Appendix B.) Predictably, the FBI tracked small socialist and communist publications. They also viewed civil liberties as a left-wing cause and subscribed, for example, to the American Civil Liberties Union's

"Feature Press Service," as well as three other related publications (*Civil Liberties*; *Civil Liberties Docket*; and *Civil Liberties in New York*).[127] The FBI paid close attention to the CP press (the *Daily Worker* and *People's World*).[128] They equated Party journalism with its "pamphlets"—that is, printed material directed to build solidarity and membership. In Philadelphia, the FBI office estimated that its reading of the *Daily Worker* allowed information to be "disseminated to the files" of about 100 individuals.[129] The files on reporters and editors included Lester Rodney, the long-time sports editor.[130] Louis Budenz, the *Daily Worker's* labor and managing editor between 1936 and 1945, served the FBI by supplying the names of about 400 American communists.[131]

Radical newspapers unaffiliated with political parties were monitored, such as *PM* and the *National Guardian*. The *Guardian's* executive editor, James Aronson, recalled that circulation reached about 54,000 by the onset of the Korean War but dropped almost in half after the newspaper opposed U.S. involvement. "We learned that the FBI had been visiting subscribers asking them if they were aware of the true nature of the *National Guardian*. Local post offices apparently were cooperating with the FBI and, in violation of the law, permitting examination of mail bundles of the paper. . . . A sympathetic telephone company employee informed us that all our office phones were being tapped. We assumed this was true also of our home phones."[132]

Independent progressive journals with a theoretical orientation were viewed as a threat, including *Dissent* and *Science and Society*. The FBI file on *Dissent* begins soon after its founding in 1954. The bureau wrote: "The accent of 'Dissent' is 'radical' and its tradition is the tradition of democratic socialism, with editorial emphasis on reestablishing socialist thought. It is felt that the publication is of sufficient investigative importance to warrant its regular receipt and handling."[133] A separate file on *Dissent's* founding editor Irving Howe covers the period 1953 to 1959. Howe's background included writing for both socialist publications such as *Labor Action* and *The New International* as well as mainstream magazines such as *Time*, where he served as a literary critic. His 141-page file documents an interview by agents in 1954.

Subject states that his activities in the Independent Socialist League was a matter of public record and that he saw no need to further discuss them. He then stated that he would be happy to sit in his car and discuss ideologies. He continued that this was as far as he would go with the interviewing agents and that he had no intention of identifying or "involving" others in view of what he described as the "misuse" of the Smith Act by the Department of Justice and the use of Executive Order 10450 to "Blackball radicals" and prevent them from earning a living. He declined to further specify these remarks.[134]

During the early 1960s, the FBI kept track of the journal's criticism of it. In the Winter 1963 issue, contributing editor Daniel M. Friedenberg called for the creation of a special court to handle FBI illegal surveillance. In the same issue, Norman Mailer, a frequent FBI critic, also expressed the view that the FBI did more damage to America than the Communist Party.[135] The FBI's Mailer files totals 446 pages.[136] By the end of the 1960s, the FBI used *Dissent* to study Left ideas. "It is one of the best magazines we receive which illustrates the thinking of the New Left particularly as related to the college student," the head of the New York FBI office said. It "gives view of how leftists view current events. It enables supervisors to follow trends in the socialist movement, not only in the U.S., but on the international level as well."[137]

The bureau compiled a list of all editors, writers, and advertisers of the Marxist journal *Science and Society* and opened investigations on anyone not already subject to monitoring. They located bookstores that sold the journal, which had a printing of several thousand copies. Although labeled a communist-front publication, an FBI memo in 1958 indicated: "Review of [FBI files] did not disclose any evidence that [*Science and Society*] is controlled or dominated by the CP. Furthermore, the files did not indicate that [it] is used to recruit individuals into the CP or for Soviet espionage."[138] Still, the FBI remained opposed to the distribution of Marxist publications. When several editors of the journal published a book of essays, *Philosophy for the Future* (1948), the bureau objected to the detrimental influence of "materialists" on the "minds of countless youth." A 1957 memo said:

"It is not unlikely that the majority of the educated enemies of the Bureau who are regularly attacking or opposing us in one form or another are philosophic materialists. And, they are not decreasing in numbers. *Philosophy for the Future* is our problem of the future." But the journal's FBI file abruptly ends in the early 1960s because, as David H. Price speculates, "*Science and Society* was no longer seen by the FBI as a threat, a conclusion supported by the FBI's broader recognition that radical theory was less threatening than activism."[139]

The FBI's adversarial relationship to the New Left and "underground" press of the late 1960s substantiates this view. The bureau believed this media, consisting of more than 400 local papers with a readership up to about 4 million, served as a "communication center" for radicals by disseminating information on activism. One memo noted: "New Left underground newspapers, especially those oriented toward the Weatherman philosophy, be afforded intensive investigation due to their apparent role as a communication center."[140] In 1968, the FBI began a special campaign to surveil and undermine as many newspapers as possible. Headquarters told local offices to compile intelligence on staff and printers, as well as advertisers and develop counterintelligence operations to force these publications to fold. Moreover, other entities besides the FBI attacked the underground press—local police, the CIA, politicians, and vigilantes—which further eroded their ability to survive. John McMillian in *Smoking Typewriters* (2011) noted these largely uncoordinated efforts made the overall suppression *more* effective since the press "could be attacked on multiple fronts, by a range of enemies that were sometimes hard to discern."[141]

The FBI, as well as the CIA, infiltrated the staff of the popular *Ramparts* in Berkeley, California, and wrote articles for the newspaper. The investigation opened in 1966, when the paper had a monthly circulation of about 65,000, and lasted a decade, generating a 1,572-page file. The paper's vocal anti-war sentiment, as well as the involvement of several writers and editors the FBI already identified as subversive (including I.F. Stone, Fred J. Cook, and Irving Beinin), initially prompted the inquiry. A 1967 memo to assistant director William C. Sullivan, the supervisor of COINTELPRO operations, referred to *Ramparts* as a "West Coast publication whose articles have been strongly left-wing and which have included strong criticism of the Bureau." Another memo noted that "many staff members of 'Ramparts' magazine have subversive backgrounds."

Counterintelligence against the newspaper appears to have begun in 1967, when agents in several cities contacted bank officials to detail *Rampart's* finances. As circulation grew to about 200,000 readers, the FBI speculated that "wealthy radicals" might be making "large contributions." When Warren Hinckle III became publisher, Hoover sent an order to subordinates: "What do we know about Hinckle?" Official justification for surveillance changed over time and included foreign influence and financing in violation of the Registration Act, as well as association with revolutionaries including the Weather Underground Organization.[142] The magazine's staff recognized they were under surveillance and some tried to elude it, for example, by using pay phones instead of the office's landlines.[143]

Although the *Village Voice* in New York City described itself as a "liberal weekly," the FBI labeled it a "well known 'hippie' paper" and investigated it as a New Left vehicle. In 1971, the FBI began to read each issue as part of a survey of "underground publications."[144] Among other subjects of investigation, the bureau viewed the *Yipster Times* as such a threat that staffers were placed on the Administrative Index (ADEX)—the successor to the Security Index. After obtaining the newspaper's mailing list, the FBI interviewed some subscribers.[145] The bureau also targeted the Liberation News Service with undercover informers to inhibit its work. Angus Mackenzie reported, "The FBI attempted to discredit and break up the news service through various counterintelligence activities, such as trying to make LNS appear to be an FBI front, to create friction among staff members, and to burn down the LNS office in Washington while the staff slept upstairs."[146] In 1969, Tom Forcade, head of the Underground Press Syndicate, estimated that 60 percent of alternative papers were victimized by state repression.[147]

The FBI holds files on newspapers associated with the women's liberation movement, including *Ain't I a Woman?* and *off our backs* (oob).[148] The declassified oob file lists the newspaper as "armed and dangerous—extremist." Agents tried to interview its staff in Washington, D.C., in 1973 but found the "paper has a strict policy regarding non-cooperation with the FBI, and she [a staff member] furnished no information to the agents."[149] Surveillance of feminist publications was part of the broader monitoring of the women's movement. Between 1969 and 1979, the FBI main file on the movement reached more than 3,000 pages.[150]

The FBI supported the suppression of the Black Panther Party's newspaper. An agent said the newspaper "was the voice of the BPP and if it could be effectively hindered, it would result in helping to cripple the BPP." Wiretaps were placed on the newspaper's phones and infiltrators were planted on its staff.[151] In New York City, the FBI urged the newspaper's distributor to raise its rates because the BPP "suffers from a constant shortage of funds."[152]

"Most alternative publications were operated on a shoestring budget in the 1960s and early 1970s," notes Chip Berlet, who worked with the underground press, "and there is little doubt that the added expenses caused by FBI-inspired tax audits, postal hassles, price hikes, evictions, and arrests forced many publications into insolvency."[153] Counterintelligence methods also included pressuring advertisers; harassing street vendors; destroying papers; and forging letters of complaint from "concerned parents" to university administrators to limit distribution on college campuses.[154]

The Detroit FBI office developed a plan to target the printing plant that produced New Left literature. In 1970, they designed an op to obtain in "liquid form a solution capable of duplicating a scent of the most foul smelling feces available. In this case, it might be appropriate to duplicate the feces of the specie sus scrofa [wild pig]. A quart supply, along with a dispenser capable of squirting a narrow stream for a distance of approximately three feet would satisfy the needs of this proposed technique."[155] What purpose might be achieved by this operation? In addition to ruining the paper bundles, the printer might become paranoid about the odor in his facility and cease to work with political activists. In a second case, the FBI contacted the publisher of *New*

Left Notes in Addison, Illinois, and prepared secretly to alter the SDS publication without editorial approval. "Contact has previously been had with Ad-Print and personnel there are extremely cooperative with the Bureau. If the appropriate situation presents itself, it may be possible to insert bogus information in an edition to create chaos in the organization."[156]

The FBI tracked college publications when they became associated with "student agitation" by expressing anti-war views or civil rights advocacy. In some cases, the FBI submitted bogus letters to the editor. The investigation of the College Press Service (CPS), which distributed articles to about 500 newspapers, lasted three years (1970-1973) and included surveillance of financial records and CPS staff. Hoover believed the Service's "releases contain information which discredit the Government and authority, and follow the New Left movement in expression and content."[157]

In at least one case, the FBI edited and published a newspaper and presented it as independent college journalism. *The Rational Observer* at American University in Washington, D. C., hoped to influence opinion on college campus by attacking the anti-war movement and expressing favorable views of U.S. military draft compliance.[158] In another case, the bureau put out a newsletter in Winston-Salem, North Carolina, named the *Black Community News Service* in order to draw supporters away from the local BPP.[159] Moreover, the FBI worked closely with a photo news organization, the New York Press Service, to penetrate New Left protests. The Service advertised: "The next time your organization schedules a demonstration, march, picket, or office party, let us know in advance. We'll cover it like a blanket and deliver a cost free sample of our work to your office."[160]

By 1975, the vast majority of underground newspapers had ceased publication. The FBI played a significant role in their demise. As the American Chapter of the writer's group PEN concluded in a 1981 report: "The withering of the underground press was not entirely a natural decline" because the press was victimized by "surveillance, harassment, and unlawful search and seizure by U.S. government agencies."[161]

Manipulation after the Cold War

The practice of Cold War journalism ended with the demise of the Soviet Union. The bureau embraced more open access that, ironically, led to a higher level of media misleading. Officials served as public sources for news articles, appeared on network television, and presented public speeches. Dissemination of information no longer depended on ad-hoc contacts. However, in most of these forums the FBI spread false information about peaceful political activity, which they categorized as "terrorism," naming particular groups to vilify and demonize. This strident scare politics presented exaggerated claims about the threat of mayhem and political violence, which the mainstream media too often uncritically accepted. A new War on Terror journalism, like Cold War journalism, rarely challenged the goals of the U.S. intelligence community. The FBI helped to frame the underlying assumptions that shaped the media's construction of the terrorist threat.

Shaping public opinion is a contested process. Since the mid-1970s, Americans have become aware of the FBI's history of abuse of power trampling upon constitutional rights. As historian Richard Gid Powers notes, during the 1990s conflicting representations of the FBI existed in the popular mind. Both hero and villain. "[S]o many different and contradictory images of the Bureau are in circulation that every new FBI story confirms one or another FBI stereotype. FBI officials find it difficult to present a coherent, unified message to the public."[162]

Attempts to manipulate media coverage expressed itself in full form before the arrival of the millennium. The FBI repeatedly warned about potential violence from apocalyptic groups across the political spectrum. They publicized a special report, "Project Megiddo," which referenced the threat posed by an estimated 1,000 cults in America.[163] Moreover, the new popular discourse on Weapons of Mass Destruction, which originated with the Clinton Administration, became linked by the FBI to the threat of terrorism.[164] The social construction of "what might happen" included computers crashing and bombs exploding at the New Year 2000. The FBI estimated that the prospect of terrorism from either domestic or overseas sources was about 50 percent. Rather than downplaying the threat, the FBI used the media to intensify popular anxiety and insecurity. The media compliantly reported dire warnings without much filtering.[165]

Some old habits persisted as FBI agents continued to impersonate journalists. In 2000, several agents posed as press photographers to take pictures of right-wing radicals in Idaho.[166]

It became relatively easy for the FBI to use the mass media to manufacture fear by making pronouncements about imminent threats to the homeland. The manipulation of media coverage occurred when the FBI leaked internal bulletins and other documents warning of terrorism. Television news in particular responded compliantly, magnifying threats, when the Bush administration periodically raised the color coded terror-alert level. For example, the national networks devoted about five and a half minutes of coverage when the alert level officially rose, compared to just one and half minutes when it was lowered. The media in general over reported the fear messages emanating from official sources.[167]

The "war on terror" intensified the FBI's negative portrayal of dissidents and protest. As one example, the media relied on unsubstantiated police claims that a large segment of street protestors in the anti-globalization movement were violent "troublemakers." The National Lawyers Guild concluded in 2010, "Misleading news coverage has helped the public buy the official line that protest poses a threat that necessitates a repressive and overwhelming police response."[168]

The FBI could successfully promote misrepresentations because many reporters gave up claims to objectivity in the immediate aftermath of the 9/11 attacks. As L. Brent Bozell III, a conservative media watch leader, proudly noted: "[R]eporters discarded the ridiculous notion that a journalist is a reporter first, an American second. Most journalists made known loudly, unambiguously, unapologetically, *their* outrage, *their* sorrow, *their* love of country."[169] The media increasingly became an administration ally, making no pretense to serve as an independent watchdog. In 2003, *American Prospect* editor Michael Tomasky concluded: "There have been occasional and notable exceptions to this trend, but by and large, the U.S. press has followed the government's agenda since 9/11 in a way that hasn't been the case for decades. And, it should be noted, news organizations have sometimes lowered their standards in doing so."[170]

The diversity of commentary experts, who could place the attacks in historical and transnational perspective, also seemed at a near all-time low. Very few media voices questioned whether the FBI should get enhanced spying powers. Moreover, the large news organizations began to silence liberal points of view. A leading example was NBC's decision to cancel Phil Donohue's hour-long television show in early 2003. An internal NBC report explained the political basis of the decision. Donohue represented a "difficult public face for NBC in time of war. He seems to delight in presenting guests who are antiwar, anti-Bush, and skeptical of the administration's motives." The network did not want his show to become "a home for the liberal anti-war agenda at the same time that our competitors are waving the flag at every opportunity."[171] Whether the FBI secretly put pressure on NBC to drop Donohue is unknown. The network easily could have made the decision without government interference inasmuch as it had become, like other major news organizations, a big corporation with a conservative business agenda.

ABC-TV also forced comedian Bill Maher, the host of *Politically Incorrect*, to apologize after he questioned Bush's characterization that the 9/11 hijackers were "cowards."[172] Some stations still canceled Maher's show and eventually he migrated to paid cable television. Anthony R. DiMaggio refers to the manner that "corporate media framing reinforces pro-war positions" by viewing the U.S. as a benevolent superpower which supports only humanitarianism and democracy.[173] Lisa Finnegan provides evidence that a compliant news media published pro-administration, quasi-propaganda articles that sometimes included misinformation.[174] Of course, the bias of the media to support U.S. wars was not new, but the war on terror was different: The enemies were not primarily state actors; Islamic radicalism crossed sovereign borders. As a result, the war on terror had no easy resolution. When was victory achieved?

The rise of a private "terrorism industry" within the publishing and media community also advanced FBI interests. These so-called "experts," who often work in government-funded private research groups, occupy media coverage by exaggerating the threat of political violence and advocating enhanced spying on Americans. As early as 1989, Edward S. Herman and Gerry O'Sullivan identified this media formation, which has grown in proportion in subsequent years. In addition, ex-government officials often become television journalists espousing largely official viewpoints. So, for example, former Bush Homeland Security advisor Fran Townsend served as a CNN contributor and ex-GOP Congresswoman Susan Molinari became a regular commentator for MSNBC.[175]

Journalists also worked directly with the state after 9/11 in advisory roles. When Deputy Defense Secretary Paul Wolfowitz secretly assembled a group of leading intellectuals and strategists to develop effective government responses to terrorism, the participants included Fareed Zakaria, an editor and columnist at *Newsweek*, who later hosted his own news show on CNN. (Ironically, the title of his television show is "GPS," and surveillance is associated with Global Positioning Systems.) The *Atlantic Monthly* writer Robert Kaplan also reportedly was a member of the group. In a related way, the situation of "embedded reporters" who lived with specific military units became an integral part of the government's control of media coverage during the invasion of Iraq. Rarely did these journalists report on antiwar sentiment among soldiers fearful the military might expel them.[176]

Liberal-Left media referred to print, radio, and television critically as "weapons of mass diversion," "weapons of mass distortion," and "weapons of mass distraction." The mainstream media allowed the FBI to spread false ideas (distortion) linking domestic political activity to terrorism. The hype about terrorism served as a distraction to keep popular attention away from everyday real problems. Propagating a terror scare served as a diversion to mask the high level of inequality and injustice in America.

After the Cold War, the media landscape expanded with Web journalism and a new corps of freelance writers afforded few press rights and protections. The FBI viewed independent media centers ("Indymedia") as radical journalism and often equated it with terrorism subject to warrantless monitoring. These journalists may be arrested alongside protestors as part of FBI "preventative" strategies. Indymedia was affected by some state laws prohibiting the photographing of police, which hinders effective documentation of misconduct. The NLG noted a law enforcement trend of "attaching ominous meanings to ordinary objects" like tape recorders and cameras, the common tools of Indymedia journalists. The journalist as terrorist? Did these journalists pose a true threat to society? Only a cynical government intent on suppression and unconcerned about accountability would make this claim.[177]

The FBI engaged in extensive surveillance of the Internet. This open source monitoring—no warrant is required as if one is reading a newspaper—employed analytical artificial intelligence programs looking for suspicious language. The FBI entered dozens of web sites and chat rooms to find information on political activity. Media surveillance might be at an all-time high. But there is resistance. In 2009, the civil liberties group, Electronic Frontier Foundation (EFF) issued a "Surveillance Self-Defense" on-line manual. "When the government wants to record or monitor your private communications as they happen, it has three basic options," they wrote. "It can install a hidden microphone or 'bug' to eavesdrop on your conversation; it can install a 'wiretap' to capture the content of your phone or Internet communications as they happen; or it can install a 'pen register' and a 'trap and trace device' to capture dialing and routing information indicating who you communicate with and when." They reserved special concern about text messaging over cell phones, considered highly vulnerable to government snooping. "First, just like your cell phone conversations, SMS text messages sent to and from your cell phone can easily be intercepted over radio with minimal equipment and without any cooperation from the cell phone provider."[178]

Despite this new surveillance, the Internet increased the number of critics who monitored FBI practices. In addition to the EFF, the Electronic Privacy and Information Center (EPIC) regularly reported information about FBI surveillance practices; the Bill of Rights Defense Committee (BORDC) provided a daily on-line digest of critical articles on the bureau; the Transactional Records Analytical Clearinghouse (TRAC) at Syracuse University analyzed federal law enforcement activity; Political Research Associates issued on-line reports on the FBI; as did lawyer groups such as the American Civil Liberties Union (ACLU) and the National Lawyers Guild. Progressive news and commentary web sites—HuffingtonPost and Salon—regularly featured FBI critics. In sum, the media landscape on the Internet was occupied with critics coexisting with official and proto-official FBI spokespeople. There was a diversity of viewpoints. The FBI can not effectively suppress critics in this new media form.

Web sites also posted FBI files for the public to read, an important part of a demystification process. The veil of secrecy surrounding the FBI is being lifted. Americans can read FBI records to understand the type of information collected during investigations. Some sites are critical of FBI conduct. Others provide access for educational purposes. (One of the best sites remained GovernmentAttic.org.) The FBI web site also selectively posts its own files for public consumption. Why did the secrecy-obsessed FBI participate in this transparency effort? A critical view holds that by providing a modicum of openness, the FBI boosted its reputation as a democratic entity when in fact it served as the chief vehicle for repressive politics in the government.

Appendix A

Journalists and Writers Subject to FBI Surveillance

David Brinkley
Peter Arnett
Joseph Kraft
Eric Sevareid

Charles Kuralt
David Halberstam
Haywood Broun
Walter Lippmann
Edward R. Murrow
Walter Cronkite
Harrison Salisbury
Peter Lisagor
Ben Gilbert
I. F. Stone
Joseph Alsop
Jack Anderson
Daniel Schorr
James Wechsler
Hanson Baldwin
James B. Reston
Fred J. Cook
Carey McWilliams
Art Buchwald
Max Lowenthal
Peter Matthiessen
E. B. White
Sinclair Lewis
John Steinbeck
Upton Sinclair
Carl Sandburg
Theodore Dreiser
John Dos Passos
Pearl S. Buck
Dorothy Parker
H. L. Mencken
Edmund Wilson
John Kenneth Galbraith
Herbert Block
Benjamin Ginzburg
Oliver Harrington
Wade Thompson
Douglas Dowd

Herman Wouk
Walter E. Dillion
Alan Barth
Theodore Draper
Joseph F. Dinneen
Nathan Glazer
Morris L. Ernst
Herbert Aptheker
Leo Huberman
Paul Sweezy
Norman Mailer
Irving Howe
Nat Hentoff
Betty Friedan
Studs Terkel
Lester Rodney
Daniel M. Friedenberg
Tom Forcade
Ingra Arvad
Philip Jaffe
Kate Mitchell
Mark Gayn
William Beecher
Marvin Kalb
Hedrick Smith
Leonard Lyons
Lloyd Norman

Source: Herbert Mitgang, *Dangerous Dossiers: Exposing the Secret War against America's Greatest Authors* (New York: Donald I. Fine Books 1988): Natalie Robins, *Alien Ink: The FBI's War on Freedom of Expression* (New York: W. Morrow, 1992); Athan G. Theoharis, *Abuse of Power: How Cold War Surveillance and Secrecy Policy Shaped the Response to 9/11* (Philadelphia: Temple University Press, 2011); as well as numerous press articles.

Appendix B

Publications Subscribed to by the FBI Office in New York City in 1966

ACA News
The ADL Bulletin
American Dialog
The Annals
Bulletin (Institute for the Study of the USSR)
Bulletin of International Socialism
Challenge
Civil Liberties
Civil Liberties Docket
Civil Liberties in New York
The Communist Viewpoint
Crime and Delinquency
Dissent
East Europe
Feature Press Service
Fellowship
Foreign Affairs
Freedomways
Free Student
Headline Series
Intercom
International Affairs
International Socialist Review
Jewish Currents
The Militant
Monthly Review
The Nation
National Guardian
National Review
National Review Bulletin
The New Leader
New Politics
The New Republic

New World Review
The Partisan
Party Affairs
Party Voice
Poland
Political Affairs
Publishers' Weekly
Religion in Communist Dominated Areas
The Reporter
Rights
The Russian Review
Science and Society
Scientific World
The Soviet Review
Spartacist
Studies on the Left
Studies on the Soviet Union
Survey
United Nations Monthly Chronicle
Vanguard
The Worker
Workers World
World Politics
World Trade Union Movement
Worldview
Young Socialist
Yugoslavia Facts and Views

Source: SAC New York to Director, "Publications—Handling by Research-Satellite Section, Research-Satellite Matter," Aug. 9, 1966, *Dissent* FBI file.

Notes

1. David Cunningham, "The Patterning of Repression: FBI Counterintelligence and the New Left," *Social Forces* 82 (Sept. 2003): 209-240.

2. Athan G. Theoharis et al., *The FBI: A Comprehensive Reference Guide* (New York: Oryx Press, 2000), 229; Ellen Schrecker, *Many are the Crimes: McCarthyism in America* (Boston: Little Brown, 1998), 204. See also Richard Gid Powers, *G-Men: Hoover's FBI in American Popular Culture* (Carbondale: Southern Illinois University Press, 1983); Bob Herzberg, *The FBI and the Movies: A History of the Bureau on Screen and Behind the Scenes in Hollywood* (Jefferson, NC: McFarland, 2007); and Claire A. Culleton, *Joyce and the G-Men: J. Edgar Hoover's Manipulation of Modernism* (New York: Palgrave MacMillan, 2004).

3. Frank J. Donner, *The Age of Surveillance: The Aims and Methods of America's Political Intelligence System* (New York: Random House, 1980), 467-477.

4. FBI Director, "Executives Conference," October 4, 1946, Executives Conference FBI file.

5. J. F. Malone to Mr. Mohr, "Inspection – Domestic Intelligence Division," Dec. 29, 1961, 7, Donald E. Moore FBI file.

6. U.S. Senate Select Committee to Study Government Operations (Church Committee), "Intelligence Activities and the Rights of Americans," Book II, April 26, 1976, 15; Jules Boykoff, *Beyond Bullets: The Suppression of Dissent in the United States* (Oakland, CA: AK Press, 2007), 13.

7. Heidi Boghosian, *The Policing of Political Speech: Constraints on Mass Dissent in the U.S.* (New York: National Lawyers Guild, 2010), 22-23.

8. U. S. Senate Church Committee hearings, Nov. 19, 1975, 87-89, www.aarclibrary.org/publib/contents/church/contents_church_reports_vol6.htm (accessed Oct. 20, 2009).

9. Schrecker, *Many are the Crimes*, 221-222.

10. U. S. Senate Church Committee hearings, Nov. 19, 1975, 88-89.

11. Jim Tuck, *McCarthyism and New York's Hearst Press: A Study of Roles in the Witch Hunt* (Lanham, MD: University Press of America, 1995); David Nasaw, *The Chief: The Life of William Randolph Hearst* (Boston: Houghton Mifflin, 2000), 502-506; Robert Justin Goldstein, *American Blacklist: The Attorney General's List of Subversive Organizations* (Lawrence: University of Kansas Press, 2008), 87-89.

12. Edward Alwood, *Dark Days in the Newsroom: McCarthyism Aimed at the Press* (Philadelphia: Temple University Press, 2007), 3; Alwood, "Watching the Watchdogs: FBI Spying on Journalists in the 1940s," *Journalism and Mass Communication Quarterly* 84 (Spring 2007): 137-150.

13. James Aronson, *The Press and the Cold War* (New York: Bobbs-Merrill, 1970), 6; Nancy Bernhard, *Television News and Cold War Propaganda, 1947-1960* (Cambridge: Harvard University Press, 1999); James

L. Aucoin, *The Evolution of American Investigative Journalism* (Columbia: University of Missouri Press, 2005), 43-46; Albert Abramson, *The History of Television, 1942 to 2000* (Jefferson: McFarland, 2007), 294.

14. Donner, *The Age of Surveillance*, 238; Dan Berger, *Outlaws of America: The Weather Underground and the Politics of Solidarity* (Oakland, AK Press, 2005), 71, 93.

15. Curt Gentry, *J. Edgar Hoover: The Man and the Secrets* (New York: Norton, 1991), 388-389; Schrecker, *Many are the Crimes*, 216.

16. Earl Caldwell interviewed on PBS *NewsHour*, Sept. 15, 2010, www.pbs.org/newshour/bb/media/july-dec10/photographer_09-15.html.

17. Ivan Greenberg, "Civil Rights Photojournalist Named as FBI Spy," Rowman and Littlefield, Sept. 20, 2010, www. rowmanblog. typepad.com/rowman/2010/09/civil-rights-photojournalist-named-as-fbi-spy.html; "Mixed Reaction to Civil Rights Photographer's FBI Ties," *Washington Post*, Sept. 14, 2010.

18. "New Documents Show Longtime Friendship Between J. Edgar Hoover and Paul Harvey," *Washington Post*, Jan. 23, 2010.

19. "Files Indicate Helms was 'Contact' for FBI," *Raleigh News and Observer*, May 27, 2010.

20. Ibid.

21. FBI Web site, "Walter Winchell File," www.fbi.gov/foia/ (accessed Dec. 14, 2010).

22. A. H. Belmont to D. M. Ladd, "Walter Winchell Simulcast (Radio and Television) January 10, 1954," Jan. 11, 1954, Walter Winchell FBI file.

23. A. H. Belmont to D. M. Ladd, "Walter Winchell Simulcast (Radio and Television) February 21, 1954," Feb. 23, 1954, Winchell FBI file.

24. A. H. Belmont to D. M. Ladd, "Walter Winchell Simulcast (Radio and Television) January 31, 1954," Feb. 1, 1954, Winchell FBI file.

25. A. H. Belmont to D. M. Ladd, "Walter Winchell Simulcast (Radio and Television) February 14, 1954," Feb. 15, 1954, Winchell FBI file.

26. Gentry, *J. Edgar Hoover*, 384.

27. U.S. Senate Church Committee hearings, Nov. 18, 1975 (p. 20) and Dec. 3, 1975 (p. 181), www.aarclibrary.org/publib/church/reports_vol6/pages/ChurchV6_008 (accessed Oct. 21, 2009).

28. FBI Web site, "Eric Sevareid," www.fbi.gov/foia/ (accessed Dec. 14, 2010).

29. Jon Elliston, "The Journalist and the G-Men," Nov. 26, 2003, www.localhost/gyrobase/Content?oid=20575.

30. "FBI Kept Tabs On NY Reporter Halberstam," NY City News Service, Nov. 6, 2008, www.nycitynewsservice,.com/2008/11/06/fbi-kept-tabs-on-ny-reporter-halberstam/.

31. Athan G. Theoharis, *Abuse of Power: How Cold War Surveillance and Secrecy Policy Shaped the Response to 9/11* (Philadelphia: Temple University Press, 2011), 46.

32. Joseph E. Persico, *Edward R. Murrow: An American Original* (New York: McGraw-Hill, 1988), 329-325, 472.

33. Nicholas J. Cull, *The Cold War and the United States Information Agency: American Propaganda and Public Diplomacy, 1945-1989* (New York: Cambridge University Press, 2009), 189-261.

34. "Cronkite Records Destroyed by FBI," *USA Today*, Sept. 23, 2009.

35. Myra MacPherson, *All Governments Lie! The Life and Times of Rebel Journalist I. F. Stone* (New York: Scribner's, 2006), xvi, xxiii, 191-195, 285-306, 424-425.

36. William G. Staples, ed., *Encyclopedia of Privacy* (Westport, CT: Greenwood Press, 2007), 226-227.

37. Donald A. Ritchie, *Reporting from Washington: The History of the Washington Press Corps* (New York: Oxford University Press, 2005), 149-150.

38. Athan G. Theoharis, ed., *From the Secret Files of J. Edgar Hoover* (Chicago: Ivan R. Dee, 1991), 249.

39. Daniel Schorr, "The FBI and Me," *Columbia Journalism Review* 4 (Nov./Dec. 1974): 8.

40. Ibid., 9, 14.

41. Mark Feldstein, *Poisoning the Press: Richard Nixon, Jack Anderson, and the Rise of Washington's Scandal Culture* (New York: Farrar, Straus and Giroux, 2010), 300.

42. "Records Show J. Edgar Hoover's Disdain for Columnist," *Washington Post*, Oct. 12, 2008.

43. Ibid.

44. William Safire, *Before the Fall: An Inside View of the Pre-Watergate White House* (New York: Doubleday, 1974), 168; Gentry, *J. Edgar Hoover*, 639.

45. John F. Stacks, *Scotty: James B. Reston and the Rise and Fall of American Journalism* (Boston: Little, Brown and Co., 2003), 301-302.

46. Church Committee hearings, Nov. 18, 1975, 21.

47. SAC New York to Director, "Ramparts Magazine, IS - C," March 16, 1966, Ramparts FBI file.

48. "Hoover Praised, Pilloried P-D," *St. Louis Post-Dispatch*, April 5, 2010.

49. Ibid.

50. "P-D Editorials on Kidnapping Inflamed the FBI's Hoover," *St. Louis Post-Dispatch*, April 6, 2010.

51. FBI monograph, "Smear Campaign Against the FBI: The Nation," July 1959, i. 10. See also Fred J, Cook, *Maverick: Fifty Years of Investigative Reporting* (New York: G. P. Putnam, 1984).

52. Richard Lingeman, "The Files' Tale: Redbaited by the FBI," *The Nation*, Jan. 11, 2010.

53. Fred J. Cook, "The FBI," *The Nation*, Oct. 18, 1958, 277; "Smear Campaign Against the FBI," ii-v, 149.

54. W. C. Sullivan to A. H. Belmont, Feb. 19, 1955, Henry Steele Commager FBI file.

55. D. M. Ladd to Director, "Henry Steele Commager," June 29, 1949, Commager FBI file.

56. W. C. Sullivan to A. H. Belmont, Jan. 29, 1957; A. H. Belmont to L.V. Boardman, "Henry Steel [sic] Commager, Central Research Matter," Nov. 35, 1957; M. A. Jones to Mr. Nease, "Request for Information Regarding Professor Henry Commager," June 13, 1958. Commager FBI file.

57. Commager wrote a personal letter to Hoover after the assassination of the Rev. Martin Luther King, Jr. "Three years ago you had the limitless insolence of calling Martin Luther King the Greatest Liar in America. I trust you realize that your vulgarity and irresponsibility contributed directly to the Tragedy in Memphis." M. A. Jones to Mr. DeLoach, "Henry Steel [sic] Commager," Nov. 15, 1963; FBI Liaison [name redacted] to White House, July 10, 1967; Department of State report, "Henry Steel [sic] Commager," Oct. 19, 1968; SAC Boston to Director, "Henry Steel [sic] Commager," Nov. 21, 1976; Commager to J. Edgar Hoover, April 4, 1968; M. Jones to Mr. Bishop, "Henry Steele Commager," June 29, 1970. Commager FBI file.

58. Murray Polner, "James Wechsler: The Editor Who Dared Challenge J. Edgar Hoover," Jan. 5, 2004, http://hnn.us/articles/2869.html.

59. FBI, "The FBI in Our Open Society," June 1969, 19-20, http://www.governmentattic.org/docs/FBI_In_Our_Open_Society_1953.pdf (accessed June 16, 2010).

60. Ibid., 20. In 1951, Wechsler served as editor of the *New York Post* when it published a 17-part series devoted to exposing the Red Scare tactics of Senator Joseph McCarthy entitled: "Smear Inc. – A One-Man Job." In response, McCarthy subpoenaed Wechsler to testify before Senate hearings on communist subversion. Aronson, *The Press and the Cold War*, 87-94; Alwood, *Dark Days in the Newsroom*, 69-72.

61. M. A. Jones to Mr. DeLoach, "Howard Zinn," Nov. 27, 1962; A. Rosen to Mr. Belmont, "Racial Situation Albany, Georgia," Nov. 15, 1962. Howard Zinn FBI file.

62. A. Rosen to Mr. Belmont, "Howard Zinn," Jan. 8, 1964, Zinn FBI file.

63. David Carty, "Art Buchwald Couldn't Make This Man Laugh," CBSNews.com, June 25, 2008, http://www.cbsnews.com/stories/2008/06/25/national/main4207013.shtml.

64. Buchwald's satire was closer to real life than he might have known. In 1957, Hoover considered having his secret corps join forces at the national CP convention to elect their own people to take over the party. Hoover eventually rejected the idea because if the FBI faction failed to gain party control, they might be expelled, substantially reducing the FBI's secret access. Stephen J. Whitfield, "Civil Liberties and the Culture of the Cold War, 1945-1965," in Raymond Arsenault, ed., *Crucible of Liberty: 200 Years of the Bill of Rights* (New York: Free Press, 1991), 60.

65. M. A. Jones to Mr. DeLoach, "'Playboy' Magazine, April, 1965," March 3, 1965, Art Buchwald FBI file.

66. Hugh Hefner-Playboy Magazine FBI files, http://www.paperlessarchives.com/playboy.html (accessed Jan. 17, 2011).

67. Steven E. Kercher, *Rebel with a Cause: Liberal Satire in Postwar America* (Chicago: University of Chicago Press, 2006), 47.

68. Mr. Nease to M. A. Jones, "'Herblock's Special For the Day,' Book by Herbert Block," Jan. 26, 1959, Book Review FBI file.

69. "Oliver Harrington," in Henry Louis Gates and Evelyn Brooks Higginbotham, eds., *African American Lives* (New York: Oxford University Press, 2004), 376-377.

70. SAC Los Angeles to Director, "Attacks Against the FBI, SM-C," Feb. 26, 1962, Book Review FBI file.

71. M. A. Jones to Mr. DeLoach, "Richard Drinnon," March 6, 1962, Book Review FBI file.

72. G. C. Moore to E. S. Miller, "[Text redacted]," Oct. 3, 1973, *Ramparts* FBI file.

73. Herbert Mitgang, *Dangerous Dossiers: Exposing the Secret War Against America's Greatest Authors* (New York: Ballantine Books, 1988), vii-ix, 151-162, 177-187; Natalie Robins, *Alien Ink: The FBI's War on Freedom of Expression* (New Brunswick: Rutgers University, 1982), 23-25; "FBI Tracked 'Working' Man Studs Terkel," NY City News Service, Nov. 15, 2009, www.nycitynewsservice.com/2009/11/15/fbi-tracked-working-man-studs-terkel/; John Rodden, "Wanted: Irving Howe

FBI No. 727437B," *Dissent* (Fall 2002), www.dissentmagazine.org/article/?article=568.

74. "Barney Rosset Dies at 89; Publisher Fought Legal Battles," *Los Angeles Times*, Feb. 23, 2012.

75. Claire A. Culleton, "Extorting Henry Holt & Co.: J. Edgar Hoover and the Publishing Industry," in Culleton, ed., *Modernism on File: Writers, Artists, and the FBI, 1920-1950* (New York: Palgrave Macmillan, 2009), 238.

76. W. C. Sullivan to A. H. Belmont, "Book Reviews, Central Research Matter," May 11, 1959, Book Review FBI file. Thanks to Ernie Lazar for providing material from this file.

77. Mr. Tolson to C. A. DeLoach, "'Rededication to Freedom,' Book by Benjamin Ginzburg," March 12, 1959, Book Review FBI file.

78. Ibid.

79. Ibid.

80. M. A. Jones to Mr. DeLoach, "Egghead's Guide to America," June 22, 1962, Book Review FBI file.

81. M. A. Jones to Mr. DeLoach, "Step by Step," June 6, 1965, Book Review FBI file.

82. Samuel Walker, *In Defense of American Liberties: A History of the ACLU* (New York: Oxford University Press, 1990), 176, 333.

83. J. J. Casper to Mr. Mohr, Nov. 11, 1962, Book Review FBI file.

84. Morris Ernst also identified books for the FBI to review. An official acknowledged: "On 5/9/61, Morris Ernst advised the Bureau that one of his clients, the Athenian Press of New York City, has sent him the above-captioned book for him to read for libel. He stated that the book includes severe criticism of the FBI and Ernst asked if he could send the book to the Bureau." The book in question was John Bulloch and Henry Miller, *Spy Ring: The Full Story of the Naval Secrets Case.* W. A. Branigan to W. C. Sullivan, "Gordon Arnold Lonsdale," June 7, 1961, Book Review FBI file.

85. F. J. Baumgardner to A. H. Belmont, "'The Black Muslims in America,' by C. Eric Lincoln," April 21, 1961, Book Review FBI file.

86. R. W. Smith to W. C. Sullivan, "The Fund for the Republic Book Reviews," Oct. 5, 1961, Book Review FBI file.

87. F. J. Baumgardner to A. H. Belmont, "American Communism and Soviet Russia," June 7, 1960, Book Review FBI file.

88. M. A. Jones to Mr. DeLoach, "The Price of Liberty," Oct. 23, 1961, Book Review FBI file.

89. M. A. Jones to Mr. DeLoach, "Youngblood Hawke by Herman Wouk," May 5, 1962, Book Review FBI file.

90. W.V. Cleveland to Mr. Evans, "Book Reviews," June 15, 1962, Book Review FBI file.

91. Mr. DeLoach to M. A. Jones, "'The Doorbell Rang', New Mystery Novel by Rex Stout," May 20, 1965, Book Review FBI file.

92. Mitgang, *Dangerous Dossiers*, 227-228.

93. M. A. Jones to Mr. DeLoach, "The Alternative Case," Aug. 7, 1959, Book Review FBI file.

94. Powers, *G-Men*, 270-281; Kenneth O'Reilly, *Hoover and the Un Americans: The FBI, HUAC, and the Red Menace* (Philadelphia: Temple University Press, 1983), 140-145; Theoharis, *J. Edgar Hoover, Sex, and Crime: An Historical Antidote* (Chicago: Ivan R. Dee, 1995), 37-39.

95. William Sullivan to Cartha DeLoach, March 3, 1966, Magazine Subscription FBI file. Again, thanks to Ernie Lazar for providing this material. Lazar has donated hundreds of FBI files he obtained under the FOIA to the Robert F. Wagner Archives at New York University's Tamiment Library. The guide to this material is available at http://dlib.nyu.edu/findingaids/html/tamwag/lazare.html (accessed Dec. 16, 2011).

96. SAC New York to Director, "Book Review," Aug. 22, 1960, FBI Book Review File.

97. S. B. Donahue to A. H. Belmont, "Book Reviews." Nov. 21, 1960, Book Review FBI file.

98. Gentry, *J. Edgar Hoover*, 386-387.

99. Whitefield, "Civil Liberties and the Culture of the Cold War, 1945-1965," 65-66.

100. FBI, "The FBI in Our Open Society," June 1969, 24.

101. Gentry, *J. Edgar Hoover*, 387-388.

102. Peter Matthiessen, *In The Spirit of Crazy Horse* (New York: Viking, 1991, 2nd ed), 469, 565, 589-596.

103. Church Committee, "Intelligence Activities and the Rights of Americans," 245.

104. Ibid., 244.

105. Ibid., 247.

106. Ibid., 246.

107. Loch K. Johnson, *A Season on Inquiry: The Senate Intelligence Investigation* (Lexington: University Press of Kentucky, 1985), 127.

108. Boykoff, *Beyond Bullets*, 182-183.

109. Church Committee, "Intelligence Activities and the Rights of Americans," 16.

110. Ibid., 244.

111. SAC Albany to Director, Aug. 5, 1968, http://www.icdc.com/~paulwolf/cointelpro/hoover5aug1968.htm (accessed Sept 2, 2011).

112. John Drabble and Christopher Vaughan, "Fighting Black Power: FBI Media Campaigns, 1967-1971," 2007, 10-11, http://www.allacademic.com//meta/p_mla_apa_research_citation/1/7/3/4/2/pages173426/p173426-10.php (accessed March 6, 2011).

113. Boykoff, *Beyond Bullets*, 181.

114. Church Committee, "Intelligence Activities and the Rights of Americans," 16.

115. SAC Albany to Director, "COINTELPRO – New Left," Dec. 11, 1969, New Left FBI file.

116. Church Committee, "Intelligence Activities and the Rights of Americans," 246.

117. Ibid., 244.

118. Ibid., 16.

119. Ibid., 244.

120. Ibid., 245.

121. Jane Fonda, *My Life So Far* (New York: Random House, 2005), 220.

122. Rick Perlstein, "Operation Barbarella," *London Review of Books* 27 (November 2005): 4.

123. Berger, *Outlaws of America*, 85-86.

124. Jeremy Varon, *Bringing the War Home: The Weather Underground, the Red Army Faction, and Revolutionary Violence in the Sixties and Seventies* (Berkeley, University of California Press, 2004), 176.

125. SAC WFO to Director, "COINTELPRO – New Left," Aug. 22, 1969, New Left FBI file.

126. Athan G. Theoharis and John Stuart Cox, *The Boss: J. Edgar Hoover and the Great American Inquisition* (Philadelphia: Temple University Press, 1988), 9; "[Text redacted] to C. D. Brennan, "Publications – Records Branch, Files and Communication Division," June 11, 1971, *Dissent* FBI file.

127. As Robert Justin Goldstein notes, more than 50 groups that focused on civil liberties and civil rights defense work eventually were included in the official Attorney General's List of Subversive Organizations. Goldstein, *American Blacklist*, 106.

128. A. H. Belmont to L. L. Laughan, "The Worker," July 14, 1950, the Daily Worker FBI file.

129. SAC Philadelphia to Director, "Use of Form in Disseminating Material Appearing in the Pennsylvania Edition of the 'Worker'," Feb. 14, 1949, the Daily Worker FBI file.

130. William P. Barrett, "FBI Kept Tabs for Decades on 'Press Box Red,'" *Forbes*, Dec. 23, 2010, www.blogs.forbes.com/william pbarrett/2010/12/23/fbi-kept-tabs-for-decades-on-press-box-red/ ?boxes=Homepagechannels.

131. SAC New York to Director, "William Albertson (Louis Budenz 400)," Sept. 8, 1950, William Albertson FBI file.

132. Aronson, *The Press and the Cold War*, 108. *PM*'s large FBI file is held by the Wagner Archives at the Taminent Library, New York University.

133. W. C. Sullivan to A. H. Belmont, "'Dissent – Central Research Matter," Feb. 15, 1955, *Dissent* FBI file; D. D. Guttenplan, *American Radical: The Life and Times of I. F. Stone* (New York: Macmillan, 2009), 542.

134. SAC Boston to Director, "Irving Horenstein, wa. Irving Howe, Security Matter – ISL," June 9, 1954, Irving Howe FBI file.

135. M. A. Cohes to Mr. DeLoach, "Daniel M. Freidenberg – Criticism of the FBI, Dissent Magazine," Aug. 6, 1963; A. J. Jones to Mr. DeLoach, "Norman Kingsley Mailer – Criticism of the Director, Dissent Magazine," Aug. 6, 1963. *Dissent* FBI file.

136. Robins, *Alien Ink*, 330.

137. SAC New York to Director, "Publications – Handling by Research-Satellite Section," Oct. 21, 1968; SAC New York to Director, "Publications – Handling by Research-Satellite Section," Oct. 20, 1969; SAC New York to Director, "Publications – Handling by Research-Satellite Section," Oct. 14, 1971. *Dissent* FBI file.

138. David H. Price, "Theoretical Dangers: The FBI Investigation of 'Science and Society,'" *Science and Society* 4 (Winter 2004/2005): 480.

139. Ibid., 481.

140. FBI document, "Specific Recommendations From Conference, 9/10-11/70, Concerning New Left Movement," n.d, p. 1-12, L. Patrick Gray III FBI file.

141. John McMillian, *Smoking Typewriters: The Sixties Underground Press and the Rise of Alternative Media in America* (New York: Oxford University Press, 2011), 125.

142. Mr. Wick to M. A. Jones, "[Text redacted] Ramparts Magazine, San Francisco, California," Oct. 27, 1966; D. J. Brennan, Jr. to William C. Sullivan, "Ramparts," Jan. 31, 1967; SAC New York to Director, "Communist Party USA, Counterintelligence Program, Internal Security-C (Ramparts)," April 19, 1967; SAC San Francisco to Director, "'Ram-

parts,' IS-C," March 26, 1967; M. A. Jones to Mr. Hick, "Warren Hinckle III, Publisher, Ramparts Magazine," May 1, 1967; SAC San Francisco to Director, "Ramparts Magazine, Inc., IS-C-, Registration Act.," October 31, 1969; SAG San Francisco to Acting Director, "Ramparts Magazine, IS-RA," June 8, 1973. *Ramparts* FBI file.

143. Peter Richardson, *A Bomb in Every Issue: How the Short, Unruly Life of Ramparts Magazine Changed America* (New York: The New Press, 2009), 57-59.

144. When writer Nat Hentoff wrote an article in the June 3, 1971, issue detailing FBI harassment of several film directors who were making a movie on secret surveillance and civil liberties, Congressman Ed Koch of Manhattan wrote the director to complain about the FBI's behavior. Hoover denied the harassment. Koch wrote: "It would be very helpful to me in responding to my constituents if you could detail the inaccuracies [in the article]." J. Edgar Hoover to Senator Joseph D. Tydings, Sept. 29, 1970; Edward I. Koch to J. Edgar Hoover, June 17, 1971; J. Edgar Hoover to Edward I. Koch, June 25, 1971. *Village Voice* FBI file.

145. Chip Berlet, "The FBI, COINTELPRO and the Alternative Press," Political Research Associates, www.publiceye.org/liberty/Feds/media/fbi-media-alternative.html,1 (accessed Dec. 2, 2011).

146. Angus Mackenzie, "Sabotaging the Dissident Press," *Columbia Journalism Review* (March-April 1981): 58.

147. Berger, *Outlaws of America*, 82-84; Mackenzie, "Sabotaging the Dissident Press," 61.

148. Rodger Streitmatter, *Voices of Revolution: The Dissident Press In America* (New York: Columbia University Press, 2001), 232, 270-271.

149. SAC WFO to Acting Director, FBI, "Off Our Backs Newspaper (OOB), IS –Revact," July 2, 1973, *off our backs* FBI file.

150. Robins, *Alien Ink*, 327; Ruth Rosen, *The World Split Wide Open: How the Modern Women's Movement Changed America* (New York: Viking Penguin, 2000), 247-263.

151. Berger, *Outlaws of America*, 82

152. Berlet, "The FBI, COINTELPRO and the Alternative Press," 3.

153. Ibid.

154. McMillian, *Smoking Typewriters*, 128-134.

155. SAC Detroit, "Counterintelligence Program, IS – Disruption of New Left," Oct. 13, 1970, New Left FBI file.

156. SAC Chicago to Director, "COINTELPRO – New Left," March 3, 1971, New Left FBI file.

157. Chip Berlet, "COINTELPRO and the College Press," n.d.

158. SAC Indianapolis to Director, "COINTELPRO – New Left," Aug. 11, 1969," New Left FBI file; Berger, *Outlaws of America*, 83.

159. Berlet, "The FBI, COINTELPRO and the Alternative Press," 5.

160. Mackenzie, "Sabotaging the Dissident Press," 63.

161. Quoted in McMillian, *Smoking Typewriters*, 125.

162. Richard Gid Powers, "The FBI in American Popular Culture," in Athan Theoharis, ed., *The FBI: A Comprehensive Guide*, 306.

163. FBI, "Project Megiddo," October 1999, 4, 28.

164. FBI annual report, *Terrorism in the United States*, 1997, 21; "Congressional Testimony of FBI Director Louis J. Freeh," Sept. 3, 1998, 9.

165. Ivan Greenberg, *The Dangers of Dissent: The FBI and Civil Liberties since 1965* (Lanham: Lexington Books, 2010), 159-161, 172.

166. Reporters Committee for Freedom of the Press, "FBI Agents Pose as Photographers during Aryan Nation Trial," *The News Media and the Law* (Fall 2000), www.rcfp.org/news/mag/24-4/_contents. html.

167. Brigitte L. Nacos, Yaeli Bloch-Elkon, and Robert Y. Shapiro, *Selling Fear: Counterterrorism, the Media, and Public Opinion* (University of Chicago Press, 2011), 39.

168. Boghosian, *The Policing of Political Speech*, 22-23.

169. L. Brent Bozell III, *Weapons of Mass Distortion: The Coming Meltdown of the Liberal Media* (New York: Crown Forum, 2004), 220.

170. Michael Tomasky, "Breaking the Code: Or, Can the Press be Saved from Itself?" in Cynthia Brown, ed., *Lost Liberties: Ashcroft and the Assault on Personal Freedom* (New York: New Press, 2003), 157.

171. Robert W. McChesney, *The Problem of the Media: U.S. Communication Politics in the 21st Century* (New York: Monthly Review Press, 2004), 279.

172. Elaine Tyler May, "Echoes of the Cold War: The Aftermath of September 11 at Home," in Mary L. Dudziak, ed., *September 11 in History: A Watershed Moment?* (Durham: Duke University Press, 2003), 48-49.

173. Anthony R. DiMaggio, *Mass Media, Mass Propaganda: Examining American News in the "War on Terror"* (Lanham: Lexington Books, 2008), 43.

174. Lisa Finnegan, *No Questions Asked: News Coverage since 9/11* (Westport: Praeger, 2007).

175. Edward S. Herman and Gerry O'Sullivan, *The Terrorism Industry: The Experts and Institutions that Shape Our View of Terror* (New York: Pantheon Books, 1989); Joseba Zulaika, *Terrorism: The Self-Fulfilling*

Prophecy (Chicago: University of Chicago Press, 2009); Glenn Greenwald, "The Merger of Journalists and Government Officials," Dec. 28, 2010, Salon, www.salon.com/2010/12/28/cnnn/.

176. Boykoff, *Beyond Bullets*, 298-299; Bob Woodward, *State of Denial* (New York: Simon and Schuster, 2006), 83-85; Nancy Snow and Philip M. Taylor, "The Revival of the Propaganda State: US Propaganda at Home and Abroad Since 9/11," *International Communications Gazette*, 68(5-6), 2006, 389-407.

177. Boghosian, *The Policing of Political Speech*, 2, 4; Institute for Applied Autonomy, "Defensive Surveillance: Lessons from the Republican National Convention," in Torin Monahan, ed., *Surveillance and Security: Technological Politics and Power in Everyday Life* (New York: Routledge, 2006), 171.

178. Electronic Frontier Foundation, "Surveillance Self-Defense," www.ssd.eff.org/book/export/html/14 (accessed Dec. 27, 2010).

3

Threatening Historians

J. Edgar Hoover, while holding a law degree, was known to express negative attitudes toward academics. A close associate remarked: "He was suspicious of the academic community, of any intellectual—of any scholar. He disliked them instinctively."[1] During the Cold War, the FBI surveilled academic life to a greater extent than contemporaries realized. They focused on both campus student politics and the activities of professors. Human Rights Watch (HRW) has suggested that when professors are put under surveillance for political reasons or purged from their jobs it serves "as a warning to individuals throughout society that dissent and political opposition would not be tolerated." Academics have been "disproportionately represented among the world's political prisoners and universities were favored targets of repression."[2]

Recently, American historical scholarship focuses on the FBI's adversarial relationship to colleges and universities.[3] A new approach is to study specific academic disciplines (Russian studies, Asian studies, sociology, and anthropology).[4] Uncovering the surveillance of American historians during the Cold War adds to this knowledge, providing further evidence of the FBI's massive monitoring. Using the Freedom of Information Act (FOIA), I obtained little-noticed FBI files on ten leading historians (Richard Hofstadter, Allan Nevins, Samuel Eliot Morison,

Henry Steele Commager, John Hope Franklin, C. Vann Wood-ward, Herbert G. Gutman, William Appleman Williams, Warren Susman, and Howard Zinn). The files shed light on the construction of threats and enemies and reveal different narratives for those perceived as "liberals" versus those considered "radicals." All the individuals considered here are deceased, which allowed access to their files. (No women are included in this group because relatively few taught in the academy in this period or else they still are living.) The FBI reported "no records" for five of my record requests—on John R. Commons, Selig Perlman, Christopher Lasch, Paul Wallace Gates, and Kenneth Stamp—and created obstacles to receiving the file on Harvard's Oscar Handlin.[5]

The FBI became interested in historians because, like journalists, they helped shape public opinion. By writing about the past, they informed the population of what came before so they can better frame current perspectives. More so than journalists, historians aided a theoretical understanding of a subject. From the FBI's perspective, they had a platform and could influence not only the politics of their students but also the reading public. While in these files the FBI infrequently referred to particular books or historical debates, they did notice when historians wrote for the popular press or popular journals. Popular media had the potential to influence social action, whereas scholarship—not accessible to most readers—posed less of an obstacle to FBI efforts at opinion management. In this regard, it is not surprising to find that historical journals rarely seemed to engage the FBI's interest. The bureau's FOIA office reported records did not exist for *Labor History* or *Radical History Review* and only two pages were found for the *Journal of Negro History*. By contrast, they assembled a large file (997 pages) on *Radical America*, which appealed to a broader audience linked during the late 1960s and early 1970s to a protest movement.[6]

The FBI routinely tracked political participation and associations outside scholarship and teaching, such as public speeches, petition signing, and attendance at demonstrations. They operated under the assumption that if a scholar signed a petition against the House UnAmerican Activities Committee (HUAC) or supported anti-war activity, he de facto posed a threat in the classroom. Ironically, in the files I examined there is virtually no discussion of classroom teaching—no attempt to evaluate the political content of lectures. Moreover, the FBI did not appear to prioritize subversive threats based on a subject's expertise.

The nature of the intelligence gathering was substantially different for liberals and radicals. The files on liberals were smaller in size and sometimes consisted primarily of "cross references"—that is, the subject was not under full investigation but records existed about them in connection with other investigations. By contrast, radical historians defined as subversive were put under full investigation and frequently encountered undercover informers who secretly reported on their activities. In a few cases, the FBI deployed "conspicuous" surveillance, that is, the bureau purposely and strategically let the subject know about the monitoring to induce paranoia and to serve as a warning to moderate or cease political expression. The documents detail failed efforts to interview subjects and to recruit them as informers. Apparently, none of these historians were placed under electronic surveillance.

The FBI and Liberalism

Repression in American academia was greatest during the Red Scare of the 1950s. The FBI conducted a large investigation program titled Communist Infiltration of Education, and hunted for subversives in coordination with both HUAC and college administrators. After the U.S. Supreme Court's *Dennis* case (1951), many universities issued special codes to ensure professors did not engage subversive subject matter in the classroom. *Dennis* determined that the First Amendment did not cover speech advocating the violent overthrow of the U.S. government. Like Cold War journalism, academic "objectivity" became a biased and limited construction to restrict the discussion of controversial ideas. For example, the Rutgers University administration issued anticommunist bylaws advising teachers to "remain within his own field of competence and handle controversial subjects with discretion and the 'standards of sound scholarship and competent teaching.'" Teachers who engaged in speculative thinking or offered critical commentary on current events could be found guilty of "incompetence." Incredibly, Rutgers even advised teachers to speak against the communist Left in the classroom. A professor's "utterance" included "a failure to speak in circumstances in which such appropriate conduct requires that the person should speak."[7]

Most colleges and universities capitulated to official Cold War pressures because trustees and state legislators urged administrators to purge radicals. Moreover, universities often depended on the government for science and engineering funding. The military-industrial-academic complex largely responded to the political line the FBI and HUAC gave it.[8] The FBI monitored the lectures of leftist professors, questioned their colleagues and students, and enlisted campus informers in different capacities. Many colleges designated an officer to serve as a campus liaison with the FBI.[9] In 1956, a survey of 2,451 randomly selected social science professors reported some ominous trends: 61 percent said an FBI agent had contacted them in the previous year; 40 percent worried students might misrepresent their politics; and about a quarter refrained from expressing opinions or participating in activities fearful of the government.[10] Overall, several hundred professors lost their jobs during the 1950s, including tenured faculty. (The blacklist also victimized hundreds of elementary and high school teachers.) In many respects, the political police achieved its objective of silencing critics of the status quo.

Repression survived the McCarthy period. In 1976, the U.S. Senate Church Committee reported on FBI "counter-intelligence" directed against New Left professors. One technique involved: "Sending anonymous letters or leaflets describing the activities and associations of New Left faculty members and graduate assistants to university officials, legislators, Board of Regents, and the press. These letters should be signed 'A Concerned Alumni,' or 'A Concerned Taxpayer.'"[11] In 1973, the American Civil Liberties Union attorney Frank J. Donner wrote: "The campus has been a high-priority surveillance target since the early 1960s. . . . They have deployed a nationwide corps of planted informers ('FBI scholarship boys,' they are often called) to penetrate faculty and student political activities."[12]

The bureau believed liberalism posed a primary threat when it became an ally of radicalism by challenging the supremacy of the Red Scare machinery. The FBI collected intelligence on liberal historians who signed petitions—notably, for the abolishment of HUAC—or defended communists or other leftists on free speech grounds. In these instances, the FBI equated liberal dissent with disloyalty. The "guilt by association" intelligence model also condemned liberals who joined organizations with communist members. During the 1960s, director Hoover argued that liberalism's tolerance of radical dissent enabled the New Left and the black power movements to thrive.[13] Moreover, any membership in radical organizations, even if in the distant past, remained privileged in FBI files. Several liberal historians had been radicals as young men. Their early radicalism, even if later abandoned, colored the FBI's view of them. In a few cases, liberal historians were considered for low-level presidential appointments prompting FBI background investigations. While not necessarily adversarial, these investigations generated information that could be used against a subject in the present or future.

The FBI holds small files on Allan Nevins (35 pages), Samuel Eliot Morison (19 pages), and Richard Hofstadter (33 pages). None were investigated in depth, but the bureau collected political intelligence to be retrieved during routine "name checks." The FBI wrote about Nevins, who taught at Columbia University, when he testified in 1941 on behalf of labor historian Philip S. Foner after City College of New York suspended him for communist activities. According to the FBI, Nevins told the New York Board of Higher Education he "never heard Dr. Foner make any statement which could be considered subversive. He praised Dr. Foner's teaching, scholarship, and reputation for truth and veracity." In 1948, the FBI also noted Nevins signed a petition circulated by an alleged communist group, the National Institute of Arts and Letters, protesting the methods employed by HUAC toward writers.[14] Harvard Prof. Samuel Eliot Morison signed several petitions against the state HUAC in

Massachusetts, which formed the basis of his FBI file.[15] Meanwhile, Columbia University professor Richard Hofstadter's student radicalism at the University of Buffalo during the mid-1930s was raised in connection with an FBI name inquiry requested by the State Department in 1952. Hofstadter had worked with the National Student League, which the FBI viewed as a communist-front organization.[16] In 1966, the FBI also connected Hofstadter to a petition circulated by the National Committee for a Sane Nuclear Policy (SANE) against U.S. involvement in the Vietnam War. The FBI investigated SANE since at least 1960. However, the FBI thought enough of Hofstadter's scholarship to purchase *The Paranoid Style in American Politics* for its official Washington library.[17]

Hofstadter's Columbia colleague, Henry Steele Commager, amassed a large FBI file (457 pages) covering the years 1947 to 1970. A leading public critic of FBI power and the Red Scare, the bureau investigated to determine if he participated in Communist Party activities. While they did not find evidence of membership, the FBI practiced "guilt by association": During the late 1940s he joined at least one organization cited by the Attorney General as communist, the American-Russian Institute for Cultural Relations with the Soviet Union. Assistant Director William C. Sullivan summarized the official view of Commager as "a too vocal, bombastic and misinformed liberal or 'fellow traveler' as the Director has noted. . . . [He] has shown poor judgment and a lack of discretion in his personal and organizational associations."[18]

Hoover found Commager's liberal views repugnant and agents tracked his writing for the *Nation*, the *New York Times*, and *Harper's*. The FBI questioned his loyalty when he wrote in a 1949 article: "What guaranty is there that J. Edgar Hoover may not some day be Attorney General, Hoover who recently asserted that 'so-called progressives and phony liberals' are little better than Communists? Should the designation by such men of organizations as being subversive be the standard, then?"[19] Hoover hand-wrote a note alongside an internal memo: "Above all shows another fellow-traveler is speaking his piece true to form."[20] Within a few months, FBI agents attempted to interview Commager at his summer home in Williamsville, Vermont. Neither he nor his wife were at home so the agent questioned his 14 year-old daughter. In a personal letter of protest to Hoover, Commager asked: "It would be interesting to know just how far your agents go in such interrogation. Do you draw the line at the age of 14, or 10, or do you question any one able to talk?" An FBI official who researched the incident concluded, "In view of Commager's background it appears that the purpose of his letter was to 'get a rise out the Bureau.' Based on his previous articles it is not improbable that his complaint is without foundation." Hoover concluded, "Recently he [Commager] has given renewed evidence of hostility toward the Bureau. Under no circumstances should he or any member of his family be interviewed without specific prior Bureau approval."[21]

The next year an agent interviewed Commager at his office at Columbia University. The interview created a large incident of an uncertain nature. At first, the agent questioned Commager about one of his colleagues, whose name is redacted in the declassified file. When asked if the colleague was a communist, Commager reportedly responded in a sarcastic manner. The interviewing agent wrote: "At this point, Commager became very angry and stated substantially: 'No, we've never been able to sign him up.'" The agent replied, "What do you mean sign him up? Are you a member?" Commager reportedly answered, "Sure I'm a communist! So what? Half the people in New York are communists." The FBI account indicated:

> With this, COMMAGER, according to [text redacted,] took his billfold from his pocket, withdrew a card from the billfold and threw it across the desk toward [text redacted]. The latter picked up the card and looked at it. He said that the card was a membership card in the Communist Party. He said he cannot remember what was on the card; that he believes it bore some name other than COMMAGER's true name . . . he then told COMMAGER that he would like to photstat the card and COMMAGER replied, "O.K. I can help you." With that, Commager picked up a telephone and apparently called a photostatic laboratory. Shortly a young man came into the office

and COMMAGER instructed him to take the card and make a photostat of same which he was to give to [text redacted].[22]

When contacted by his superiors, the agent who conducted the Commager interview could not find the membership card. It mysteriously had disappeared.[23] So whose name was on the card? Why would Commager carry it in his wallet? FBI officials remained uncertain about Commager's allegiances because none of their informants inside the CP reported on his membership. It seemed highly likely that he never joined the Party.

In 1955, high FBI officials engaged in a rare discussion about his scholarship after a West Point Military Academy officer asked permission to assign one of Commager's books (*Europe and America Since 1942*) in the classroom. The officer wanted to know whether Commager was a communist or ever appeared on a government blacklist. Communist authors were not allowed to be assigned at West Point. The West Point official believed "the content of the book is perfectly sound." Assistant Director William C. Sullivan concurred and admitted he owned three Commager books (*The American Mind; Living Ideas in America*; and *The Heritage of America*).[24]

In 1962, President John F. Kennedy considered Commager for an unstated government post, which led to an FBI background investigation. Hoover instructed agents: "Extreme care must be utilized to obviate any possibility of charges of character assassination being made against the Bureau."[25] The subsequent report recycled known information. It also included new consultations with CP informants who reported no familiarity with Commager. The FBI interviewed more than a dozen of his professional peers. Most offered a positive evaluation. Among the negative reports, a former colleague at Columbia warned that Commager might associate with communists. "Commager is the type of person who would select his associates on the basis of those who interest him. . . . [E]ven if a person were a Communist and Commager found him interesting, he would not hesitate to associate with him, although he [text redacted] feels Commager would not be negatively influenced in such a case." A second Columbia colleague expressed reservations. The FBI reported his view: "If Commager were to be selected for a position such as on the Civil Rights Commission he would be happy to support him. However, he does not feel Commager is the type who would make a good representative of the U.S. in a foreign land, inasmuch as he questions the appointee's wisdom and discretion in presenting his case in such matters as civil rights in the U.S."[26] Commager never received the unstated administration position.

Despite the president's interest in Commager, the FBI during the early 1960s placed him on its "Do Not Contact" list because "he has been a long-time critic of the FBI." Later in the decade, the FBI noted Commager's anti-war activity at Harvard University. He had conducted a "War Teach-In" against U.S. involvement in Vietnam. Commager continued to defend the civil liberties of radicals, which irked the FBI. The Boston office noted he signed a petition protesting contempt proceedings by New Hampshire authorities against Marxist economist Paul Sweezy. The last document in the file, dated June 29, 1970, consists of a Hoover request for updated intelligence after Commager again criticized the FBI for sanctioning repression in a *Look* magazine article. Hoover told subordinates, "Let me have a memo on Commager."[27] How Hoover used the information remains unclear.

The Kennedy administration also considered historian John Hope Franklin for an appointment. At the time, Franklin served as chairman of the history department at Brooklyn College and as a member of the editorial board of the *Journal of Negro History*. He was one of the most prominent African American historians of his generation. Six FBI field officers interviewed his colleagues and neighbors to uncover subversive activity which might disqualify him for the job. Overall, the interviews supported his loyalty. One store owner told investigators Franklin is "a completely loyal American citizen who never indicated any sympathetic interest in Communism or any subversive philosophy."[28] A neighbor said Franklin "always kept his grass cut," a metaphor to signify orderliness and respectability. However, the FBI was not pleased with some of their findings. Although none of their informers inside the Communist Party knew Franklin as a member, the bureau reported contact with communists as early as 1947. While Franklin taught at North Carolina College at Durham, he participated in the activities of the Southern Conference for Human Welfare, cited as a Party front by HUAC. On several occasions, he gave scholarly talks to alleged communist groups and associated with African American scholars and leaders under FBI investigation for subversion.

In 1953, the FBI interviewed Franklin as part of a loyalty investigation of Prof. Edward Franklin Frazier, a colleague at Howard University. Franklin "furnished favorable comments" about Frazier, who the FBI identified as "affiliated with numerous communist front organizations." Franklin defended Frazier's loyalty. "Dr. Frazier had never evidenced any communist sympathies."[29] There is one reference to Reverend Martin Luther King Jr. The New York field office noted, "[Text redacted] advised that both he and Dr. FRANKLIN took part in the Montgomery, Alabama march with Dr, King as they felt he had the right point of view during this occasion." The FBI reported that Franklin "could not see being associated with any of the other Southern groups."[30]

Franklin's published books did not garner any negative FBI comment. But his 1952 review of Herbert Aptheker's *A Documentary History of the Negro People in the United States,* which appeared in the *Journal of Negro Education,* brought condemnation. Aptheker was a known communist under bureau investigation and Franklin's positive evaluation of his work suggested some type of conspiracy. The FBI noticed the review after the *Daily Worker,* the CP newspaper, ran an excerpt. The FBI file quoted Franklin at length to suggest his sympathy for radicals. They highlighted the following passage:

> Mr. Aptheker's labors have placed all students of the history of the Negro people under obligation to him. His painstaking and exhaustive work will provide a veritable mine of information for persons interested in pursuing further the history of the Negroes. . . . We have in this book the sole source book of the political, social, and economic aspirations of the American Negro.[31]

In addition to praise for Frazier and Aptheker, Franklin's fondness for W.E.B. DuBois led to critical FBI commentary. The FBI investigated DuBois as a supporter of communist causes and Franklin wrote about him in a publication—*Freedomways*—which the FBI viewed falsely as a communist front. The FBI quoted Franklin's praise as if to demonstrate political guilt. Franklin wrote:

> I am pleased to learn that "Freedomways" is planning an issue to memorialize Dr. DuBois. For the latter portion of my life, Dr. DuBois has been an inspiration to me and to most members of my generation. . . . His impeccable scholarship, his fearlessness as a leader, and his determination to secure freedom for all peoples, were the hallmarks of his great and illustrious life. I am certain that he will continue to wield enormous influence through his immortal writings.[32]

Such praise for a communist should not be tolerated. In a memo to the White House, the FBI called Franklin an "apologist" for DuBois, who "sponsored communist fronts" and finally "joined the Communist Party at the age of 93."[33]

During the FBI background investigation, Franklin's white colleagues defended him by insisting he was not a race man. A Cornell history professor, who knew Franklin for 15 years, "regards the appointee as a fine and able historian and as an extremely broadminded person who has never allowed the racial issue to bother him and who has never held any bitterness toward anyone because of his racial background."[34] Another white colleague said Franklin was not outspoken on race questions in his scholarship. In fact, the FBI reported: "One close associate states that some Negroes have been critical of Franklin's publications as they felt he had not 'sufficiently sided with the Negro.'"[35] Another professor indicated Franklin did not have "a chip on his shoulder because of his race."[36] In the minds of these white scholars, deemphasizing a racial identity and consciousness was intended as a compliment.

One of the last documents in the file reveals that when Richard M. Nixon became president, the FBI wrote negatively about Franklin to legal counsel John D. Ehrlichman. The FBI reported on a Franklin lecture sponsored by Concerned Black People (CBP). "Several leaders of CBP have reportedly had Communist Party affiliations and it has openly opposed United States foreign policy in Vietnam."[37]

In contrast to Commager and Franklin, the FBI withheld the majority of its file (80 pages out of 101) on C. Vann Woodward, the prize-winning scholar of the American South and race relations. Fortunately, a detailed Naval Intelligence file (76 pages) outlines the contours of the government's monitoring. Once again, the FBI became interested in his political activism, not scholarship, when he publicly defended communists and criticized HUAC.

The FBI wrote about him on at least four occasions. In the early 1930s, while teaching at the Georgia School of Technology in Atlanta, Woodward participated in the legal defense of Angelo Herndon, a 19-year-old African American labor organizer arrested for communist activity. Woodward was drawn to the case for reasons related to free speech and civil rights. When a court found Herndon guilty of inciting insurrection, the CP led a national campaign to free Herndon and made "Angelo Herndon and the Scottsboro boys!" a rallying slogan for the mid-1930s Left.[38] While the FBI never found that Woodward joined the CP, as a young man he acted as a "soap box orator" at the courthouse "standing around in groups arguing with anyone who would listen that Herndon and the others had a right to assemble to discuss anything they wished to." Although Naval Intelligence could find no one who "ever heard WOODWARD make any remarks indicating that he was a member of the Communist Party, WOODWARD did say that he was a Socialist." Woodward apparently told one source he considered himself a "rebel" and "the U.S. Constitution guaranteed the right of all Americans to foment and lead a revolution and that 'George Washington was a revolutionist.'" He called the prosecution in the Herndon case a "Tool of Capitalism" and "used the terms 'Capitalist Slavery,' 'Tyranny of Capitalism' and once made the remark that 'the courts are slaves of capitalism.'"[39] Like Franklin, Woodward also participated in the activities of the Southern Conference for Human Welfare.

In 1954, he taught at John Hopkins University and the FBI investigated his association with communists. The bureau contacted four informants "familiar with CP matters in the Baltimore area" and all reported "negative results." The Baltimore field office told Hoover: "It is not believed that a security investigation is warranted. . . . This case is, therefore, being placed in a closed status."[40]

During the early 1960s, the FBI gathered intelligence about his political activities after he signed a petition circulated by the American Civil Liberties Union calling for the abolishment of HUAC. Woodward also signed a legal affidavit on behalf of Julius Irving Scales, a communist convicted under the Smith Act, asking for a reduction in his prison sentence.[41] As a result of the redactions in his file, we do not know if the FBI tracked his participation in Left scholarly activity. In 1961, Woodward wrote a sympathetic blurb for *Studies on the Left*, which was then under FBI investigation. In 1966, Woodward spoke at the second annual Socialist Scholars Conference. The FBI monitored the conferences between 1966 and 1970, generating an 838-page file. Woodward, who long championed the underdog, remained open to the ideas of the New Left and favorably reviewed an important book by historian Barton Bernstein, *Towards a New Past*, claiming radical historians "deserve a full hearing and close reading. . . . They have much to say that is relevant to the correction of a complacent and nationalist reading of our past."[42]

The FBI and Radicalism

Of course, the FBI disagreed with Woodward's assessment: Radical historians not only made no contribution to understanding the past, but formed an enemy intent on destroying the nation. Whereas the FBI tracked liberal historians for critiquing the government Red Scare machinery, radicals earned the FBI's wrath as the actual enemy itself: subversives which the machinery directly targeted for neutralization.

Most studies of radical historians do not cite government spy files.[43] Without such a reference, an understanding of their historical experience is incomplete. For example, a great deal has been written about social historian Herbert G. Gutman,[44] who died in 1985, but it is not fully appreciated that Gutman lived in the shadow of the FBI for about 20 years. Overall, five FBI offices tracked Gutman—New York City, Milwaukee, Newark, Buffalo, and San Francisco with investigations at seven colleges. In addition to placement on the Security Index, the FBI early on listed Gutman in the Communist Index. The FBI believed he joined the Party briefly in 1949 before the age of twenty and remained connected to communist-infiltrated groups for many years. A critical reading of Gutman's 441-page FBI file tells us why the government put him under surveillance and what they hoped to achieve.[45] The political intelligence concentrates on activism during the late 1940s and early 1950s. The subsequent material in the file provides periodic updates until to the late 1960s.

The file opens when Gutman attended Queens College, CUNY, in New York City as an undergraduate. In 1948, Gutman served on the Student Council and voted in favor of a charter for American Youth for Democracy (AYD), an alleged communist group the college faculty tried to ban. Gutman's support for the AYD led the FBI to contact the college administration to obtain his school record. An FBI informant on campus also observed Gutman distributing pamphlets put out by the Civil Rights Congress that, in the FBI's words, "dealt with some anxiety regarding academic freedom and Negro discrimination." The FBI considered the Congress a communist group.[46]

The FBI's interest in Gutman increased after he graduated from Queens College and spent the summer of 1949 as an adult counselor at Camp Kinderland. Identified as a communist camp for children, the FBI infiltrated Kinderland and Gutman encountered informants who later would testify against him. In the fall, he began a year at Columbia University studying for a master's degree in history under Richard Hofstadter. The Gutman file (as well as the Hofstadter file) does not refer to his time at Columbia University, although it seems likely the FBI still watched his activities. While a doctoral candidate and teaching assistant at the University of Wisconsin at Madison, the FBI placed Gutman on a list of communists among the faculty and conducted an "investigation concerning the subject's possible Communist affiliation and activities at the University."[47] They found that "GUTMAN has been reported as showing an interest in racial groups."[48] A civil rights activist, affiliated with the Wisconsin Civil Rights Congress, stayed at Gutman's apartment. So did a speaker for the Labor Youth League (LYL) on the Madison campus. For the FBI, these visits confirmed that Gutman remained in close contact with communists.[49]

The FBI's evaluation of Gutman's days at Madison is summed up in a five-page memo dated June 20, 1955:

> Detroit anonymous advised that HERBERT and [text redacted] avoided open attendance of LYL meetings or other suspect groups at the University of Wisconsin during their stay in Madison from 1950 to 1953, but they were friendly to Communist and pro-Communist individuals at the University, particularly to the group of such individuals active in the University Chapter of the LYL. The GUTMANS were also said to profess interest in racial equality and to have attended some of the meetings of the University of Wisconsin Chapter of the National Association for the Advancement of Colored People.

> Detroit anonymous, report SA [text redacted] Milwaukee, 10/12/53, believed that the GUTMANS were at least pro-Communist in sentiment but very careful concerning their activities and statements in public because of their connections with the University of Wisconsin faculty.

The college administration gave the FBI material from his school file, including the essay Gutman wrote for admission to the graduate school. Although a resident of Madison, the FBI consulted their informants inside the CP in New York to determine if Gutman remained active in left politics. They found he was not active in New York.[50] Gutman later recalled that while at Madison he drifted away from Old Left ideas, but the FBI did not seem to notice the shift.[51] By 1953, Gutman remained on the Communist Index and the FBI collected voter registration records on his immediate family. The bureau reported their registration as members of the American Labor Party, except for Gutman's father, Joseph, listed as a Democrat.[52]

In the mid-1950s, the investigation took two new turns. In 1954, the FBI tried to interview Gutman to enlist him as an informer. He refused to talk to the agents. The FBI also tried to interview and recruit his wife, Judith. In September, three different "attempts to interviews subjects . . . have been unproductive. Difficulty has been encountered in contacting subjects so they could be interviewed simultaneously but separately. However, continued efforts will be made to interview subject in the near future."[53] By early October, the FBI had conducted the Gutman interview, displeased by the result. The New York FBI office reported: "Subject interviewed by Bureau agents on 10/5/54, at which time he declined to discuss his activities without the aid of legal counsel . . . GUTMAN, at this time, declined to answer any questions regarding the Communist Party."[54] A second memo offers more detail.

> [T]he subject had no prescribed working hours and apparently spends most of his time at his residence, working on research papers. . . . At 9:00 P.M. the subject was observed leaving his apartment, whereupon he deposited some trash in the basement incinerator and returned to the apartment. Agents [text redacted] and [text redacted] thereafter approached the subject at his apartment and identified themselves. The subject was apprized [sic] by the interviewing agents of the nature of their inquiry, to which he replied, "I have nothing to discuss with you."
>
> The subject was advised that in view of his past activities and associations, it was believed that he could provide valuable information regarding the CP, and that his Government would welcome his cooperation. However, the subject remained adamant, and stated that "I will answer none of your questions without an attorney." Repeated efforts to engage the subject in a discussion of his activities were unproductive and the interview thereafter terminated . . .
>
> Continued efforts will be made to interview subject's wife, JUDITH GUTMAN, under existing Bureau instructions and a

report reflecting same will be submitted to the Bureau in the near future.

In view of the subject's recent activity with a group sympathetic to the CP cause, as well as his uncooperative attitude upon interview, he is being recommended for inclusion in the Security Index and an FD 122 is being submitted reflecting this request.[55]

The effort to recruit Gutman was not unusual. Informants were the first choice of the bureau for intelligence gathering. Under COINTELPRO (Counter Intelligence Program), the FBI used informers in 83 percent of its domestic security investigations.[56]

In 1955, HUAC subpoenaed Gutman to testify during hearings devoted to "Communist Camps in the United States." His appearance followed Stanley Wechkin, a one-time friend who spoke about Gutman's effort to recruit him into CP front groups while attending Camp Kinderland.[57] HUAC asked Gutman standard questions: Was he ever was a member of the CP? Congressmen raised his employment at Camp Kinderland as evidence of communist allegiance and charged he recruited campers into the Labor Youth League, the Jefferson School in Manhattan, and the 1948 Wallace presidential campaign.[58] Gutman refused to answer HUAC's questions, citing both the First and Fifth Amendments. At one point, Gutman scolded the committee for their witch-hunt, which prompted a question about why he was willing to criticize Congress but not the Communist Party.

The FBI never blacklisted Gutman. By the mid-1950s, they recognized he was not a card-carrying communist and had not yet obtained a full-time teaching position. However, after the HUAC appearance the bureau continued to track his activities. For example, when Gutman traveled overseas in 1959 on a funded grant, the FBI searched his passport records and notified overseas FBI Legal offices and the CIA about his itinerary. The bureau noted that Gutman again refused to indicate past CP involvement. "Subject did not answer the questions in his passport application pertaining to present and past membership in the CP."[59] The file says the CIA conducted physical surveillance of Gutman in at least one nation, Turkey.[60] After the ten-week trip ended, the FBI reported no subversive activity by Gutman overseas. "In connection with the subject's foreign travel, the following legats advised that no information came to their attention while the subject was traveling abroad. The legats are identified as follows: Madrid, Paris, London. Rome and Bonn. . . . The subject was not reinterviewed because he was uncooperative when interviewed on 10/5/54. In addition, his spouse, who is the subject of Bufile 100-401424 and New York File 100-115754, was uncooperative on 4/8/60."[61] We have this description of the Judith Gutman interview:

> Subject was contacted on 4/8/60, by SAS of the FBI for the purpose of interview. Upon learning the identity of the agents and the purpose of the contact subject stated that she did not desire to talk to the FBI and walked away. Further efforts to engage the subject in conversation were negative. Although subject was uncooperative, she did not appear hostile or nervous at the time of the contact. She was emphatic in her refusal to be interviewed. In view of the subject's uncooperative attitude no additional contacts with her are contemplated at this time.[62]

During the 1960s, the FBI reported that Gutman engaged in little organized political activity at several colleges where he taught—Fairleigh-Dickinson University, SUNY Buffalo, and the University of Rochester. Campus informers reported Gutman was not active in subversive activities. In New York City, informants also found no activism. A Jan. 26, 1961, memo said, "Informants familiar with some CP activities in the NYC area advised that during October and November, 1960, they could furnish no information concerning the subject."[63] But the stigma of prior communist association persisted. In 1962, Gutman was listed among "Alleged communist Infiltration of Faculty of Fairleigh-Dickinson University."[64] In 1964, Gutman was placed on a list of "Subversives Employed by the State of New York."[65] The FBI again considered a recruitment effort, but decided it would not be fruitful. "GUTMAN, an Associate Professor of History at SUNYAB, has not come to the attention of any of our sources at that school. [Sentence redacted.] Similar negative information was furnished on 5/12 by [text redacted]. A review of this file does not reveal reason which would justify a reinterview attempt or indicate that GUTMAN should be considered for PSI [Potential Security Informant] development. He should continue to be carried in Section A of the Reserve Index because of his 1949 CP membership, his teaching position and also because of past hostility to the FBI and the HUAC."[66] When he taught at Stanford University in 1966, the FBI again noted he did not engage in subversive activity.[67]

The FBI never mentioned Gutman's published scholarship. Moreover, the background material in Gutman's file does not refer to any political activity after 1955. However, the FBI withheld 237 pages, claiming this material consisted of duplicate pages. During the 1960s, the FBI continued to view Gutman as an Old Left figure who did not evolve from the communist politics of his youth. The file ends in 1968 at a time when the FBI only recently started its extensive and disruptive New Left COINTELPRO campaign.[68] Gutman was not yet a well-known scholar, a status he received in the mid-1970s with the publication of *Work, Culture and Society in Industrializing America* and *The Black Family in Slavery and Freedom*. Apparently, the Gutman file was not reopened. His influence on young New Left scholars studying "history from the bottom up" remained beyond the FBI's understanding.

Howard Zinn's FBI file

Howard Zinn's political activism spanned six decades. He remains the best selling American historian, with over 1 million copies sold of *A People's History of the United States*. After his death in 2009, the FBI posted his 423-page file on its web site documenting surveillance from the late 1940s until at least the late 1960s.

After serving two years in the U.S. military during World War II, Zinn returned to his native New York City and became involved in radical politics. The FBI discovered him in 1948 at the age of 26 when he struck up a conversation with an undercover informer during a street protest. He admitted regularly attending CP meetings in Brooklyn. The FBI consulted 15 informers who infiltrated the New York CP and eight knew of his activism. One informer confirmed Zinn's name appeared on a membership list at CP Headquarters. As a result, the FBI placed him on the Security Index.[69] While a doctoral candidate at Columbia University, the FBI twice interviewed Zinn to recruit him as an informer. This effort failed. An agent reported:

> ZINN again stated that he did not believe in the principle of force and violence and knew of no one who did advocate this principle. He stated that he did not consider himself or any of his friends to be a threat to the security of the nation.
>
> He stated that under no circumstances would he testify or furnish information concerning the political opinion of others.[70]

Zinn denied CP membership but admitted to past participation in several groups the FBI considered Party fronts. The agent concluded that "additional interviews with ZINN would not turn him from his current attitude."[71] The next year the FBI removed him from the Security Index.[72]

The investigation moved to Atlanta in 1956 when Zinn obtained a full-time teaching job at Spelman College, an historically black institution. The FBI wrote that his CP membership had ended in 1953 and their informants familiar with Spelman College could find nothing on him. However, in the early 1960s Zinn's name resurfaced when he was quoted in the press about the bureau. His comments focused on the failure of the FBI to protect African Americans in the South against white racial violence. "Negroes tend to distrust the FBI," Zinn had said. "With all the clear violations by local police of Constitutional rights, the FBI has not made a single arrest on behalf of Negro citizens."[73] In a speech, he also stated: "Our Attorney General is callous and the FBI incompetent to deal with civil rights problems."[74] After Zinn wrote an article in the *Nation* in 1964 about police brutality and civil rights in Hattiesburg, Mississippi, Hoover asked "why Zinn's name is not included in the Security Index." A week later the FBI again placed Zinn in the Index. Since he did not belong to any revolutionary organizations, "Subject's activities make this a close case as to whether he belongs on the Reserve Index or Security Index." But the FBI concluded that Zinn qualified "as a dangerous individual who might commit acts inimical to the national defense and public safety of the United States in time of an emergency."[75] At the time, Zinn served on the executive board of the Student Nonviolent Coordinating Committee (SNCC). He was not aware of the FBI's surveillance.[76]

Staughton Lynd, a colleague in the Spelman History Department, is referenced in the Zinn file in 1963. FBI informants had gathered intelligence on Lynd since at least 1953 while he was at Harvard University. One informant reported that Lynd "had never been permitted to join the Communist Party while at Harvard because he could never seem to make up his mind that the Party was worthwhile." The FBI reported also on Lynd's activism at Spelman when he hosted in 1961 a visiting Soviet youth delegation at the college. In 1962, he helped organize national protests against nuclear weapons testing and participated in a local march against the U.S. blockade during the Cuban Missile Crisis. In 1963, an informer reported that the Spelman Peace Committee, a group organized in favor of nuclear disarmament, "met in the on-campus apartment of STAUGHTON LYND and that LYND and ZINN were very active in this committee."[77]

After Spelman College fired Zinn, he secured a teaching post at Boston University and the FBI followed him up north. Until his file allegedly was closed in 1969, more than a dozen memos trace the wide scope of his activism against U.S. military involvement in Vietnam and his association with the civil rights, black power, and New Left movements.[78] The FBI holds material on Zinn in 14 files other than his own suggesting his broad influence. Several cite "communist infiltration" even though the FBI found that Zinn did not participate in CP activities during the 1960s. The files are:

Roslyn Zinn
Communist Infiltration of the American Veterans Committee
Herbert Yanowitz

Communist Infiltration in Racial Matters
Communist Infiltration of the Student Non-Violent Coordinating Committee
Japan Peace for Vietnam Committee
Stop the Draft Week!
Ernest P. Young
National Mobilization Committee to End the War in Vietnam
Communist Infiltration of the Southern Student Organizing Committee
Anti-Draft Activities
Communist Infiltration of Students for a Democratic Society
Demonstrations Protesting U.S. Intervention in Vietnam
Student Mobilization Committee[79]

Zinn criticized the FBI for much of his career. A 1993 article, "The Federal Bureau of Intimidation," received wide distribution. He wrote:

> I thought it would be good to talk about the FBI because they talk about us. They don't like to be talked about. They don't even like the fact that you're listening to them being talked about. They are very sensitive people. . . . And one of the things that makes it [the U.S.] not quite a democracy is the existence of outfits like the FBI and the CIA. Democracy is based on openness, and the existence of a secret policy, secret lists of dissident citizens, violates the spirit of democracy . . . the only thing you can do with the FBI is expose them to public understanding, education, ridicule. They deserve it. They have "garbologists" ransacking garbage pails. A lot of interesting stuff in garbage pails. They have to be exposed, brought down from that hallowed point where they once were. And, by the way, they have been brought down. That's one of the comforting things about what has happened in the United States in the last 30 years.[80]

William Appleman Williams

William Appleman Williams was an avowed Marxist (or neo-Marxist) active in socialist groups. In writings and speeches he expressed revisionist views of U.S-Soviet relations, blaming the U.S. for the Cold War, and critiqued American imperialism. As Jon Wiener writes, "his graduate seminar [at Madison] provided the intellectual arena in which New Left History in the United States first developed." In 1959, students in Williams' class started the influential journal, *Studies on the Left*. The journal "wanted to make history illuminate the present. Its editors argued that liberalism, the ideology by which the corporate elite had established its hegemony, was becoming increasingly authoritarian."[81] Although Williams was a popular, if controversial, figure in his profession, elected president of the Organization of American Historians in 1980, the FBI viewed him as an enemy and placed him on the Security Index. His declassified FBI file totals 99 pages for the period 1958 to 1972.

In 1957, Williams started teaching in the History Department at the University of Wisconsin, and it was not long before the FBI noted his presence.[82] They pointed to his membership in the National Council of the Emergency Civil Liberties Committee, dating at least from 1954, claiming it represented "communist activity." In addition, his service on the National Committee of the American Forum for Socialist Education, as well as his role as a contributing editor of the *American Socialist*, earned notes in his file. The FBI also developed information from his prior teaching post at the University of Oregon. On one occasion, Williams lectured at the Oregon Federation for Social Action on the topic, "Natural History of the Cold War." In an unusual practice, the FBI summarized this lecture based on an informant's notes. It was noted that Williams allegedly called the Soviet Union a "free society." In a second lecture, "Re-consideration of Soviet Conduct and Relating American Policy," Williams urged détente, a heretical point of view as the Cold War raged across the globe under Eisenhower. The FBI wrote:

> According to the informant, Professor WILLIAMS spoke of the struggle of the Soviet leaders and people against poverty and for social security. He maintained that the West must negotiate with Russia, because there cannot and must not be an atomic war. He advocated aid to Russia's satellites through the United

Nations. He also suggested that Russia be allowed to overcome her struggle against poverty and to build security. He also was reported as having stated that the policy of containment was very bad, and if Russia were pushed too far, she would fight.[83]

While teaching at Madison, Williams attended meetings of the Wisconsin Socialist Club, which the local FBI office placed under investigation. On February 13, 1958, he spoke on the topic, "Has America a Socialist Future?" The official documentation says: "In view of WILLIAMS' apparent connections with and interest in the new all inclusive types of national and local socialist groups. . . . Bureau authority is granted to investigate the subject, such investigation being limited to the contacting of reliable established sources at the University of Wisconsin and confidential informants in the Madison, Wisconsin, area."[84] It did not help his cause that his name appeared on a petition to President Eisenhower asking for clemency for Morton Sobell, imprisoned during the Rosenberg atomic spy case. Sources on campus reported Williams in a public speech "criticized American troops in Lebanon as dangerous and a policy based on force." The FBI was uncertain if Williams was pro-Soviet in sentiment and consulted a historian who told them that while a socialist ("probably Marxian in a philosophical sense"), he was not pro-communist in political activity. In August 1958, the FBI contacted "informants acquainted with communist and pro-Communist activities in the Madison, Wisconsin, area" and "none of these informants knew the Subject and none had any information concerning him." The FBI also received information on Williams from the college administration.[85]

When he received a $1500 grant from the Fund for Social Analysis, the FBI escalated its tactics. The Fund was devoted to exploring Marxist theory in the social sciences. HUAC summoned Williams to testify about the Fund on April 28, 1961. Prior to his appearance, he told a group of graduate students about the summons. An FBI source among the graduate students reported:

Williams stated that he had been under investigation by the FBI for several years and was not surprised that he was being summoned. He said that he has not been informed of the nature of the inquiry to be made of him. He told the group further that he would appear at the hearing and would read a prepared statement, which would set forth that he is not and never has been a member of the Communist Party, but that he is an American radical in the tradition of [text redacted] and in the tradition of true Marxist Socialism.

This source further advised that Williams also stated that he feels strongly that the HUAC has no right to engage in its current activities and that he is not obligated to say anything. He stated that he will of his own violation tell what he is willing to tell but will not answer any questions.[86]

FBI memos also indicate Williams praised Marx at a meeting of the Socialist Club on campus. Petitions he signed to recognize communist China and East Germany and to urge the abolishment of HUAC were noted in his file. The FBI tracked many of his speaking appearances, referred to published articles, and noted radical journals to which he subscribed.[87] For unknown reasons, no material in the declassified file covers the years 1962 to 1966. In 1967, the FBI stated it never tried to interview him or recruit him as an informer. He remained on the Security Index "because he is a university professor and has been most critical of U.S. foreign policy and reportedly has been invited to visit Cuba. Because of his profession, in time of national emergency, he would be in a position to influence others against the national interest."[88]

On April 29, 1967, Hoover determined that Williams' posed a threat to the president and notified the Secret Service of his "expressions of strong or violent anti-U.S. sentiment."[89] After Hoover died in 1972, Williams remained a high priority subject included in Administrative Index (ADEX)—an emergency detention list that replaced the Security Index. The official documentation highlighted his "very critical" view of U.S. policy in Vietnam and he "has been described as a Marxist historian."[90] The new FBI director, L. Patrick Gray III, affirmed Hoover's earlier assessment that Williams posed a threat to the president. "Potentially dangerous because of background, emotional instability or activity in groups engaged in activities inimical to U.S."[91] The file abruptly ends with this Gray letter.

Warren Susman, too, was connected to the University of Wisconsin at Madison earning a doctoral degree and identified as part of the New Left. Susman became a leading cultural historian who challenged the consensus view of American history which identified little conflict in the American past. As Michael Denning writes, "if we wish to understand American culture less as the story of the hegemony of the middle class, than as the condensation of class conflicts—at turns mediated, or displaced by the new industries of culture—then we must pay close attention to Susman's practice of cultural history."[92] In 1961, the FBI first mentioned Susman for sponsoring a public appeal to President Kennedy against nuclear arms testing in the atmosphere as a member of the Raritan Valley Committee for a Sane Nuclear Policy. FBI files also tracked a petition he signed in 1962 protesting the conduct of HUAC and noted his involvement in *Studies on the Left*. An FBI memo lists all editorial board members and contributors to *Studies*, including Susman. "If Bureau files reflect any significant information of any of these individuals, such information should be furnished to Milwaukee in documentary form in order that it may be incorporated into the next report on STOL."[93]

While teaching at Rutgers University, Susman's name also surfaced several times for activity in opposition to U.S. involvement in Vietnam. In 1965, the FBI in Newark, New Jersey, tracked the Inter-University Committee for a Public Hearing in Vietnam, which supported demonstrations. In 1967, Susman signed a petition, along with more than 60 other Rutgers faculty and students, voicing opposition to the Vietnam war. The petition indicated that signees would refuse to serve in the armed forces if called; Susman was listed as one of the faculty supporters. In 1967, the bureau also noted that Susman participated in an anti-war demonstration in Washington, D.C, which included SDS members from Newark.[94] Left scholarly activity was noted in 1967 and 1968 in connection with the Socialist Scholars Conference. The FBI spied on both conferences, conducting background checks on all program participants. In 1968, the Newark office noted Susman participated on a panel with Christopher Lasch of the University of Rochester on "The Role of Intellectuals in Social Change."[95]

Susman helpd organize the First Socialist Scholars Conference held at Columbia University in 1965. The conference became an annual event, and the FBI attended: The bureau holds an 838-page file covering the years 1966 to 1970. Although no FBI personnel attended the first conference, "patriotic" American Alice Widener sent Hoover an article she wrote to alert him to the subversion she witnessed at the conference. Hoover took immediate action, writing the New York FBI office: "The Bureau desires that New York, through its sources, attempt to obtain a list of individuals present at this Conference. . . . It also is desired that efforts be made to obtain a complete transcript of the remarks made by speakers at this Conference." U.S. Senator Frank J. Lausche of Ohio also read about the conference in *Barron's* business magazine and penned an outraged letter to Hoover, asking "Did or did you not have anyone in attendance? . . . The purpose of this letter is to learn from you whether or not transcripts of the speeches delivered at this Socialist Scholars Conference are available." Hoover responded by noting that only one FBI informant attended but "his report was not complete" because this informant, based in Newark, went to only one session at the two-day event. The New York office tried to identify the conference sponsors, but with little success. "A canvass of the informants of the NYO in security matters has failed to disclose that this conference was sponsored by any of the organizations of interest to the Bureau in the security field." In other words, the CP and the Socialist Workers Party (SWP), as well as some small splinter groups, were not involved. Hoover told a New York special agent, "The Bureau and your office had no advance notice of this conference," which from the FBI point of view constituted an intelligence failure.[96]

The bureau was better prepared when the conference met the next year. Attendance was high, about 2,000 people, and a 26-page FBI memo lists all the conference speakers with a summary of each person based on available information from their files. Hoover wrote Senator William Proxmire, who inquired about the Conference, "we are currently identifying all individuals in attendance. . . . The conference was attended by a large number of university professors as well as communists, socialist, and extreme liberals."[97] When the conference convened in the fall of 1967, the FBI opened a formal investigation about six months before its scheduled opening. Why so early? They worried for the first time that the CP would play a significant role. An informant discovered an internal CP memo suggesting, "The Party feels it important to participate in this conference and to seek the inclusion of CP ideas among those presented for discussion." The CP largely had ignored the 1966 conference, sending only eight members to attend. The FBI recognized that the organizers of the conference actively resisted CP involvement.[98]

The FBI tracked the Steering Committee, chaired by historian Eugene D. Genovese. An unidentified woman provided information to the bureau. The FBI also checked the records of the New York County Clerk's office and the Credit Bureau of Greater NY looking for information. The FBI reviewed the bank account of the conference to locate the source of its funding. The balance of the account on March 10, 1967, was only $1120.21.[99]

About 3,000 people attended the 1967 conference. The FBI kept track of the different organizations with literature tables. Their earlier worry about communist infiltration proved unfounded. FBI sources estimated that only 11 members of the CP attended as well as about 40 members of the SWP. True to its purpose, the conference embraced a non-sectarian point of view.[100]

The FBI provided full coverage of the Fourth Annual Conference in the fall of 1968. Again, they conducted background research on all speakers. Some questions remained about the socialist allegiances of participants. The FBI had trouble determining which faction on the left was dominant. As a result, the New York office noted, "There is no Bureau approved characterization of the Socialist Scholars Conference."[101] The Fifth Annual Conference drew the attention of Nixon's Justice Department. Assistant Attorney General J. Walter Yeagley wrote Hoover asking for information. Hoover wrote back: "Individuals in the Security Index have participated in these conferences in the past."[102] For the Sixth Annual meeting in 1970, the FBI prepared a glossary of individuals associated with the conference, detailing their radical ties. Fifty-five individuals are included in the glossary, a virtual who's who of the nonsectarian, intellectual Left.[103]

Notes

1. Gilbert Geis and Colin Goff, "Lifting the Cover from Undercover Operations: J. Edgar Hoover and Some of the other Criminologists," *Crime, Law and Social Change* 18 (1992): 91.

2. Human Rights Watch notes: "Researchers, scholars, teachers and students in dozens of countries continued to be harassed, censored, dismissed, imprisoned, and, in worst cases, tortured or killed for openly expressing their views or addressing controversial issues." Human Rights Watch, "Human Rights Watch World Report 2000: Academic Freedom," Dec. 1999, 1.

3. Ellen Schrecker, *No Ivory Tower: McCarthyism and the Universities* (New York: Oxford University Press, 1986); Noam Chomsky et al., *The Cold War and the University: Toward an Intellectual History of the Postwar Years* (New York: New Press, 1997); Christopher Simpson, ed., *Universities and Empire: Money and Politics in the Social Sciences During the Cold War* (New York: New Press, 1998); Philip Zwerling, ed., *The CIA On Campus: Essays on Academic Freedom and the National Security State* (Jefferson, NC: McFarland, 2011); Rebecca S. Lowen, *Creating the Cold War University: The Transformation of Stanford* (Berkeley: University of California Press, 1997); Robin W. Winks, *Cloak and Gown: Scholars in the Secret War, 1939-1961* (New York: William Morrow, 1987); and Sigmund Diamond, *Compromised Campus: The Collaboration of Universities with the Intelligence Community, 1945-1955* (New York: Oxford University Press, 1992).

4. Michael Forrest Keen, *Stalking the Sociological Imagination: J. Edgar Hoover's Surveillance of American Sociology* (Westport: Greenwood Press, 1999); David H. Price, *Threatening Anthropology: McCarthyism and the FBI's Surveillance of Activist Anthropologists* (Durham: Duke University Press, 2004); Diamond, *Compromised Campus*, 50-109; Bruce Cummings, "Boundary Displacement: Area Studies and International

Studies During and After the Cold War," in Simpson, ed., *Universities and Empire*, 165-167.

5. When I requested Oscar Handlin's file, the FBI responded in an irregular way that blocked access. They wrote in a letter: "Based on the information you provided, we conducted a search of the Central Records System. We were unable to identify main file records responsive to the FOIA request...Unfortunately, we are unable to access the manual indices of the FBI Headquarters at this time as they are currently being prepared for automation. Additionally, records responsive to your request regarding COINTELPRO were previously processed for another requestor. In order to avoid charging duplication fees unnecessarily, we have made these records available on the FBI public website, http://vault.fbi.gov." However, the FBI did not post the Handlin records on its web site by the time this book went to press.

6. In 1971, the FBI called *Radical America* "a New Left theoretical journal." SAC Milwaukee to Director, "Radical America," Sept. 14, 1971, *Radical America* FBI file.

7. Schrecker, *No Ivory Tower*, 175.

8. During the 1950s, the American Association of University Professors (AAUP) issued an official statement sanctioning the firing of faculty who supported communism. The AAUP statement, engineered by Yale President Whitney Griswold, insisted that faculty should be "united in loyalty to the ideal of learning, to the moral code, to the country, and to its form of government...free enterprise is as essential to intellectual freedom as economic progress." This policy echoed Yale's, where communists would not be hired. The prominent historian Daniel Boorstin, later the Librarian of Congress, also testified before HUAC in 1953 that communists should not be allowed to teach in American universities. Jonathon R. Cole, *The Great American University* (New York: Public Affairs, 2009), 359-363.

9. Cummings, "Boundary Displacement," 165-167.

10. Milton Schwebel, "Comments on the Cold War and the Human Mind," paper presented at a conference sponsored by the American Civil Liberties Union ("Ending the Cold War at Home"), 1991.

11. Clarence M. Kelley with James Kirkpatrick Davis, *Kelley: The Story of an FBI Director* (Kansas City: Andrews, McMeel, and Parker, 1987), 173; Jerry Berman, "FBI Charter Legislation: The Case for Prohibiting Domestic Intelligence Investigations," *University of Detroit Journal of Urban Law* 55 (Summer 1978), 1056.

12. Frank Donner, "Political Informers," in Pat Watters and Stephan Gillers, eds., *Investigating the FBI* (Garden City, NY: Doubleday, 1973), 358.

13. Devin Fergus, *Liberalism, Black Power, and the Making of American Politics, 1965-1980* (Athens: University of Georgia Press, 2009), 1.

14. FBI Name Check, Nov. 16, 1955, Nevins FBI file.

15. FBI Name Check, "Samuel Eliot Morison," May 21, 1959, Morison FBI file

16. FBI Name Check, "Richard Hofstadter," Feb. 1, 1952, Hofstadter FBI file.

17. SAC, Miami to Director, "Voter's March, May 14-15, 1966," May 11, 1966; SAC, New York to Director, "Book Reviews," Nov. 24, 1965, Hofstadter FBI file; Guenter Levy, *The Cause that Failed: Communism in American Political Life* (New York: Oxford University Press, 1990), 226.

18. W. C. Sullivan to A.H. Belmont, Feb. 19, 1955. Henry Steele Commager FBI file.

19. B.E. Sackett to Director, "Professor Henry S. Commager, Internal Security," March 8, 1941; M.S. Jones to Mr. Nichols, "Henry Steele Commager," Sept. 23, 1947; D.M. Ladd to Director, "Henry Steele Commager," June 29, 1949. Commager FBI file.

20. D. M. Ladd to Director, "Henry Steele Commager," June 29, 1949, Commager FBI file.

21. Henry Steele Commager to J. Edgar Hoover, Oct. 14, 1949; D. M. Ladd to Director, "Henry Steele Commager," Feb. 1, 1950. Commager FBI file.

22. R. P. Kramer to Director, Feb. 16, 1950, Commager FBI file.

23. D. M. Ladd to Director, "Henry Steele Commager," March 9, 1950. Commager FBI file.

24. W. C. Sullivan to A.H. Belmont, Feb. 19, 1955, Commager FBI file.

25. Director to SACs, "Henry Steele Commager," July 27, 1962. Commager FBI file.

26. New York FBI report, "Henry Steel [sic] Commager," Aug. 8, 1962; SAC New York to Director, Aug. 15, 1962. Commager FBI file.

27. Commager wrote a personal letter to Hoover after the assassination of Martin Luther King, Jr. "Three years ago you had the limitless insolence of calling Martin Luther King the Greatest Liar in America. I trust you realize that your vulgarity and irresponsibility contributed directly to the Tragedy in Memphis." M. A. Jones to Mr. DeLoach, "Henry Steel [sic] Commager," Nov. 15, 1963; FBI [name redacted] to White House, July 10, 1967; Department of State report, "Henry Steel [sic] Commager," Oct. 19, 1968; SAC Boston to Director, "Henry Steel [sic] Commager," Nov. 21, 1976; Commager to J. Edgar Hoover, April

4, 1968; M. Jones to Mr. Bishop, "Henry Steele Commager," June 29, 1970. Commager FBI file.

28. The FBI Headquarters file totals 497 pages. SAC New York, "Report of [text redacted], John Hope Franklin," Jan. 18, 1962, 7, John Hope Franklin FBI file.

29. [text redacted] to [text redacted], "John Hope Franklin, Special Inquiry – State Department," Feb. 5, 1962, 1, 9, Franklin FBI file. On the Frazer investigation, see Keen, *Stalking the Sociological Imagination*, 84-104.

30. SAC New York, "Report of [text redacted], John Hope Franklin," Oct. 10, 1965, 10. Franklin FBI file.

31. SAC Washington, "Report of [text redacted], John Hope Franklin," Jan. 19, 1962, 1-2, Franklin FBI file.

32. SAC Chicago to Director, "John Hope Franklin," May 6, 1965, 1, 3, Franklin FBI file.

33. [Text redacted] to Marvin Watson, July 22, 1965, Franklin FBI file.

34. SAC Albany, "Report of SA [text redacted], John Hope Franklin," Jan. 18, 1962, 2, Franklin FBI file.

35. John Hope Franklin, Special Inquiry – State Department," Feb. 5, 1962, 1, 9, Franklin FBI file.

36. [Text redacted] to Marvin Watson, Nov. 5, 1965, Franklin FBI file.

37. [Text redacted] to John D. Ehrlichman, April 21, 1969. Franklin FBI file.

38. FBI memo [author redacted], "Comer Vann Woodward," Nov. 10, 1964. Comer Vann Woodward FBI file; Frederick T. Griffins, "Ralph Ellison, Richard Wright, and the Case of Angelo Herndon," *African American Review* (Winter 2001): 615-636; Charles H. Martin, "The Angelo Herndon Case and Southern Justice," in Michal Belknap, ed., *American Political Trials* (Westport: Greenwood Press, 1994), 159-178.

39. Naval Intelligence report, "Comer Van [sic] Woodward," Aug. 22, 1951, Woodward FBI file.

40. FBI memo [author redacted], "Comer Vann Woodward," March 12, 1953; SAC Baltimore to Director, "Comer Vann Woodward, Security Matter-C," April 28, 1954. Woodward FBI file.

41. FBI memo [author redacted], "Comer Vann Woodward," April 2, 1963, Woodward FBI file.

42. Jon Weiner, *Professors, Politics and Pop* (New York: Verso, 1994), 212; C. Vann Woodward, "Wild in the Stacks," *New York Review of Books*, Aug. 1, 1968, 8-12.

43. See Paul Buhle, ed., *History and the New Left: Madison, Wisconsin, 1950-1970* (Philadelphia: Temple University Press, 1989); Buhle and Edward Rice-Maximin, *William Appleman Williams: The Tragedy of Empire* (New York: Routledge, 1995); Henry Abelove et al., *Visions of History* (New York: Pantheon Books, 1983); A.A.A. Van Der Linden, *A Revolt Against Liberalism: American Radical Historians, 1959-1976* (Amsterdam: Rodopi BV Editions, 1996); Weiner, *Professors, Politics and Pop*, 175-217; and Kenin Mattson, *Intellectuals in Action: The Origins of the New Left and Radical Liberalism, 1945-1970* (Pennsylvania State University Press, 2002).

44. For a sympathetic treatment of Gutman's scholarship, see Ira Berlin's Introduction to Gutman, *Power and Culture: Essays on the American Working Class* (New York: New Press, 1987), 3-69. For a critical view, see the symposium published in 1988 and 1989 in the journal *Politics, Culture and Society* with articles by Herbert Hill, Steve Brier, Irving Bernstein, Nick Salvatore, and Albert Fried.

45. Gutman never requested a copy of his FBI file. The FBI first processed a records request in 1988.

46. SAC New York memo, Aug. 24, 1949; Milwaukee FBI office, "Security Matter, Herbert George Gutman," March 26, 1953. Gutman FBI file.

47. SAC New York to FBI Director Nov. 1, 1951, Gutman FBI file.

48. SAC Milwaukee to FBI Director April 28, 1953, Gutman FBI file.

49. FBI Report, Milwaukee, Wisconsin, "Security Matter," Oct. 12, 1953; SAC New York to FBI Director June 20, 1955. Gutman FBI file

50. Milwaukee FBI office, "Security Matter, Herbert George Gutman," March 26, 1953, Gutman FBI file.

51. Herbert G. Gutman, "Learning About History," in Buhle, ed., *History and the New Left*, 47-48.

52. SA [deleted] to SAC New York, Oct. 29, 1953. Gutman FBI file,

53. SAC New York to FBI Director, Sept. 27, 1954. Gutman FBI file.

54. New York FBI report, "Security Matter, Herbert George Gutman," Oct. 10, 1954, Gutman FBI file.

55. SAC New York to FBI Director, Oct. 10, 1954, Gutman FBI file.

56. David Garrow, "FBI Political Harassment and FBI Historiography: Analyzing Informants and Measuring the Effects," *The Public Historian* 10 (Fall 1988): 7, 14.

57. L. B. Nichols to Clyde Tolson, July 15, 1955, Gutman FBI file.

58. Later FBI memos note Gutman acted as a petition canvasser for the Campaign Committee of the Communist Party in 1949 to elect candidates to the New York City Council. He also apparently encour-

aged "the singing of Communist songs" at Camp Kinderland. Buffalo FBI office to Civil Service Commission, Jan. 26, 1965, Gutman FBI file.

59. SA [deleted] report, Washington D.C., "Herbert George Gutman," May 29, 1959; SAC, New York to FBI Director, June 15, 1959. Gutman FBI file.

60. Legat, London to FBI Director, Aug. 26, 1959; Deputy Director, [CIA] to FBI Director Aug. 31, 1959. Gutman FBI file.

61. New York FBI office report, "Security Matter, Herbert George Gutman," Jan. 1, 1961, Gutman FBI file.

62. New York FBI report, "Security Matter," April 28, 1960, Gutman FBI file.

63. New York FBI office report, Jan. 26, 1961, Gutman FBI file.

64. SAC New York to FBI Director, Dec. 12, 1961, Gutman FBI file.

65. SAC, Buffalo to FBI Director, June 28, 1964, Gutman FBI file.

66. FBI memo from SAC [name deleted] to SAC (100-18396), May 14, 1965, Gutman FBI file.

67. SAC Buffalo to FBI Director, Oct. 17, 1966; SAC San Francisco to FBI Director, Oct. 27, 1967. Gutman FBI file.

68. SAC [text redacted] to SAC (100-18396), March 20, 1968; SAC Buffalo to FBI Director, March 25, 1968. Gutman FBI file.

69. New York FBI office report, "Howard Zinn," March 9, 1949; New York FBI office report, "Howard Zinn," Aug. 21, 1950. Howard Zinn FBI file.

70. NY SAC to Director, "Howard Zinn," Feb. 24, 1954, Zinn FBI file.

71. Ibid.

72. NY SAC to Director, "Howard Zinn," Aug. 10, 1955, Zinn FBI file.

73. A. Rosen to Mr. Belmont, "Racial Situation Albany, Georgia," Nov. 15, 1962, Zinn FBI file.

74. A. Jones to Mr. DeLoach, "Howard Zinn," May 21, 1963, Zinn FBI file.

75. J. F. Bland to W. C. Sullivan, "Howard Zinn," May 18, 1964, Zinn FBI file. See also Matthew Rothschild, "The FBI's File on Howard Zinn," *The Progressive*, July 31, 2010, http://www.progressive.org/wx073110.html.

76. Howard Zinn, "The Politics of History in the Era of the Cold War: Repression and Resistance," in Chomsky et al., *The Cold War and the University*, 52.

77. Atlanta FBI field office report, "Howard Zinn," July 31, 1963, Zinn FBI file. See also Carl Mirra, *The Admirable Radical: Staughton Lynd and Cold War Dissent, 1945-1970* (Kent, OH: Kent State University Press, 2010).

78. Thomas D. Maning, Boston FBI office report, "Howard Zinn," March 7, 1968, Zinn FBI file.

79. FBI, "Correlation of Summary, Howard Zinn," June 9, 1969, Zinn FBI file.

80. Howard Zinn, "The Federal Bureau of Intimidation," *Covert Action Quarterly* 47 (Winter 1993-1994), http://mediafilter.org/MFF/FBI.html.

81. Weiner, *Professors, Politics and Pop*, 184, 186-187.

82. Buhle and Rice-Maximin in *William Appleman Williams* (p. 28-29) cite an earlier incident where Woodward may have come to the attention of the FBI. In mid-1940s, he produced a newsletter for the NAACP in Corpus Christi, Texas, while a young naval officer. The FBI talked to his commanding officer to warn him about his activism and may have notified his landlord. This incident is not mentioned in Woodward's FBI file.

83. Milwaukee FBI office report, "Professor William Appleman Williams, Security Matter- C," April 22, 1958, Williams FBI file.

84. SAC Milwaukee to Director, "William Appleman Williams," June 5, 1958; Ibid. June 23, 1958. Williams FBI file.

85. Milwaukee FBI report, "Professor William Appleman Williams," Aug. 29, 1958, Williams FBI file.

86. SAC Milwaukee to Director, "William Appleman Williams," July 2, 1961, Williams FBI file.

87. Milwaukee FBI report, "William Appleman Williams" April 26, 1961; SAC Milwaukee to Director, "William Appleman Williams," May 26, 1961. Williams FBI file.

88. Milwaukee FBI report, "William Appleman Williams" April 25, 1967, Williams FBI file.

89. J. Edgar Hoover to Director of the Secret Service, April 29, 1967, Williams FBI file.

90. SAC Portland to Director, "William Appleman Williams," May 11, 1972, Williams FBI file.

91. L. Patrick Gray, III, to Director of the Secret Service, June 19, 1972, Williams FBI file.

92. Michael Denning, "Class and Culture: Reflections on the Work of Warren Susman," *Radical History Review* 36 (1986): 110-111.

93. SAC Newark to Director, "Inter-University Committee for a Public Hearing on Viet Nam," May 17, 1965; SAC Newark to Director, "Socialist Scholars Conference," Oct. 10, 1968; SAC Milwaukee to Director, "Studies on the Left," May 16, 1962; SAC Milwaukee to New York, "Studies on the Left," Feb. 27, 1963. Warren Susman FBI file.

94. SAC Newark to Director, "Inter-University Committee for a Public Hearing on Viet Nam," May 17, 1965; SAC Newark to Director, "Advertisement," May 9, 1967; Newark FBI report, "Demonstrations Protesting US Intervention in Vietnam," Nov. 15, 1967. Susman FBI file

95. SAC Newark to Director, "Socialist Scholars Conference," Dec. 12, 1967; SAC Newark to Director, "Socialist Scholars Conference," Oct. 10, 1968. Susman FBI file.

96. [Text redacted] to J. Edgar Hoover, Sept. 20, 1965; Director to SAC New York, "First Annual Socialist Scholars Conference (Internal Security)," Sept. 29, 1965; Senator Frank J. Lausche to J. Edgar Hoover, Sept. 29, 1965; J. Edgar Hoover to Senator Frank J. Lausche, Oct. 5, 1965; SAC New York to Director, "First Annual Socialist Scholars Conference," Nov. 16, 1965; Director to SAC New York, "Socialist Scholars Conference," Aug. 25, 1966. Socialist Scholars Conference (SSC) FBI file. The CIA also took an interest in the event, writing a nine-page memo to Hoover to describe "Communist and Trotskyist thought on attitudes and activities within the present academic world in the United States." James Angleton to FBI Director, Nov. 2, 1965, SSC FBI file.

97. FBI report, "Socialist Scholars Conference," Sept. 16, 1966; J. Edgar Hoover to Senator William Proxmire, Oct. 4, 1966. SSC FBI file

98. SAC New York to Director, "COMINFIL, Socialist Scholars Conference," March 15, 1967; SAC New York to Director, "COMINFIL, Socialist Scholars Conference," April 18, 1967. SSC FBI file.

99. SAC New York to Director, "COMINFIL, Socialist Scholars Conference," April 18, 1967, SSC FBI file.

100. SAC New York to Director, "Socialist Scholars Conference," Oct. 10, 1967; New York FBI report, "Socialist Scholars Conference," Oct. 13, 1967. SSC FBI file.

101. SAC New York to Director, "Socialist Scholars Conference," Aug. 30, 1968. SSC FBI file.

102. J. Walter Yeagley to FBI Director, Sept. 23, 1969; FBI Director to J. Walter Yeagley, Sept. 25, 1969. SSC FBI file.

103. New York FBI report, "Sixth Annual Socialist Scholars Conference," July 20, 1970, SSC FBI file.

In 1927, barbers in Brooklyn, NY, marched to protest the execution of Nicola Sacco and Bartolomeo Vanzetti. The two Italian American anarchists had been arrested for murder in 1920 and their case become a major cause for liberals and the Left during the 1920s. The FBI collected political intelligence on the defendants, their supporters, and the lawyers in the case. Before the execution, FBI Headquarters alerted local offices around the nation to evaluate the state of radical activities, fearing disturbances.

Credit: New York World-Telegram and Sun collection at the Library of Congress

In 1932, the hard times associated with the Great Depression prompted veterans of World War I, as well as other low-income Americans, to form the Bonus Army to de-mand relief from the federal government. They set up an encampment in Washington, DC, and sometimes clashed with police, as shown here. The FBI investigated the Bonus Army to discredit them as communists and criminals, and noted their alliances with organizations of farmers and the unemployed.

Credit: New York World-Telegram and Sun collection at the Library of Congress

Longtime FBI Director J. Edgar Hoover is shown in the 1936 FBI documentary, "You Can't Get Away With It." Despite this depiction, Hoover rarely was known to carry a weapon and rarely, if ever, used one in the line of duty.

UNITED STATES GOVERNMENT

MEMORANDUM

TO: SAC (100-18645)(P)   Date: 6/3/65

FROM: SA ███████████████

SUBJECT: DEMONSTRATIONS PROTESTING
            U. S. INTERVENTION IN
            VIET NAM
            INFORMATION CONCERNING
            (INTERNAL SECURITY)

   Re Buffalo airtel, 5/28/65, to which was attached
for the Bureau sets of memoranda containing information about
individuals either on the Security Index or the Reserve Index
of the Buffalo Office and also connected with an institution
of higher learning. Each memorandum contain a concise subversive history of the person and where applicable his participation in any activity protesting U. S. action in Viet Nam or the
Dominican Republic.

   By this memo a copy of the memo sent to the Bureau on
each particular subject fitting the aforementioned categories
is being placed in the appropriate file. The information set
forth in each subject's memo is self-explanatory.

RECOMMENDATION

   Channelize with copy of instant memo a copy of the
memorandum furnished the Bureau by airtel 5/28/65, as explained
above.

1 - 100-18035
1 - 100-11809
1 - 100-18512
1 - 100-15762
1 - 100-18396 (HERBERT GEORGE GUTMAN)
1 - 100-18257
1 - 100-18498
1 - 100-18541
1 - 100-17840
1 - 100-16865
1 - 100-16863
1 - 100-18227
1 - 100-12887
1 - 100-17496
1 - 100-18631
1 - 100-18632
1 - 100-12062
1 - 100-18023
1 - 100-10462

(21)

ALL INFORMATION CONTAINED
HEREIN IS UNCLASSIFIED
DATE

100-18396- 47

Searched
Serializ
JUNE 8 1965
FBI BUFFALO

100- 57748- 36

In 1965, a memo from the FBI file on historian Herbert G. Gutman indicates that numerous individuals associated with higher education institutions in the Buffalo, NY,
region had been placed on the Security Index, which authorized indefinite detention
by the American government during a national emergency. Although the names of
the individuals are redacted, their official file numbers are indicated at the bottom left
side of the document.

F B I

Date: 8/27/69

Transmit the following in _____
(Type in plaintext or code)

Via   AIRTEL
(Priority)

TO: DIRECTOR, FBI (100-449698)

FROM: SAC, NEW HAVEN (100-19687) (P)

SUBJECT: COINTELPRO - NEW LEFT

Re: Bureau airtel to Albany, 8/20/69.

As a result of the arrest of the leadership of the Black Panther Party in New Haven, Connecticut, on a charge of murder and conspiracy to commit murder, the organization has suffered from confused disorganization and lack of discussion. Its principal concern has been and continues to be the defense of its 8 leaders presently in jail.

To date, there has been little to indicate that the BPP in New Haven and the SDS have been so closely alied, that the announcement by ████ and ████ would have any strong impact.

Sources have furnished no information to indicate that either is aware of ████ and ████'s comments.

However, sources will be canvassed for any information bearing on this situation, and should there be an indication of any strained relationship, this office would be in a good position to capitalize on it through the medium of ████████████ ████████ for WNHC TV, a highly reliable established contact of this office.

No action will be taken without prior Bureau approval.

2 - Bureau
2 - New Haven
RRM/lec
(4)

REC-56   100-449678-32-12

EX-105

62 AUG 29 1969

5 SEP 9 1969

Approved: _____   Sent _____ M   Per _____
          Special Agent in Charge

A 1969 memo in the New Left FBI file shows efforts to inhibit the political activity of the Black Panther Party in New Haven, Connecticut, by arresting its leadership. The FBI also was prepared to use friendly media contacts at a local television station to create division between the Panthers and Students for a Democratic Society.

Former FBI official W. Mark Felt appears on CBS' "Face the Nation" in Washington on Aug. 30, 1976. In 2005, Felt was revealed to be "Deep Throat," the long-anonymous source who leaked secrets about President Nixon's Watergate cover-up to the Wash-ington Post. Felt worked with several other top FBI officials in this successful effort to oust Nixon from office.

"WE BROKE THE LAW? WE ARE THE LAW!"

Credit: A 1995 Herblock Cartoon, copyright by The Herb Block Foundation

Among the few dissenting voices in the war on terrorism, a group of artists associated with Refuse and Resist assembled on September 22, 2001, in Manhattan wearing dust masks and signs that read, "Our grief is not a cry for war." Jim Costanzo took this photograph as part of a performance developed to respond to the terrorist attack on the World Trade Center.

Credit: Photo from the Library of Congress

4

The Ideology of the FBI

For the FBI leadership, dissidents created disunity, and the latter, if politically charged, threatened to generate unwanted disorder. In order to understand surveillance in America, it is necessary to study its ideological roots: the beliefs, attitudes, and worldview that framed leadership decisions governing political monitoring. Although a large bureaucracy keenly interested in preserving (and expanding) its administrative autonomy and jurisdiction, the FBI did not lack ideas of its own and issued many statements that might be found in a political party platform. It functioned as a political actor and made policy in large ways. In this chapter, I focus on the period immediately following the death of J. Edgar Hoover. My analysis is based on public speeches and, secondarily, on internal communications and documents. Over a three-year period (1972 through 1974) FBI directors L. Patrick Gray III and Clarence M. Kelley presented more than 50 addresses. In litigation, *Greenberg v. FBI* (2008), I obtained the full text of these talks and treat them as a set of "ideological data" to mine for political meaning.

Since FBI directors rarely spoke in public, their speeches became important occasions for the American people to see and hear them. These "cloak and dagger" men came out from the shadows to present a public representation of what their organization stood for and how it carried out its functions. To an extent these speeches were propaganda—but even so, we can read them as a form of political messaging. They are not "empty words" because language and discourse serve as critical structuring agents to understand the world. The study of the language of government officials can illuminate how leaders choose to communicate to the people. Interrogating FBI language use becomes part of a critique of domination when approached from the perspective of the subjects of investigation.

When Gray and Kelley took over the bureau, oppositional social movements had assumed a large presence in the society. As a result, their speeches widely engaged questions of protest and dissent in response to pressing political mobilization. During the period 1965 to 1975, more than six million Americans engaged in social protest. Civil conflict in the United States was more widespread and intensive than in most other Western democracies. Some scholars call this period the Second Civil War.[1]

The directors devoted substantial attention to articulating the nature of the threat facing the nation and justifying the FBI's response. The bureau believed it was fighting to roll back the beginnings of a domestic revolution. Gray and Kelley championed a politics of government protection that viewed most adversarial challenges to existing power arrangements as threats to the well-being of the society. For example, Gray belittled radicals as "uninformed," "naive," and "emotionally unstable." They were objectified as enemies to be neutralized, rather than viewed as opponents or critics with legitimate views. This intolerant view of dissent extended even to civil libertarians, who were called "extremists" if they criticized police misconduct.

The FBI leadership had difficulty embracing pluralist traditions. Only their views were correct and those with whom they disagreed should be suppressed. It did not seem to matter if they engaged in deception to advance their views. In this regard, the directors baldly denied the FBI gathered political intelligence and used informers to disrupt political activity. They were unwilling to criticize Hoover's leadership and/or engage in a critical dialogue about official abuse of power. In fact, in order to control the public discourse surrounding their speeches, they almost never took questions from the media or the audience, limiting their expression to a carefully crafted text. In all likelihood, they did not write their own speeches. They were counseled by other FBI officials not to improvise or stray from the prepared remarks.

Both Gray and Kelly viewed city police and FBI agents as patriotic "peace officers" helping to prevent and resolve conflict in society. But, of course, associating "law and order" with peace maintenance is a politically paradoxical position. The policing of protest often included violent methods with the deployment of tear gas, batons, water hoses, canine units, and occasionally bullets. There is a "politics of violence": Some forms by official entities such as police receive legitimation, while other forms by subordinate groups are criminalized.[2] During the early 1970s, movements for social change often fomented disorder to create a context in which people in power are compelled to reform society. They believed leaders would pass new laws and hand out concessions when confronted with intensive social action. By contrast, it is not surprising that an FBI director would express disdain for those who showed "disrespect for the law" and "contempt for authority."[3] Ironically, both Gray and Kelley interpreted the "rule of law" so loosely it incorporated state-sanctioned repression, including illegal acts. Kelley defended COINTELPRO as necessary to fight illegitimate violence. He exaggerated the degree of violence associated with the New Left and the black power movement in order to demonize almost all forms of protest. Like communists of an earlier era, he believed violent radicals infiltrated and took over legitimate political groups turning them into threats to the society.

Gray Becomes Director

President Richard Nixon named Gray acting FBI director the day after Hoover died. At the time, Gray served in the Justice Department as the assistant attorney general in charge of the Civil Division. Just prior to Hoover's death, Nixon nominated Gray for a different job—deputy attorney general and his nomination unanimously cleared a Senate committee. But Nixon then changed his plans for Gray, who he viewed as a trusted servant. Critics say Gray was too loyal to Nixon and the selection process confirms this view. Nixon thrust the job at him without prior warning and Gray barely had time to consider his selection before Nixon rolled him out to face the media. Gray recounted this process in one of his speeches. Attorney General Dick Kleindienst called him at 11:40 am to arrange a meeting in Kleindienst's office for 2:15 pm. Gray recalled:

> I thought it was just another meeting where we would discuss some more of the transition business. And I was there at the appointed time and, as was my custom, I tapped and walked straight in. I didn't see him as I usually did see him seated behind his desk. He was standing in the center of his office. And, as I moved in, he just said, "I'm going to appoint you Acting Director of the Federal Bureau of Investigation." I stopped. Just looked at him. My first reaction, of course, was at least what I consider to be a normal human reaction. It was to tell this man that he had to be kidding, but I didn't. The situation in the Department and the circumstances—it had to be. And I looked to the left of his desk and I saw seated there Assistant Attorney General Ralph Erickson, who at that time was in charge of the Office of Legal Counsel in the Department, the Department's conscience or the lawyer's lawyer in the Department. And I asked him, I said, "Ralph, what are you doing here?" I saw he had some papers in front of him. He said, "I have copies of the Appointing Statutes of the United States and . . . " He was not permitted to say anymore because Mr. Kleindienst said, "The President wants to see you right away. Let's go."[4]

Almost immediately, Gray embarked on the first of 37 public speeches during his short eleven months as director. While it is not clear who penned his talks—in all likelihood it was not Gray—they still stand as documents which can be analyzed for messaging in a public forum. In a speech on May 17, 1972, Gray recounted being "stunned" that he was named acting director. "My name had not been among those prominently mentioned as the possible successor to J. Edgar Hoover, and the thought had, frankly, not even occurred to me." Gray, who had once worked on Nixon's vice presidential staff, acknowledged: "There has been some speculation that my appointment is somehow part of a scheme for the President to gain political control of the FBI." He denied such a role in blunt terms. "I am not a political advisor or counselor to President Nixon. . . . I am not a crony of President Nixon's. . . . In fact, when I met with the President he gave me only one instruction—that the FBI and the Director continue to be absolutely non-political. . . . As long as I head the FBI, it will not come under political influence nor will it ever try to exert political influence."[5] These comments about the non-political nature of the FBI raise the first major issue to contest.

The FBI's National Security Division arguably functioned as the most politically charged agency in the government. Historically, it expressed a bias against all critics of the status quo, including both reformers and revolutionaries. Dissent in general was viewed as suspect and the FBI went beyond fact-based intelligence gathering to focus on sabotage and dirty tricks. The operative strategy of COINTELPRO—"disrupt, destroy, neutralize"—indicated the FBI's goals regarding speech and political activity it found objectionable. The bureau did not restrict its focus exclusively to communists, as much of the general population assumed.

By making the claim the FBI did not "exert political influence," Gray's reference frame was limited mainly to the two-party system. In his view, the FBI did not interfere with the activity of the Republicans and Democrats; it did not become a vehicle of either party. Of course, the FBI gathered intelligence on mainstream political leaders. However, it rarely directed counter-intelligence operations against them. Such efforts were reserved for political groupings outside the two-party system, which were viewed as illegitimate and defined in anti-American terms. Indeed, in these instances the exertion of political influence by the bureau often crossed the line into criminal activity.

In several speeches, Gray denied ongoing and persistent political intelligence gathering. Gray said, "One of the first inquiries I made of top FBI officials was about the possible existence of files that might be called secret files or political dossiers. Both of these phrases have a sinister connotation. I have been informed, as a result of my preliminary inquiries, that there are no secret files or dossiers."[6] Why cannot the director publicly recognize the FBI's secret intelligence files? Many people inside and outside of government already recognized the large scope of FBI intelligence gathering, although few knew details of its vast dimensions. How many secret files existed? Almost one million separate domestic security investigations were opened between 1955 and 1975 under the "subversive" or "extremist" category. Scholars estimate that as many as 20 million Americans were mentioned in FBI spy files in this period.[7] Collecting political intelligence indeed is "sinister" because it undermined the intent of the Bill of Rights and democratic traditions. While the effort to confuse the public about the FBI's political role was not new, Hoover's successor embraced this deception as if nothing had changed at the bureau. They routinely made false statements as they worked in the area of opinion management.

Significantly, Gray never expressed a critical view of Hoover. Instead, he opened many talks with two or three paragraphs of praise for the recently deceased director. This easy embrace signaled Gray was not bringing large-scale changes to the bureau. He was not appointed to be a "reformer." In 1972, the sins of the FBI were not yet exposed, so Gray did not see a need to distance himself from Hoover and the massive abuse of power that occurred during the prior 25 years. He certainly did not get orders from Nixon to criticize Hoover. On May 25, 1972, Gray opened a talk to a law enforcement conference in Biloxi, Mississippi, in the following terms: "The past three weeks have been the most interesting and enlightening of my career. They have provided me a unique insight into the talent, energy, and insight with which J. Edgar Hoover directed the FBI for nearly 48 years. His legacy to us is an investigative agency free of scandal or corruption, sound in principle and organization, and thoroughly dedicated to prompt, efficient, and impartial service to the American people."[8]

These general platitudes are not meaningless. They signify elements of government ideology. After all, the director is a top official of the executive branch, a key leader in the intelligence community, and the top law enforcement officer in the nation. Despite objections to the contrary, the FBI functioned as a national police force with respect to domestic intelligence. Its conduct set an example for the approximately 391,000 state and local law enforcement officers then policing the nation.

For Gray to note the absence of "scandal and corruption" under Hoover continued the FBI practice of protecting their own leaders and their reputation. In this speech, as well as in others, Gray never acknowledged the existence of COINTELPRO or reckoned with this major source of corruption in the federal government. This approach helped construct what scholars identify as the Blue Wall of Silence. The usual reference is to city police, who lie or mislead to protect the crimes of fellow officers. The director's speeches largely served the same purpose. The FBI's Blue Wall of Silence shielded not only their political disruption but also their ideological conservatism. As one example, Gray claimed that Hoover's FBI provided "impartial service" and served all the people. This deception was great: The bureau certainly did not provide impartial service to critics of capitalism and African Americans. In fact, enemies often were afforded few, if any, any legal protections. On the issue of race, Hoover long viewed African Americans as second-class citizens living in a majority white nation. As a result, the FBI narrowly viewed civil rights as a states rights issue, which helped protect the system of racial inequality and oppression.

Gray reluctantly introduced one substantive liberal change departing from Hoover's tenure. The FBI for the first time began to hire women as special agents. This change was "in the air" during the early 1970s: New civil rights laws forbid workplace discrimination based on sex in the private and public sector. Both the Immigration and Naturalization Service and the Bureau of Narcotics and Dangerous Drugs recently opened their ranks. The FBI was last major federal investigative agency not to hire women on equal terms with men. Gray reluctantly accepted the inevitability of the change and noted FBI culture would be impacted. "In the past such a step has been resisted on the argument that women should not be placed in occupations involving physical danger. I am told, however, that many women consider such protective impulses to be a clear case of male chauvinism, and are perfectly willing to take their chances with the men.

While it may prove a difficult mental adjustment for some of us, this step must and will be taken." Yet, only 41 women became agents by 1976 out of 8,619—very slow progress, indeed. In addition, the number of African American, Latino and other minority FBI agents remained very low. By 1976, only 104 blacks and 117 Latinos served as agents.[9] White males continued to supervise and work most security and criminal investigations.

In 1958, Hoover and his staff published a book, *Masters of Deceit*. Although it focused on American communists, it might as well have been about the FBI itself. The idea of being a "master" is a staple FBI concept integrated into its constructs and discourse. As the lead agency for social and political control within the government, it unilaterally engaged in blacklists, imposed economic sanctions, and distributed misinformation. So it is not surprising Gray titled a June 16, 1972, speech delivered at Pepperdine University, "Masters of Change," in which social control over people, ideas, and process was fundamental. "Can we become MASTERS OF CHANGE? . . . So whether we like it or not, change is a Great Issue which confronts us. How are we going to cope with it? Are we going to be overwhelmed? Frustrated? Are we to become embittered, alienated, frightened? . . . If we do not master the forces of change, these forces will master us. And they will propel us headlong in directions that even their creators never intended." Gray's apocalyptic comments included a long tirade against movements for social change, especially the New Left. He referred to "wanton destruction" and the prevalence of revolutionary violence. "Today we hear angry voices claiming that change cannot be accomplished through our existing institutions. This claim is used as the excuse for trying to effect change through riot, bombing, and wanton destruction." It is useful to quote Gray at length to capture the texture and distortion of inherited democratic values in his presentation.

> Today we hear strident and bitter voices from a very small, though highly articulate minority that the historic institutions of America should be destroyed completely as if the Huns or Vandals had passed through.

These voices, especially those of the extremist "New Left," assert that our democratic institutions are corrupt and not worth saving. We are told that our American way of life is repressive. These raucous voices proclaim there is no freedom in this country. They assert that there is no avenue for change within the existing political process. Reform is not good enough for them. They demand that the system itself be overturned.

There are even a few—such as the adherents of the Weatherman faction of the old Students for a Democratic Society—who do not hesitate to employ the guerrilla tactics of the bomb to show their contempt for our society and their desire for a violent revolution. And let me emphasize that these few are infinitely small in numbers, even among their own generation.

Proudly, these extremists claim credit for bombing our Capitol building and the Pentagon—and say more is still to come.

It is ironic, of course, that this system which they despise provides the very means by which they can speak out so freely and drench the people of this Nation with their vitriol.

Through the First Amendment of our Constitution they may say anything and print anything they desire, including instructions to revolutionaries on how to procure and use guns and how to make and use bombs.

Through the Fifth Amendment they can, at the other extreme, refuse to say anything at all when they feel they might be incriminated.

In many instances they have used their right of free speech to shout down and deny free speech to others . . .

These few claim the right to harass the law enforcement officer and to impede him in the legitimate exercise of his duties. If they don't like a law, they claim the right to violate it and then blatantly proclaim that any penalty is "wrong." When they are brought to justice for breaking the law they call themselves "political prisoners." And when they receive a fair trial, they proclaim that a fair trial is no trial at all.

These are excuses for those who think they can effect change by the easy and direct means of the bullet, rather than by the more laborious and demanding method of the ballot.

The genius of our society is that every individual is able, within the range of his own abilities and talents, to influence the community and the society in which he lives.[10]

If we interrogate the text, it is clear Gray's words ring hollow in several ways. His deliberate contempt for popular social movements was exemplified by comparisons to the Huns. Protestors are "strident," "bitter," and "raucous," especially the New Left, which the FBI despised. In 1968, the bureau opened a special section of COINTELPRO to surveil and attack its leaders. He referred to the First Amendment and its abuse by radicals who "shout down" others, rather than acknowledge the bureau's own suppression. Can Americans really "say anything and print anything" without facing retribution by the government? Gray denied that attacks on civil liberties emanated from the seat of government.

It is misleading to associate most social movements with revolution. It is a form of scare politics. While Gray admitted the Weathermen represented only a small dimension of the era's political activism, they posed an immense challenge to law and order. Revolutionary violence was directed "so the system itself be overturned." The Weathermen's bombings of the Capitol and Pentagon were given great importance and "more is still to come." Rather than downplaying their significance, the FBI leadership sought to highlight bombings to discredit dissent and any organized opposition.

Gray simplified and distorted protest goals by claiming radicals favored the bullet over the ballot. Of course, there were other methods to achieve change. To begin with, electoral strategies were only one means. During the 1960s and early 1970s, protest movements often sought to put pressure on leaders, and change popular consciousness, not to elect their own members to office. They organized from below to influence elites to pass civil rights legislation and end the war in Vietnam. Moreover, when the New Left advocated revolution, they almost never laid out a blueprint on how to bring about a transformation of society. Even the Weathermen deliberately did not target civilians during their campaign of political violence. Neither the bullet nor the ballot were the favored methods embraced by the "angry voices" or "articulate minority" in this period. Rather, street protests in the form of either nonviolence or "days of rage" proved central to effect change.

It seems ironic that Gray complained radicals "harass the law enforcement officer" when for decades the FBI harassed thousands of law-abiding people. He expresses contempt when activists challenged the legitimacy of laws and called themselves "political prisoners."

Gray's speech, "The Image of Law Enforcement," singled out "extremist organizations" as "vendors of ideologies alien to our society who place rule by mob above rule by law." What was mob rule? Why call the New Left alien? These characterizations reflected intolerant bias. Gray again used scare tactics when he labeled all critics as enemies if they charged the FBI with undermining rights. Disparaging references to civil libertarians and social justice lawyers illustrated contempt for those who presented a negative image of police. "I refer to the abrasive verbal assaults made against our profession by misguided libertarians who labor under an apparent misapprehension that efficient enforcement of the law is inconsistent with the cause of civil liberties." His dislike of progressive attorneys was evident, especially their "demeaning treatment accorded peace officers. Incessant disparagements—allegations of 'police brutality' shouted as a reflex action, without regard for the facts—have the unavoidable effect of impairing the image of law enforcement officers in the minds of the inexperienced, the easily led and misled, the uninformed and the naïve." The use of multiple insults reflected the organization's authoritarian mentality.

Responding to verbal attacks on police formed a major theme in many of these speeches. Gray derided anti-police speech almost as much as physical assaults carried out in a few instances by radical groups. Since police suffer attack, they may employ excessive tactics to defend themselves. "The law enforcement profession finds itself constantly under attack by extremists. We are called 'pigs.' We are accused of repressing the rights of citizens. Every opportunity is seized to portray our police, our courts, our judicial system as cold, insensitive, unfair and bigoted." His reliance on language to express the FBI point of view was inadequate; consumed with anger, words cannot fully express his feelings. "My command of the English language does not enable me to express my indignation when I hear police officers called 'pigs.'"[11] The division of the world into us and them, good guys and bad guys, and supporters and opponents of the police demanded a strong and expansive FBI to contain violent enemies. As they patrol the streets as well as the political sphere, the image of the police must be above reproach. "It is not enough that law enforcement agencies consistently *be* right. Like Caesar's wife, we must *look* right, as well."[12]

Undermining the Rule of Law

The idea of the rule of law dates to the ancient Greeks and became the basis of liberal constitutionalism. In short, all people and the government should be ruled by the law and obey it. Laws are public and enacted and enforced in a transparent manner.[13] "The rule of law is the DIVIDING LINE separating a government of free people from tyranny on the one hand and from anarchy on the other hand," Gray said. Acting in the role of historian, he asked: "Why then has the rule of law—with only one major challenge during the 1860s—worked so effectively over these two centuries? Because the vast majority of citizens respect the law! And the law deserves our respect." Historians and legal scholars might question this interpretation. The rule of law often is treated as an "ideology" and the FBI itself may not abide by it. As scholar Cameron Stuart writes, "Unfortunately, the modern history of Western democracies has shown that the rule of law was not able to prevent some of the worst behavior of states or individuals within states. It is not surprising that critics of modern Western democracies have taken the rule of law as a key target." Indeed, the rule of law has been used to cover up abuse of power by government. "For Marxists it is a legitimating ideology which disguises the class-based hegemonizing function of law. For feminists, its talk of equality and generality merely serves to continue the 'maleness' of law and the disregard of law for the oppression of women in the private sphere. For critical legal studies movements, the rule of law paints over the fundamental contradictions of modern life, including the tension between the need to be free and the desire to live in community."[14] Gray did not consider such complex ideas, concerned only with maintaining the status quo, which was under stress. He concluded: "Today, unfortunately, we see extremists—a small percentage of our population, to be sure—including some members of the legal profession actively seeking to disrupt and harass our judicial process. . . . They revile the peace officer and claim the right to harass and impede him in the legitimate exercise of his duties."[15]

The Church Committee concluded in 1976, after conducting 21 public hearings and about 800 interviews, that the FBI's adherence to the law of rule never was firm. As the agency built dossiers, ignoring civil liberties and legal considerations became institutional practice. The Church Committee wrote: "Legal issues were often overlooked by many of the intelligence officers who directed these operations. . . . Even when agency officials recognized certain programs or techniques to be illegal, they sometimes advocated their implementation or permitted them to continue nonetheless."[16] The FBI's attitude toward the rule of law can be evaluated by its response to the New Left; specifically, the New Left's growing challenge to the legitimacy of the legal system. As early as 1970, the bureau distributed two internal monographs on the subject—"The Struggle Against Lawlessness" (56 pages) and "Extremists Attack the Courts" (8 pages). Both recently have been declassified. While the former document referred primarily to violent crime, it noted "social unrest, racial tensions, attacks on constituted authority, mass disrespect for the law, and lack of positive and effective support for police by much of the public" contributed to crime escalation.[17] The monograph ended with a discussion on the "steadily increasing incidence of civil disorder." In the FBI's view, the problem of "student and racial unrest" expressed itself in "riots, violent demonstrations, civil disobedience, and the like" producing major challenges for police.

> Using the Vietnam War and the so-called black liberation movement as instruments to generate conflict, new left and black extremists, through their insurrectional activities, have contributed to the development of a lawless atmosphere in our society. This atmosphere is characterized by a growing contempt for established authority and increased criminal behavior marked by violence.[18]

The FBI refused to acknowledge that police brutality and repression provided a central grievance of protestors. City police misconduct had sparked many of the urban race riots. FBI repression of the New Left and the black power movement contributed to the rise of revolutionary factions within these groups which endorsed violence, such as the Weather Underground and the Black Liberation Army.[19] The mind-set of the FBI refused to take seriously the reasons behind the formation of social movements and the legitimate grievances of the "insurrectionists." As guardians of law and order, the police decried challenges to established authority including peaceful civil disobedience. Ironically, the FBI worked outside the rule of law in order to defend the rule of law against attack. As a result, it situated the rule of law in a suppression framework.

In the second monograph, the FBI asserted it must actively fight the New Left and "black militants," who posed a "definite threat to the continued peace and order of the Nation." Although the radicals' so-called "attack" on the courts was peaceful, the challenge to legal authorities in any form must be contained by the government. For the FBI, the Chicago Conspiracy trial of 1969 became the leading example of dangerous protests against legal authority. The defendants—Tom Hayden, Abbie Hoffman, David Dellinger, Bobby Seale, Jerry Rubin, Rennie Davis, John Froines, and Lee Weiner—were arrested at the time of the 1968 Democratic Party convention and charged with conspiracy to encourage riots in the streets of Chicago. Their trial lasted five months and the defendants, represented by progressive attorneys William Kunstler, Leonard Weinglass, Arthur Kinoy, and others, viewed the case as a "political trial." The FBI in turn viewed the trial as an example of lawlessness. The monograph described the behavior of the defendants as a "concerted assault on the judicial process."

> From the beginning it was apparent that the defendants and their defense attorneys were conspiring to bring the protest of the streets and the campuses into the court. Cries of anguish from the defendants, scuffles, melees, infantile demeanor, and crude retorts, all condoned by defense counsel, melded into a concerted assault on the judicial process. . . .
>
> While it was the contention of the defense that their antics represented a symbolic expression of free speech and an assertion of the rights of the accused, the truth of the matter was admitted by Abbie Hoffman, another defendant in the trial, after he was sentenced. Hoffman stated, "We cannot respect an authority that we consider illegitimate."[20]

From the FBI's perspective, street demonstrations in support of the defendants in Chicago, led by Students for a Democratic Society and the Black Panthers, were not legitimate First Amendment activity but "designed to frustrate justice." A special note about Kunstler was included in the report. "Since the late 1950s, [he] has been attracted to the defense of those who oppose the capitalist system or who have chosen to resort to violence to change it." All of the defendants were under FBI surveillance at the time of the trial.[21]

A second criminal court case underscored the contemporary contempt for judicial authority. Again, the methods of the defense attorneys and their clients questioned the integrity of the legal proceeding. In the "Panther 21" trial in New York City in 1970, the lawlessness originated with the police, who arrested nearly two dozen members of the Black Panther Party on false criminal charges to disrupt their political activity and deplete their resources. In New York City, the police had kept black militants under heavy surveillance.[22] During the trial, activists used the court to publicize social justice issues employing a new style of "cause lawyering." The FBI in turn reacted with profound shock and anger. Put simply, the bureau never had experienced this kind of resistance to their counterintelligence tactics. The behavior of the defendants in Chicago and New York undermined the effectiveness of political policing. The monograph stated: "From the opening day, it was evident that the same tactics used in Chicago would be deployed in New York. The general demeanor of the defendants and their supporters in the courtroom forced the trial judge to clear the court and declare a recess on several occasions." The Panthers engaged in verbal rebellion and physical confrontation.

> Though the judge directed the defendants to be quiet, he was greeted with their shouted replies of, "We are already in jail," and "There will be blood all over this courtroom." In the days that followed, the court was witness to such scenes as five separate fights between Panther defendants and officers and hurled invectiveness, such as "Fascist pigs," "Power to the people," "This is nothing but an electric circus," "You should have white robes and a hood," and "Yeah, and a cap with KKK on it."

The resistance spread to courtroom spectators. The FBI reported: "One spectator, seized by court officers on orders from the bench after making a clenched fist salute, was asked why he made the salute in court. He stated, 'I don't recognize this court as representing the people; therefore, I have no respect for this court and I will say what I feel like saying.'"[23]

The FBI feared defiance of the courts might become widespread. In addition to these two cases, they referred to other examples by New Left and black activists (in Buffalo and Los Angeles). They noted street protests against court authority organized by the New Mobilization Committee and the National Lawyers Guild in the cities of Los Angeles, San Francisco, New Haven, Washington, Atlanta, Chicago, New York City, Seattle, and Detroit. The FBI studied the rhetoric of radicals objecting to their use of the term "political prisoners." They quoted a writer in the August-September 1969 issue of *Liberation* magazine, who wrote: "We need to attack the legal system of the United States—courts, grand juries, legislative committees, the ideology itself—

just as we attacked its fraternal institutions, the University, and the Selective Service System." In the monograph, the FBI also quoted a speaker at the 1970 convention of the Student Mobilization Committee to End the War in Vietnam who expressed contempt for the legal system and favored using court trials to highlight government misconduct. The anti-war speaker had said: "It is the job of movement activists to use a political trial as an opportunity to demonstrate to the masses of Americans that civil liberties are being threatened, as a means of defeating any attempts by the ruling powers to deny us those rights." [24]

According to the New Left, courts were not impartial bodies but demonstrated an interest in maintaining racial oppression, the war in Vietnam, inequality, and other abuses in American society. Recent scholarly literature points to patterned police misconduct in court proceedings, including perjury ("testilying") and coercion of witnesses. In several known cases, the FBI withheld exculpatory evidence that might have exonerated defendants. The exculpatory evidence usually consisted of secret surveillance records or memos withheld during the discovery phase of a case. For many years the bureau also spied on activist lawyer groups, including the National Lawyers Guild and the American Civil Liberties Union, which demonstrated manipulation of the legal process.[25]

The rule of law certainly did not apply to the FBI practice of warrantless, illegal break-ins. As official William C. Sullivan admitted in a 1966 memo, "We do not obtain authorization for 'black bag' jobs from outside the Bureau. Such a technique involves trespass and is clearly illegal; therefore, it would be impossible to obtain legal sanction for it. Despite this, 'black bag' jobs have been used because they represent an invaluable technique in combating subversive activities of a clandestine nature aimed at undermining and destroying our nation."[26] While the bureau refused to call itself a "secret police," their efforts in security matters almost always were clandestine. Until the mid-1970s, their refusal to let anyone from outside the bureau inspect their records—even in closed investigations—reflected a secret police mentality, as did their routine destruction or purging of spy records.[27] In some respects, the bureaucracy acted like a military organization by demanding total compliance and obedience from its employees.

On June 22, 1972, Gray prepared to give a speech in Connecticut before the New London County Bar Association, but for an unknown reason cancelled the engagement. The Watergate break-in occurred just five days earlier. Perhaps Gray needed to be in Washington. We still can analyze this important text. First, Gray again discussed his relationship to Nixon, expressing devotion but repeating his independence. "I am not a political animal. I am not a political manipulator. I am not a political crony of President Nixon in any sense of the word. I do respect, admire, and have a deep affection for the President. It has been my privilege to help some of his programs and to work in his administration in managerial and administrative assignments. I believe the President respects my ability to carry out an assignment." He then addressed critics/enemies in a dismissive manner. "I recognize the FBI has critics—even enemies. . . . Some of the criticism of the FBI comes from those who do not even know that they know nothing; who, without regard for the law, and without regard to all the other demands on the FBI, would remake that organization in whatever image they desire to attain their particular objective, be it social, political or criminal." The difference between an FBI critic and an enemy seemed blurred. As I suggested in chapter 2, the FBI investigated critics who wrote articles and books that depicted the bureau in unfavorable ways.

Gray continued falsely to assert the "nonpolitical" nature of the bureau. "The FBI should never be an instrument of social policy or social change. It must remain purely an investigative agency whose function is solely to develop and report the facts fairly, promptly, and impartially." While this description might apply to criminal detective work, the G-man's extralegal persecution of dissidents placed it in a different category. "Other agencies and other officials have the responsibility for making policy or deciding which prosecution is warranted. The FBI provides the information—the raw material—without recommendation, with objectivity, and without partisan flavor."[28] Such boldly misleading assertions denied their political policing functions.

Political policing embraced deception, not objectivity. There was an obvious "partisan flavor" as they made policy and secretly decided on their own who to persecute through covert operations.

The difference between persecution and prosecution is fundamental. The former consists of systematic mistreatment without public accountability, while the latter is done according to stated rules and procedures under the rule of law. Those who suffer persecution rarely can openly defend themselves. Is it fair to conclude that the FBI for decades engaged in lawless persecution based on political disagreements?

In another speech, Gray took aim at Ramsey Clark, the former Attorney General under President Lyndon B. Johnson. Clark recently charged police engaged in a program "to control blacks and other minorities instead of protecting them against the crime that often wrecks their neighborhoods." Gray became livid at these remarks, especially Clark's view that, "If we seek to use the police simply to make people keep their places . . . then we will know violence, and we should." Again, Gray tells the audience about his frustrated emotional response. "Reactions swell so fast within me that I have difficulty deciding which to speak of first." This trope served his scare politics. After regaining his composure, he suggested "we should discuss this subject from a professional standpoint, and not in political terms." Of course, it is a cliché to separate politics from "professional" work. Gray also praised police for the recent decline of crime, according to official statistics. The so-called "ghetto dweller" should view crime reduction as beneficial. Gray then delved into a deeper issue. "Yet what the critics are really saying is that law enforcement is somehow anti-social. Ignoring the fact that crime impacts most heavily against the disadvantaged, and ignoring the alarming rise in crime for the past dozen years, they interpret society's efforts to combat crime as being repressive." He attacked an article in the *New Yorker* that echoed the view of Ramsey Clark—crime control programs were efforts to "keep Negroes in their place." Gray voiced "outrage" rejecting "these monstrous accusations. . . . To equate law enforcement with repression is one of the most dangerous threats to a free society." Once more he cannot tolerate critics associating them with "monstrous allegations" and "dangerous threats." These critics did not speak for the "disadvantaged." He summarized their arguments by expressing little tolerance for opposing views. "Their inference is that crime is simply an expression of discontent, and they attempt to legitimize this expression by discrediting our efforts to curb it. The disadvantaged communities do not need friends of this stripe."[29]

Besides Ramsey Clark, Gray attacked Harvard law professor Alan M. Dershowitz. Dershowitz had criticized the indiscriminate arrest of antiwar protestors during the 1971 May Day activities in Washington, D.C., Dershowitz viewed the street protests as legal, protected behavior. Gray defended the police action calling the event a violent disorder. "I do not know whether Professor Dershowitz was in Washington during the May Day riots. But no one observing the protest activities on that day could possibly call them peaceful—unless the burning and over-turning of automobiles, the physical obstruction of motorists, and countless other acts of arson and vandalism may be called peaceful." The difference of opinion between Dershowitz and Gray was based on the fact that police did not arrest particular individuals guilty of vandalism but arrested a whole group in a sweep. Gray admitted: "In the vast majority of cases, convictions were not possible only because there was insufficient evidence." But the director's harsh words for the law professor implied he supported violence. "The generalization made by Professor Dershowitz does not but urge Americans to ignore the difference between peaceful dissent and mob violence."[30]

The Pig Question

Gray engaged what might be called the Pig Question. He derided contempt for police and believed the majority of Americans agreed with his point of view. "Society resents—and rightfully so—the contemptuous language which refers to peace officers as 'pigs.'" The term had been in circulation for about five years. Its first use probably dated to May 1967, when it appeared in the

Black Panther Party newspaper as part of a call for community control. Panther leader Huey Newton said,

> This defining of the police as pigs will hopefully make some of them think, and oppose what the racists in the police departments are unjustly doing. It will spread to millions and millions of people who know that the cops are "pigs" and will hopefully generate some political movement for real community control of the police. The police departments are acting like the old German Gestapo who the world called "swine," which is the same as "pig."[31]

The term connoted stench, filth, laziness, meanness, and ugliness. Pigs acted as agents of repression. Panther leader David Hilliard offered a similar history of the term.

> We invented the term "pigs" in reference to the cops in order to rhetorically reduce the police force to its lowest common denominator. Although "pigs" was a harsh and contemptuous term, we felt that anybody who so flagrantly ignored the civil liberties of black people deserved such a scurrilous description, especially, Huey insisted, one devoid of profanity.[32]

The term soon spread along race and gender lines. Chicago street protestors adopted it during the 1968 Democratic Convention. At Lincoln Park on Aug. 25, 1968, as police tried to evict them from their encampment, protestors chanted "Pig, Pig, Fascist Pigs" and "Pigs Eat Shit." Yippie leader Jerry Rubin recounted in *Do It!* (1970) of his arrest during the Chicago protests. "They took me to pig headquarters. A small room, the public office of Amerika's political police, the Red Squad." Panther leader Eldridge Cleaver wrote in 1970: "What kind of ceremony are we going to stage to celebrate our triumph over the pigs? It won't be another Fourth of July! At least on a Kindergarten level, it may be a bad idea to stage the Inauguration of Pigasus or explain to the little hip tots by saying, 'Once upon a time, a class of exploiters and oppressors ruled our country and the people called them pigs. They called them pigs because . . .'" Hippies and the anti-war movement widely adopted the term "pigs" and it appeared in many of the nation's counterculture newspapers.[33] During the Stonewall Riot in 1969, a pivotal event in gay and lesbian history, the crowd yelled "Police Brutality! Pigs" as police made arrests. The Brown Berets, a Chicano group with as many as 60 chapters, also began using the term in 1969. They referred to police as "white pigs."[34]

Some protestors began to use the more provocative expression "off the pigs" during the murder trial of Newton in 1968. Protestors believed police should be prosecuted, not Newton, for the murder of African Americans. Demonstrators sang, "No more pigs in our community/ Off the pig/ It's time to pick up the gun." According to this view, black Americans should patrol their own neighborhoods as a form of community control. However, Panther leader Bobby Seale offered a more militant interpretation in *Seize This Time* (1970). In his view, "Off the pigs" meant "Kill the slavemaster."[35] Still, he was writing in metaphorical terms. Even the FBI recognized the rhetoric against the white power structure rarely was acted upon. Hoover reported to Nixon in a May 26, 1971, meeting that police slayings "were not indicative of a national conspiracy (although there was a lot of talk by Black Panthers and other militant groups to kill police, they didn't plot out individual killings in a conspiratorial fashion)."[36]

The term pigs even made it into an official COINTELPRO propaganda effort in early 1970. In New Orleans, the FBI mailed a bogus letter to the editor of *Challenge* newspaper purportedly from a member of the Progressive Labor Party (PLP), a small socialist group. The FBI letter concluded: "I'm making sure my name doesn't get on any pig records, just yet anyway."[37]

What was Gray's best defense of the so-called peace officer? Police were noble because they risked their lives to protect and save the lives of others. He provided statistics on officer fatalities. From 1962 to 1971, an estimated 722 officers were "murdered" in the line of duty. Reference to police fatalities provided the basest reason to justify almost any conduct by law enforcement. No one would deny, as Gray said, "Peace officers are human beings serving in a tough and demanding profession." But did they really protect all the people or did they enforce the will of a repressive government? "A profession which reduces crime, protects the community and scrupulously respects the rights of the individual can hardly be an instrument of repression."[38] Many of his contemporaries disagreed: Police sacrificed rights to maintain order; the lower classes were prosecuted more than the upper classes; and the National Security Division tirelessly tried to contain many forms of dissent. In thousands of cases, the FBI acted secretly as protectors of privilege to suppress freedom.

In key respects, radicals had begun to influence the thinking of the FBI. Gray's speeches became a response to the popularity of the new social movements. The director felt compelled to engage (and reject) the ideas advanced by these movements. He said in a speech, "Freedom under Law":

> We are told that American society is "sick" and that law is used to repress freedom. This is demogoguery, pure and simple. It is a slander and a lie.
>
> But still, the questions persist: What are these United States today, and where are we going? How do we as American citizens evaluate *ourselves*? Do we *believe* in our form of government? Does government care about people? Is our society out of control? Are the law officers of the nation the tools of an oppressive ruling establishment?
>
> Well, what are the answers? I want to tell you what *mine* are.[39]

His response, consisting of nine pages of text, included attacks on historian Henry Steele Commager and Kunstler. Both Commager and Kunstler supported protest movements and criticized repression in society. Gray alternately claimed he respected free speech for all Americans, yet those who advocated radical change did not deserve such rights. The FBI and city police were at war with protest movements. "The peace officer must combat those in our society who have repeatedly demonstrated monumental contempt for the rights to which each citizen is entitled. He battles daily against the small band of its own citizens who have declared war on America." He bitterly called radicals "bombers, burners, and looters"—a reference not only to the New Left or the Black Panthers but also urban minority residents who rioted during the "long hot summers" of the late 1960s. "'Off the pigs' is the exhortation used by today's revolutionaries to inflame their followers to kill an officer." The followers of radical leaders were "easily misled, emotionally unstable, misfits of society." By contrast, "responsible citizens" owed a "great debt to my predecessor as leader of the FBI, America's unforgettable G-man, the late J. Edgar Hoover."[40]

Gray acknowledged the FBI's credibility and legitimacy was questioned on many college campuses. But, critics of the bureau were mistaken to evoke an Orwellian Big Brother. "I know there have been fears and allegations on the college campus and elsewhere that the FBI is a 'Big Brother,' hovering about in Orwellian style looking over the shoulders of citizens, checking on their every move, maintaining secret dossiers and undermining academic freedom. These allegations simply are not true." Another misleading statement followed: "I have found no evidence at all that the FBI has gone out and investigated beyond its jurisdictional perimeters or taken the law into its own hands to move in a dictatorial manner across our landscape."[41]

The new social movements influenced the FBI on the issue of dress style. In several speeches, Gray noted the organization's tolerance of more casual attire for agents but stated in no uncertain terms this was not a retreat from "discipline." He said, "Occasionally I have heard that the new Acting Director is determined to convert the FBI into the communal life style of dress—that badges are 'out' and love beads 'in'—and that discipline is one of the old archaic concepts that has been relegated to the archives." It cannot be so since the FBI continued to operate like a military organization. "After 23 weeks I do not observe the men and women of the FBI going 'mod' with the medallions, the beads, the frayed blue jeans, and the sandals, even though it is true that the traditional FBI standards of attire have been somewhat modified. Colored shirts, hair worn a bit longer, and mustaches are not going to wipe out the fierce pride that exists within the hearts and minds of the men and women of the FBI."[42]

After about seven months on the job, and on the occasion of his 25th public speech, Gray referred to his own frequent speaking engagements. "From time to time I hear that the Acting Director of the FBI is making far too many speeches. . . . My point of view is that the FBI belongs to all the people of the United States, serves all the people of the United States, and that all the people of the United States are entitled to hear about the FBI—if they want to."[43] After his 36th speech, he uncharacteristically answered questions from the media and the topics touched on several subjects outside the usual purview of his talks. Asked about the unfolding scandal of Watergate, the director got defensive. A reporter asked: "Do you feel the FBI should really have a role in this Watergate investigation?" He answered in an aggressive manner as if the FBI was implicated in the scandal. "Absolutely . . . your question presupposes that all public officials are guilty of something but what that something is no one yet really, you know, has the guts to right come out and accuse us of being guilty of this something." He defended Nixon as if the attack against the president was an attack on the FBI. Asked if incidents like Watergate have occurred in previous elections, Gray believed it was likely. "It has been sort of like a developing situation in our country over the years where political parties have undertaken these kinds of operations."[44] The chief spymaster had made an unusual reference to surveillance in American politics.

The Director and the Terrorist Threat

Gray's tenure as director came to a close on April 17, 1973. He resigned at Nixon's urging over a scandal involving file destruction. Several days after the Watergate break-in, Gray destroyed two files from the safe of Howard E. Hunt at the behest of the White House. While Gray insisted these documents did not involve Watergate, the revelation of their destruction before a Senate committee made his leadership of the FBI untenable. What was in these files? They had been described by White House aides as "political dynamite" that "should not see the light of day" allegedly referencing President John F. Kennedy. [45] William Ruckelhaus, administrator of the Environmental Protection Agency, was chosen temporarily to succeed Gray. He served less than three months. As soon as Clarence M. Kelley, a former FBI agent and chief of police in St. Louis, became director he also embarked on a public speaking tour. He gave fewer speeches than Gray—about 15 during 1973 and 1974.

When we compare Gray and Kelley's speeches, it is evident that both directors presented new material in each engagement. They rarely recycled the text. Notably, both directors almost never discussed the domestic Red Menace. The communist issue did not engage FBI ideology as détente with the Soviet Union became a major priority under Nixon. Moreover, Kelley rarely referred to Hoover and his legacy. Whereas Gray offered lengthy praise, Kelley was silent because Hoover's tenure as director had begun to generate controversy as details of his spying programs slowly reached public consciousness. Kelley also made shifts in rhetoric. He did not refer to police as "peace officers" and rarely used the term "repression" to summarize the view of FBI critics. Kelley mentioned by name the new social movements more often than Gray with frequent references to the Weathermen, the Black Panthers, and the New Left. In a major change, Kelley talked about the threat posed by "urban guerillas" and "terrorists." The beginning of a discourse about terrorism proved historically important since the bureau in later years fully developed a terrorism framework to justify most domestic security investigations. Terrorists were considered even more dangerous than communists because they were associated with violence.

Even though he served as director, Kelley did not have the autonomy to speak freely. In his speeches, he had to abide by a series of guidelines developed by officials from the Correspondence and Crime Research Section. First, Kelley was instructed to give speeches based on a prepared text and to avoid "question-and-answer type radio and television appearances which generally seek to exploit the guest being interviewed regarding controversial matters currently of major public interest." Open communication with the public and the media continued to be tightly controlled.[46] Second, Kelley's speeches should have "no political tinge." He should not speak to any groups that were "overtly political" or even "may in some other way have political connotations." The framing of "political" was remarkable for its narrow conception. The FBI leadership did not believe, for example, that speaking to a gathering of police chiefs qualified as a political setting. Moreover, the speeches should be used as "forums of dignity which will properly project the standing of the Bureau." He should talk only where the context for reception excluded conflict. "This means that extreme care must be exercised in choosing which engagements the Director should accept; and, if any doubt exists as to the advisability of acceptance, the invitation should be declined." It would be damaging if the director faced hecklers or boos from the audience or if protestors assembled outside on the street. Public criticism should be circumvented. "The Director would not want to appear in any situation where controversy surrounds either his appearance or the group which is the sponsor." Such "controversy" might advance public knowledge about the FBI's secret spying.

In order to present a public image free of politics, which served to obfuscate a political policing role, Kelley also avoided speaking to sympathetic far right-wing groups. "He should be very careful about accepting invitations from groups espousing an extremist viewpoint, even though the group is highly patriotic and bears a good reputation." So extremists can be patriotic and have a "good reputation" but only if positioned on the Right. The overriding ideological objective in choosing sites for speeches was to avoid "criticism that the Director has a narrow viewpoint." On the topic of the speeches themselves, FBI officials suggested Kelley not stray too far in his remarks and the subject "should be within the realm of his profession." Kelley did not object to these internal controls. In the declassified FBI file, he acknowledged reading the guidelines and handwrote a note: "I agree to all of above and have nothing to add."[47]

One of his first speeches, titled "Receptiveness to Change," took place before the International Association of Chiefs of Police. The setting was safe since he was speaking to friends. The director had more than 30 years of law enforcement experience. In order to meet the challenge of change, Kelley advocated professional training for police to keep up with the times. The stakes were high to respond effectively to maintain law and order.

Kelley posed three pertinent questions, which reflected the bureau's anti-democratic view of itself.

> How does one combine in a single organization, especially a law enforcement agency, the ability to deliver services effectively and the ability to change constantly?
>
> How does one combine those characteristics in a police organization which for a variety of reasons tends to work in defense of the status quo?
>
> Further, how does one accomplish this in an organization which, to a degree, will always be authoritarian and secretive?

He did not explain why the FBI had to be authoritarian and secretive or why it must defend the status quo. These underlying assumptions about organizational practices and motives are consistent with descriptions of a secret police.

Kelley, like Gray, lamented the recent rise of anti-police community sentiment. This sentiment helped create the "urban guerrilla," who engaged in violent attacks on police.

> There are elements in the community today which do not like us. They gloat over our mistakes. They clap their hands in glee when we find ourselves in situations of embarrassment. A few—the extremists—injure, maim and kill our officers.

He strongly derided domestic "acts of terrorism." He grouped together speech expression with physical violence. Those who "kill our personnel" and those who "hurl epithets" both were viewed as terrorists. He belittled radical speech as "chatter" and viewed it as abusive. Speech becomes subversive when radicals "encourage others to disobey the law."

> Officers are today, as never before, targets of terrorist groups which deliberately seek to ambush patrol cars, to bomb precinct stations, to kill our personnel. They chatter a constant stream of abuse against law enforcement. They encourage others to disobey the law and hurl epithets against the men in blue.

Who are these terrorists? What kind of mentality of hatred do they espouse? What are the tactics of the urban guerrilla?

In order to promote professional training, the FBI Academy developed a course to address terrorism. "Ten or fifteen years ago urban guerrillas and violence-prone extremists were peripheral in law enforcement concern," Kelley said. "This is no longer true. Riots, demonstrations, mass rallies, the general unrest of recent years suddenly deposited this new born baby, so to speak, on our doorstep." He proudly noted that almost 1,300 agents already attended the Anti-Sniper and Survival course at Quantico. [48]

Speaking before a group of journalists, Kelley argued that the effectiveness of police work depended on the cooperation of the public. Press portrayals of police proved critical in building popular support for the FBI.

> When an FBI Agent or a policeman knocks upon a citizen's door seeking information relating to a crime in your community, how will the lawman be received?
>
> Will the citizen slam the door in the lawman's face?
>
> Will the citizen merely be wary and suspicious?
>
> Or will the citizen cooperate fully, realizing the vital responsibility the lawman has to try to keep the community a safe place in which to live? Realizing, too, the lawman may forfeit his life in the effort?
>
> The articles and editorials you publish are a contributing factor.[49]

We can extend Kelley's argument in a critical respect. The FBI wanted the media to construct a positive police image to help in the recruitment of informers. When ordinary people served as moles and stool pigeons, they passively accepted the narrative of crime and subversion offered to them by the authorities. The media should not undermine that narrative with critical reporting.

Kelley attempted to humanize the bureau to improve its reception. "We are an organization of human beings, and human beings are notoriously imperfect. We will make mistakes, though we try our utmost to avoid them." He promised an "open stance" toward reporters in contrast to the past, but stopped short of criticizing Hoover. "Now I am aware that in the past the FBI has had something less than a wide open press policy. I intend no criticism of that policy in my remarks today." He again spread disinformation by denying disruption of First Amendment political activity through the use of agents provocateurs. Such provocateurs stood outside the rule of law, so Kelley concealed their history of unethical and illegal conduct. He devoted several paragraphs to perpetuate the cover-up.

> Occasionally, a salvo of criticism directed at the FBI is utterly groundless, yet the initial barrage lights up the skies so spectacularly the public may be indelibly impressed by the display.

> A case in point is the allegation that the FBI uses agents provocateurs as a clandestine investigative expedient . . .

> Permit me to state emphatically that under no circumstance does the FBI use agents provocateurs.

> Do we use informants? Certainly. We would be remiss as an investigative agency if we shunned them. But we keep check on them. We do everything within our power to assure that they don't develop into agents provocateurs. The services of informants are terminated if they display a tendency toward over-zealousness . . .

> I hope that clears up the myth of FBI agents provocateurs.[50]

As I already have noted, covert operatives were directed to act in nefarious ways before the Justice Department developed guidelines for their use. Informers committed crimes. They tried to get subjects to break the law. Informers advocated violence and even planned acts of violence to discredit subjects of investigation.[51]

Kelley hoped to remake the FBI's image by deemphasizing its clandestine nature. "All too frequently," he told the Missouri Bar Association, "I find citizens—and this includes some in your profession—may have an incorrect image of the

FBI. The FBI has been viewed strictly as a 'cloak and dagger' organization." He referred to a distorted image generated by popular culture. "Maybe this impression comes from reading spy books or thrill novels." He conceded: "Certainly, we have investigations which must be conducted clandestinely. . . . Yet, on the other hand, if you examine the FBI very closely you will find that we are not an esoteric, strange, mysterious, far-away organization." The adjectives "mysterious" and "far away" were appropriate since government oversight of the FBI did not exist at this time. Very few people inside or outside government were allowed to examine the FBI up close, that is, inspect its spy files. Spy books may underestimate the level of counter-intelligence conducted under the color of the law. "A primary aim of my leadership of the FBI is to encourage our citizens, wherever they live, to know more about our agency—what it is, how it operates, how it can help them." [52] Yet, the bureau's culture of secrecy never crumbled under Gray or Kelley. Kelley assumed a constitutional approach. "Along these lines the FBI Agent is also not, as some people may feel, upset or angry about constitutional rules which govern his behavior as an investigator." He pushed the point much too hard. It was patently false to make the claim: "We do not go on exploratory or fishing expeditions for information. . . . We do not pursue an oppressive-type investigatory path which leads to the violation of the rights of the individual." Rather than functioning as a secret police intent on political containment, he again emphasized professionalism. "Our profession is like your profession—or any other profession." [53]

Although COINTELPRO ended in 1971, spying continued against a broad range of domestic dissidents. In 1973, the FBI conducted 21,414 security investigations of Americans. [54] In a speech titled, "We Serve Freedom," Kelley directly rebutted the political policing charge becoming popular at the time.

> We are accused—falsely—for example of conducting "political investigations," maintaining political dossiers on prominent government officials, "snooping" and invading the privacy of Americans—exceeding our lawful authority . . .

> Let me emphasize again the FBI is not, as some critics claim, usurping, arrogating or assuming an investigative authority which is illegal.

These claims were almost all false. Later, Kelley offered "frank" words about social control to prevent the development of revolutionary sentiment.

> Let's be frank.

> There are individuals and groups in this nation that are hostile to our democratic form of Government.

> They seek in every possible way to discredit, undermine and disrupt the orderly processes of the law . . .

> Our duty under law is to start an investigation when we receive information that individuals or groups are engaged in activity which, if uninterrupted, could result in an act injurious to the national security.

> Does this make the FBI a Gestapo or a national police?[55]

In contrast to the Gestapo, the bureau was an "open investigatory agency." He again spread misinformation: "We do not compile political dossiers."[56]

In 1972, the FBI organized the first national conference on police-community relations. The social control function was explicit: Improving community relations helped to fight the appeal of radical grassroots politics and aided in gathering intelligence on subversives to solve the "disorder" problem. The origin of what later was labeled "community policing" occurred as a reaction to social and political conflict.

> The object of an effective police-community relations program, as I see it, is not to convince the public we lawmen are knights in shining armor. The object is to solve problems—very real problems confronting both the police agency and the community it serves.

I refer to the problems that gave rise to disdain for legally constituted authority, disenchantment with the so-called 'establishment' on the part of our youth, and a decline in respect for law and order, evolving out of the 1960s. I refer also to the problems fostered by these attitudes.

We in law enforcement have found ourselves dealing with large, angry groups whose grievances often have been expressed in disorder and violence.[57]

Thus, the politics of community policing relations were not neutral. Police used community outreach programs to burnish their image, restore legitimacy, and reduce popular contempt for "legally constituted authority." Ultimately, political pacification became a goal to deal with "large, angry groups," which embraced "disorder and violence."

On March 29, 1974, Kelley finally referenced COINTELPRO prompted by increased media attention to FBI crimes during the Hoover era. His words were measured. Kelley defended FBI activity without much critical analysis.

Perhaps you have seen the recent mention in the press about the FBI and its policies on internal security—and by internal security we mean our efforts to protect you and other Americans from the foreign spy, the saboteur, the urban guerrilla, the terrorist. The media has recently carried stories utilizing the term "cointelpro"—which is an FBI term relating to certain aspects of internal security.[58]

Kelly tried to reframe the issue to emphasize terrorism. COINTELPRO began in 1956 to combat the U.S. Communist Party, which never engaged in political violence, and expanded to spy on other peaceful political activity. Was Martin Luther King, Jr. a terrorist? His approximately17,000-page Headquarters file did not document any instance of urban guerrilla activity or other violent actions. Yet, the FBI bugged his phone and hotel rooms, tried to break up his marriage, and anonymously urged him to commit suicide. [59] The efforts against King were only one example where political policing had nothing to do with the "foreign spy, the saboteur, the urban guerrilla, the terrorist." Elsewhere, Kelley reiterated that acts of political violence justified the FBI response under COINTELPRO. He referred to the "crisis" of the 1960s and early 1970s when "violent revolution" posed a serious threat. Privileging the terrorism threat constituted a major historical distortion.

> When we talk about internal security, the FBI's position—and my position personally—is that we must never allow any subversive group of terrorists or individuals advocating violence to bring this great nation to its knees. . . . No terrorist group, or organization threatening violence, should ever be allowed to subvert our historic principles of free government.

> The government had to protect our society. If the extremist groups, and their mentality of terrorism, were allowed to gain even a temporary ascendancy, great damage might be done to the freedoms which form the lifeblood of our democratic society.

> As a result of this crisis in the 1960s and early 1970s, the FBI instituted a program called "cointelpro" which is an abbreviation which simply means "counterintelligence program." This program was a positive effort to reduce and lessen the extremist danger. It was designed to bring under control and weaken extremist groups, such as the Students for a Democratic Society (SDS), the Weatherman and other revolutionary organizations, and to protect the rights of innocent citizens. The gospel of violent revolution and insurrection had to be halted. If permitted to proliferate, it could seriously jeopardize our constitutional system of government.[60]

Kelley directly aligned himself with these social control efforts, proud the FBI "did not stand idly by and allow our freedoms to be jeopardized. It took positive action." Kelley echoed Gray by mistakenly categorizing most protest as violent, demonstrating a complete lack of faith in the First Amendment and the judgment of the American people. The single-minded focus on terrorism blurred meaningful issues of injustice in American society.

I feel strongly that the FBI's "cointelpro" or counterintelligence program contributed substantially to neutralizing these extremist elements in this period of revolutionary strain and tension in the 1960s and early 1970s.

Today, civil disorder has greatly subsided. As we all know, the fancy on campuses today is streaking, not burning buildings. We no longer have riots which burn up large areas of our cities. Major civil disturbances have not recently occurred.

What I am saying is that we must gather intelligence-type information, for example, about groups and individuals who may outwardly appear innocuous and law-abiding but who are liable to undertake serious acts of violence as a part of an effort to interfere with or destroy our democratic form of government.[61]

COINTELPRO helped to pacify campus politics. Kelley preferred that college students engage in frivolous behavior (streaking or running naked) rather than develop serious political commitments.

How did the FBI mind justify their attack on the First Amendment with their defense of "freedom" and "democracy"? Was any peaceful protest possible in American society? Their ideological framework placed the sinister work of subversives and extremists in most forms of dissent. These sinister forces invaded political groups and took them over. As a result, protest from the bottom up remained suspect. In a speech ironically entitled, "In Pursuit of a Delicate Balance," Kelley tipped the scales toward repression by providing justification for state control of political activity outside the major political parties.

On occasions we hear complaints that the FBI has investigated people who have merely been involved in non-violent, peaceful demonstrations.

Let's examine this point of view a little more closely.

As we all know, there are frequent instances when groups are formed in a community to protest some issue of the day. This is legitimate. This is the citizen's right.

> Experience, however, has taught that all too often violence-prone subversive groups attempt to exploit the activities of these legitimate organizations.
>
> What happens?
>
> The legitimate group is infiltrated, if not completely taken over, by extremists. Adherents of the original and worthy group simply drop out. The extremists, those persons who do not respect the law and refuse to accept restraints, become dominant. Within the group a transition has occurred from a peaceful and lawful posture to one of potential or actual violence.[62]

He raised the issue of individual privacy. He seemed to believe that a "delicate balance" can exist between the preservation of privacy and the agency's imperative to collect intelligence. In practice, most subjects of investigation were demonized as enemies and their privacy was not a matter of consideration. Kelley said that since no commonly accepted definition of privacy existed in American society, the FBI ignored this issue. "Some people say the right of privacy is this; others say it is that." Of course, the Fourth Amendment prohibited "unreasonable searches and seizures" by government. Like Gray, Kelley referred to the depiction of totalitarian government in Orwell's *1984* as a straw man. The FBI does not deny privacy in this dystopian manner.

> I remember reading George Orwell's *1984*, which paints the terror of the dictatorial state. Here Big Brother hovers everywhere and there is absolutely no privacy in either home or office. Every minute of an individual's life, awake or asleep, is monitored by the inevitable scrutiny of the dictator.[63]

At the time of this speech, Congress debated the passage of the Privacy Act of 1974 to reform FBI record systems. Kelley promised the FBI would adhere to new privacy legislation. Yet, he had harsh words for civil libertarians. "Are they correct in their assessment that the individual is helpless before Gargantuan Federal and local law enforcement agencies which, in addition to their numbers, and their specialists, have access to successive generations of electronic technology?" The civil libertarian approach was not as balanced as the FBI's. "We must have a balance that protects both the rights of the individual and the rights of society." Framing a rights discourse only in "security" terms, Kelley was certain that "Lawlessness is an enemy of individual liberties." The director will "contribute to strengthening the security of the Nation and thereby assure the individual liberties of our citizens."

Ironically, Kelley viewed himself in military terms. The military, of course, negated the rights of the individual by objectifying its opponents, assuming the power to freely kill individuals to advance the supremacy of the nation-state. In American history, civil liberties almost always were reduced during wartime. "As Director of the FBI, I have come to think of the FBI in much the same way was Robert E. Lee thought of his army. They can do almost anything." That he chooses the top Confederate army general as his peer, a senior advisor to Jefferson Davis during the Civil War who wanted to preserve slavery at any cost, seemed profoundly regressive. Did slaves, as property, have individual civil rights? The answer to that question is as obvious as the FBI's cynical attempt to deny its political role.

Notes

1. By 1970, police arrested more than 100,000 people for political activity (including rioting and looting). Ted Robert Gurr, "Protest and Rebellion in the 1960s: The United States in World Perspective," in Gurr, ed., *Violence in America: Protest, Rebellion, Reform* vol. 2, (London: Sage Publications, 1989), 105, 121; Maurice Isserman and Michael Kazin, *America Divided: The Civil War of the 1960s* (New York: Oxford University Press, 2000).

2. Jennifer Carlson, "A State of Violence? A Historical Look at Civilization, Criminalization and the Politics of Legitimate and Illegitimate Force in Michigan," in Jeff Shantz, ed., *Law Against Liberty: The Criminalization of Dissent* (Lake Mary, FL: Vandeplas Publishing, 2011), 11-13.

3. L. Patrick Gray III, "Challenges We Face Together," May 25, 1972, 6, 11, Gray FBI file.

4. L. Patrick Gray III, comments to Employees of the Richmond [FBI] Office, Oct. 30, 1972, 2-5, Gray FBI file.

5. L. Patrick Gray III, address before the Thomas Moore Society, Washington, DC, May 17, 1972, 1-3, Gray FBI file.

6. Gray, address before the Thomas Moore Society, 6.

7. William Preston, *Aliens and Dissenters: The Federal Suppression of Radicals, 1903-1933* (Urbana: University of Illinois Press, 1994), 290.

8. Gray, "Challenges We Face Together," 1.

9. Rhodri Jeffreys-Jones, *The FBI: A History* (New Haven: Yale University Press, 2007), 204.

10. L. Patrick Gray III, "Masters of Change," June 16, 1972, 3, 8-12, Gray FBI file.

11. L. Patrick Gray III, "A Nation that Cares," Sept. 7, 1972, 3, 10, Gray FBI file.

12. L. Patrick Gray III, "The Image of Law Enforcement," June 19, 1972, 5-6, 8-9, Gray FBI file.

13. As David K. Shipler recently noted, the rule of law must not exist only on paper. "Every element of the Bill of Rights had its counterpart in the constitution of the communist Soviet Union, where no element of the Bill of Rights existed in practice." In fact, Article 56 of the Soviet constitution established strong privacy provisions. "The private life of the citizen, the secrecy of letters, telephone conversations and telegraph communications are protected by law." Shipler, *The Rights of the People: How Our Search for Safety Invades Our Liberties* (New York: Alfred A. Knopf, 2011), 29. See also the discussion in Allan Hutchinson and Patrick Monahan eds., *The Rule of Law: Ideal or Ideology* (Toronto: Carswell, 1987).

14. Cameron Stuart, "The Rule of Law and the Tinkerbell Effect: Theoretical Considerations, Criticisms, and Justifications for the Rule of Law," *Macquarie Law Journal* 4 (2004): 135.

15. L. Patrick Gray III, "The Rule of Law – Dividing Line Between Freedom and Chaos," Sept. 22, 1972, 4-5, Gray FBI file.

16. U.S. Senate Select Committee on Intelligence [Church Committee], *Intelligence Activities and the Rights of Americans,* vol. 2, 140, 141, 155. See also Loch K. Johnson, *A Season of Inquiry: The Senate Intelligence Investigation* (Chicago: Dorsey Press, 1988); Leroy Ashby and Rod Gramer, *Fighting the Odds: The Life of Senator Frank Church* (Pullman: Washington State University Press, 1994); Kathryn S. Olmsted, *Challenging the Secret Government: The Post-Watergate Investigations of the CIA and the FBI* (Chapel Hill: University of North Carolina Press, 1996).

17. FBI monograph, "The Struggle Against Lawlessness," May 4, 1970, i.

18. Ibid., 56.

19. Akinyele Omowale Umoja, "Repression Breeds Resistance: The Black Liberation Army and the Radical Legacy of the Black Panther Party," in Kathleen Cleaver and George Katsiaficas, eds., *Liberation, Imagination, and the Black Panther Party* (New York: Routledge, 2001), 3-19; Jeremy Varon, *Bringing the War Home: The Weather Underground, the Red Army Faction, and Revolutionary Violence in the Sixties and Seventies* (Berkeley: University of California Press, 2004).

20. FBI monograph, "Extremists Attack the Courts," April 17, 1970, 2-3.

21. Ivan Greenberg, *The Dangers of Dissent: The FBI and Civil Liberties since 1965* (Lanham, MD: Lexington Books, 2010), 274.

22. Danny O. Coulson and Elaine Shannon. *No Heroes: Inside the FBI's Secret Counter-Terror Force* (New York: Pocket Books, 1999), 37-38, 49-50.

23. "Extremists Attack the Courts," 4.

24. Ibid., 1, 5-7.

25. Ann Fagan Ginger and Eugene M. Tobin, eds., *The National Lawyers Guild: From Roosevelt through Reagan* (Philadelphia: Temple University Press, 1988); Percival R. Bailey, "The Case of the National Lawyers Guild, 1939-1958," in Athan G. Theoharis, ed., *Beyond the Hiss Case: The FBI, Congress, and the Cold War* (Philadelphia: Temple University Press, 1982), 133; Samuel Walker, *In Defense of American Liberties: A History of the ACLU* (New York: Oxford University Press, 1990).

26. Athan Theoharis, ed., *From the Secret Files of J. Edgar Hoover* (Chicago: Ivan R. Dee, 1991), 129.

27. Athan G. Theoharis, "Secrecy and Power: Unanticipated Problems in Researching FBI Files," *Political Science Quarterly* 119 (2004): 283; David Garrow, *The FBI and Martin Luther King, Jr: From "Solo" to Memphis* (New York: W.W. Norton, 1981), 231; "Judge Blocks FBI From Destroying 30 Years of Documents in Archives," *Washington Post*, Jan. 11, 1980; Ann Mari Buitrago and Leon Andrew Immerman, *Are You Now or Have You Ever Been in the FBI Files* (New York: Grove Press, 1981), 35-41; Theoharis, "'In-House Cover-up,'" in Theoharis, ed., *Beyond the Hiss Case*, 35-55.

28. L. Patrick Gray III, speech before the New London County Bar Association, June 22, 1972, 11-12, 16, Gray FBI file.

29. L. Patrick Gray III, "Law Enforcement and Social Progress," June 30, 1972, 2, 6, 8, 9-10, Gray FBI file.

30. Ibid., 2, 6, 8, 9-10, Gray FBI file.

31. Bobby Seale, *Seize the Time: The Story of the Black Panther Party and Huey Newton* (1970; Baltimore: Black Classic Press, 1995), 404-405. See also Laura Pulido, *Black, Brown, Yellow and Left: Radical Activism in Los Angeles* (Berkeley: University of California Press, 2006), 149-150; Curtis J. Austin, *Up Against the Wall: Violence in the Making and Unmaking of the Black Panther Party* (Fayetteville: University of Arkansas, 2006).

32. David Hilliard, *Huey: Spirit of a Panther* (New York: Basic Books, 2005), 51.

33. Marty Jezer, *Abbie Hoffman: American Rebel* (New Brunswick: Rutgers University Press, 1993), 154-155; Todd Gitlin, *The Sixties: Years of Hope, Days of Rage* (New York: Bantam, 1993), 334; Allen J. Matusow, *The Unraveling of America: A History of Liberalism in the 1960s* (New York: Torchbooks, 1986), 421; Jerry Rubin *Do It!* (New York: Simon and Schuster, 1970), 9, 182.

34. David Eisenback, *Gay Power: An American Revolution* (New York: Carroll and Graf, 2006), 90-91; Ian F. Haney Lopez, *Racism on Trial: The Chicano Fight for Justice* (Cambridge: Harvard University Press, 2003), 189-191.

35. Seale, *Seize This Time*, 404, 407.

36. White House Memorandum for the President's File, Aug. 23, 1971, Gray FBI file.

37. SAC New York to Director, "COINTELPRO–New Left," Feb. 4, 1970, New Left FBI file.

38. L. Patrick Gray III, "Law Enforcement: Protector of Our Liberties," July 11, 1972, 3, 6, Gray FBI file.

39. Before Gray agreed to give this speech, there was a political discussion about its presentation between White House and FBI officials. According to the White House, "With Ohio being critically vital to our hopes in November [elections], we would hope you will assign this forum some priority in planning your schedule." An FBI official noted, "The Club is dominated by liberals and these are the type of people we should be contacting in an effort to 'convert them.'" L. Patrick Gray III, "Freedom Under Law," Aug. 11, 1972, 3; Patrick E. O'Donnell to L. Patrick Gray, June 13, 1972; Mr. A. Jones to Mr. Bishop, June 16, 1972. Gray FBI file.

40. L. Patrick Gray III, "America is Worth Fighting For," Aug. 23, 1972, 6-8. Gray FBI file.

41. L. Patrick Gray III, "The FBI in a Free Society," Feb. 15, 1973, 4-6, Gray FBI file.

42. L. Patrick Gray III, "A Standard of Excellence," Oct. 13, 1972, 8-9, Gray FBI file.

43. Ibid., 1.

44. Gray, "The FBI in a free society."

45. L. Patrick Gray III with Ed Gray, *In Nixon's Web: A Year in the Crosshairs of Watergate* (New York: Times Books, 2008), 3-4, 7; Richard Gid Powers, *Broken: The Troubled Past and Uncertain Future of the FBI* (New York: Simon and Schuster, 2004), 298-301.

46. Mr. Marshall to G. E. Malmfeldt, "Suggested Policy for Handling of Speech Matters and Related Commitments of the Director," July 7, 1973. Clarence M. Kelley FBI file.

47. Mr. Callahan to R. J. Baker, "Guidelines Regarding Speeches by the Director of the FBI," Aug. 14, 1973, Kelley FBI file.

48. Clarence M. Kelley, "Receptiveness to Change," speech before the International Association of Chiefs of Police, San Antonio, Texas, Sept. 25, 1973, Kelley FBI file.

49. Clarence M. Kelley, "An Alliance for Truth," speech before the National Newspaper Association, Hot Springs, Arkansas, Oct. 11, 1973, Kelley FBI file

50. Ibid.

51. Ward Churchill and Jim Vander Wall, *The COINTELPRO Papers: Documents from the FBI's Secret War Against Dissent in the United States* (Boston: South End Press, 1990); Garrow, "FBI Political Harassment and FBI Historiography," 5, 9; Davis, *Spying on Americans: The FBI's Domestic Counterintelligence Program* (New York: Praeger, 1999), 57, 88,102; Davis, *Assault on the Left : The FBI and the Sixties Antiwar Movement* (Westport: Greenwood Press, 1997), 141; Jerry J. Berman, "FBI Charter Legislation: The Case for Prohibiting Domestic Intelligence Investigations." *University of Detroit Journal of Urban Law* 55 (Summer 1977): 1070.

52. Clarence M. Kelley, "The FBI – An Agency for the People," speech before the Missouri Bar Association, Kansas City, Missouri, Oct. 12, 1973, Kelley FBI file.

53. Ibid.

54. Office of the Inspector General, "The Federal Bureau of Investigation's Compliance with the Attorney General's Investigative Guidelines (Redacted)," September 2005, 5.

55. Clarence M. Kelley, "We Serve Freedom," speech before the Kansas City Press Club, Kansas City, Missouri, Nov. 4, 1973, Kelley FBI file.

56. Ibid.

57. Clarence M. Kelley, speech before the Second National Symposium on Police-Community Relations, FBI Academy, Quantico, Virginia, Nov. 7, 1973, Kelley FBI file.

58. Clarence M. Kelley, "The FBI's Role in Protecting America," speech at the University of Kansas, Lawrence, March 29, 1974, Kelley FBI file.

59. Three top FBI leaders discuss the King incident in their memoirs. William C. Sullivan with Bill Brown, *The Bureau: My Thirty Years in Hoover's FBI* (New York: W.W. Norton, 1979), 142; W. Mark Felt, *The FBI Pyramid From the Inside* (New York: Putnam, 1979), 126-127; Oliver "Buck" Revell and Dwight Williams, *A G-Man's Journal: A Legendary Career Inside the FBI* (New York: Pocket Books, 1998), 453. See also Garrow, *The FBI and Martin Luther King, Jr: From "Solo" to Memphis* (New York: W.W. Norton, 1981); Garrow, *Bearing the Cross: Martin Luther King, Jr., and the Southern Christian Leadership Conference* (New York: HarperCollins, 2004); and Theoharis, ed., *From the Secret Files of J. Edgar Hoover* (Chicago: Ivan R. Dee, 1991), 102-103.

60. Clarence M. Kelley, "In Pursuit of a Delicate Balance," speech at the University of Missouri at Kansas City Law School, Kansas City, Missouri, Nov. 29, 1973. Kelley FBI file.

61. Clarence M. Kelley, "The FBI's Role in Protecting America," speech at the University of Kansas, Lawrence, Kansas, March 29, 1974, Kelley FBI file.

62. Kelley, "In Pursuit of a Delicate Balance."

63. Clarence M. Kelley, "Right of Privacy—Rights of Society—A Delicate Balance," speech before the American Society of Newspaper Editors, Atlanta, Georgia, April 18, 1974, Kelley FBI file.

5

The Deep Throat Faction

Over the course of its history, the FBI developed uneasy relationships with many American presidents. This especially is true after World War II when the FBI sought to expand its autonomy and conduct surveillance without significant outside oversight. Although the FBI director served as a subordinate to the president, and could be replaced, Hoover in particular attempted to use secret intelligence as leverage or intimidation to assert and maintain power. For the FBI, the ascendancy of Richard M. Nixon posed a particular challenge. The former anti-communist crusader and Red-hunter shared many of the same views about security threats as Hoover and was an advocate of unbridled spying on Americans.[1] However, Nixon as president wanted to conduct spying independent of the FBI. His advocacy of the so-called Huston Plan in 1970, which Hoover and most other top FBI leaders successfully opposed, would have created a new and separate surveillance apparatus run directly by the White House. Nixon's subsequent establishment of the "plumbers" spying group in 1971 also alienated the Hoover Old Guard at the bureau, which came to resent Nixon. After Hoover died, power struggles within the FBI and between the bureau and Nixon reached a new level that eventually led to a major constitutional crisis.

Hoover died in his sleep of natural causes on May 2, 1972. Just six weeks later, on June 17, 1972, bungling White House burglars broke into Democratic Party offices at the Watergate Hotel in Washington, DC. These two near simultaneous events unsettled the federal government. In this chapter, I analyze the FBI's critical role in the unraveling of the Nixon administration. Secret surveillance, counterintelligence operations, and media manipulation all played a part in shaping Nixon's decision to become the only president in U.S. history to resign from office. Based on a close reading of newly declassified FBI documents—including W. Mark Felt's 3,500-plus-page official file—we can write a new narrative of these seminal events. From a civil liberties perspective, FBI conduct in the Watergate scandal, as orchestrated by Felt, was unaccountable and constituted a major abuse of power. Nixon committed high crimes, but so did FBI officials.

To begin with, when Felt's role as Deep Throat first became public in 2005 few in the media, with the exception of the *Albany Times Union*, adequately appreciated he did not act alone. At least three other top-level FBI officials or agents worked with him to coordinate leaks to the press. What properly might be called a "coup" inside the government, led by Felt, helped force the president from power. The actions of this FBI "faction" were extraordinary. Instead of targeting political liberals or radicals, they went after the chief executive using information as a weapon.

Felt viewed himself as a patriotic whistleblower acting to preserve the integrity of government. Nixon broke the law during Watergate and so the president should be exposed. Critics see less noble purposes. Felt resented being passed over for the director's job after Hoover's death. He targeted the president because of this snub. In addition, Felt acted as a vigilante because the president continued to run "dirty tricks" intelligence operations bypassing the FBI altogether. The latter point is critical: Felt hoped to preserve the dominant role of the FBI to spy on Americans. Felt called it preserving the bureau's "independence."

Felt worked secretly against the orders of Director L. Patrick Gary III—that is, practicing insubordination—because he viewed Gray as a Nixon crony not worthy of respect. Moreover, Felt and other Hoover loyalists found Gray's leadership style offensive. As one official recalled: "Many of these [early] sessions we were having with Mr. Gray with regard to Watergate were what I would now describe as 'rap sessions' because in the days of Hoover whenever any discussion was had it had to be supported by facts and this was a new approach to me. Therefore, in these 'rap sessions' many names, theories and possibilities came up."[2] Felt held a different vision about how the FBI should be run.

The Felt faction engaged in a high level of deception within the bureau to protect its secret contact with the press. Soon after the Watergate break-in, Gray put Felt in charge of finding sources of FBI leaks to the media. In short, the fox had been put in charge of protecting the chickens. On several occasions, Felt and his collaborators investigated others knowing they had no part in the leaks. For example, in the summer of 1972 an agent working with Felt conducted several dozen interviews of FBI personnel in the hunt for the leaker.[3] In another instance, Felt wrote a bogus memo suggesting that the source of leaks to the *Washington Post* came from outside the bureau.[4] In a different memo dated Sept. 11, 1972, Felt told one of his conspirators to "forcibly remind all agents of the need to be most circumspect in talking about this case with anyone outside the Bureau."[5]

Students of government study its dynamics, including conflicts. It becomes a critical inquiry when the topic engages federal power at the top levels. In this case, the resignation of a president occurred in a context of pitched battle within the executive branch. Furthermore, critical civil liberty issues are raised. Is the power of the FBI so massive in U.S. society that it secretly can help to change a president without any accountability? Were Felt's actions legal? Is Deep Throat part of the long history of unconstitutional behavior by the bureau? Why the political police undid Nixon, a fellow dirty trickster, needs further explication.

A Hoover Loyalist

As assistant and associate FBI director, Felt remained a Hoover loyalist throughout his career. During the late 1960s he headed the Internal Inspection Division empowered to investigate agent misbehavior and irregularity. The final report of the U.S. Senate Church Committee has a jarring discussion about Felt.

> Internal inspection at the FBI has traditionally not encompassed legal or ethical questions at all. According to W. Mark Felt, the Assistant FBI Director in charge of the Inspection Division from 1964 to 1971, his job was to ensure that Bureau programs were being operated efficiently, not constitutionally: "There was no instruction to me," he stated, "nor do I believe there is any instruction in the Inspector's manuals, that inspectors should be on the alert to see that constitutional values are being protected." He could not recall any program which was terminated because it might have been violating someone's civil rights.[6]

Known inside the FBI as the "King of Conduct," he was familiar with COINTELPRO operations and did not use his power to restrain them. In my view, a more appropriate nickname for Felt should be the "King of Unconstitutional Conduct." Felt sanctioned any necessary acts, including cover-ups, to protect the FBI's public reputation.[7]

Felt advanced at the bureau to become the de facto director at the time he leaked classified information to the press. A graduate of George Washington University Law School, Felt was admitted to the bar in the District of Columbia in 1941. He worked in field offices in several cities before returning to Washington in 1962 to help oversee the FBI Academy. He directed the education of new agents in "counter-intelligence tactics." In short, he became an expert in covert action methods, including illegal techniques, and mastered the art of deception. He was skilled at his work, earning a promotion in 1964 to assistant director of the bureau. Felt assumed many of the duties of the long-time No. 2 man at the bureau, Clyde A. Tolson, who was ill.

He expected to be named director after Hoover died. However, to the surprise of many people Nixon passed over Felt and appointed a bureau outsider—L. Patrick Gray III—as Acting Director. Nixon bypassed Felt because he wanted to distance himself from the Hoover loyalists and select a leader who he might be able better to control. Felt, like Hoover, had opposed the Huston Plan in the summer of 1970. While Nixon wanted the authority to conduct wiretaps and break-ins against political targets independent of the FBI, Hoover and Felt were determined to keep domestic spying the exclusive province of the bureau. The fight over the Huston Plan strained relations between the president and the FBI leadership. Felt writes in his memoir: "The record amply demonstrates that President Nixon made Pat Gray the Acting Director of the FBI because he wanted a politician in J. Edgar Hoover's position who would convert the Bureau into an adjunct of the White House machine."[8]

As expected, Felt worked to protect Hoover's reputation after the director's death by helping to destroy his personal files. Felt initially took possession of Hoover's "Personal/Confidential" files totaling about 17,750 pages. He stored them in his office. Hoover had instructed his personal secretary, Helen W. Gandy, to destroy these files after he died with no thought of the need to preserve them for historical purposes. The files were housed in 10 to 12 file cabinets of five drawers, each secured with special locks. The key was kept in a locked cabinet. Felt easily could have read the files, privy to Hoover's secrets. FBI official John P. Mohr, when interviewed by the Senate Committee on Intelligence Activities in 1975, indicated he "had no idea of many files Mr. Felt collected as a result of Hoover's instructions." In addition to these Hoover files, Gandy sent to Felt's office "a number of Bureau monographs together with bound 'interesting case' write-ups." The destroyed files became "confidential trash" and were "scattered over the streets of Southwest Washington." Their loss is a major deficit limiting an understanding of how Hoover used political information. The files contained material on political leaders, including Nixon. Felt shared Hoover's penchant for secrecy. In 1975, Felt admitted to Congress that he witnessed the destruction of Hoover's papers. "There's no serious problems if we lose some papers. I don't see anything wrong and I still don't."[9]

Gray knew of the file destruction and did nothing to stop it despite his assurance to the media that all secret Hoover files would be preserved. We have this account by an FBI inspector:

"[W]hen L. Patrick Gray III, who had been appointed Acting Director, came through on a tour of the Director's office [immediately after Hoover's death], Miss Gandy told him that she was destroying Mr. Hoover's personal correspondence files and that Mr. Gray told her to continue with that destruction."[10]

Felt's power at the FBI rivaled that of the new director. Gray promoted him to associate director just two weeks before the Watergate break-in. Gray frequently traveled out of town to visit local FBI offices and, additionally, ill health, including hospitalization, kept Gray from his duties for part of the fall and early winter of 1972. In his absence, Felt became the de facto director, given authority to run day-to-day operations. He was positioned strategically to initiate a coup against Nixon without Gray's knowledge.

History changed on June 17, 1972, with the arrest of the Watergate burglars. The FBI began an investigation of the break-in, which lasted for about one year. Agents showed up at the crime scene, researched the backgrounds of the burglars, and conducted dozens of interviews. A 12-page memo from Gray, dated July 21, 1972, summarized the progress of the bureau's Watergate investigation. The memo confirmed that within a month of the break-in the FBI leadership recognized the White House had direct ties to the Watergate burglary. Gray established that Nixon's aides, and perhaps the president himself, organized a conspiracy to bug the Democrats' executive conference room and to photocopy their records.[11] The importance of this memo is enormous contradicting Gray's repeated denial of early knowledge of Nixon's ties to the break-in.

On several points the Gray memo is a seminal document. We learn that the FBI interviewed all the Watergate burglars, who used aliases and refused to indicate for whom they worked. But it did not take long before the bureau uncovered their identities with direct ties to the president. "[James Walter] McCord, who appears to be the leader of this group, [text redacted], and at the time of his arrest he was Chief of Security for the Committee to Reelect the President. The remaining subjects are all known to have Cuban backgrounds and [text redacted]." After a police search of the rooms of the burglars in the nearby Howard Johnsons motel, the name of Howard Hunt, Jr., surfaced in two ways. The FBI found a check from Hunt left in one of the rooms. His name and a White House telephone number appeared in the address book of one of the burglars. As Gray noted, for about nine months "Hunt was employed on a consultant basis by the White House staff, working with Mr. James R. Young and Mr. Charles W. Colson." The memo added, "Information was developed that on the recommendation of a member of Mr. Colson's staff, Hunt was terminated as a consultant effective April 1, 1972, and was to be hired immediately thereafter by '1701' (1701 Pennsylvania Ave., N.W., is the address of the Committee to Reelect the President.)"[12]

So there is little doubt that Gray understood that the break-in was tied to Nixon and CREEP. In the five months prior to the break-in, Gray noted that Hunt was in "regular and frequent" contact with G. Gordon Liddy pursuing secret efforts in the area of "political espionage." "Investigation further developed that Hunt, frequently utilizing the alias Ed. J. Hamilton, together with George Gordon Liddy, who frequently used the alias George Leonard or G. Leonard, traveled extensively around the United States contacting former CIA employees for the purposes of setting up a security organization for the Republican Party dealing with 'political espionage.'"[13] Despite his inability to enact the Huston Plan, Nixon still sought to establish a political espionage apparatus. He relied on Liddy, a former FBI agent, employed by the White House staff and CREEP. Liddy's employment with CREEP terminated *after* the break-in when he declined to be interviewed by FBI agents.

The FBI followed the money trail and documented the involvement of several people close to the president. Maurice Stans, Chair of the Finance Committee for CREEP, gave a $25,000 check to Kenneth H. Dahlberg, a regional finance chairman for CREEP. Dahlberg then turned the check over to Liddy. The FBI developed eyewitness evidence that Liddy gave a large sum of money to McCord before his arrest.[14]

Gray's memo indicated that McCord staked out the Watergate complex from his motel room across the street for about six weeks prior to the break-in. McCord's room faced the suite

occupied by the Democratic Party so he could conduct reconnaissance. Alfred Carleton Baldwin III, a former FBI agent, also
stayed in the room and "advised that during a period of this
time he monitored, through the use of electronic equipment set
up by McCord, telephone conversations of Spencer Oliver, a
Democratic Party official. McCord told Baldwin that four exten-
sions of Oliver's telephone . . . were being monitored."[15]

The FBI established a direct link between Liddy, Hunt, and
McCord. All three were in Baldwin's hotel room when "Liddy
took an envelope from his suit jacket and counted out about
$16,000 to $18,000 in $100 bills, which he gave to McCord."
While the break-in occurred shortly after midnight, Baldwin
served as a lookout. As the memo noted, "McCord told Baldwin
to watch and if anything unusual occurred to contact McCord
by walkie-talkie."[16]

Hunt and Liddy were on the scene during the break-in but
were not detained by District of Columbia police. There is a
remarkable paragraph in the declassified record describing the
intimate events of the crime:

> About 2:15 a.m, June 17, 1972, Baldwin noticed lights going on
> in the Watergate Apartments and subsequently police begin-
> ning to arrive. He attempted to utilize the walkie-talkie to alert
> McCord and received a response in a whisper, "We hear you,
> they got us." About this time Baldwin noticed two men leaving
> the alley on the east side of the Watergate and identified them
> as Hunt and Liddy. Hunt came to Room 723 [at Howard John-
> sons] and used the phone to contact an attorney. Hunt told
> Baldwin to telephone Mrs. McCord and advise her that her
> husband had been arrested. He also told Baldwin to pick up
> the electronic gear and deliver it to Mrs. McCord in McCord's
> panel truck which was parked in the basement of the Howard
> Johnson Motel. He further told Baldwin to pack up his own
> belongings and go home. Baldwin delivered the electronic
> equipment together with McCord's wallet which had been left
> in the room to Mrs. McCord at about 4:00 a.m., June 17, 1972.
> She drove him back to his own car and he thereupon drove to
> his home in Connecticut.[17]

Felt Secretly Leaks to the Press

According to journalist Ronald Kessler, FBI agents were "amazed to see material in Woodward and Bernstein's stories lifted almost verbatim from their reports of interviews a few days or weeks earlier."[18] Felt read the daily summaries of the investigation as well as documents about agent interviews. He knew every detail and could use it as he pleased. Recent speculation asserts that White House Counsel John W. Dean also fed Watergate-related information to Felt. However, Dean has not confirmed this role.[19]

During the first week after the break-in Gray castigated all agents working on the case about possible press disclosures. When the leaks continued, Gray interviewed several dozen additional FBI employees. None named Felt. The director seemed to suspect that a rat existed inside the bureau. In 1974, an internal FBI report noted: "Allegations of leaks concerning the Watergate investigation began in the first week of our investigation and continue to the present time. Although there has been much speculation concerning the source of these leaks, hard facts pinning down these sources have not as yet to come to light."[20]

The White House suspected Felt soon after the break-in. In an Oct. 19, 1972, meeting in the Oval Office, J. R. Haldeman informed Nixon that his sources named Felt as the likely source of Bob Woodward and Carl Bernstein's *Washington Post* articles. Haldeman's remarks are captured on one of the many tape recordings Nixon surreptitiously made.

> You can't say anything about this because it will screw up our source and there's a real concern. [Attorney General John] Mitchell is the only one who knows about this and he feels strongly that we better not do anything because . . . if we move on him [Felt], he will go out and unload everything. He knows everything that is to be known in the FBI. He has access to absolutely everything.[21]

Although speculation about Deep Throat's identity had begun to circulate within the executive branch, Nixon decided not to tell the FBI Director. Nixon said, "The danger is telling Gray if Felt is getting ready to blow his stack." Haldeman also informed Dean about Felt's betrayal. Dean, too, did not want to punish Felt in any way. Felt had not committed a crime. Apparently, Nixon shared the same sentiment. "I don't want him [Felt] to go out and say the White House tried to squelch him and all the rest."[22] Nixon worried Felt might write a book or appear on network television.

> I'm going to recommend to Gray—I know you might want to say [inaudible] give Mark Felt another position. Well, that's all I want to hear about. That's how we are going to deal with it. I knew somebody would break on it. It's hard to think what would make him [Felt] do that, but there may be bitterness over there that we didn't put Felt in the top spot. [23]

Nixon searched for additional reasons for Felt's betrayal. He focused on his religion, disparaging both Catholicism and Judaism.

> "Is he Catholic?" Nixon asked.
>   "I don't know," Haldeman responded.
>   "Find out. [inaudible] Catholic [inaudible], believe me."
>   Haldeman countered, "I think he's Jewish."

Nixon becomes alarmed. "Christ! I'm not going to put another Jew in there. Mark Felt is certainly a Jewish name. Well, that would explain it, too."[24]

Gray, deeply loyal to Nixon, aided the White House's obstruction of the FBI investigation into the break-in by allowing Dean to sit in on all FBI interviews of White House personnel. "[H]aving Dean at interviews undoubtedly had the effect of limiting the furnishing of pertinent information to our agents," an FBI report later concluded. Gray also allowed Dean to read FBI reports and communications on Watergate, which aided the White House cover-up. "[A]ccess by Dean to our investigative reports would logically indicate to him what information had been developed which would enable him to work out strategy to cover up the case."[25] FBI officials recognized the White House deliberately thwarted their inquiry.

There can be no question that the actions of former Attorney Generals Mitchell and Kleindienst served to thwart and/or impede the Bureau's investigative effort. The actions of John W. Dean at the White House and Jeb S. Magruder at the Committee to Re-Elect the President were purposely designed to mislead and thwart the Bureau's legitimate line of inquiry. At every stage of the investigation there were contrived covers placed in order to mislead the investigators.[26]

The White House's belief that Felt was acting against their interests may help to explain their obstructionism. Nixon was not going to aid an enemy challenge his hold on power.

Gray soon confronted Felt about his possible role as Deep Throat. Gray told him, "You know, Mark, [Attorney General] Dick Kleindienst told me I ought to get rid of you. He says White House staff members are concerned that you are the FBI source of leaks to Woodward and Bernstein."

Felt reassured Gray. "I haven't leaked anything to anybody."[27] He reiterated the lie in his 1979 memoir and speculated about the motive for his subterfuge, as advanced by the White House.

I was supposed to be jealous of Gray for having received the appointment of Acting Director instead of myself. They felt that my high position in the FBI gave me access to all the Watergate information and that I was releasing it to Woodward and Bernstein in an effort to discredit Gray so that he would be removed and I would have another chance at the job. Then there were those frequent instances when I had been much less cooperative in responding to requests from the White House which I felt improper. I suppose the White House had tagged me as an insubordinate.[28]

It is not known which White House requests Felt considered "improper."

A Conspiracy to Bring Down Nixon

Soon after Felt confirmed his identity as Deep Throat in 2005, a former FBI agent named Paul V. Daly alleged a sensational conspiracy: Felt had at least three accomplices. Daly got his information from a fellow FBI agent named Richard E. Long, who had confided to him almost two decades earlier. Now that Felt had admitted his role, Daly believed it was time to reveal what he knew. Long, an official at the General Investigative Division, was one of the co-conspirators. He also named Charles Bates and Robert G. Kunkel as key players working with Felt. Long, Bates, and Kunkel are all deceased so they could not confirm or deny this account. But my research in government documents suggests that at least these three people formed with Felt a secret faction at the FBI intent on ruining Nixon.

Bates, an assistant director of the Criminal Division, supervised the Watergate break-in investigation at the bureau. He was a top player who controlled how the FBI handled its investigation and the extent that it might implicate Nixon. Bates could decide on interviews of subjects and also frame the questions to be asked. Meanwhile, Kunkel headed the local Washington FBI office.

The Felt faction assumed an oppositional relationship to both the White House and the director. Several months before Nixon resigned in 1974, an FBI report found: "Messrs. Bates, Felt and Kunkel, when queried by the Inspection Staff in June, 1973, about the matter of White House involvement in the cover-up, advised there were a number of discussions with Mr. Gray during the early investigation at which time concern over the lack of complete cooperation at the White House and CRP [Committee to Re-elect the President] was voiced."[29]

In his memoir, Gray also recalled the teamwork of Felt/Bates/Kunkel. Just five days after the break-in, "I held the first of what would be a continuing series of conferences. I needed these conferences in order to keep me up with the [Watergate] investigation, since I had from the outset of my tenure assigned the day-to-day operation of the Bureau to Mark Felt." While the faction met with Gray, they already worked behind his back by secretly leaking to the press. About two weeks after the break-in, Gray said, "I called Mark Felt, Charlie Bates, and Bob Kunkel to my office for a ninety-minute meeting to go over the entire Watergate investigation to date . . . we still had not narrowed down our theories, even though we had made substantial investigative progress." Felt was put in charge. "When it became apparent that the White House was involved, I would turn control of the investigation over to Mark, recusing myself because of my assumed relationship with Nixon and my position as a presidential appointee."[30]

My critical focus on the anti-Nixon forces in no way suggests approval of the Nixon presidency. Recounting these details is critical to suggest the routes and roots of power. Who knew who and who told who—these relationships are important since the power struggle inside the government eventually led to a constitutional crisis. The secret role of the Felt faction is as big a story as the Watergate break-in and cover-up itself.

Agent Daly, who headed the Albany, NY, FBI office during the early 1980s, provided the important context for learning of Deep Throat's identity. The *Albany Times Union* reported that Long "shared the story of Deep Throat during a meeting in 1978 in Washington, D.C., where they were discussing the disclosure of documents and potential testimony in the pending prosecution of Felt, Gray and Edward S. Miller, who was an assistant director with the FBI's intelligence division." The three officials were on trial for authorizing illegal break-ins against the Weather Underground. Daly worked the case for the FBI helping to prepare documents for the trials. Long told Daly "there might be a problem should Felt opt to testify at his trial. Long then spelled out how he, Bates, Kunkel and others had funneled information to Felt that was then leaked to the press.[31] How many "others"?[32]

In terms of operational details, the Felt faction "met regularly in their Washington, D.C., offices to discuss what information they would reveal to fuel media interest."[33] Their meeting place at FBI Headquarters suggested confidence of their power, unafraid of being exposed. No secret garage meetings, which only were reserved for journalists. Other small details also suggested a conspiracy. For example, Bob Woodward indicated he had communicated with Felt by moving flower pots each morning on his outdoor balcony to acknowledge receiving messages. Apparently, Felt assigned a subordinate to coordinate the surveillance of Woodward's residence. Moreover, who delivered the secret messages to Woodward in his morning newspaper? Again, it seemed that several people worked with Felt on practical matters.

Daly believed Felt and his accomplices had good intentions. "These were men determined to protect the integrity of the FBI as an institution and to protect the integrity of a criminal investigation," he said. "I don't agree with what they did, but I believe they had a noble purpose."[34] Woodward recounted in *All the President's Men* that Deep Throat objected to the "switch-blade mentality" at the White House—the use of dirty tricks against opponents.[35] The irony of this explanation is outstanding. After all, the switch-blade mentality framed COINTELPRO and so many other actions against dissidents which Felt helped supervise. Felt was a master of the knife, cutting up or sabotaging social movements based on political disagreements. Moreover, Felt never discussed the role of Bates/Kunkel/Long in either of his memoirs, *A G-Man's Life* (2006) or *The FBI Pyramid from the Inside* (1979). He chose secrecy and a cover-up with little respect for historical truth and understanding.

The Faction's Formation

Felt/Bates/Kunkel/Long worked in concert sharing the same goals so this sense they constituted a political grouping—a "faction." There do not appear to be any other factions that formed in opposition to Felt's grouping. They tried to keep their work secret and appeared to have evaded detection. Felt led this covert faction and dominated its behavior, deciding not to delegate the role of leaker to one of these subordinates. As a result, he played the key role in the dissemination of information to journalists. He also made the critical decision *not* to disseminate information about Nixon's crimes to members of Congress or prosecutors in the Justice Department. The Watergate crisis might have unfolded very differently.

How early did the Felt faction form? Felt was engaged from the beginning. He had leaked to Woodward for the first story published on the break-in. It is unclear when Bates and Kunkel agreed to collaborate with Felt, but both agents were involved in the break-in investigation from its inception. In an early meeting between Gray and the members of the faction the topic of leaks was raised—ironically, leaks by the White House, not the FBI. Bates noted: "SAC Kunkel broached the theory that this [break-in] was in furtherance of the White House efforts to locate and identify 'leaks.' It was admitted this was a theory. Mr. Gray said we should, of course, consider this but not let it influence our complete investigation. I assured him the investigation was going full speed and I would keep him briefed on any developments."

Bates also wrote about the initial meeting Gray called to clamp down on leaks. Bates adopted a disingenuous, anti-leak position in official communications. "I met with Mr. Gray, SAC Kunkel, and 27 WFO [Washington field office] Agents. Mr. Gray pointed out the seriousness of this leak to the news media concerning our investigation. He said he would not put up with this, that there was no excuse for it, and he wanted it to be stopped. He said there was no place in the FBI for loose-lipped Agents. Mr. Gray was very forceful about this, and rightly so."[36] Gray also recalled this meeting. "I was in no mood for niceties." He recalled telling the group:

> I will not put up with this. There is no excuse for it, and I want it stopped right now. What we need in the FBI are dedicated professionals, not a bunch of little old ladies in tennis shoes. There is no place in the FBI for flip-jaw special agents, and if I catch one in the act of leaking to the press or anywhere else, that agent will be brought before me and dismissed immediately. Now go out there, do your jobs, and keep your mouths zipped.[37]

So the Felt faction acted against the specific orders of the director. And, they kept their work secret in official bureau communications. The faction's goal of ousting Nixon required a thorough investigation of the break-in, which they reiterated to Gray. Gray initially thought the CIA might be responsible for the break-in. If not the CIA, then it was part of some type of "political operation." Bates reported on their meeting:

> Mr. Gray said that after his detailed review of all the information in this matter he was convinced that it [break-in] was a CIA or a political operation or both. Both Mr. Felt and I pointed out it was extremely important that the FBI continue its aggressive, thorough investigation until we determine the motive, reasons, and identity of all persons concerned. We pointed out that Mr. Gray may possibly be called to testify at some later date before a congressional committee and we could not afford to have the FBI accused of not pursuing this matter to the end. Mr. Gray agreed completely. As a matter of fact he indicated this position to Mr. [John] Dean on the telephone. [38]

The faction cared only about preserving the FBI's independence and would undermine the director to get their way. Bates wrote: "Mr. Felt and I both pointed out that the FBI's reputation was at stake as well as Mr. Gray's position; that we did not feel we should hold back under any circumstances unless the reasons therefore were publicly expressed." Although Gray wanted Felt and Bates to know he was not a patsy for the White House, the faction remained unconvinced. "Mr. Gray made it plain that he would not hold back the FBI in this investigation at anyone's request, including the President of the U.S., and if he were ordered to do so he would resign."[39] Felt could not be persuaded that Gray would ever turn against Nixon.

The Felt faction, by controlling the entire FBI investigation into the leaks, abused their power. When Gray told Bates to "personally grill the men under oath" during his interviews of agents, one wonders if Bates also was under oath during this charade. In official memos, Felt and Bates diverted attention away from their role. Felt's mendacity was evident when he told Bates he was investigating an "article which appeared in the *Washington Post* this morning [which] appears to have been taken from the FD-302 of our interview with former SA Baldwin. You advise that you are making an analysis of this matter which analysis should be incorporated in your memorandum replying to me." Felt also contacted Bates to spread lies in his official capacity. "I personally contacted SAC Kunkel to point out that it appeared the *Washington Post* or at least a reporter had access to the Baldwin FD-302. I told him he should forcibly remind all agents of the need to be most circumspect in talking about this case with anyone outside the Bureau."[40]

In February 1973, Gary ordered an investigation into a *Post* story alleging White House officials involved in Watergate "regularly reviewed information from national security wiretaps." Felt again spread the order to others under false pretenses. In a memo to Edward S. Miller, head of the Domestic Intelligence Division, Felt indicated his need to find out if the story was accurate and the identity of the *Post*'s source. "The article, which was written by Bob Woodward and Carl Bernstein, states that E. Howard Hunt, Jr., and G. Gordon Liddy regularly reviewed information from national security wiretaps while they worked at the White House during 1971 and 1972. Mr. Gray instructed that a detailed analysis be prepared of the article." Later that month, Gray urged Felt to expedite their investigation, which prompted Felt to offer an evaluation of Woodward and Bernstein. The level of Felt's deception continued to be outstanding referring to "fiction and half truths." He wrote: "As you know, Woodward and Bernstein have written numerous articles about Watergate. While their stories have contained much fiction and half truths, they have frequently set forth information which they attribute to Federal investigators, Department of Justice sources, and FBI sources . . . On balance and despite the fiction, there is no question but that they have access to sources either in the FBI or in the Department of Justice." In the same memo, Felt was compelled to pass on an order from the director to investigate the *Post* story. "The Acting Director has instructed that you immediately institute an analysis of this article to determine those portions which could have come from FBI sources and in such instances to set forth the persons having access to that particular bit of information."[41]

On Oct. 10, 1972, Woodward and Bernstein published a blockbuster story, "FBI Finds Nixon Aids [sic] Sabotaged Democrats." The outline of the big picture on Watergate was beginning to emerge based on Felt's coaching. The article reported: "FBI agents have established that the Watergate bugging incident stemmed from a massive campaign of political spying and sabotage conducted on behalf of President Nixon's re-election campaign and directed by officials of the White House and the Committee for the Re-election of the President." Gray expressed outrage at the story and specifically sought out Bates. "I marked up our file copy of the article with ten specific questions and gave it to Charlie Bates," Gray later wrote. Bates submitted a memo on the matter a week later careful to skirt the issue of his involvement. He wrote falsely that the story was based on "conjecture" and some of it was "simply false." In his view, prosecutors may have leaked material from secret grand jury testimony. Bates knew this speculation was patently false, but it served to direct attention away from the FBI.[42]

Felt again concealed his role after major stories in *Time* magazine and the *Washington Post* published one week before the general election claimed Nixon aide Dwight Chapin tried to disrupt the McGovern campaign. Nixon was livid. "I just had a conference call with the attorney general," Felt told Gray. "The president is on the ceiling about this leak, and Kleindienst thinks it's someone after you." Someone wanted to undermine Gray's leadership. Indeed, this assessment was accurate. Felt cared little about Gray's tenure as director. He told Gray matter-of-factly to cease his traveling. "His advice is that you should be here in Washington between now and election time as much as possible."[43]

Bates also pretended not to know the identity of Deep Throat when he authorized a meeting between agent Angelo Lano and Carl Bernstein to extract from Bernstein the identity of Deep Throat. This effort failed. Agent Charles Bolz, an aide to Felt, wrote to Bates:

> [Lano] met with Bernstein in the vicinity of the Treasury Building for the specific purpose of having Bernstein identify his source. Bernstein again attempted to interview SA Lano concerning certain aspects of this case but SA Lano pointed out his only purpose in meeting with Bernstein was he had promised to give a clue to his source of his information. To this all Bern-

stein would say was "I have a very high source," but he would not identify the source or the agency to which he belonged.[44]

The Felt faction could breathe a sigh of relief. Their cover was preserved for now despite an attempt to intimidate Bernstein. "He [Bernstein] was told, as he was on October third last, that the Washington Post ought to stop stealing FBI material and printing it in their paper because someday there will be investigation of the matter and maybe the department will come looking for him."[45]

Gray remained oblivious to Felt's press manipulation. He still considered Felt a loyal deputy and defended him on several occasions against White House accusations of leaking. For example, he praised Felt's handling of a prior investigation into a "ring of homosexuals" at the White House. The FBI, which long investigated gays in the federal government, found no evidence to establish this charge. The inquiry included assessing the sexual orientation of Haldeman and Erlichman. Felt closed the investigation without public embarrassment.[46] Gray also resisted pressure by Nixon to compel Felt to submit to a lie-detector test. Nixon later recalled the conversation.

> "'Pat,' I said. 'I want you to check these leaks.'
> "He said, 'Oh, they couldn't be from the Bureau.'
> "I said, 'Yes they are . . . some are.' And I said, 'We have from very good authority that they're from Felt.'
> "'Oh, they could not be from Felt.'
> "I said, 'Damn it, they may be' and I said, 'You ought to give him a lie-detector test.'"
> "'Oh, we can't do that,' he said. 'But,' he said, 'I vouch for Felt.'"[47]

Gray described this meeting as a 30-minute "tirade" by Nixon against leaks coming from the FBI. Nixon repeatedly named Felt, and cited a lawyer for Time, Inc. as his source, but Gray still refused to accept his view of the source of the leaks.[48]

Despite Gray's reluctance to act against Felt, Nixon still believed the director was squarely on his side. He once remarked, "Oh God, I wish we had, I wish we had more Pat Grays."[49] But the two were not close socially and Nixon compared Gray unfavorably to Hoover. Nixon told Dean about eight months after the break-in: "They constantly say that Gray is a political crony, and a personal crony of the President's. Did you know that I have never seen him socially. . . . Edgar Hoover, on the other hand, I have seen socially at least a hundred times. He and I were very close friends. . . . Hoover was my crony and friend. . . . But as for Pat Gray, Christ, I never saw him."

Dean praised Hoover to the president. "While it might have been, uh, a lot of blue chips to the late Director, I think we would have been a lot better off during this whole Watergate thing if he'd been alive because he knew how to handle the Bureau."

Nixon agreed. "Well, if, if Hoover ever fought—He would have fought, that's the point. He'd have fired a few people or he'd scare them to death. He's got files on everybody, god damn it." Hoover would not have tolerated the bureau "leaking like a sieve . . . and Gray denies it. Just says it's not coming from the Bureau. Just who in the hell is it coming from? How in the hell could it be coming from anybody else?"[50]

It seems unlikely Felt would have leaked to the press against the director's orders if Hoover still held power. But, how would Hoover have dealt with Nixon's crimes? In all likelihood, he would not have acted publicly to expose the president. In Hoover's view, government spying was not a matter for public knowledge. As a result, Nixon's role in the Watergate break-in probably would have been concealed. The president would not have needed to engage in a cover-up and never would have resigned.

Several months later Nixon seemed poised to strike out against Felt. Nixon's antipathy toward Felt, tempered only by fear of his power, increased as the leaks intensified and the crimes of Watergate unfolded. On May 11, 1973, the president and Alexander Haig, his new chief of staff, discussed their approach to Felt.

Haig said, "We've got to be careful as to when we cut his nuts off."

Nixon responded, "He's bad." Nixon wanted to blow Felt's cover and then get him fired.

"Everybody's got to know he's a goddamn traitor and just watch him damn carefully."

Nixon wanted his new FBI director, William Ruckelshaus, to "clean house" and get rid of Felt. "And he [Felt] has to go, of course, because it's now obvious. You see, we had these reports—An interesting thing [is that] I had these reports out. I got them directly, you know, from the—that he [Felt] was leaking it to *Time* magazine, from their attorney. That was, oh, months ago."[51]

Felt is Forced Out

Ruckelshaus, who just had replaced Gray, soon pressured Felt officially to retire. Gray left the director's job on April 27, 1973. Felt filed his retirement papers less than three weeks later. He left with his big secret still intact.

Ironically, Felt's career ended after his admission of leaking internal FBI documents to the *New York Times* on a different subject. Felt exposed illegal FBI wiretapping requested by Secretary of State Henry Kissinger, with Nixon's approval, against 17 people—including five journalists—suspected of obtaining information from members of the National Security Council. Why did Felt assume this role? Again, he allegedly held a noble purpose and took it upon himself to effect change in government by using the press. In his memoir, Felt indicated he long compared himself to the lead protagonist in the television show, "The Lone Ranger." An FBI official described Felt's intention to "protect Mr. Hoover's and the Bureau's image." Felt had learned that "[text redacted] mentioned that Mr. Hoover was going to 'blackmail' the Administration because of illegal wiretaps and Felt said he became upset over this statement and other parts of the story and he began to 'set the record straight.'"[52] His leaks would save Hoover from a confrontation with Nixon.

After resigning, Felt played the role of victim. He denied the leak admission and informed FBI investigators that the director had gotten the story wrong. It was Felt's belief that assistant director William C. Sullivan informed to the *Times*. However, in all likelihood the director and Felt arranged a quid pro quo to avoid embarrassment to the bureau. Ruckelshaus declined to recommend criminal charges contingent on Felt's decision to retire. To protect this secret deal, Ruckelshaus refused to discuss the details of his meeting with Felt other than to reassert that Felt admitted to the leak. An FBI memo offered the following account: "Ruckelshaus advised that at first Felt denied furnishing information to [text redacted] but subsequently admitted it as a service to the FBI. Ruckelshaus indicated he was upset, agitated, and disgusted. . . . According to Ruckelshaus, Felt submitted his letter of retirement on 5/16/73 [the next day] and Ruckelshaus took no further action."[53]

A second memo confirmed an "understanding" between the two leaders. "He [Ruckelshaus] indicated that he had an unspoken understanding with Felt that no further action would be taken in this matter because of Felt's retirement and he did not want to renege on his word."[54]

Felt viewed the inquiry into the *Times* leak with grave concern, fearful his broader role as Deep Throat also might be exposed. Soon after being interviewed by FBI agents about the *Times* leak, Felt wrote a blistering "personal" letter to the new director, Clarence M. Kelley, to clear his name. He referred to charges of "disloyalty" made against him and continued to view himself as a protector of the FBI's image. He denied leaks not only in this case. "My contacts with the press have been limited." He added as an aside that he was not Deep Throat as some speculation asserted. "Incidentally, I am not Deep Throat either." And, he displayed a complete lack of integrity by asserting: "I have been candid and truthful." The letter stands as an important example of disinformation written by a master of the technique.

PERSONAL

Dear Clarence:

To be treated as a prime suspect in a sordid example of crass disloyalty to the FBI is a humiliating and degrading experience. I am disappointed that you do not know me better. In view of the conglomeration of Bureau documents circulating in the media, I quite understand the need for an aggressive inquiry, but remember that all but one, and possibly all, of your suspects are innocent and completely loyal to the Bureau. This makes it very important not to lose sight of the human considerations.

My contacts with the press have been limited. On only one occasion did I ever "leak" information and that was years ago and on instructions from the Bureau. I have never given Bureau documents to unauthorized persons. On the very few times when I did discuss impending news stories with a reporter, it was in an attempt to guide the story along more accurate lines and, hopefully, lines more favorable to the FBI. I have just completed a year of lectures and debates defending the FBI. I have spoken highly of you at all times and will continue to do so.

For me to be suspected of stealing a miscellany of Bureau documents for release to a member of the news media is ridiculous. Incidentally, I am not "Deep Throat" either, as speculated about by a reporter for the "Washingtonian."

I have cooperated to the fullest extent with your inquiry. I have been candid and truthful. I will continue to cooperate no matter how distasteful it is to me. I am anxious to have this matter resolved because I deeply resent having to bear the burden of suspicion of my former friends and associations. Unfortunately, this type of case is often difficult to solve.

Sincerely,

Mark [signed][55]

How did Kelley respond? Two weeks later, the director told Felt he was only one of several people under suspicion. Although no hard evidence suggested Felt had functioned as Deep Throat, the FBI was looking into the matter. He should not "feel that you are being singled out for particular attention without any basis whatsoever for the inquiry."

Dear Mark:

I am responding to your letter of June 20, 1974. I do not think that the interview with you [on June 13, 1974] has any significance other than that it was felt for us to round out this investigation it would be necessary to interview you. I always try to keep in sight human considerations as you mentioned them, but having served so long in the Bureau, I am sure you understand that also we are committed to the conduct of very thorough and probative investigations.

I am sure that some of the recent news articles concerning "Deep Throat" are very disturbing to you, and I hope that your experiences in this do not make you feel that you are being singled out for particular attention without any basis whatsoever for the inquiry. A number of our people are being interviewed and we are only trying to do our job as we see it.

Please give my regards to Audrey and the best of luck to you.

Sincerely,

Clarence [signed][56]

Kelley asked the Inspection Division to conduct a formal investigation into the identity of Deep Throat in conjunction with the investigation into the *Times* leak. The investigation is referenced in two internal communications. According to official J. J. McDermott, "[T]he FBI is conducting investigation to identify 'Deep Throat' to determine if former Acting Associate Director W. Mark Felt was, in fact, 'Deep Throat' and to identify any leaks from the Bureau to newsmen [text redacted]."[57] In the second memo, Assistant Director O. T. Jacobson said: "There are indications that certain Bureau materials relating to the Watergate matters were leaked. This is the subject of a continuing Inspection Division inquiry."[58] What did the FBI eventually find? The inquiry led nowhere. The Blue Wall of Silence did not come down. Those inside the FBI who knew Felt was Deep Throat kept it a secret.[59]

Soon before Felt left the FBI, he and Bates wrote several other officials—Leonard Walters and Charles Nuzman—to cover their tracks. While evaluating Gray's obstructionism, they again concealed their own press contacts. The official paper trail left no hint that Deep Throat was inside the FBI. For example, there was debate about the effect of the *Post* articles. Nuzum, the supervisor in the General Investigative Division, called the role played by Woodward and Bernstein "a myth of monumental proportions." He did not hold the press in high regard. "Those newspaper reporters undoubtedly did more to publicize this case than did the FBI since the FBI does not make press releases detailing advances made in a pending matter. The FBI was well ahead of all matters reported in the press with regard to the Watergate incident . . . "[60] Well, of course, since the Felt faction directed the press coverage. Nuzum also seemed unaware that Felt served as Deep Throat.

Walters, an assistant director of the Inspection Division, ruminated about Watergate, which was rare in FBI memos. He did not believe the FBI investigation of the break-in was a failure. "It is simply a fact of life that thinking that one is being lied to does not provide evidence and if no one involved in a conspiracy will talk truthfully, the only way to obtain a breakthrough in the development of truth is in the method used in this case; i.e., development of an airtight case against the defendants who can be convicted, coupled with the courageous action of the courts in giving maximum sentence to the convicted criminals."[61] From this narrow point of view, the eventual prosecution of all the Watergate burglars showed that law and order was achieved.

Felt and Kunkel also viewed the investigation as an overall success. To say anything else might jeopardize their cover-up. If they said it is a failure, additional internal inquiries might follow. They preferred to close it down as fast as possible. To some extent, the whitewash is typical of the lack of critical thinking at the bureau. But motivations below surface were strongly at play. The Felt insurgents engaged in doublespeak to protect themselves. Walters summarized Kunkel's point of view.

> SAC Kunkel advised that from the inception of this case he felt the FBI and his Agents in particular vigorously pursued all facets of the investigation. It was handled from the beginning

as a special with various techniques being used in WFO, such as special indices on individuals, phone numbers, and other items which would facilitate the necessary checks and investigations to be made. He stated the only lesson in his opinion the FBI could learn from the Watergate investigation would be that under no circumstances should the Bureau have permitted various legal counsel at the White House and CRP to sit in on interviews of certain personnel conducted at both places. He stated he voiced his opposition to this arrangement with Gray and other officials at the Bureau by observing that the individuals interviewed were naturally inhibited by the attorneys present. [62]

Felt's attitude was as equally misleading. According to Walters: "Felt stated that he considered this investigation to be indeed noteworthy in spite of the difficulties encountered. He stated it was a penetrative, very detailed and completely thorough investigative effort which subsequently resulted in a successful trial wherein all seven defendants were found guilty."[63]

In its original formation the faction lasted less than a year, but by then their leaking had played a critical role against Nixon. In September 1972, Kunkel was told he was to be reassigned after the mishandling of a protest demonstration in Washington unconnected to Watergate. But it took another several months before his transfer to St. Louis. At about the same time, Bates asked to be transferred to the San Francisco office accepting a demotion to SAC. He wanted out of the conspiracy, although the official reason given to Gray was a cover. Gray wrote that Bates "had a strong desire to return to the field, he told me, because he hated the paperwork and lack of action at FBI headquarters."[64] Lack of action? Meanwhile, Felt remained in charge of the anti-Nixon conspiracy, working with Long and unnamed others until he was forced to resign.

After Felt Left the FBI

Some officials inside the bureau suspected Felt continued to engage in press leaks after his retirement. On Jan. 19, 1975, an article in the *Washington Post* prompted Felt to defend himself again to Kelley. He admitted speaking to a *Post* reporter but apparently did not offer any new information. "I want you to know that I am not the source of the unfortunate [text redacted] stories appearing yesterday and today in the Washington Post. [Text redacted] did call me and I tried to talk him out of writing the story but we both know that front page by-lines sometimes become more important to reporters than the facts."[65] In this case, Kelley knew that Felt was not the source of the leak and told him that the stories came from the U.S. Senate Watergate Committee. The problem of leaks at this time proved substantial as the Church Committee prepared public hearings on abuse of power by the intelligence community. "This is only one of several recent revelations," Kelley said, "and we are struggling in order that we might keep our position in a less vulnerable state. To be perfectly frank, it is taking a great deal of our time."[66]

Felt embarked on a substantial paid college speaking tour soon after retiring, giving 15 speeches within less than a year. In order to help prepare these talks, Felt requested statistical information from the FBI: The number of name check requests conducted each year, as well as the total number of files maintained at Headquarters. Bureau records were not yet subject to the FOIA, so Felt used his unique access to gain the material. At Rutgers University in Camden, N.J., he revealed the bureau held more than 6 million dossiers. He engaged in revisionist history promoting the idea that he resigned because "there was too much interference from the White House" after the death of Hoover. It was a subtle jab at Nixon. While Felt hid his role in ousting the president, he called Watergate "the worst abuse of the government I've ever heard of." He promoted one reform: enhanced congressional FBI oversight through the establishment of a special congressional watchdog panel. However, unlike a standing committee of Congress, it would not be able to write legislation or hold hearings. The Rutgers students did not greet his appearance with enthusiasm. Only 12 people attended his speech according to an FBI source at the university.[67]

Felt began work on a professional memoir. Once again, he contacted his former colleagues for information. At this time,

FBI records recently had become subject to the FOIA and FBI officials told him to use the Act rather than rely on them. They offered no preferential treatment for the former No. 2 man when he asked for information (not actual records) on White House meetings about the Huston Plan as well as classified correspondence by former official William C. Sullivan. Director Kelley told Felt: "I must advise you that the nature of this information which you seek is such that it only can be released to you pursuant to the provisions of the Freedom of Information Act. I am sure you understand and sympathize with our policy of treating every request on an equal basis by processing such requests in chronological order, according to the date that they are received . . . [also] bearing in mind the volume of requests we have received to date."[68]

A few months later Felt again contacted Kelley and aired resentment toward the critical Church Committee hearings. "If you are replaced—which would certainly be no reflection against you—it will be an excellent time for you to strike out against the Bureau's detractors," he wrote. "The Senate Intelligence Committee report is filled with error and bias." In the style of Hoover, who tolerated little public criticism of the bureau, Felt attacked two recent books. "The 'American Police State' by [David] Wise is merely an amplification of the bias in the Church report. Sanford Ungar's book is replete with error."[69] The King of Conduct refused to acknowledge the existence of FBI crimes.

By the end of 1978, Felt completed a draft of his memoir, *The FBI Pyramid from the Inside*. Although Felt had not signed a prepublication review contract, he voluntarily sent a small part of the manuscript to William H. Webster, who recently assumed the director's job.[70] Chapter 23 raised legal issues since it discussed a Weather Underground criminal case (the "Washington Three") in which the U.S. Department of Justice had issued a gag order. "This is not a request for FBI approval," Felt wrote Webster. "I am merely expressing my willingness to discuss any changes which you may feel desirable."[71] A security officer at the FBI reviewed the chapter and found "five paragraphs to be classifiable up to 'Secret' as they relate to intelligence sources and methods impacting on joint investigation with Central Intelligence Agency (CIA)." While Felt agreed to sanitize the chapter as requested, he and his publisher, G. P. Putman and Sons, refused to comply with the bureau's voluntary request to review other portions of the book.[72]

Ironically, the Carter administration targeted Felt for legal prosecution in 1978 on a matter entirely separate from Deep Throat. As part of an effort to reform the FBI, the Justice Department charged Felt and two other FBI officials—Gray and Edward Miller—for authorizing illegal break-ins. For the first time in American history government leaders faced prison for engaging in political spying. Felt and Miller had approved nine "black bag jobs" against Weather Underground leaders and associates in New York and New Jersey. The government charged Gray because he served as director, even though he had no advance knowledge of the entries. In a strange twist, Nixon took the stand during the two-month trial to defend Felt's authority to spy on radicals. It did not matter that Felt had conspired to drive him from office. Nixon viewed all forms of spying against the Left as legitimate, including illegal techniques. These political views outweighed the sense of betrayal he held toward Deep Throat. Nixon's testimony had little impact. Felt and Gray were found guilty. They escaped prison when the new president, Ronald Reagan, summarily pardoned the former FBI leaders in 1981.[73]

Felt submitted two other manuscripts to the FBI for prepublication review. In 1986, the FBI reviewed *An Unexpected Turn of Events*. In 1990, the FBI looked at a study titled *Thirteen True Stories About the FBI*. The bureau approved both books concluding that "no sensitive information" was revealed.[74] Neither manuscript ever made it into print. By the early 1990s, Felt developed Alzheimer's disease with serious memory problems. He had been working on a rewrite of his memoir, which appeared in 2006 under the title *A G-Man's Life*. A family friend, attorney John O'Connor, helped put the manuscript together and wrote the introduction.

What "Noble" Purpose?

Deep Throat helped change the course of American history. There are several speculative questions to consider. What if Woodward and Bernstein, as well as other reporters, proved unable to unravel the crimes of Watergate? Did the Felt faction have a contingent plan? How far were they willing to go to sabotage the president? In the past, FBI officials shared secret intelligence with congressional committees and individual congressman. Would Felt leak to Congress?

In all likelihood, he would have found a way to expose Nixon. His favored method consisted of contacting the press because it allowed maximum control over the development of the inquisition. Felt guided reporters in a way that would not have been possible with Congress. The coup was conducted *on his terms*. Felt not only was spared public identification as an anti-Nixon patriot. He avoided the ordeal of testifying about the FBI's Watergate investigation. Moreover, Felt's strategy of leaking in slow pieces did not hurt Nixon's prospects in the 1972 elections. Felt preferred that Nixon win a second term and then be removed rather than help liberal Democrat George McGovern obtain a victory. This strategy assured that a Republican would succeed Nixon. Gray, too, protected Nixon's electoral prospects. By the end of July 1972, Gray had enough knowledge of Watergate to connect Nixon to the crime, but decided to keep a lid on the story.

The FBI leadership's antipathy toward Senator McGovern became clear during the Democratic presidential primaries. On several occasions, McGovern had criticized Hoover and FBI spying, which prompted several agents to send private letters of protest to the presidential candidate. On March 5, 1971, Kunkel wrote McGovern: "Your continuing paranoiac crusade of vilification of Mr. Hoover and the FBI has finally brought me to writing this letter." The letter, filled with insults, approached intimidation.

> I would normally ignore such unwarranted and unfounded criticism on the basis that it was an unthinking, emotional out-

burst from one who would eventually get his facts straight . . . I find it incomprehensible that a United States Senator who has aspirations of becoming President of the United States would make criticisms, allegations and charges based not on any documentation. . . . As an avowed "liberal" Senator, you are indicting both Mr. Hoover and the FBI in public without any background knowledge or investigation and yet I seem to recall raging criticism of others who engaged in the same tactics. . . . I can only say that it makes me sick at heart when people like you use your position to degrade it by either perversion of the truth or by lack of interest in developing the truth.[75]

Kunkel's letter further underscored that FBI leaders had a very hard time tolerating public criticism. In their minds, if a liberal like McGovern became president, the security of the nation would be placed at risk.

What "noble" purpose? Felt represented the consummate FBI spymaster skilled at covert dirty tricks deployed against a broad range of peaceful and lawful political activity. He opposed racial justice and movements for equality, deeply committed to the conservative politics of the bureau. Notably, Felt never leaked any negative information to the press about the big crimes of COINTELPRO. For Felt, illegal activity, including break-ins, was legitimate as long as it aided information collection. Yet, in his view only the FBI should conduct them. Nixon's burglars had botched the Watergate job, which risked discrediting an important technique of the intelligence community.

What about Bob Woodward's independence as a reporter? Did Felt or one of his subordinates try to recruit Woodward as an informer? That is, they told Woodward they would supply him with critical information only if he agreed to work for them. Did the FBI infiltrate newspapers in this era? As chapter 2 suggests, the answer is yes. Moreover, the FBI maintained informal "contacts" with friendly reporters with whom they shared information from classified files. In the Woodward case, a top FBI leader took this covert dealing to a new level to pursue his own personal and political agenda.

Why could Woodward be used? Before becoming a reporter, he had been a former Navy officer with special clearance to work in the White House as a courier. In that capacity, he first met Felt near the Oval Office and developed a relationship. The young Woodward came to view the older Felt as a mentor. As a reporter, he used Felt as a source in articles prior to Watergate.

The propriety of the Woodward-Felt relationship requires further comment. Felt as mentor manipulated Woodward. The reporter became a vehicle for larger actors in government. What if Woodward had changed the perspective of the story and asked different questions? Could the *Post* have established that a top FBI leader tried to discredit the president to advance FBI power?[76]

Historian Richard Gid Powers raises other pertinent questions. "How did Felt (and the FBI, for that matter) know the substance—sometimes the very words—of conversations in the Oval Office almost as they were taking place? Were Nixon's tapers themselves being taped? Did Deep Throat know more than he told Woodward, more than anyone has ever learned about the ways of Watergate?"[77] Scholars have yet to document that the FBI routinely bugged the Oval Office or the walls of Congress. But in specific cases it appeared they bugged congressional offices.[78] Have they ever planted informers inside the White House?

Leonard Garment, who succeeded Dean as Nixon's White House counsel, speculated about Felt in his book, *In Search of Deep Throat* (2000). Deep Throat's identity was not yet revealed but Garment made a good argument for Felt. "Mark Felt was the prototypical career FBI man. He was, in this theory, understandably angry [at Nixon] on behalf of not only himself but his agency. He was also believed by some of his colleagues, and therefore by Deep Throat theorists, to be a big leaker to the press. These characteristics were a good fit." But Garment was not certain. "The trouble with Felt's candidacy was that Deep Throat in *All the President's Men* simply did not sound to me like a career FBI man."[79] Garment came to believe that the source was inside the White House. "Deep Throat's unique contribution was to talk with Woodward about Nixon's White House. . . . Deep Throat knew about the clockwork craziness in that place. He knew the sound of Nixon angry; he knew things about the character of various people involved in the cover-up. This type of information was not accessible to a member of the Bureau, even one in a high position."[80] Apparently, this type of information was at Felt's disposal. How he knew the inner workings of the Nixon administration remains a mystery.

Felt wrote about Watergate in his memoirs in a self-serving and misleading manner. He compared himself to the Lone Ranger—a single, heroic individual pursuing justice. "What we needed was a 'Lone Ranger,' who could bypass the administration's handpicked FBI director and Justice Department leadership and derail the White House cover-up." But, as we have noted, he did not act alone. Moreover, he was not an outsider like the Lone Ranger, but a key top leader in the government. What type of "justice" did Felt pursue? In his jaundiced view, he protected the FBI's independence which Nixon's political corruption had threatened.[81] But Felt's vision was just as corrupt as Nixon's. The only difference is that Nixon intruded on the FBI's terrain, which the Hoover old guard fought to the point of total conflict—bringing down the president.

Felt never wrote directly about his role as Deep Throat. When he mentioned Kunkel and Bates investigating the break-in, he neglected the dynamics of their conspiracy. Instead, he offered this obfuscation in his memoir: "Numerous times when Gray was out of the city, John Dean, the White House legal counsel, called me and demanded that I take other steps to silence the leakers. I refused and pointed out to him that some of the leaks could not possibly have come from the Bureau, since they included information to which we were not privy." At one point, he claimed meeting with Woodward only once during the whole Watergate investigation and purportedly refused to confirm Woodward's information about the break-in.[82]

O'Connor offered an explanation for Felt's silence. "When Mark Felt last wrote for publication in the mid-1980s, he still was holding his identity as Deep Throat secret. Since then, his memories of the period have almost entirely faded. As a consequence, he has never revealed three important aspects of his story: why he initiated his high-stakes meetings with Woodward, how he planned and managed these meetings, and how he escaped detection at the FBI."[83] O'Connor suggested a key Felt strategy: to get the media to report that Watergate was only one incident among many dirty tricks organized by the White House, which the Justice Department and the FBI's top leadership, both loyal to Nixon, refused to acknowledge.

O'Connor does not shed much light on the Felt faction other than by noting, "By February 1973, senior FBI Watergate investigators, including Bates, [Charles] Bolz and Washington SAC Kunkel, has been transferred—either because they pressed the case too strongly or were suspected of leaking."[84] Felt survived this purge because he was an "escape artist." There is nothing more on this topic.

My research using the Freedom of Information Act included obtaining not only Felt's FBI file but also the declassified files on Bates and Kunkel. In a lawsuit, I obtained the FBI files on directors Gray and Kelley. More than 16,000 pages of the FBI file on the Watergate break-in already is available to the public. As an activist researcher, I mined these documents looking for all memos authored by the Felt insurgents. There is now enough information to conclude that the Felt faction not only violated the orders of their director, but they abused power to protect their efforts by assuming the official role to investigate themselves. Deep Throat was not a hero but can be interpreted as a major villain in the long history of FBI misconduct.

Notes

1. For example, in early 1960 vice president Nixon sent Hoover as a gift a copy of Russell Amos Kirk's book, *A Program for Conservatives* (1954), and inscribed an inside page: "To J. Edgar Hoover who is such an intelligent advocate of some of the conservative principles set forth in this book. From his friend, Dick Nixon." Mr. DeLoach to M. A. Jones, January 25, 1960, Book Review FBI file.
2. L. M. Walters to Felt, June 6, 1973, Watergate FBI file.
3. C. W. Bates to Mr. Bolz, June 22, 1972, Watergate FBI file.
4. W. M. Felt to Mr. Gebhardt, Feb. 21, 1973. Watergate FBI file.
5. W. M. Felt to Bates, Sept. 11, 1972, Watergate FBI file.

6. The Church Committee reported on the FBI's systematic violation of civil liberties. *Intelligence Activities and the Rights of Americans, Final Report of the Select Committee to Study Governmental Operations,* Vol. 2, 1976, 140, 141, 155; Athan G. Theoharis, ed., *A Culture of Secrecy: The Government Versus the People's Right to Know* (Lawrence: University Press of Kansas, 1998), 22.

7. W. Mark Felt and John O'Connor, *A G-Man's Life: The FBI, Being 'Deep Throat,' and the Struggle for Honor in Washington* (New York: Public Affairs, 2006), xxxv, xxxvii.

8. W. Mark Felt, *The FBI Pyramid From the Inside* (New York: Putnam, 1979), 245; Felt, *A G-Man's Life,* xvii-xviii, 103-105.

9. FBI memo, "Interview of Helen W. Gandy, former Executive Assistant to the Director of the FBI, by SSC Staff Members," June 12, 1975, Mohr FBI file.

10. FBI Inspector Hunter E. Helgeson memo, June 9, 1975, John P. Mohr FBI file.

11. Gray's memo, declassified on March 3, 2009, was stored in a June Mail file -- the most sensitive FBI material outside the bureau's central filing system. J. Edgar Hoover established the special June Mail classification in 1947 to conceal certain secret surveillance operations, frequently illegal, in order to avoid potential "embarrassment" for the bureau. Only top leaders at the bureau had access to June Mail and certainly Felt would have read it. Office of the Director, "James Walter McCord, Jr., and Others, Burglary of the Democratic Party National Headquarters, Washington, D.C., June 17, 1972, Interception of Communications," July 21, 1972, L. Patrick Gray III FBI File.

12. Ibid.

13. Ibid.

14. Ibid.

15. Ibid.

16. Ibid.

17. Ibid.

18. Ronald Kessler, *The FBI: Inside the World's Most Powerful Law Enforcement Agency* (New York: St. Martin's Press, 2003), 199.

19. Philip T. Mellinger, "Deconstructing Deep Throat," *Washingtonian,* Nov. 17, 2011, www.washingtonian.com/articles/capitalcomment/21589.html.

20. FBI Office of Planning and Evaluation, "FBI Watergate Investigation," May, 14, 1974, 47, Watergate FBI file.

21. Nixon Tapes, Conversation Number 370-9, Oct. 19, 1972. See also Felt, *The FBI Pyramid From the Inside,* 225; Richard Reeves,

President Nixon: Alone in the White House (New York: Simon and Schuster, 2001), 532; Richard A. Moss, ed., "Nixon and the FBI: The White House Tapes," National Security Archive, June 3, 2005.

22. Nixon Tapes, Conversation Number 370-9.

23. Ibid.

24. Ibid.

25. "FBI Watergate Investigation," 44.

26. O. T. Jacobson to FBI Director, July 5, 1974, Watergate FBI files.

27. Felt, *A G-Man's Life*, 225-226.

28. Felt, *The FBI Pyramid From the Inside*, 278.

29. Jacobson to FBI Director.

30. L. Patrick Gray III with Ed Gray, *In Nixon's Web: A Year in the Crosshairs of Watergate* (New York: Times Books, 2008), 65, 84.

31. "Account Adds Intrigue to Deep Throat Story," *Albany Times-Union*, June 7, 2005.

32. Tim Weiner in *Enemies* says FBI official Charles Nuzum also was part of the Felt conspiracy. His name rarely surfaces in the thousands of pages of FBI files I reviewed. Weiner, who devotes only a couple of pages to Deep Throat, relies primarily on oral history sources. He mistakingly claims that "Felt and his allies began leaking the secrets of Watergate" only a "few weeks before the November 1972 elections" (p. 315). Weiner, *Enemies: A History of the FBI* (New York: Random House, 2012).

33. "Deep Throat's Tale Revealed," *Albany Times-Union*, June 6, 2005.

34. Murray Waas, "FBI Cleared W. Mark Felt of Watergate Leaks," *Village Voice*, June 10, 2005.

35. Leonard Garment, *In Search of Deep Throat: The Greatest Political Mystery of Our Time* (New York: Basic Books, 2000), 126.

36. C. W. Bates to Mr. Bolz, June 22, 1972, Watergate FBI file.

37. Gray, *In Nixon's Web*, 75.

38. Bates to Bolz.

39. Ibid.

40. W. M. Felt to Bates, Sept 11, 1972. Watergate FBI files. See also "The Deep Throat File," National Security Archive, June 22, 2005.

41. W.M. Felt to Mr. Gebhardt, Feb. 21, 1973, Watergate FBI file.

42. Gray, *In Nixon's Web*, 124-127.

43. Ibid., 132.

44. C. Bolz to Mr. Bates, Oct 12, 1972, Watergate FBI file.

45. Washington Field Office to Acting Director, Oct. 25, 1972, Watergate FBI file.

46. "Watergate and the Two Lives of Mark Felt," *Washington Post*, June 20, 2005.

47. Nixon Tapes, Conversation Number 165-10, May 12, 1973.

48. Gray, *In Nixon's Web*, 151-175.

49. Fred Emery, *Watergate: The Corruption of American Politics and the Fall of Richard Nixon* (New York: Touchstone Books, 1995), 244-248.

50. Nixon Tapes, Conversation Number 865-14, Feb. 28, 1973.

51. Nixon Tapes, Conversation Number 165-10, May 12, 1973.

52. O. T. Jacobson to Mr. Callahan, "Watergate – Alleged Leak to New York Times Re [text redacted] Matter," June 20, 1974, Felt FBI file.

53. Ibid.

54. H. N. Bassett to Mr. Callahan, "Watergate – Alleged Leak to New York Times Re [text redacted] Matter," July 31, 1974, Felt FBI file. See also, "F.B.I. Seeks Sources of Watergate Press Leaks, *New York Times*, September 26, 1974.

55. W. Mark Felt to Clarence M. Kelley, June 20, 1974, Felt FBI file.

56. Clarence M. Kelley to W. Mark Felt, July 3, 1974, Felt FBI file.

57. J. J. McDermott to Mr. Jenkins, "[Text redacted] New York Times," Oct. 10, 1974, Felt FBI file.

58. Jacobson to FBI Director.

59. In 1979, Felt filed a records request under Freedom of Information Act (FOIA) on the Deep Throat investigation. This file totaled 217 pages but only 131 pages were declassified. T. H. Bresson to Mr. Bassett, "Freedom of Information-Privacy Acts (FOIPA) Request of W. Mark Felt Regarding Alleged Leaks of FBI Documents to New York Times," Feb. 2, 1979, Felt FBI file.

60. L.M. Walters to Mr. Felt, May 23, 1973, Watergate FBI file.

61. L. M. Walters to Mr. Felt, June 6, 1973, Watergate FBI file.

62. Ibid.

63. Ibid.

64. Gray, *In Nixon's Web*, 117-119.

65. W. Mark Felt to Clarence M. Kelley, Jan. 20, 1975, Felt FBI file.

66. Ibid, Feb, 4, 1975.

67. W. Mark Felt to Clarence M. Kelley, Dec. 12, 1973, Felt FBI file; W. G. Campbell to Mr. Callahan, "Request for Public Source and Statistical Type Information by Former Acting Associate Director W. Mark Felt," Aug. 15, 1973, Felt FBI file; "Ex-Hoover Aide Says White House Meddled with FBI," *Courier Post*, Oct. 11, 1973; SAC Newark to Director, "W. Mark Felt," Oct. 12, 1973, Felt FBI file.

68. W. Mark Felt to Clarence M. Kelley, March 9, 1976; Clarence M. Kelley to W. Mark Felt, March 19, 1976. Felt FBI file.

69. Sanford J. Ungar, *FBI: An Uncensored Look Behind the Walls* (New York: Atlantic Monthly Press, 1976); W. Mark Felt to Clarence M. Kelley, Dec. 18, 1976, Felt FBI file.

70. Legal Counsel to Director, "W. Mark Felt," March 23, 1979; William M. Baker to W. Mark Felt, March 19, 1986, Felt FBI file.

71. W. Mark Felt to William H. Webster, Feb. 15, 1979, Felt FBI file.

72. D. Ryan to Mr. O'Brien, "W. Mark Felt, Safeguarding of National Security Information and Material," April 4, 1979; Philip B. Heymann to Director, "W. Mark Felt, Former Acting Associate Director, FBI (Safeguarding of National Security Information)," July 27, 1979. Felt FBI file.

73. I discuss this case at length in *The Dangers of Dissent: The FBI and Civil Liberties since 1965* (Lanham: Lexington Books, 2010), 97-105.

74. William M. Baker to W. Mark Felt, March 19, 1986; Robert B. Davenport to W. Mark Felt, June 28, 1990. Felt FBI file.

75. Robert G. Kunkel to Senator George S. McGovern, March 5, 1971, Robert G. Kunkel FBI file.

76. Alicia C. Shepard notes that the reporting of the Watergate scandal, by relying so heavily on the use of anonymous and confidential sources, helped change journalism. Shepard, *Woodward and Bernstein: Life in the Shadow of Watergate* (Hoboken: John Wiley and Sons, 2007), 112-113.

77. Richard Gid Powers, "Secret Agent Man," *Washington Post*, April 23, 2006.

78. Interview with Ronald V. Dellums, KQED-TV, April 24, 1973, www.diva.sfsu.edu/bundles/189474; Ronald V. Dellums and H.L. Halterman, *Lying Down with Lions: A Public Life from the Streets of Oakland to the Halls of Power* (New York: Random house, 2000); Gerald Myer, "The FBI Surveillance of Congressman Vito Marcantonio," *Our Right to Know* (Fall/Winter 1984-85), 16-18.

79. Garment, *In Search of Deep Throat*, 147.

80. Ibid., 1

81. Felt, *A G-Man's Life*, xv, xxvii, 194.

82. Ibid., 199-202.

83. Ibid., 213-214.

84. Ibid., 217, 222-223.

6

Surveillance Society Policing

The last half of the 20th century has seen a significant increase in the use of technology for the discovery of personal information. Examples include video and audio surveillance, heat, light, motion, sound and olfactory sensors, night vision goggles, electronic tagging, biometric access devices, drug testing, DNA analysis, computer monitoring including email and web usage and the use of computer techniques such as expert systems, matching and profiling, data mining, mapping, network analysis and simulation. Control technologies have become available that previously existed only in the dystopic imaginations of science fiction writers.[1]

Gary T. Marx

The sociologist Gary T. Marx, who helped pioneer the study of surveillance in the United States, wrote the above passage for the launch issue of the academic journal *Surveillance and Society* in 2002. Marx, who taught for many years at the Massachusetts Institute of Technology, had brought attention to the topic as early as 1988 in his important book, *Undercover: Police Surveillance in America*.[2] By the end of the 1980s popular and scholarly writers (and a few political leaders) first began to notice that the Information Society, a development of the last several decades, was being transformed into something else: Large entities (government and business) used technology to become "watchers" over the society. They deployed new surveillance systems for their own objectives. For government, surveillance enabled new levels of social control ("security") over disorderly populations. There is an irony that state surveillance continued to advance even though the Cold War had ended and an enemy had yet to be defined overseas. During the "bubble in time" decade of the 1990s, as historian William L. O'Neill calls it, government laid the groundwork to track the communication patterns of the general population as a whole, in addition to the political activity of particular groups and individuals.[3]

President Bill Clinton (1993-1998) signed the Communications Assistance for Law Enforcement Act (CALEA) in 1994, which can be viewed as a key development solidifying the new surveillance society. The president and Congress set in motion what would develop in later years: The wholesale surveillance of the nation's communication systems. CALEA stated it was "a telecommunications carrier's duty to cooperate in the interception of communications for Law Enforcement purposes, and for other purposes." The so-called "other purposes" was a euphemism for intelligence agencies, notably the FBI. It focused on *electronic* surveillance: Telecommunications carriers and manufacturers of their equipment were compelled to modify and design facilities and services to ensure that they had built-in surveillance capabilities. The FBI demanded to be able to simultaneously wiretap almost 60,000 phones at any time or nearly 4 percent of the nation's 160 million phones. This very high level of potential wiretapping raised troubling questions: Why demand that capability since the FBI never before wiretapped phones on such a massive scale? Now, the FBI would be able to listen to *millions* of conversations. Moreover, the FBI subsequently gained approval to apply CALEA standards not only to telephones but also all broadband Internet services.[4] The federal judiciary sanctioned such surveillance by refusing to rule it violated the Fourth Amendment.

Near the end of the 1990s the FBI deployed new Internet spying systems labeled DIRT, Carnivore, Red Hook, and Magic Lantern. They gained access to records of individual emails, navigation online, as wells as files in hard drives. Break-ins of homes and offices became necessary to fight encryption by planting keystroke recorders directly in computers. Police searched the Web looking for radical expression, people, and groups. They treated Web sites like newspapers—public spaces not requiring a warrant to enter—and joined computer chat rooms and bulletin boards not only to read messages but also with active infiltration, posing as fictitious people to engage suspects in conversation. The Web was formless and agents spent their days on broad fishing expeditions casting wide and far. Computer Trojan programs and worms also began remotely to snoop inside individual computer hard drives.

By the year 2000, nearly a dozen scholarly books focused on the decline (or end) of privacy in America. These books included references to "the unwanted gaze," "total surveillance," and "the transparent society."[5] They discussed the new "politics of visibility." The public had begun to comprehend the detrimental effects of surveillance on sane living. Transparency increasingly left the individual no place to hide or rest. Electronic surveillance technology could follow the individual into the home via phone and computer. Huge databases were linked to generate secret portraits of people and their activities to maximize top-down tracking. Did Americans retain the right to control the dissemination of information about their lives? Stealing this right attacked individual autonomy. Sometimes, government stole with malice.

21st-Century Surveillance Systems

In 1998, President Clinton established a new political surveillance standard for domestic large events by designating them National Special Security Events (NSSE). This designation applied to meetings of foreign dignitaries and business officials as well as the national conventions of the major political parties. It sanctioned law enforcement to use heavy-handed tactics against protestors, including pre-event surveillance and mass arrests during demonstrations.[6] The NSSE became a means to

crack down on dissident activity against meetings and conferences of transnational elites from the World Trade Organization
(WTO), Free Trade Areas of the Americas, International Monetary Fund, the World Bank, as well as the G-20 Summit.

Surveillance of the anti-globalization protest movement
soon emerged as a major initiative. In 1999, large demonstrations by labor, environmental, and human rights groups in
Seattle outside the meetings of the WTO, resulting in more than
500 arrests, elevated the movement in both public consciousness
and as a top government surveillance target. The "lessons of
Seattle" from a law enforcement perspective included enhanced
pre-event spying and raids.[7] Although the FBI did not say so
explicitly, it became empowered by American political leaders
to protect the capitalist market economy by cracking down on
critics. As criminologist Jeff Shantz notes, "The criminalization
of dissent has been a common feature of neoliberal governance
in the current period of capitalist globalization."[8] In Seattle, and
elsewhere, FBI intelligence helped uniformed law enforcement
to police demonstrations in increasingly violent ways with tear
gas, pepper spray, rubber bullets, and concussion grenades.[9]

The Seattle protests occurred the year before the Millennium.
The 9/11 attacks occurred less than a year after its arrival. At
the Millennium, government officials worried computers might
crash, unable to cope with numeric change, affecting not only
the individual user but also the nation's critical infrastructure.
Moreover, the FBI believed Biblical-based apocalyptic visions
might grip a segment of the population at home or overseas
leading to political violence. Top officials publicly predicted that
the likelihood of a terrorist attack was about 50 percent. They
did not anticipate war from a sovereign nation. Rather, the FBI's
special "Project Megiddo" report concluded the chief threat
came from American cults and radical right-wing groups. The
FBI used the Millennium to consolidate its power by spreading
a security culture dominated by fear. They conducted a major
internal reorganization establishing several new divisions.

The 9/11 attacks should be placed within the context of the
Millennium. While the leaders of al Qaeda were not Christian,
and cared little about the Second Coming of Christ, it seemed

likely they, too, were caught up in the millennial craze. For example, the following expression about being "Y to K compliant, the Islamic way" appeared on an Islamic educational website.

> Often we are more concerned about how our electronic gadgets and systems will perform come year 2000 but we always forget our own performances. How is our performances on this earth come yaumal kiyamah? Will we pass the test from ALLAH SWT and be declared as "JANNAH" COMPLIANT? Hence, just do not adjust your computer systems only but please also adjust yourself to be Y to K compliant, the Islamic way.[10]

In all likelihood, most Muslims felt Y2K had nothing to do with their religion. Faithful adherents do not celebrate New Years. Another Internet posting criticized such celebrations in Arab nations as expressions of disloyalty.

> What is our relationship as Muslims to the celebration of Y2K? These are celebrations which have nothing to do with Islaam or the Muslims, and the celebrations done in its name by some Muslim countries is prohibited . . . There is no doubt that imitating the disbelievers and attending their religious celebrations or the celebration of their religious festivals such as Y2K in the Muslim countries is nothing but an indication and confirmation of love of the disbelievers.

This posting suggested the Millennium heightened Muslim resentment against interfaith efforts by Jews and Christians. Y2K was associated with evil.

> The Jews and Christians will exert intensive efforts during the occasion of Y2K to propagate their beliefs through the media which will ensure that this gets wide coverage, which will increase the possibility of the penetration of these false beliefs into the hearts of people, especially those with weak souls . . . with the upcoming occasion of Y2K, the evil call for interfaith will reoccur; this phenomenon which aims to mix the truth with falsehood, destroy Islaam and make the Muslims apostate from their religion.[11]

How widespread this sentiment was in the Muslim world is hard to determine. What if its adherents included the followers of bin Laden? From a Western perspective, it seems hard to ignore the timing: The preoperational planning for the destruction of the World Trade Center lasted for months—perhaps even several years—before the Millennium. Moreover, al Qaeda's formation and rise to prominence on a global level occurred as the 20th century ended. Supporters in Afghanistan could date their first counter-insurgency experience to the anti-Soviet war of the late 1980s. "[T]he Afghan war did for militant Islam what the Spanish civil war [1936-1939] did for the Communists," notes journalist Daniel Schorr. "It gave the veterans a spirit de corps [sic], it radicalized them and gave them a sense of further mission, and with the Soviets gone, the freedom fighters' mission now turns westward."[12] Their terrorist acts increased during the 1990s with the bombing of two American embassies in Africa in 1998 and the attack on the battleship U.S.S. *Cole* in Yemen in 2000.[13]

September 11 led to a major expansion of surveillance practices despite the bureau's intelligence failure prior to the attacks. The revelation of an internal memo from early August 2001, "Bin Laden Determined to Attack in the United States," embarrassed the bureau as did other pre-attack indicators: A July 2001 FBI report of potential terrorist interest in aircraft training in Arizona; and the August 2001 arrest and release of plotter Zacarias Moussaoui while he attended a flight school in Minnesota.[14] Many critics believed the bureau had enough prior warning to stop the attacks. However, the Bush administration, promoting an aggressive "wartime" posture, gave the FBI even greater secret spying powers. The popular refrain—"Nothing Will Ever Be the Same"—seemed to give new legitimacy to government efforts to sacrifice rights under the banner of national security. The "war on terror" necessitated a reduction in civil liberties not only for select high profile targets but also for the general domestic population whose email, phone, and other communications were collected and data-mined.

The FBI began to impose gag orders in its dealings with the public sanctioned by the USA Patriot Act. It experienced reduced oversight of its activities by other coordinate branches of government and increased its overseas activities as part of an American-led effort to protect/dominate the world. Preventing terrorism became the official reason to encroach on the rights of a broad spectrum of the population. The "connect the dots" mentality of the American government did not lead to greater transnational understanding, but instead expressed a narrow mindset intent on controlling many forms of protest in society.

Most Americans seemed to support passage of the USA Patriot Act in October 2001, although Congress acted without any public hearings or debate. Within the U.S. Congress, Representative Barney Frank (D-Mass.) was among only a handful of dissenters and noted the Act was "drafted by a handful of people in secret, subject to no committee process . . . immune from amendment." The Senate voted 98 to 1 to pass the Patriot Act. Russell Feingold (D-Wis.) cast the sole no vote. He said, "The new law goes into a lot of areas that have nothing to do with terrorism and a lot to do with the government and the FBI having a list of things they want to do."[15] The FBI was given expanded authority to conduct telephone, Internet, and street surveillance, and to obtain third-party records without warrants through the use of special National Security Letters.

However, the American public expressed resistance to some new post-9/11 surveillance practices. In 2002, the Bush administration cancelled two broad spying programs after public opposition.[16] The TIPS program proposed by the U.S. Justice Department encouraged Americans to spy on one another. TIPS stood for Terrorism Information and Prevention System. The U.S. House Republican leader Bob Barr of Georgia, known as a libertarian, called the program a "snitch system." "A formal program organized, paid for and maintained by our federal government to recruit Americans to spy on fellow Americans smacks of the type of fascist or Communist government we fought so hard to eradicate in other countries in decades past."[17] Eventually, Congress refused to support the program, but it nonetheless was implemented in other forms—often called "suspicious activity reporting" or SAR. Similarly, public opposition to the Pentagon's Total Information Awareness (TIA) program led Bush to cancel it. TIA would use advanced data-mining technology to establish a centralized database on Americans. Undersecretary of Defense Peter Aldridge described its goal to discover "connections between transactions"—surveying phone records, passports, drivers' licenses, credit cards, airline tickets, rental cars, gun purchases, chemical purchases, and criminal records. However, the Bush administration secretly put TIA into practice under other names and jurisdictions in subsequent years.[18]

A growing number of communities also formally condemned the Patriot Act. By 2005, the elected bodies of more than 330 cities, towns, and counties, as well as four states (Maine, Vermont, Alaska, and Hawaii), passed resolutions against the Act. (By 2012, the number of resolutions reached 414). Professional organizations of librarians, journalists, and attorneys also voted to condemn aspects of the legislation that infringed on their autonomy.[19]

Surveillance technology in the post-9/11 period was programmed to conduct "total" forms of monitoring: Very little beyond eye or ear. Of course, this goal was hard to achieve, but the threat it posed to privacy was real. Particular individuals and groups were watched, as occurred in the past, although new intrusive methods increased the effectiveness of such monitoring. Statistics on the number of individual investigations remained a secret. While it may be lower than during the 1950s and 1960s, generalized surveillance now gathered information on tens of millions of people. Their records were sorted and analyzed looking for patterns that the watchers found objectionable. The new term "dataveillance" entered the discourse. As Reg Whitaker notes, "Databases can 'talk' to one another and in doing so, create the capacity for decentralized 'dataveillance,' a surveillance society in which the 'files' exist in no central location, and are perhaps under no central control, but which in their totality may exercise far more intrusive capacity to gaze into the private space of individuals than the Big Brother surveillance state of the past."[20] For example, anytime a city police officer noticed something "suspicious," they could conduct name checks through readily accessible computer databases to determine if an individual should be detained or referred for investigation.

After 9/11, computer data mining became integral to FBI surveillance practices. The database known as Investigative Data Warehouse (IDW) contained millions of entries on Americans, including biometric characteristics, for use by police. President Bush also created the Terrorist Surveillance Program to gather data on hundreds of thousands of emails and telephone conversations within the nation looking for "suspicious" patterns to locate terrorists or political troublemakers. Agents did not read the content of email, but gathered the sender and receiver addresses. Nonetheless, this form of mass surveillance was unrelated to investigations of specific individuals or groups. The FBI also relied on private data mining companies to aid their own intelligence gathering. These efforts led to profiling and discrimination.[21] Moreover, if the IDW system was programmed to sort information along lines of race, ethnicity, class, or any other category (for example, gun owner or subscriber to *Mother Jones* magazine), it could be used to create blacklists. What if the FBI "interrogated the data" by asking the computer for a list of all black males under 30 years who bought the rap music of Brother Ali or Jay-Z? Can the IDW generate a list of all people who bought my prior book, the *Dangers of Dissent*, on Amazon? Did the FBI retain a list of all labor union members in the nation? All people who donated money to Ralph Nader for President in 2000? Government profiling of this nature entered the domain of a centralized police state. At present, the public does not know what questions are being asked and how the information is being used.

Surveillance of the Web sites of political groups also became commonplace. For example, a Los Angeles agent wrote on September 4, 2003: "Surveillance of the Internet found three websites that currently are promoting protests against the upcoming 2004 Republican National Convention (RNC) in New York. At least one of these sites is operated by a group known to have participated in illegal and disruptive demonstrations against political and economic gatherings in the United States." This memo referenced the protest groups Global Exchange, United for Peace and Justice, and the RNC Welcoming Committee.[22]

The intelligence community also systematically monitored social media online (such as Facebook, Twitter, and blogs) without warrants. Again, this mass surveillance can be unrelated to specific investigations. A Department of Homeland Security (DHS) document from 2010 indicated they were "capturing public reaction" to news events involving government anti-terror efforts. DHS seemed to be tracking any opinion critical of the U.S. government.[23] Meanwhile, the FBI began the development of a social networking monitoring system using geospatial mapping tools to identify place in addition to speech.[24]

The hacking tools to accomplish surveillance of electronic communications became part of a five billion dollar retail market developed almost entirely after 9/11. The technologies of surveillance included: "massive intercept" devices to capture tens of thousands of simultaneous phone conversations from cellular networks and programs to retrieve data from individual computers and smart phones. In one innovation, a mobile suitcase-size device was capable of monitoring Web use on nearby public Wi-Fi networks. Bogus cellphone towers also allowed for the interception of phone calls within a three-mile radius. Private companies sold these products to both democratic and repressive regimes. In 2011, representatives from more than 43 nations attended the annual "Wiretappers' Ball" held outside Washington, DC, to showcase the trade in surveillance technology. The *Washington Post* reported that "the overwhelming U.S. government response has been to engage in the event not as a potential regulator but as a customer."[25]

Facial recognition technology emerged as another innovation that threatened privacy. A new "politics of identification" involved how images of our faces were collected and used by the government. The engineering of social control increased the individual's visibility to official power. Police databases were able to store digital mug shots to identify suspects in crowds. The civil liberties group, Electronic Privacy Information Center (EPIC), described the way the computer-based system works.

> The first step for a facial recognition system is to recognize a human face and extract it from the rest of the scene. Next, the system measures nodal points on the face, such as the distance between the eyes, the shape of the cheekbones and other dis-

tinguishable features. These nodal points are then compared to the nodal points computed from a database of pictures in order to find a match. Obviously, such a system is limited based on the angle of the face captured and the lighting conditions present. New technologies are currently in development to create three-dimensional models of a person's face based on a digital photograph in order to create more nodal points for comparison. However, such technology is inherently susceptible to error given that the computer is extrapolating a three-dimensional model from a two-dimensional photograph.[26]

While the FBI from late 1960s through the 1980s assembled small "terrorist photo albums" of people under active investigation,[27] the new databases by contrast hoped to include a photographic image of *all* people living in the nation. How did the government assemble so many mug shots? Congress passed the Real ID Act of 2005 mandating that a computer chip be placed in every driver's license issued after May 2008 containing a digital photograph for facial recognition purposes.[28] The same type of computer chip could be added to all new passports.

The total forms of monitoring included street-level CCTV cameras. An FBI analyst noted that legal warrants were not needed for their use. "An effective law enforcement technique, especially in circumstances where suspects engage in counter-surveillance or where physical surveillance by law enforcement is operationally impractical, is to affix a video camera to a utility pole . . . as long as the video surveillance is of a public area, there is no Fourth Amendment concern."[29] Concealed cameras placed in public places vastly increased during the last decade. No one knows for certain the number of government/police security cameras embedded across the nation. Including private entities, at least 30 million new security cameras have been purchased since 9/11.[30]

The idea of an "eye in the sky" can now be taken literally.[31] While satellites have served as tracking and spying tools since the early 1960s, new ways of seeing included unmanned aerial drones equipped with cameras operating covertly, undetected by the subject of surveillance. It is well known that spy drones have been used in overseas locations flying high above

Afghanistan or China, for example, to record place and movement outdoors. Some spy balloons or blimps flying 15,000 feet above ground can transmit live video. Less well known are new Pentagon efforts to develop spy drones the size of birds and insects that fly close to the ground. These "spy flies," equipped with sensors and micro-cameras, are designed to act like inhabitants of the natural world to blend into the environment.[32] Recently, aerial drones have begun to be deployed by domestic law enforcement. In 2011, the ACLU described the surveillance drone known as "Hummingbirds":

> A tiny drone called the Nano Hummingbird was developed for the Pentagon's Defense Advanced Research Projects Agency (DARPA) by AeroVironment. Intended for stealth surveillance, it can fly up to 11 miles per hour and can hover, fly sideways, backwards and forwards, for about 8 minutes. It has a wingspan of 6.5 inches and weighs only 19 grams—less than a single AA battery.[33]

Whether these miniature drones already have been used inside the U.S. to surveil political protests is a matter of debate.

Of course, the FBI also used human infiltration to watch public places. Operatives posed as private street vendors, building or street repair workers, or the homeless. The bureau also established "listening posts" in commercial establishments both in conjunction with specific investigations and also independently of them.

The changes in intelligence structures led to increased centralization and cooperation. As Political Research Associates, a progressive Web-based research group, notes: "Horizontal and vertical information systems and coordinating entities such as federal task forces, joint terrorism task forces, and intelligence fusion centers link many organizations in a web of data collection sharing and coordinated enforcement efforts. . . . Agencies at all levels of government and the private sector had roles in domestic security activities."[34] Although it was not the only domestic entity that collected intelligence, most information gathered elsewhere found its way to the bureau, which sorted and evaluated it.

The category of "terrorism" continued to be misapplied to peaceful and lawful protest politics on a broad scale. Moreover, the FBI definition of terrorist activity often differed from that of other federal agencies. As researchers at Syracuse University's TRAC noted, "federal agencies can't seem to agree on who is a terrorist and who is not. The failure has potentially serious implications, weakening efforts to use the criminal law to combat terrorism and at the same time undermining civil liberties." In 2008, government prosecutors declined to bring charges against 73 percent of the criminal cases referred to them for terrorism, up from 61 percent in 2005. In other words, the FBI often created weak charges against subjects that did not stand up in court.[35] Nonetheless, these types of cases proved useful for the FBI to generate popular fear and political insecurity. False criminal charges served as a disciplinary mechanism.

FBI investigations can be started based on the low threshold of "advocating violence," including casual inflammatory remarks. While hyperbolic political expression is protected by the First Amendment and rarely resulted in arrest, the FBI used it to justify intelligence-gathering operations. Did demonstrators who chanted "No Justice, No Peace" have the intent to engage in political violence? Protestors at the 2008 Republican Convention used the slogan, "Swarm, Seize, Stay," in their political literature, which the FBI interpreted as evidence of violent intentions.[36] Additionally, the more serious speech category of "true threats" can be misapplied. Heidi Boghosian, president of the National Lawyers Guild, writes:

> "True threats" is a legal standard that provides police with the presumptive justification they need to conduct surveillance, execute search warrants on organizing spaces, and charge individuals with serious offenses such as conspiracy to riot. Police portray activists as either "peaceful" or "violent." Those determined violent are characterized as security threats that trigger aggressive police and prosecutorial response.[37]

The FBI's "terrorism" classification has been questioned even within the U.S. Justice Department. In a recent report, the Office of the Inspector General reviewed FBI surveillance of five domestic political advocacy groups conducted from 2001 through 2006. The groups were:

Thomas Merton Center
People for the Ethical Treatment of Animals (PETA)
Greenpeace USA
The Catholic Worker
Religious Society of Friends (Quakers)

The Justice Department concluded that while the misapplied terrorism classification did not violate any federal law, it "relied upon potential crimes that may not commonly be considered as 'terrorism' (such as trespassing or vandalism) and that alternatively have been classified differently, such as under the classification for crimes on government reservations." (See Textbox 6.1) The consequences of such labeling went beyond "stigma" because "persons who are subjects of domestic terrorism investigations are normally placed on watch lists, and their travels and interactions with law enforcement may be tracked."[38]

Meanwhile, the level of FBI misconduct during terror investigations remained high. The Electronic Frontier Foundation (EFF) obtained through litigation internal FBI documents indicating that as many as 40,000 violations of the law or government regulations occurred during the presidency of George W. Bush (2001-2008). The FBI operated "without meaningful oversight" to protect citizen constitutional rights. For example, the Justice Department reported in 2006 on "significant noncompliance" by the FBI with Attorney General Guidelines. EFF called them "flagrant violations of a variety of legal authorities." This included false statements by FBI agents in written court declarations; improper evidence used to obtain grand jury subpoenas; the improper use of a subject's username and password to access account information; and searching password-protected computer files without a warrant. Indeed, EFF's findings may understate the level of abuse of power because the bureau applied the "inconsistent and arbitrary practice of redacting and withholding documents" to prevent a full study of its behavior.[39]

Textbox 6.1

In September 2010, the Office of Inspector General at the U.S. Department of Justice issued a critical report about FBI surveillance practices ("A Review of the FBI's Investigations of Certain Domestic Advocacy Groups").

The FBI classified many of the investigations we reviewed as pertaining to "acts of domestic terrorism" and, in one case, as a Terrorism Enterprise investigation. These classifications raised questions about whether the FBI has expanded the definition of domestic terrorism to people who engage in mainstream political activity, including nonviolent protest and civil disobedience. As described in this section, the consequences of being identified as the subject of a "terrorism" investigation may include being placed on a terrorism watchlist. In subsequent chapters, we discuss some specific cases in which the FBI's naming of individuals as subjects of terrorism investigations have led to their being placed on terrorism watchlists . . .

In sum, the evidence in our review did not indicate that the FBI targeted any of the groups for investigation on the basis of their First Amendment activities. However, we also concluded that the factual basis for opening some of the investigations of individuals affiliated with the groups was factually weak. Moreover, in several cases there was little indication of any possible federal crimes as opposed to state crimes. In some cases, we also found that the FBI executed the duration of investigations involving advocacy groups or their members without adequate basis, and in a few instances the FBI improperly retained information about the groups in its files. In some cases, the FBI classified some investigations relating to nonviolent civil disobedience under its "Acts of Terrorism" classification.

Since 9/11, the level of suspicion in society amplified to very high levels. Increased police surveillance in civic life heightened public perception of risk, which "can produce effects such as increased anxiety, avoidance of public conveyances, avoidance of crowds, and increased suspicion of others."[40] Elites manufactured what Torin Monahan calls a top-down "culture of insecurity" that increasingly enlisted the "individual as the first line of defense in securing the homeland."[41] In this effort, both police and the general public were instructed to report "suspicious activity." It matters greatly who did the reporting and how they defined such behavior. There were set criteria for police authorities at the local, state, and federal level. But police do not always follow them. There has been a lowering of the standard of when people can be detained and questioned. Meanwhile, the general public participated in suspicious activity reporting to police without specified standards. They were urged to join "watch" programs. Employees in specific occupations (emergency responders, truck drivers, real estate agents, doormen, fisherman, store clerks, and utility workers) were told to remain alert to report anything "out of place" or if a person "just does not seem to belong" in a particular context.[42] The result was both police reporting without reasonable suspicion and uninformed popular reporting which may be based on race or ethnic difference or cultural misunderstanding.

What activity is a precursor to terrorism? The police programs included such behavior as "using binoculars, taking pictures, drawing diagrams and taking notes." The ACLU said, "SAR programs increase the probability that innocent people will be stopped by police and have their personal information collected for inclusion in law enforcement and intelligence data bases."[43] Tens of thousands of SAR reports were filed each year with Fusion Centers. For example, in 2010 the Department of Law Enforcement in Florida alone processed more than 5,700 reports. There is no sound evidence that such behavioral detection is effective in preventing terrorism.[44] The FBI sorted through thousands of reports to determine a "nexus to terrorism" warranting their investigative involvement. From July 2004 through November 2007, the FBI looked at almost 108,000 potential terrorism-related threats and suspicious incidents."[45] The overcollection of information can be counterproductive. The ACLU referred to "an ocean of data about innocent individuals that will overwhelm the investigative resources of the authorities."[46] That is, unless the authorities vastly expand their current capabilities—a prospect that would be very worrisome.

Suspicious activity reporting also applied to financial activity. The Treasury Department operated a special mass surveillance system called FinCen. Bush charged it with looking into terrorist financing after 9/11 and it has grown dramatically. By 2008, FinCent sent 1.2 million reports to the FBI for inspection.[47] Obama proposed to increase the Treasury Department's surveillance operations to track all money transfers across U.S. national borders. Information on transfers would be fed into a giant database using artificial intelligence to locate patterns associated with terrorist financing.[48]

The institutional intelligence apparatus Bush put in place, and Obama has enhanced, included Fusion Centers run by individual states. The "fusion" metaphor is appropriate: The centers brought together disparate information from police contact with the civilian population—ranging from traffic stops to city police infiltration of political groups—and made it available within the law enforcement community. By 2011, more than 70 centers operated under the auspices of the new Department of Homeland Security (DHS). The typical center established an information sharing network based on the work of the county sheriff, city police, state police, the National Guard, FBI, DHS, as well as private sources. As Thomas Cincotta notes, "At first glance, smaller, more diffuse centers might seem to pose a smaller threat to civil liberties than a KGB-like national force. In truth, however, this decentralized network may be more dangerous because it obscures lines of authority, subverts congressional oversight and privacy guidelines, and turns numerous state and local police into intelligence agents."[49] By mandating that different police agencies work together, the centers helped transform the culture of intelligence gathering, breaking down barriers that separated agencies.

Fusion Centers wrongly labeled peaceful political speech and protest as terrorist threats. In Tennessee, it placed the ACLU on a map of "terrorism events and other suspicious activity" because the civil liberty group sent a letter to school officials cautioning that holiday celebrations focusing only on one religious tradition, such as Christianity, amounted to an unconstitutional endorsement of religion.[50] The North Central Texas Fusion Center labeled Muslim-American lobbyists as a threat to public safety. "A number of organizations in the U.S. have been lobbying Islamic-based issues for many years" and these lawful efforts "provide an environment for terrorist organizations to flourish." The Center cited the Council on American Islamic Relations (CAIR) as a threat. It also singled out the International Action Center (IAC), founded by former U.S. Attorney General Ramsey Clark, as an "international far Left group" in sympathy with Muslim terrorists and noted that former Congresswoman Cynthia McKinney was a delegate at a recent conference. "The IAC also has operations in the United States including one of the main anti-war and anti-Israel protest movements in the U.S. called ANSWER, Act Now to Stop War and End Racism. Law enforcement should be aware of activities in their area."[51] In Maryland, the state police classified 53 nonviolent political activists as terrorists and entered their names into their Fusion Center database. Undercover troopers used aliases to infiltrate the Maryland Campaign to End the Death Penalty as well as the Baltimore Pledge of Resistance, an anti-war group, without evidence of criminal conduct.[52] In this environment, the Center for Constitutional Rights reissued in 2009 a pamphlet for activists advising them how to respond if federal agents tried to interview them. (See Textbox 6.2.)

Surveillance as Harassment

The FBI's "October Plan" provided a prime example of "surveillance as harassment." In announcing the Plan about six weeks before the 2004 presidential election, the FBI helped place the terror scare into presidential politics. The bureau had no advance intelligence on any terrorist plot, but, as CNN news reported: "The FBI is putting together an aggressive plan that includes rousting people suspected of supporting violent extremists. Federal lawmen may jail some who have committed minor crimes or immigration violations and question or tail others if only to let them know the government can find them."[53] Known also

Textbox 6.2

In 2009, the Center for Constitutional Rights, a progressive lawyers' organization founded in 1966, reissued a pamphlet advising political activists about FBI surveillance and harassment. The following excerpt from *If an Agent Knocks* notes different "dirty tricks" employed to fight social movements.

Federal law enforcement agencies like the Federal Bureau of Investigation (FBI) have a dark history of targeting radical and progressive movements. Some of the dirty tricks they use against these movements include: infiltration of organizations to discredit and disrupt their operations; campaigns of misinformation and false stories in the media; forgery of correspondence; fabrication of evidence; and the use of grand jury subpoenas to intimidate activists. Today's activist must know and understand the threat posed by federal law enforcement agents and their tactics as well as several key security practices that offer the best protection.

Federal agents have many tools at their disposal to target activists. While it is important to know and understand these tools and tactics, it is of critical importance that you resist any paranoia of government surveillance or fear of infiltration, which will only serve to paralyze you or your organization in your quest for social change. If fear of government repression prevents you from organizing, the agents of repression will have won without even trying.

The Center for Constitutional Rights (CCR) created *If an Agent Knocks* to provide advice to activists likely to be targeted by FBI agents or other federal investigators. Since its original release in 1989, *If an Agent Knocks* has been widely circulated in progressive activist communities across the country. This guide includes both the timeless advice included in the original version and extensive updates to reflect the current state of the law and law enforcement tools. This updated edition also includes a comprehensive discussion of today's technology, including cell phones, e-mail and Web browsing. This guide should be seen as a resource for the information needed to protect yourself and other activists from government investigation and to empower you to continue the struggle.

as the 2004 Threat Task Force, it embraced "aggressive—even obvious—surveillance." This is the language of official repression. "Aggressive" is a keyword for harassment. "Obvious" is a keyword for overt or open surveillance to promote fear and paranoia. Interviews also functioned as harassment if they became a pretext to issue warnings to change behavior.

The October Plan directed special attention to Arabs and Muslims in America with more than 2,000 interviews.[54] Before addressing the main elements of the October Plan, it is important to note the difficulties I faced obtaining FBI documents under the Freedom of Information Act. On two occasions, the FBI denied that they held any material on the subject by claiming their search produced "no records." I filed an administrative appeal after each denial with the Office of Information at the U.S. Department of Justice. After more than two years the FBI began to release the documents, which total 2,734 pages. Their denials appeared to constitute a delay strategy. After all, the Plan was not a secret.

The files reveal the historical reasoning used by the bureau to monitor American Arabs and Muslims. An FBI agent in Charlotte, North Carolina, wrote:

> According to the Islamic lunar calendar, November 2, 2004, is the anniversary of the Battle of Badar (sic). This battle was the first battle fought in the name of Islam. It was fought against the enemies of Allah. Mohammed, the prophet and his forces, battled in the holy city of Mecca. Of course, November 2, 2004 is the U.S. election day.[55]

The October Plan included Operation Tripwire. In July 2004, the bureau said: "To identify potential terrorist sleeper cells, Operation Tripwire commissions all JTTFs to ask specific questions of specific industries (e.g., suspicious behavior of airline passengers) and then looks for patterns from the collected data. We're collecting and analyzing data on radicalism in prisons. We're coordinating new initiatives for railroads and cruise ships."[56] They also looked at the crop-dusting industry, storage facilities, and the transportation of hazardous materials. Tripwire had 12 subcategories:

Maritime
Hotels
Sporting Events
Transport
Department of Motor Vehicles
Military
Storage
Chemical, Biological, Radiological, and Nuclear (CBRN)
Correction
Aviation
Mosques
Malls[57]

From a civil liberties perspective, religious profiling took place when only one set of religious institutions (mosques) were under widespread surveillance.

In Dallas, an individual was told during an interview that the FBI "was engaging in a public outreach to promote efforts in building a stronger relationship with the Muslim community." The subject, a licensed taxicab driver, was born in Karachi, Pakistan, and had resided in the U.S. for 14 years. The FBI asked questions to gather information related to both potential crimes as well as religious beliefs and organizational politics. First, they wanted to know his opinion of FBI efforts to contact the local Muslim community. How he answered that question could shape the nature of the interview—whether he was considered a friendly or hostile subject. The agents then asked a series of scripted operational queries.

Had he observed any criminal activities and was he willing to contact the FBI if he noticed any?
Did he know of any person "who might be in place to conduct or facilitate an attack"?
Did he know of anyone "making inquiries or taking actions to procure or store dangerous chemicals, weapons, or explosives"?

Did he know of anyone "attempting to acquire or modify SUV's or other heavy vehicles"?

Did he know of anyone "who may possess a commercial drivers' license with authority to transport hazardous materials"?

Did he have knowledge of anyone "who has shown interest in or has attempted to acquire radiological materials from labs, medical, or disposal facilities"?

Finally, did he have any "information to indicate he had knowledge of anyone who may be conducting surveillance of potential U.S. targets"?

The agents noted that the subject "has not been solicited, nor has he any knowledge of anyone being solicited to support radical Islamic individuals or organizations."[58] Again, from a civil liberties perspective the routine surveillance of religious radicalism in the form of individuals or organizations is objectionable. Why assume that radicals of either a religious or political nature de facto support violence? This assumption not only is flawed but undermines constitutional protections embedded in the First Amendment.

The FBI targeted the Islamic Center of San Francisco (ICSF). The FBI tried to interview its leadership but reported resistance.

On 10/21/2004, [text redacted], DOB [text redacted], telephone number [text redacted], contacted SA [text redacted]. [Text redacted] is a [text redacted] of the ICSF. [Text redacted] advised that the board members at ICSF are worried about the FBI's interest in talking to them. They believe the interviews are really interrogations, and that an interview with the FBI could lead to further investigation and ultimately deportation from the United States. They have been advised by the ACLU not to talk to the FBI.[59]

A very important point was raised here: Did outreach interviews really serve as hidden interrogations? Can immigrants trust the FBI when it engaged in public community efforts? Outreach programs could become pretexts to gather intelligence and recruit informers.

On Oct. 1, 2004, two FBI agents met with members of the Masjid Muhammed mosque in Louisville, Kentucky. An FBI memo about the meeting noted: "Logical topics were discussed to address directive to enhance intelligence collection, and examine opportunities to develop assets within the community."[60] In a separate interview, an agent interviewed the spiritual leader of the Faisal Mosque in Louisville to gather intelligence on congregants. However, the agent did not reveal that this religious leader already was a subject of investigation. "[Text redacted] was identified as a Category I subject, 'Subjects who have been the focus of long-term intelligence investigation, which have . . . yet to develop solid links to terrorism.' Louisville plans to implement several investigative actions [text redacted] on subject in the near future, but also felt an interview of [text redacted] as a recognized Islamic leader, would be beneficial." The leader told the agent that Islam is "a religion of peace and terrorists do not represent Islamic people." The leader also said "if someone that they considered dangerous or behaved suspiciously came to their attention, they would contact writer."[61]

In Los Angeles, the local FBI office was instructed by headquarters to interview 60 terrorism subjects considered sympathetic to Islamic extremism. The office used "proactive investigative techniques" on a case-by-case basis to "maximize disruptive impact." Local agents also formulated plans to identify new suspects. "Many ideas were discussed, with a focus on new, creative, out of the box techniques."[62]

In San Diego, agents initiated a "disruption plan" against a male Muslim subject who had been under investigation for more than two years. The subject allegedly had made phone calls to suspected terrorists. Two agents "confronted the subject at a computer lab located at San Diego State University and handed him a copy of the 9/11 Commission Report. [Text redacted] was told that he should read the highlighted portion of the book."[63] The interview blew the cover on the surveillance serving as a form of intimidation.

The Brooklyn, NY, mosque known as Iman Albaani Masjid was put under investigation. The FBI researched the individual who paid the institution's rent and obtained financial documents from the New York Community Bank in connection with the probe. Reference also was made to a mosque in Jamaica, Queens, along with efforts to recruit informers. One memo revealed networks of surveillance:

> [Text redacted] has known [text redacted] for more than three years. He first met [text redacted] at the MASJID (MOSQUE) AHLUL KORAN WA SUNNA, located in Jamaica, Queens, New York. [Text redacted] was an Imam at the MASJID (MOSQUE) AHLUL WA SUNNA and developed a relationship with [text redacted]. According to [text redacted] preached a pure version of Islam and "warned against troublemakers." [Text redacted] possesses an FI (student) visa and is currently in status. Attempts to recruit [text redacted] as an asset have not been successful, although [text redacted] continues to speak to agents and detectives. An individual by the name of [text redacted] recently moved to Schenectady [New York] because FBI agents had approached [text redacted] a few times at the Mosque.[64]

An interview could become a recruiting opportunity. In Milwaukee, an agent interviewed a male employee of Shelter for Life International (SFLI), a nonprofit relief organization that provided aid to refugee camps overseas funded by the U. S. State Department. The individual, who emigrated from Afghanistan, had been contacted by agents twice in the past. Although he could not provide the FBI with current intelligence on any terrorist activity, the agent reported he "agreed to stay in contact with the FBI, and was provided a business card." The agent "anticipates opening [text redacted] as an asset." The degree of indirect or direct coercion faced by recent immigrants in such contexts was clear. This individual had petitioned to become a permanent resident. Would a decision not to inform affect his status?

Some subjects refused to talk to agents without an attorney. A long-time employee of the University of Pittsburgh obtained the services of the ACLU to be present at the FBI interview. She worked as the International Studies and Outreach Director for the Consortium for Educational Resources on Islamic Studies

(ICP) in charge the administration of foreign students. As is typical in many of these interviews, the FBI agent asked about local Muslim attitudes toward law enforcement. The agent wrote:

> [Text redacted] informed the Muslim community has been under extreme scrutiny since the terrorist events of 09/11/2001. If speaking with law enforcement will help clear their names, then they will speak. . . . [Text redacted] advised that every time meetings or prayer services are held at the ICP, people wonder who in the crowd is actually an FBI agent. However, [text redacted] claims because of this paranoia, individuals including herself strive very hard to keep the image of the ICP "squeaky clean."[65]

Most subjects negotiated the situation on their own by refusing to inform for the FBI but cooperating to an extent in the interview. A subject associated with Indiana University of Pennsylvania had come to the attention of the bureau because of paid translation work for *Al Jumuah*, a Muslim lifestyle magazine. The subject also contributed money to his local mosque. An agent asked about the views of the Indiana Muslim community toward the FBI. The agent wrote:

> [Text redacted] explained some of the Muslim community members feel insulted when the FBI comes to talk to them. This is not his opinion. [Text redacted] wishes to help as much as possible. On one occasion, [text redacted] was discussing this with his relative who lives in Virginia and felt somewhat uncomfortable. According to [text redacted], he and his relative discussed this issue and agreed they must cooperate if they could and help the FBI.[66]

However, the subject made it clear he did not want to become an informer. As the agent reported: "[Text redacted] stated he could be recontacted but did not wish to maintain a continual relationship with the FBI."[67]

Fear of the government investigation impacted Arab-American economic behavior, particularly contributions to organizations within their communities. An FBI agent described an interview with a man in Arlington, Texas.

> [S]ince the arrests of the Holy Land Foundation, many mosques including his do not allow collections from outside the Mosque. [Text redacted] said that lately people are not even giving enough money to pay electric bills at the mosque, and that it is very upsetting. [Text redacted] said that people are afraid to give money to the mosque because they believe that their names will be placed onto an FBI list. [Text redacted] said that giving money to the needy is a large part of being Muslim, and now people are afraid.[68]

Shortly after 9/11 the Bush administration shut down the Holy Land Foundation, the largest Islamic charity in the United States, by freezing its assets. Attorney General John Ashcroft described the Foundation as "the North American front for Hamas" and a federal judge upheld the administration's crackdown. In 2008, five leaders of the Foundation were found guilty of overseas terrorist-financing.[69]

False leads also led to detention. In Burlington, North Carolina, the owner of a country store called police "regarding two Arabic males. . . . The two entered the store and wanted to buy numerous bags of fertilizer. When asked by [text redacted] what they were going to do with all the fertilizer, one replied, 'blow something up.'" The store owner refused to sell the fertilizer to the men, who were driving an ice cream truck. The FBI investigated and found that the men actually were Israeli citizens and had not made any threats. One had joked about "growing weed." Two other Israeli men registered to the truck also were interviewed. In the end, at least two of the men were taken into custody for immigration status violations.[70]

On occasion, local FBI agents acknowledged the detrimental impact of their interviews. In Butte, Montana, the JTTF interviewed a male Muslim clerk at Brown's book store based on rumor. A source had reported that the subject "hates America and has a picture of Osama Bin Laden in his apartment." After an interview, the FBI decided the man expressed "delusional beliefs," but was not a threat. ("He discussed various psychic abilities which both he and his father possess, and his unequivocal belief that he will be elected President of the United States in 2008.") The FBI decided not to interview the father, who allegedly "suffers from 'flashbacks' associated with his treatment in a Moroccan jail in the 1970s. . . . A visit from the FBI appears more likely to stimulate such an event [violent act], rather than to serve any intelligence-gathering objective."[71]

The scare politics spread to hobby shops and toy airplane clubs. The FBI believed remote-controlled (RC) models of airplanes and boats could be programmed to wage a terrorist attack. The threat seemed unlikely, as a Baltimore FBI agent reported: "[T]he use of RC model airplanes would not be very effective due to the minimal amount of payload carrying capability and tremendous amount of skill required to operate the airplanes with any great degree of precision." Most RC airplanes have a wingspan of less than 5 feet. Few have the capability for more than 15 minutes of air travel and the models typically weigh about 6 pounds. Yet, the FBI pursued the matter as if it constituted a top security threat. It contacted all the shops in Delaware selling RC model airplanes, which spread fear in the RC and hobby community. The Baltimore agent reported: "In general, the RC clubs and hobby shops have been watchful of suspicious individuals inquiring about RC model airplanes and other related devices."[72] Again, the keyword "suspicious" is raised: What exactly is suspicious activity and do cultural differences lead to misunderstanding?

Immigrants disproportionately were targeted by the FBI. Before Bush left office, the U.S. Justice Department issued another set of FBI guidelines expanding spying power. The new guidelines, which took effect on Dec. 1, 2008, lowered the standard to authorize surveillance prompting civil liberty concerns about profiling based on race, religion, gender, or ethnic background. FBI agents began collecting intelligence on businesses, behaviors, lifestyle characteristics, and cultural traditions in ethnic communities.[73] The Brennan Center for Justice at NYU Law School noted the likelihood of police officers "making decisions based on two factors, such as ethnicity and gender, like investigating males of Arab descent *because* they are males of Arab descent."[74] (See Textbox 6.3.)

Textbox 6.3

The danger to civil liberties posed by FBI profiling is discussed by Emily Berman in "Domestic Intelligence: New Powers, New Risks" (2010), published by Brennan Center for Justice at NYU School of Law.

Dangers of Profiling

Permitting investigations without factual predicate and with limited supervisory involvement is overwhelmingly likely to lead to profiling on the basis of race, religion, ethnicity, national origin, or political belief. In the absence of constraints imposed by a standard such as reasonable suspicion or probable cause, FBI agents are now free, in many situations, to rely on their own discretion. As we have seen time and again, individuals permitted such discretion in making law enforcement decisions are influenced by their conscious or subconscious biases. And this reliance on bias can lead to profiling. Historically, when law enforcement officials have been able to collect intelligence on groups and individuals suspected—without any objective basis—of harboring ill will toward the U.S., the burden of that investigative activity has fallen on groups that espouse disfavored ideologies, minorities, or others who are perceived as threatening.

Justice Department officials have assured both Congress and the public that "department rules . . . forbid predicating an investigation simply based on somebody's race" or "solely for the purpose of monitoring activities protected by the First Amendment." The question is not, however, whether investigative activity will be motivated by race, religion, national origin, or political belief *alone*. Problematic profiling consists not only of relying entirely on characteristics like race or religion, but of taking them into account, in the absence of any particularized suspicion indicating that such characteristics are relevant, and making law enforcement decisions based even in part on such factors. Reliance on that criteria—that an officer has engaged in racial profiling only when the single factor, i.e., race, religion, ethnicity, etc., is used to make a law enforcement decision—comes close to defining the problem out of existence. It would not prohibit many inappropriate uses of these characteristics. For instance, it would not prohibit an officer from making decisions based on two factors, such as ethnicity and gender, like investigating males of Arab descent because they are males of Arab descent. Nor would it bar decisions based on the use of race and place, such as pulling over black drivers in white neighborhoods because they are blacks in white neighborhoods.

Moreover, the new guidelines allow agents in local field offices to conduct physical surveillance, recruit informers, and interview friends of subjects without supervision. The FBI began to investigate people simply to determine if they would make effective informants. In the latter instance, the FBI tried to dig up incriminating evidence on a person in order to coerce them to snitch. The FBI General Counsel stated that the new guidelines "are the culmination of prior efforts to revise the FBI's operating rules in the wake of the September 11 terrorist attacks." The FBI will "proactively look for threats within the country . . . moving beyond a reactive model (where agents must wait to receive leads before acting). "[75] It is too early to know how "proactive" spying will differ from "reactive" spying.

Agents were instructed at the FBI academy in Quantico, Virginia, about Islam in biased ways. The teaching lesson plans on this topic, which were obtained by an online news organization, indicated that the more "devout" a Muslim, the greater the likelihood he is "violent." An instructional presentation added: "Any war against non-believers is justified" under Muslim law; a "moderating process cannot happen if the Koran continues to be regarded as the unalterable word of Allah." A presentation titled "Militancy Considerations" contrasted Islam with Judaism and Christianity in its relationship between piety and violence. The FBI taught that while the followers of the Torah and the Bible move from "violent" to "non-violent" over time, this "moderating process has not happened" for devotees of the Koran. According to this interpretation, religious Muslims always would form a terrorist threat. Moreover, FBI agents were taught that the Prophet Mohammed was a "cult leader." This type of disrespect for religion empowered agents to view Muslim-Americans as dangerous. "Seeing the materials FBI agents are being trained with certainly helps explain why we've seen so many inappropriate FBI surveillance operations broadly targeting the Muslim-American community, from infiltrating mosques with agents provocateur to racial- and ethnic-mapping programs," commented Mike German, a former FBI agent who worked for the American Civil Liberties Union. "Biased police training can only result in biased policing."[76]

Surveillance of Peace Activists

Between 2008 and 2010, the FBI and local and state police aggressively targeted peace and anti-war activists in Iowa, Minnesota, Pennsylvania, and Illinois. Again, the bureau misapplied the terrorist label to justify the crackdown. Ex-FBI agents Coleen Rowley and Mike German both expressed reservations about these investigations. According to Rowley, who exposed the bureau's intelligence failure before the 9/11 attacks and was named *Time* magazine's Person of the Year in 2002: "Agents are now given a green light, for instance, to check off 'statistical achievements' by sending well-paid, manipulative informants into mosques and peace groups. Forgotten are worries about targeting and entrapping people not predisposed to violence."[77] German said, "Unless the rules regulating the FBI are strengthened to safeguard the privacy of innocent Americans, we are all in danger of being spied on and added to terrorist watch lists for doing nothing more than attending a rally or holding up a sign."[78]

For nine months in 2008 the FBI set up a surveillance network in Iowa City, a small college town, to monitor activists associated with the Wild Rose Rebellion. The bureau identified the group as an "anarchist collective" planning protests to disrupt the upcoming national conventions of one or both major political parties—the Democrats were to meet in Denver in August and the Republicans in St. Paul in September. Declassified FBI documents reveal informer infiltration, staking out the homes of members, investigating their garbage, examining cell phone, email, and motor vehicle records, as well as secretly photographing and videotaping them. The FBI identified where activists worked. They directed clerks in local stores to listen to conversations. David Goodner, one of those under investigation, later exposed the surveillance after obtaining FBI files under the FOIA. He said the Rebellion group had modest, nonviolent social action plans to organize peaceful civil disobedience, such as street blockades, outside the Republican National Convention (RNC). "Nonviolent civil disobedience is an American as apple pie. . . . It's what this country was founded on; it's what every social movement in U.S. history has used to create a more just and democratic society." He questioned the logic that led "the FBI to claim that peace organizers who were doing tried and true methods of civil disobedience were somehow domestic terrorists or threats to national security."[79]

Is peaceful civil disobedience an "act of terrorism"? Technically, blocking traffic might break the law but its severity does not seem very great. Moreover, in this case the number of people participating in the protest—about 25—was so small it is hard to label it any kind of security threat.[80]

In the past, undercover FBI informers inside groups often sought leadership roles. This pattern was replicated within the Wild Rose Rebellion. Goodner said an informer gave public speeches against the war in Iraq and "played a very high-profile role in our group. . . . He knew the activist lingo. He could speak the slang." The informer also served as moderator at some group meetings and went to the convention to function as a medic for the protestors in the event of police violence. Robert Ehl, who helped found the Wild Rose Rebellion, said the informer was present at the very first meeting of the group. "We would go and hang out with him—me and him and a couple of people at a bar or somebody's apartment."[81] Ehl raised the idea of a government "green scare." "The documents released to us by the FBI also show that it attempted to connect our organizing work to animal and environmental liberation activities, something authorities have been criminalizing to a greater degree in recent years, called by some the 'green scare.'"[82] Indeed, the misapplication of "terrorism" to protest activity was written into law in the Animal Enterprise Terrorist Act (AETA) of 2006. The government viewed property sabotage or vandalism as a form of terrorism, as well as any effort to "physically disrupt" the functioning of a business or research center related to animals. Two groups—the Animal Liberation Front (ALF) and the Earth Liberation Front (ELF)—were identified as leading "eco-terrorists" responsible for hundreds of nonlethal criminal acts.[83]

Surveillance associated with the RNC also focused on local groups in St. Paul. The local city police and sheriffs' department infiltrated several organizations thought to be planning protests, such as the RNC Welcoming Committee. Prior to the convention, police traveled around the country to collect intelligence on people who might travel to St. Paul. They "took thousands of pictures and organized pretextual traffic stops of individuals and groups" such as Code Pink, Sisters Camelot, the Campus Antiwar Network in Iowa, and new Students for a Democratic Society.[84] Before the convention opened, Indymedia journalists who documented police misconduct were stopped and searched on the street. Police raided the offices of I-Witness Video as well as the home of one of its leaders, Michael Whalen, based on an informer's erroneous report about the stockpiling of weapons. In addition, the FBI worked with city police to raid the office of the RNC Welcoming Committee and the homes of some of its activists, seizing computers and political literature. Another raid occurred at the protestors' Convergence Center where 60 people were preemptively detained. Eight activists—known as the RNC 8—were charged with the felony offense of conspiracy to riot in furtherance of terrorism based, again, on erroneous informer reports. According to the National Lawyers Guild, the informers claimed the "activists sought to kidnap delegates to the RNC, assault police officers with firebombs and explosives, and sabotage airports in St. Paul."[85] Such wild, unfounded charges to justify arrests were clear examples of official repression.

One of the informers who worked for the FBI was paid almost $50,000; another earned more than $21,000. Resembling COINTELPRO tactics, the Bloomington Police Department created a phony protest group—Indy-TACT—to infiltrate and discredit dissident activity. The hyperbolic rhetoric of the fake group is revealing. They identified as "red zone activists" with "red hot malevolence." The police composed a political manifesto for Indy-TACT which referred to a "Freedom from Capitalism" flag.

> Attention all Capitalists, Imperialists, Racists, Sexists, Homophobes, and most of all—Republicans! The status quo has just been replaced by a new order of autonomy, mutual aid, and direct democracy! Indy-TACT, a group of Fort Wayne, Indiana anti-capitalists, anti-authoritarians, and antiwar activists are

beginning our Freedom from Capitalism flag in the fertile soil of St. Paul as we stand in solidarity in our adoption of Sector 2 in St. Paul, Minnesota, the host of the RNC.[86]

After the convention ended, five separate civil rights lawsuits were brought against the FBI, city police, and the City of St. Paul. Protestors won all of them, with settlements totaling more than $75,000. They found that police affidavits for the raids were of dubious value. As one example, an FBI agent wrote that the delivery of 21 boxes to one home "contained weapons that are to be used during the R.N.C." based on "information from a liable [sic] source." No weapons were found. Rather, the boxes contained political literature with such titles as "Wash Your Own Dishes" and "Activists Guide to Basic First Aid."[87]

In late September 2009, world leaders met for a week at the G-20 Summit meetings in Pittsburgh. Federal, state, and local police cast a wide surveillance net and hyped unjustified fears of street violence. The campaign began several months before the Summit meetings when local newspapers, based on biased police sources, began to raise the specter of protest violence. Overall, about 6,000 uniformed police officers and 2,500 National Guardsmen were deployed to prevent disorder. The size of this paramilitary force, which used tear gas, pepper spray, smoke bombs, canine units, and Long Range Acoustic Devices (LRADs) for crowd control, rivaled the total number of protestors marching in the street. The National Lawyers Guild believed this was the first domestic use of LRADs as a weapon. Sound cannons mounted on police trucks emitted a high frequency—which can cause long-term hearing loss—to disperse crowds.[88]

In *The Policing of Political Speech* (2010), the NLG argues that the experience of repression at the RNC and G-20 Summit reflects an "increased intolerance for protest." Preemptive arrests by law enforcement posed a threat to the rule of law. The NLG noted: "Many have refrained from political activism out of fear of the threat of arrest and prosecution. It is likely that the demonstrations we have seen would have been much larger but for the fear instilled in those who oppose one or another government policy but are reluctant to engage in robust speech. Legal defense against false arrests and litigation to redress violations can hold the line but can never fully restore the ability of the people to exercise their rights."[89]

The shadow of the RNC protests lasted into 2010, when FBI agents conducted raids against the homes of several dozen activists in Chicago and in Minneapolis. In Minneapolis, the individuals associated with two groups: the Anti-War Committee and the Freedom Road Socialist Organization. They had helped organize protests at the RNC and also against U.S. military involvement in Iraq and Afghanistan. Jess Sundin, whose home was targeted, reported: "They spent probably about four hours going through all of our personal belongings, every book, paper, our clothes, and filled several boxes and crates with our computers, our phones, my passport—with which they left my home." The FBI claimed the searches were necessary to find evidence of "material support" for overseas terrorism.[90]

The alleged threat posed by "anarchists" has become a top FBI priority. What exactly is anarchism in the 21st century? During the late 19th and early 20th century, when anarchism first developed as a political philosophy, its proponents believed social change and revolution could be achieved through strategic acts of violence. They called it "propaganda by the deed," which served as a catalyst for the masses to rise up and rupture the system. Since the revival of anarchism during the late 1960s, its proponents generally embraced ecology, environmentalism, antiwar activity, and anti-globalization—not propaganda by the deed. The FBI's perception of anarchism seems to be stuck in the era of World War I and the Palmer raids.

In the case of Scott Crow of East Austin, Texas, the FBI conducted extensive monitoring without evidence of any criminal activity or plans for violence. The *New York Times* featured Crow, an activist in anti-corporate demonstrations, in a rare article addressing ongoing political policing. The newspaper reported that Crow "is among dozens of political activists across the country known to have come under scrutiny from the F.B.I.'s increased counterterrorism operations since the attacks of Sept. 11, 2001." Most of these operations were kept secret. "When such investigations produce no criminal charges, their methods rarely come to light publicly."[91]

However, Crow requested his FBI file under the FOIA and the bureau acknowledged their surveillance, declassifying 440 pages. He learned that the FBI kept track of his friends and associates by recording the license plates of cars parked outside his home. The bureau also installed outdoor Closed Circuit Television (CCTV) to record the visitors to his dwelling. An FBI memo noted the CCTV "will be remote monitoring, in that the camera will not be physically held by an Agent or consenting party. No consenting party is required to be in the area to be viewed for this CCTV- NO SOUND authority. . . . The camera will be located outdoors and no trespass is required to install."[92] The FBI also researched his tax returns looking for evasion, rather than just under reporting of income. They searched his garbage, especially the paper recycling portion, and made notations of what they found. "A desk calendar page for April 4, 2006, with the notes 'taxes?', 'call fire dudes,' 'go to ecoplace for games (illegible),' and 'send money order.'" They also highlighted, "Several communications form Working Assets, a San Francisco based organization involved in a number of different social/political causes."[93]

Crow worked at a recycling center and became an advocate for peaceful civil disobedience. He had been arrested about a dozen times during political demonstrations, but never convicted of anything more serious than trespassing. The FBI also noted he helped run an annual training camp for peaceful protestors called the Radical Encuentro Camp. An FBI infiltrator at the Camp described the group in negative terms. "Most attendees dressed like hippies, had dread locks (both men and women) and smelled of bad odor."[94]

The FBI called him an "eco-terrorist." They investigated his travels in nine states during the period since 9/11. He said the FBI used five informants against him. "I don't like the state," Crow told the *Times*. "I don't want to overthrow it, but I want to create alternatives to it."[95] Crow later wrote a book, *Black Flags and Windmills* (2011), about his life as a grassroots activist.[96]

In the 21st century, top FBI targets like Crow became subject to day-to-day monitoring. This was not new. When the FBI established the New Left section of COINTELPRO in 1968, they established the category of "key activist." Those so designated—about 80 people—were put under intensive electronic and human surveillance with efforts to pin criminal charges on them. In addition to monitoring their political activities, the FBI tracked their lives on an everyday basis in their communities and at their workplaces. The FBI deployed non-lethal "neutralization" tactics to curtail the influence of these people. While the FBI currently claims they do not maintain a key activist list, they still target select individuals for the same type of coverage. The number of people abused in this manner is unknown.

Privacy and Surveillance Oversight

U.S. Supreme Court Justice Louis Brandeis wrote in his famous dissent in *Olmstead v. U.S.* more than 80 years ago that the right to privacy is "the most comprehensive of rights and the right most valued by civilized man."[97] Privacy is critical to the "development of human individuality," law professor Jeffrey Rosen recently noted. "We are beginning to learn how much may be lost in a culture of transparency: the capacity for creativity and eccentricity, for the development of self and soul, for understanding, friendship, even love." No less than the well-being of the individual is at stake. Professor Anita Allen added. "It is not simply that people need opportunities for privacy; the point is that their well-being, and the well-being of the liberal way of life, requires that they in fact experience privacy." One cannot live long if they are denied the right to enjoy anonymity, solitude, and intimacy. Helen Nissenbaum has raised the political question of limiting surveillance and restricting access to personal records "to curtail such evils as government intimidation and totalitarian-style incursions into private life."

The preceding quotes from Brandeis, Rosen, Allen, and Nissenbaum were contained in a Brief of *Amici Curiae* submitted by the Electronic Privacy Information Center in the recent

U.S. Supreme Court case, *NASA v. Nelson* (2011). This humanistic privacy argument did not sway America's highest court, which ruled federal employees have no "informational right to privacy" surrounding employment background investigations. Robert M. Nelson, a federal contract employee at the Jet Propulsion Laboratory operated by the California Institute of Technology, had objected to written questions about his treatment for illegal drug use and refused to authorize the government to collect his personal information from schools, employers, and others during a background investigation. He lost the case.[98]

After 9/11, a new popular debate related to security versus privacy engaged the public. Unfortunately, many people asked the wrong questions. For example, the popular refrain, "I have nothing to hide," became a short-sighted and incomplete response to government's increased spying powers. People should not assume that if one has done nothing wrong, it matters little if government snooped. Secret information-gathering programs created an imbalance of power between the populace and the state. As Daniel J. Solove writes in *Nothing to Hide* (2011):

> Exclusion occurs when people are prevented from having knowledge about how information about them is being used, and when they are barred from accessing and correcting errors in that data. Many government national-security measures involve maintaining a huge database of information that individuals cannot access. Indeed, because they involve national security, the very existence of these programs is often kept secret. This kind of information processing, which blocks subjects' knowledge and involvement, is a kind of due-process problem. It is a structural problem, involving the way people are treated by government institutions. . . . To what extent should government officials have such a significant power over citizens? This issue isn't about what information people want to hide but about the power and the structure of government.[99]

Without significant checks, secret spying will continue to challenge the integrity of privacy in society. The detrimental effects of privacy invasion may be incremental. As Solove notes: "Privacy is rarely lost in one fell swoop. It is usually eroded over time, little bits dissolving almost imperceptibly until we finally begin to notice how much is gone."[100] The FBI, by embracing a regressive politics of visibility, believed that eradicating privacy was acceptable as long as government did not engage in political censorship. These are different types of constraints on civil liberties. But what if the FBI attacks *both* privacy and expression?

Few argue that government should never engage in surveillance. Rather, agencies such as the FBI should get a warrant or have probable cause that a crime will be committed. No evidence suggests the effectiveness of surveillance will be greatly diminished by enhanced accountability measures. When the government mentions "terrorism," its policies too often remain unquestioned.[101] The libertarian Cato Institute concluded in *Leashing the Surveillance State* (2011) that after 9/11 "it should not be surprising that we erred on the side of granting government more power with fewer restrictions. Now, with the benefit of a decade's experience, we have an opportunity to do better."[102]

Several government mechanisms exist that could improve accountability of FBI surveillance. In most instances, the federal government has declined to utilize them to provide meaningful and effective oversight. For example, the federal judiciary has proved reluctant to place restrictions on FBI spying. The courts generally deferred to the FBI and began with the presumption that FBI conduct was legitimate. They rarely decided cases concerning the civil liberties of subjects of FBI investigations. In addition, the Justice Department oversees the FBI by issuing guidelines for its conduct. Only once have FBI Guidelines had a restraining effect: The Levi Guidelines issued in 1976 sought to end political spying and succeeded in ways never before imagined. But succeeding presidents beginning with Ronald Reagan revised the Levi Guidelines to empower the FBI once again to conduct political policing.

Within the Justice Department, the Inspector General (IG) also investigated FBI misconduct. Glenn A. Fine served as IG during the Bush administration and for the first two years of the Obama administration. His most critical report on FBI conduct involved the improper use of National Security Letters.[103] Yet, IG reports seemed to have little overall impact within the government. They led to a few modest procedural reforms but did not change the overall practice of political policing. Fine has refused to question the FBI's political motives.[104] In sum, the IG serves as a weak regulatory mechanism.

Congress has abdicated its legislative responsibility to check FBI abuse of power. It never passed an FBI Charter Act first proposed in the late 1970s by the Carter Administration. It almost always approved large budgetary increases for the bureau. While congressional committees since the mid-1970s have held critical hearings on FBI conduct, the legislative body rarely mustered the courage to change the way the bureau operated. In fact, after 9/11 Congress gave the bureau a virtual blank check to wage the war on terrorism. Congress also established special "commissions" touted for being independent and above narrow party conflict, which almost always bolstered spying from a bipartisan perspective.[105]

During the rise of the surveillance society, presidents from Clinton to Obama have posed few obstacles to the expansion of political policing. "The buck stops here" read a sign on President Harry Truman's desk in the Oval Office. As he explained in his farewell address to the American people in January 1953: "The President—whoever he is—has to decide. He can't pass the buck to anybody. No one else can do the deciding for him. That's his job."[106] The president retains ultimate control over the FBI and can hire and fire the director at his discretion. As one example of Bush's and Obama's support for FBI practices and indifference to civil liberties, neither president has followed the recommendation of the 9/11 Commission and allowed the newly created Privacy and Civil Liberties Oversight Board (PCLOB) to function. Congress established the board in 2004 to provide new oversight of the intelligence community. Coleen Rowley noted that Bush "assured its powerlessness and later dismantled it. Obama has thus far totally ignored the issue by not appointing anyone to the PCLOB."[107]

Most scholars view the bureau as a huge "bureaucracy." That designation did not mean that the organization lacked political objectives. Despite lack of accountability to democratic

standards and resistance to outside oversight, the FBI developed
many internal guidelines, regulations, and operating procedures
to guide the conduct of agents and other personnel. Recently, a
list of their policy documents was released under the FOIA. In
2010 and early 2011, the FBI issued 135 documents in this area
including the following titles:

> Surreptitious Entries Policy Implementation Guide
> National Security Undercover Operations Policy Implementation Guide
> Legal Review of Intelligence Information Reports
> Community Outreach in Field Offices
> Inspection Division Statement of Authorities and Responsibilities
> Intelligence Dissemination Policy Implementation Guide
> Handling of Unsolicited Proposals
> Civil Rights Policy Implementation Guide
> FBI Ethics and Integrity Program Policy Implementation Guide
> FBI Whistleblower Policy
> Image Capturing Devices within FBI Controlled Facilities
> National Name Check Derogatory Information Policy
> Protection of FBI Information Transmitted via Facsimile
> Protection of Human Subjects in Research Conducted or Supported by the FBI
> Security Clearance Requirements Access to FBI Information System[108]

There are references to "surreptitious entries" or break-ins. In
contrast to the Hoover era, the FBI now applied for legal warrants to conduct them. There are guidelines for "undercover
operations," but this does not prevent legal violations, especially
in the use of informers. Efforts at "community outreach," as I
have noted, often incorporated the gathering of intelligence. The
ACLU recently has elaborated this point noting that in California
the FBI collected Social Security numbers and other identifying
information, as well as political views, while working with the
local Muslim community.[109] The bureau's documents referred to

"ethics," "integrity," internal "inspection," and "whistleblower policy"—yet the FBI remained challenged in these areas to live up to the nation's democratic ideals.

After Hoover died in 1972, most lawmakers agreed he served too long and amassed too much power. In order to prevent another "boss" or "strongman" from holding the job, Congress limited the term of the FBI director to ten years. As a result, it has been difficult for another cult of personality to develop. Bush appointed Robert Mueller as director a week before the September 11, 2001, attacks. After Obama won the 2008 election, he ratified Mueller's terror scare leadership by not replacing him. In fact, when Mueller's ten-year term expired in 2011, the president took the unusual step of asking Congress for a two-year extension.[110] Liberal editorial pages, represented by the *Washington Post*, as well as civil liberty groups, questioned Obama's judgment. The ACLU listed five main points of disagreement with Mueller's leadership. The FBI significantly misused its authority as sanctioned by Congress under the both Patriot Act and the Foreign Intelligence Surveillance Act. It infiltrated religious institutions such as mosques. It used the material witness statue to protect abuse of power. It surveilled peaceful and lawful political groups. Lastly, it mishandled official watch lists.[111] Although the relationship between Mueller and Obama needs further study, what appears to be a strong partnership developed to fight terrorism, significantly setting back civil liberties in the United States.

Obama and the Surveillance State

In the *Dangers of Dissent*, I held open the possibility that President Obama might chart a different course than his predecessors and pose obstacles to the bipartisan construction of an American surveillance state. Obama, an African American constitutional law professor and arguably the first "bottom up" president in modern U.S. history, at first signaled he might place restraints on the wide array of government spying. For example, he shed the exaggerated rhetoric of the "war on terror." He talked about the importance of civil liberties. He promised a new era of openness in government. However, by now it has become clear there is more continuity than discontinuity with Bush on these matters. In 2011, Obama signed an extension of the Patriot Act for another four years. It did not matter that Osama bin Laden recently had been killed in Pakistan. As New York University law Professor Karen Greenberg asked: "Now That Bin Laden is Dead, Can We Have Our Freedoms Back?"[112] Yale Professor David Bromwich concurred: "The tone of the present administration is more soothing than that of its predecessor. But ever since Obama gave his National Archives Speech, in May 2009, the continuities with Cheney-Bush have been unmistakable."[113] In that speech, the president claimed to embrace a "common sense" (not ideological) approach eschewing both the left and the right. He said:

> On the one side of the spectrum, there are those who make little allowance for the unique challenges posed by terrorism, and would almost never put national security over transparency. And on the other end of the spectrum, there are those who embrace a view that can be summarized in two words: 'Anything goes.' Their arguments suggest that the ends of fighting terrorism can be used to justify any means, and that the President should have blanket authority to do whatever he wants—provided it is a President with whom they agree.

> Both sides may be sincere in their views, but neither side is right. The American people are not absolutist, and they don't elect us to impose a rigid ideology on our problems. They know that we need not sacrifice our security for our values, nor sacrifice our values for our security, so long as we approach difficult questions with honesty and care and a dose of common sense. That, after all, is the unique genius of America.[114]

This common sense approach was an abdication. It occurred in a context where government lawbreakers rarely were held accountable. Obama's common sense became a centralist ideology that sanctioned a "post-legal" America. As Tom Engelhardt notes:

> The National Security Complex has access to us, to our lives and communications, though we have next to no access to it. It has, in reserve, those enhanced interrogation techniques and when trouble looms, a set of what might be called enhanced legal techniques as well.
>
> Theoretically, the National Security Complex exists only to protect you. Its every act is done in the name of making *you* safer, even if the idea of safety and protection doesn't extend to your job, your foreclosed home, or aid in disastrous times.
>
> Welcome to post-legal America. It's time to stop wondering whether its acts are illegal and start asking: Do you really want to be this "safe"?[115]

Obama should have discarded the Attorney General Guidelines for the FBI developed by Bush. The guidelines posed a threat to civil liberties for several reasons. In a new development, they empowered the bureau to gather intelligence based on race, ethnicity, and religion. That an African American leader should tolerate such profiling seemed out of order, an injustice of great magnitude. His Justice Department under Attorney General Eric Holder, also the first African American to hold the job, placed a priority on enforcement of civil rights laws and hired lawyers with civil rights backgrounds, in contrast to Bush.[116] Yet, the surveillance state under Obama and Holder has been expanded.

The 2008 FBI Guidelines that Obama refused to revise also included open-ended "assessment" investigations, one of the greatest challenges to civil liberties in decades. Almost any reason can be stated to trigger an assessment inquiry, including gathering information to recruit new informers, and it is unclear how long they can last. During the four-month period December 2008 to March 2009, the FBI initiated 11,667 assessments, which led to only 427 regular investigations. About one-third of these assessments resulted from vague tips of suspicious activity. From April 2009 to April 2011, the bureau opened 42,888 terrorist assessments resulting in only 1,986 investigations. In sum, the FBI has been given great leeway to impose itself into American life without even the minor constraints that govern its regular investigations. They roam the public space checking leads and conducting recruiting sessions.[117]

The Obama administration sanctioned the FBI's revision of its Domestic Investigative and Operations Guide (DIOG) in a way which further eroded privacy protections. DIOG is distributed to special agents as a reference guide for conducting investigative activity. In 2011, the FBI made changes allowing for dumpster diving or trash inspection without any restrictions when they evaluate a subject as a potential informant. Why? So they can find incriminating evidence to use to compel a subject to work for them. Does this mean that the FBI soon will take over garbage collection around the nation? In addition, the FBI will be able to deploy "surveillance squads" to track a subject without restriction during an assessment inquiry. These squads coordinated monitoring to keep watch on people on a 24-hour basis. Lastly, the new manual made it easier for informers or agents secretly to attend the meetings of a suspect group. FBI operatives can attend up to five meetings before any rules take effect that might limit their presence. Overall, the new changes sanctioned political intelligence gathering on a broad level without firm evidence of any criminal wrongdoing. Such activity already occurred; now it has a legal backing. For example, the FBI could scrutinize a whole ethnic community without any evidence of potential security threats.[118] The new keywords, beside "proactive," include "intelligence-driven"—the bureau says it needed near limitless authority to collect information on Americans. While it denied it harassed people based on this information, many subjects of investigation would disagree.

Civil liberty critics pointed to sting operations or "agents provocateur" cases, which have proliferated during the Obama administration, as an abuse of power. Since 2009, the FBI arrested 41 people on terrorism charges along these lines employing what defense lawyers believe was "entrapment." The FBI encourages crime as a "test" on subjects. Undercover agents or informers enticed subjects into plans to break the law, which may even include providing phony bomb materials. Police were prepared to make arrests if the subjects showed any interest in the FBI's plans.[119]

Two other Obama spying initiatives shed dim light on the president's respect for privacy, openness, and civil liberties. First, several Democratic senators charged that his FBI applied a secret interpretation of the Patriot Act so broad that it almost amounted to a whole different law. Senators Ron Wyden of Oregon and Mark Udall of Colorado believed the secret interpretation vastly expanded federal surveillance power in ways the public did not comprehend. They warned of "unfettered" FBI access to bulk citizen data. Again, the issue does not appear to involve dossiers on particular individuals, but mass data collecting on the population as a whole. In 2011, the senators proposed an amendment to the reauthorization of the Patriot Act stressing public accountability: "United States Government officials should not secretly reinterpret public laws and statutes in a manner that is inconsistent with the public's understanding of these laws, and should not describe the execution of these laws in a way that misinforms or misleads the public."[120] Secret laws fundamentally undermined democratic accountability by preventing voters from knowing how their leaders acted on their behalf.

The second issue involved the retention of data by Internet service providers. The Justice Department urged Congress to mandate subscriber data be kept for one year, as opposed to 90 days. Why? So law enforcement and intelligence agencies could have greater opportunity to access these records. The type of information stored included customer names, addresses, phone numbers, credit card numbers, account numbers, as well as records of Web navigation. The information represents "a data bank of every digital act by every American," said Congressman Zoe Lofgren of California, who opposed the act. The FBI could "find out where every single American visited Web sites." Moreover, the Congress engaged in Orwellian doublespeak by naming the legislation the Protecting Children from Internet

Pornographers Act of 2011. Most privacy advocates and civil libertarians opposed the measure.[121]

The issue of "geolocation" tracking by government has begun to be addressed in the Congress. New technologies—cell phones, smart phones, laptops, and auto navigation devices—usually were equipped with Global Positioning Systems (GPS). While they may offer benefits to consumers, the ability of law enforcement to use the data to track and log the travels of Americans posed a major privacy threat. To date, the FBI has not applied for legal warrants to access this data because federal laws or federal courts have not mandated it. When Senator Wyden introduced the Geolocation Privacy and Surveillance Act in 2011, the Obama Justice Department opposed its provisions to require the use of warrants. The administration went further towards the erosion of privacy by urging the U.S. Supreme Court to allow the warrantless placing of GPS tracking devices on vehicles.[122]

Conclusion

The radical argument that the both the Democratic and Republican parties embraced a "permanent war" since World War II in order to maintain their hegemony seems even stronger now than during the Cold War.[123] At least during the Cold War the U.S. faced a hostile superpower intent on contesting U.S. expansionism. After the Cold War, the U.S. remained the only world superpower not facing a major threat to its territory from a sovereign nation. In this environment, the government under both Bush and Obama seized on the terror threat to unite the population around existing structures and to impose a political framework where progressives and radicals come to be viewed as extremists and terrorists. In sum, the scare politics of the war on terror served to contain dissent. When people act in opposition to government, they were likely to be framed as violent antagonists intent on political chaos and mayhem. Political expression outside the two-party system was relegated to the category of fanatical extremism.

The structures of surveillance have never been as large. It no longer was a matter of dossiers gathered on individuals. Mass data-mining extended monitoring to the general population as a whole. We all were under suspicion. A week after Obama won the 2008 presidential election, director Mueller gave a speech explaining the FBI's total information awareness goals. He said: "In the FBI, we have a mantra: 'Know Your Domain.' Knowing your domain means understanding every inch of a given community—its geography, its populations, its economy, and its vulnerabilities."[124] Government should know every inch of a community? If taken literally, it was a blueprint for a police state.

One way for Americans to monitor the development of a police state is to track the number of government employees working for the domestic intelligence apparatus. Indeed, by 2011 the number of FBI agents had increased by about 40 percent since 9/11 (from about 10,000 to 14,000). Almost half of all agents have been hired since 9/11.[125] Another indicator of creeping authoritarianism was the dramatic increase in the bureau's budget—about 130 percent rise since 9/11 (from $3.3 billion in fiscal 2001 to $7.9 billion in fiscal 2012).[126] Other changes currently being advocated within the intelligence community, but which Congress has not yet sanctioned, would tear down the wall between the FBI and CIA. (The Patriot Act already helped tear down the wall between the FBI and city police.) Every time a "wall" was torn down within the law enforcement and intelligence community, the new cooperation in government leaves civil liberties at greater risk. In this new vision, the CIA would be able to operate domestic spying, forcing the FBI and state and city police to become integrated into a new intelligence system.[127] The establishment of the Department of Homeland Security in 2004 already pushed in this direction. How far off is the imposition of new police state organizational structures in the name of fighting a largely phantom, amorphous terror threat?

Placing the modern U.S. state in a transnational perspective we do not find domestic "killing fields" and it is rare for elements of the domestic population to "disappear."[128] However, the role of the FBI as an authoritarian entity within the government, operating with broad sanction by the two-party system, prompts serious questioning about the nature of what is possible is America and the political limitations that the nation's leaders impose on the people. Is it legitimate for Americans to stand in opposition to the FBI or, more generally, the policies of the government? Does opposition equal disloyalty? A few months after 9/11, Attorney General John Ashcroft told the U.S. Senate Judiciary Committee that support for civil liberties equaled support for terrorism: "To those who scare peace-loving people with phantoms of lost liberty, my message is this: Your tactics only aid terrorists . . . they give ammunition to America's enemies."[129] Has that sentiment faded over time? The Obama administration would never publicly make such a foolish assertion. But its policies, as carried out by the FBI, demonstrate tacit agreement. The administration's failure to act on behalf of civil liberties was partly the result of a lack of mobilization by the American people. An anti-spying social movement has not arisen since 9/11. While a large segment of the American population embraced a "rights consciousness" on many issues, it did not seem to include protesting government spying or protecting free speech and assembly. At present, bipartisan government discourages the people from viewing the Constitution, and specifically the Bill of Rights, as a dynamic document that might empower them to oppose the "prevent, preempt, and disrupt" strategy that hinders the growth of progressive politics in the United States. A new popular consciousness is needed to oppose the expanding scope of surveillance in America. Once the people mobilize, government must change its behavior or risk being cast aside by a new social order.

Notes

Portions of this chapter were previously published in the following:
"The FBI and the Making of the Terrorist Threat," *Radical History Review*, Volume 111, pp. 35-50. Copyright, 2011, MARHO: The Radical

"Safeguarding Neoliberal Politics: The FBI's Attack on Dissent," in Jeffrey Shantz, ed., *Protest and Punishment: The Repression of Resistance in the Era of Neoliberal Globalization* (Durham, NC: Carolina Academic Press, 2012).

1. Gary T. Marx, "What's New About the 'New Surveillance'? Classifying for Change and Continuity," *Surveillance and Society* 1 (Late 2002): 9, http://www.surveillance-and-society.org/ articles1/ whatsnew.pdf.

2. Gary T. Marx, *Undercover: Police Surveillance in America* (Berkeley: University of California Press, 1988).

3. William L. O'Neill, *A Bubble in Time: America during the Interwar Years, 1989-2001* (Chicago: Ivan R. Dee, 2009); Kristie Ball and Frank Webster, eds., *The Intensification of Surveillance: Crime, Terrorism and Warfare in the Information Age* (Sterling, VA: Pluto Press, 2003).

4. Whitfield Diffie and Susan Landau, *Privacy on the Line: The Politics of Wiretapping and Encryption* (Cambridge: MIT Press, 2007), 219-223; David K. Shipler, *The Rights of the People: How Our Search for Safety Invades Our Liberties* (New York: Alfred A. Knopf, 2011), 194-196.

5. See, for example, Reg Whitaker, *The End of Privacy: How Total Surveillance is Becoming a Reality* (New York: New Press, 2000); Charles J. Sykes, *The End of Privacy: Personal Rights in the Surveillance Society* (New York: St. Martin's Press, 1999); Jeffrey Rosen, *The Unwanted Gaze: The Destruction of Privacy in America* (New York: Random House, 2000); Amitai Etzioni, *The Limits of Privacy* (New York: Basic Books, 1999); Whitfield Diffie and Susan Landau, *Privacy on the Line: The Politics of Wiretapping and Encryption* (Cambridge: MIT Press, 1998); David Brin, *The Transparent Society* (Reading, MA: Perseus Books, 1998); John J. Gilliom, *Surveillance, Privacy, and the Law: Employee Drug Testing and the Politics of Social Control* (Ann Arbor: University of Michigan Press, 1994); Williams Staples, *The Culture of Surveillance* (New York: St. Martin's Press, 1997); David Flaherty, *Protecting Privacy in Surveillance Societies* (Westport: Greenwood Press, 1989).

6. Heidi Boghosian and the National Lawyers Guild, *The Policing of Political Speech: Constraints on Mass Dissent in the U.S.* (New York: National Lawyers Guild, 2010), 25.

7. Abby Scher, "The Crackdown on Dissent," *Nation*, Jan. 19, 2001. The ACLU in Washington state drew very different lessons from the Seattle protest. See "Out of Control: Seattle's Flawed Response to Protests Against the World Trade Organization," Nov. 21, 2000,

http://www.acluwa.org/sites/default/files/attachments/WTO%20 Report%20Web.pdf.

8. Jeff Shantz, ed., *Law Against Liberty: The Criminalization of Dissent* (Lake Mary, FL: Vandeplas Publishing, 2011), 1. See also Shantz, ed., *Protest and Punishment: The Repression of Resistance in the Era of Neoliberal Globalization* (Durham, NC: Carolina Academic Press, 2012).

9. Luis A. Fernandez, *Policing Dissent: Social Control and the Anti-Globalization Movement* (Piscataway: Rutgers University Press, 2008).

10. "Are We 'Islam Compliant' as Much as We are Y2K Compliant?" n. d. http://www.themodernreligion.com/index1.html (accessed Feb. 5, 2011).

11. "Y2K," Zer YT! Media Sociale Shiqiptare, n. d. http://www.zeriyt.com/y2k-t27168.0.html (acessed Feb. 5, 2011).

12. Daniel Schorr, *Come to Think of It: Notes on the Turn of the Millennium* (New York: Viking Press, 2007), 47.

13. Brian M. Jenkins, "The Organization Men: Anatomy of an Attack," in James F. Hogue Jr. and Gideon Rose, *How Did This Happen? Terrorism and the New War* (New York: Public Affairs, 2001), 9-10.

14. *The 9/11 Commission Report: Final Report of the National Commission on Terrorist Attacks Upon the United States* (Washington, DC: U.S. Government Printing Office, 2004): 347.

15. Quoted in Lewis H. Lapham, *Gag Rule: On the Suppression of Dissent and the Stifling of Democracy* (New York: Penguin Press, 2004), 7.

16. Schorr, *Come to Think of It*, 246.

17. Quoted in James Bovard, *Terrorism and Tyranny: Trampling Freedom, Justice and Peace to Rid the World of Evil* (New York: Palgrave Macmillan, 2003), 155.

18. Bovard, *Terrorism and Tyranny*, 157; Shane Harris, *The Watchers: The Rise of the American Surveillance State* (New York: Penguin, 2010).

19. Richard Maxwell, "Surveillance: Work, Myth, and Policy," *Social Text* 83 (Summer 2005): 6; Bill of Rights Defense Committee (BORDC), "Resolutions Passed and Efforts Underway, by State," http://www.bordc.org/list.php; http://www.bordc.org/involved/orgs/ (accessed Jan. 31, 2012).

20. Reg Whitaker, "After 9/11: A Surveillance State?" in Cynthia Brown, ed., *Lost Liberties: Ashcroft and the Assault on Personal Freedom* (New York: Free Press, 2003), 55. See also, David Lyon, *Surveillance After September 11* (Malden, MA: Blackwell Publishing, 2003).

21. Oscar Gandy Jr., "Data Mining, Surveillance, and Discrimination in the Post-9/11 Environment," in Kevin D. Haggerty and Richard V.

Ericson, eds., *The New Politics of Surveillance and Visibility* (Toronto: University of Toronto Press, 2006), 374-376.

22. Los Angeles, CT-6 to Counterterrorism Boston, New York, Los Angeles, Sept. 3, 2003. This FBI memo is contained in a report by the American Civil Liberties Union, "History Repeated: The Dangers of Domestic Spying by Federal Law Enforcement," May 29, 2007. http://www.aclu.org/national-security/history-repeated-dangers-domestic-spying-federal-law-enforcement.

23. "DHS Monitoring of Social Media Concerns Civil Liberties Advocates," *Washington Post*, Jan. 13, 2012. See also Lori Andrews, *I Know Who You Are and Saw What You Did: Social Networks and the Death of Privacy* (New York: New Press, 2012).

24. "FBI Looking to 'Friend' Terrorists," TechNewsworld.com, Jan. 30, 2012, http://www.technewsworld.com/story/74295.html.

25. "Trade in Surveillance Technology Raises Worries," *Washington Post*, Dec. 1, 2011; "Document Trove Exposes Surveillance Methods," *Wall Street Journal*, Nov. 19, 2011.

26. Electronic Privacy Information Center, "Face Recognition," n.d., www.epic.org/privacy/facerecognition/ (accessed Aug. 22, 2011).

27. See the declassified file, "FBI Terrorist Photo Album," at www.vault.fbi.gov/FBI%20Terrorist%20Photo%20Album (accessed July 29, 2011).

28. For a general discussion, see David Lyon, *Identifying Citizens: ID Cards as Surveillance* (Cambridge: Polity Press, 2009).

29. "Pole Cameras and Surreptitious Surveillance," *FBI Law Enforcement Bulletin* 78 (November 2009): 23, 32.

30. "Post 9/11, Surveillance Cameras Everywhere," MSNBC.com, Aug. 23, 2011, www.today.msnbc.msn.com/id/44163852/ns/business-us_business.

31. The term "eye in the sky" received popular currency with the publication of Philip K. Dick's 1957 novel of that name.

32. "War Evolves with Drones, Some as Tiny as Bugs," *New York Times*, June 19, 2011; "Dragonfly or Insect Spy? Scientists at Work on Robobugs," *Washington Post*, Oct. 9, 2007. See also Gary T. Marx, "Electric Eye in the Sky: Some Reflections on the New Surveillance and Popular Culture," in David Lyon and Elia Zureik, eds., *Computers, Surveillance and Privacy* (Minneapolis: University of Minnesota Press, 1996), 193-226; Dwayne A. Day, John M. Logsdon, and Brian Latell, eds., *Eye in the Sky: The Story of the CORONA Spy Satellites* (Washington, DC: Smithsonian Institution Press, 1998).

33. American Civil Liberties Union, "Protecting Privacy From Aerial Surveillance: Recommendations for Government Use of Drones," December 2011, 3, http://www.aclu.org/technology-and-liberty/report-protecting-privacy-aerial-surveillance-recommendations-government-use.

34. Political Research Associates, "Suspicious Activity Reporting: A Window into the Domestic Security Infrastructure," http://www.publiceye.org/liberty/matrix/reports/sar_initiative/suspicious-activity-reporting.html.

35. TRAC, "Who is a Terrorist? Government Failure to Define Terrorism Undermines Enforcement, Puts Civil Liberties at Risk," Sept. 28, 2009, 1-2, http://trac.syr.edu/tracreports/terrorism/215/.

36. Boghosian, *The Policing of Political Speech*, 3.

37. Ibid., 1.

38. Office of Inspector General, U. S. Department of Justice, "A Review of the FBI's Investigations of Certain Domestic Advocacy Groups," September 2010, 1-2, 188.

39. Electronic Frontier Foundation, "Patterns of Misconduct: FBI Intelligence Violations from 2001-2008," 1-10, https://www.eff.org/pages/patterns-misconduct-fbi-intelligence-violations (accessed Jan. 31, 2011).

40. William Bloss, "Escalating U.S. Police Surveillance after 9/11: An Examination of Causes and Effects," *Surveillance and Society* 4 (Mid 2007): 221, http://www.surveillance-and-society.org/articles4(3)/escalating.pdf (accessed Jan 31, 2011).

41. Torin Monahan, *Surveillance in the Time of Insecurity* (New Brunswick: Rutgers University Press, 2010), 20.

42. American Civil Liberties Union, "The Surveillance-Industrial Complex: How the American Government Is Conscripting Businesses and Individuals in the Construction of a Surveillance Society," August 2004, 4-6.

43. American Civil Liberties Union, "More About Suspicious Activity Reporting," June 29, 2010, 1, http://www.aclu.org/spy-files/more-about-suspicious-activity-reporting; American Civil Liberties Union, "Sounding 'Suspicious': Making Sure the FBI Protects Americans and Our Liberties," Aug. 25, 2011, http://www.aclu.org/blog/national-security/sounding-suspicious-making-sure-fbi-protects-americans-and-our-liberties.

44. ACLU, "More About Suspicious Activity Reporting," 3.

45. U.S. Department of Justice, Office of Inspector General, "Report to Congress on Implementation of Section 1001 of the USA Patriot Act," Feb. 2009, 9-10, www.justice.gov/oig/special/s0902/index.htm.

46. Ibid.; FBI, "Privacy Assessment for the e-Guardian Threat Tracking System," April 13, 2005, 3, www.foia.fbi.gov/eguardian_threat. htm.

47. Ivan Greenberg, *The Dangers of Dissent: The FBI and Civil Liberties since 1965* (Lanham: Lexington Books, 2010), 203.

48. Dina Temple-Raston, "Treasury Seeks to Cast a Wider Net for Terrorists," National Public Radio, Sept. 29, 2010, http://www.npr.org/templates/story/story.php?storyId=130197341.

49. Thomas Cincotta, "Intelligence Fusion Centers: A De-Centralized National Intelligence Agency," Political Research Associates, 2, http://www.publiceye.org/magazine/v24n4/intelligence-fusion-centers.html (accessed Jan. 6, 2011).

50. "ACLU Calls Anti-Terrorism Agency Map Placement 'Disturbing,'" *The City Paper*, Dec. 21, 2010, http://nashvillecitypaper.com/content/city-news/aclu-calls-anti-terrorism-agency-map-placement-disturbing.

51. North Central Texas Fusion System Prevention Awareness Bulletin, Feb. 19, 2009, 4-5, http://nashvillecitypaper.com/content/city-news/aclu-calls-anti-terrorism-agency-map-placement-disturbing.

52. "Md. Police Put Activists' Names on Terror Lists," *Washington Post*, Oct. 8, 2008.

53. "Election Heightens Terrorism Offensive," *Washington Post*, Sept. 27, 2004; "FBI Pursues a Tough New Anti-Terror Strategy in the Run-up to November," CNN.com, Sept. 27, 2004 (no longer on-line); "FBI's Anti-Terror 'October Plan,'" CBSNEWS.com, Sept. 17, 2004, www.cbsnews.com/stories/2004/09/17/eveningnews/main644096.shtml.

54. "Inquiry Targeted 2,000 Foreign Muslims in 2004," *Washington Post*, Oct. 31, 2008.

55. Raleigh Resident Agency, SA [text redacted] to Counterterrorism, Charlotte, "FBI National Initiatives," Oct. 5, 2004, October Plan FBI file.

56. FBI, "Protecting America from Terrorist Attack," July 2004, http://www.fbi.gov/news/stories/2004/july/njttf070204.

57. Columbia Squad 4/JTTF SA [text redacted] to Columbia, "Columbia Division Prevention Plan; Reporting Requirements," Oct. 5, 2011, October Plan FBI file.

58. Dallas Counter-Terrorism/ Fort Worth RA to Counterterrorism Dallas, "[Text redacted] IT- UBL/Al-Qaeda," Oct. 21, 2004, October Plan FBI file.

59. San Francisco Squad 17A, SA [text redacted] to Counterterrorism, "2004 Threat Task Force – Prevention Plan," Oct. 29, 2004, October Plan FBI file.

60. Louisville Squad 4/JTTF to Counterterrorism, "2004 Threat Task Force – Prevention Plan (Community Outreach)," Oct. 4, 2004, October Plan, FBI file.

61. Louisville, Squad 4 [text redacted] to Counterterrorism, "2004 Threat Task Force, Prevention Plan, Subject Interviews," Oct. 29, 2004, October Plan FBI file.

62. Los Angeles, CT-6 to Los Angeles, "Fall 2004 Prevention Operations for Threats to Los Angeles," Oct. 22, 2004, October Plan FBI file.

63. San Diego, Squad 21 SA [text redacted] to San Diego, "2004 Threat Task Force – Prevention Plan," Oct. 21, 2011, October Plan FBI file.

64. New York, IT-2 SA [text redacted] to Albany Counterterrorism, "[Text redacted] IT-Other, AL-QAEDA," Oct. 35, 2004, October Plan FBI file.

65. Pittsburgh Squad 4/JTTF to Counterterrorism, "[Text redacted] IT-Other," October 19, 2004, 3, October Plan FBI file.

66. Pittsburgh Laurel Highlands RA to Counterterrorism, "[Text redacted] IT-URL/AL Qaeda," Oct. 12, 2004, October Plan FBI file.

67. Ibid.

68. Dallas CTFW/ Fort Worth Resident Agency to Dallas, "2004 Threat Task Force Prevention Plan," Oct. 12, 2004, October Plan FBI file.

69. "Islamic Charity Says F.B.I. Falsified Evidence Against It," *Washington Post*, July 27, 2004; "Five Convicted in Terrorism Financing Trial," *Washington Post*, Nov. 25, 2008.

70. Charlotte, Greensboro RA to Counterterrorism, "2004 Threat Task Force Prevention Plan," Oct. 14, 2004, October Plan FBI file.

71. Salt Lake City SA [text redacted] to [text redacted], "Salt Lake City 2004 Threat Task Force Prevention Plan," Oct. 10, 2004, October Plan FBI file.

72. Baltimore Squad 17/Wilmington RA to Counterterrorism Baltimore, "2004 Threat Task Force—Prevention Plan," Oct. 22, 2005, October Plan FBI file; RC Hobbies Online, www.rchobbies.org/rc_airplanes.htm (accessed Jan. 30, 2011).

73. American Civil Liberties Union, "ACLU Seeks Records About FBI Collection of Racial and Ethnic Data in 29 States," July 27, 2010, www.aclu.org/national-security/aclu-seeks-fbi-records; FBI, "Domestic Investigations and Operations Guide," Part I, Dec. 16, 2008 http://foia.fbi.gov/diog/domestic_investigations_and_operations_guide_part1.pdf.

74. Emily Berman, "Domestic Intelligence: New Powers, New Rules," Brennan Center for Justice, New York University Law School, Jan. 18, 2011, 30.

75. Valerie Caproni, statement before the Senate Select Committee on Intelligence, Sept. 23, 2008, 1-2, www.centerforinvestigativereporting.org/files/FBItestimony; "Terror Plan Would Give F.B.I. More Power," *New York Times*, Sept. 13, 2008; "Justice Dept. Completes Revision of F.B.I. Guidelines for Terrorism Investigations," *New York Times*, Oct. 4, 2008; "Rule Changes Would Give FBI Agents Extensive New Powers," *Washington Post*, Sept. 12, 2008.

76. Spencer Ackerman, "FBI Teaches Agents: 'Mainstream' Muslims are 'Violent , Radical,'" Wired.com, Sept. 14, 2011, www.wired.com/dangerroom/2011/09/fbi-muslims-radical/.

77. Coleen Rowley, "We're Conflating Proper Dissent and Terrorism," *Minneapolis Star Tribune*, Jan. 15, 2011, http://www.startribune.com/opinion/commentary/113637589.html.

78. American Civil Liberties Union, "FBI Improperly Spied On Activists, Says Justice Department Inspector General," Sept. 20, 2010, http://www.aclu.org/free-speech-national-security/fbi-improperly-spied-activists-says-justice-department-inspector-gener.

79. "FBI Files on Investigation of Iowa City Peace Activists Made Public," *Iowa Independent*, Sept. 23, 2010, http://iowaindependent.com/43846/fbi-files-on-investigation-of-iowa-city-peace-group-made-public.

80. "FBI Defends 2008 Probe in Iowa City," *Des Moines Register*, Sept. 21, 2010.

81. Mathew Rothschild, "FBI Infiltrates Iowa City Protest Group," *Progressive*, May 26, 2009, http://www.progressive.org/print/131130 .

82. Robert Ehl, "FBI Tactics Can Suppress Dissent," Oct. 2, 2010, http://thegazette.com/2010/10/02/fbi%E2%80%99s-tactics-can-suppress-dissent/. See also Will Porter, *Green is the New Red: An Insider's Account of a Movement Under Siege* (San Francisco: City Lights, 2011).

83. Department of Homeland Security, "Domestic Terrorist Newsletter" 1 (2006): 1-2, www.naiop.org/governmentaffairs/newsletter/dtnewsletter.pdf (accessed June 11, 2010); "Eco-Terrorists, Too, May Soon Be on the Run," *Christian Science Monitor*, Feb. 15, 2002.

84. Boghosian, *The Policing of Political Speech*, 27.

85. Ibid., 30.

86. Ibid., 33.

87. "Settlements End Suits Over Raids by Officials," *New York Times*, June 3, 2011.

88. Boghosian, *The Policing of Political Speech*, 39-44.

89. Ibid., 65.

90. Amy Goodman, "FBI Raids and the Criminalization of Dissent," Sept. 28, 2010, http://www.truthdig.com/report/item/fbi_raids_and_the_criminalization_of_dissent_20100928/; "F.B.I. Searches Antiwar Activists' Homes," *New York Times*, Sept. 24, 2010.

91. "For Anarchist, Details of Life as F.B.I. Target," *New York Times*, May 29, 2011.

92. San Antonio, CT-2/CTXJTTF/ Austin Resident Agency to San Antonio, "SAC Authority is Requested for Closed Circuit Television (CCTV) Monitoring Without Sound During a Surveillance," March 3, 2007, Scott Crow FBI file.

93. San Antonio, Squad CT-2/CTXJTTF/ Austin Resident Agency to San Antonio, "Scott Crow; AOT-DT Animal Rights; Eco Extremism," July 16, 2007, 3-4, Crow FBI file.

94. FBI FD-302 form, April 4, 2007, Crow FBI file.

95. "FBI to Expand Domestic Surveillance Powers as Details Emerge of its Spy Campaign Targeting Activists," "Democracy Now!", June 14, 2011, http://www.democracynow.org/2011/6/14/fbi_to_expand_domestic_surveillance_powers; "For Anarchist, Details of Life as F.B.I. Target."

96. Scott Crow, *Black Flags and Windmills: Hope, Anarchy, and the Common Ground Collective* (Oakland: PM Press, 2011).

97. *Olmstead v. U.S.* 277 U.S. 438, 478 (1928).

98. Brief of Amici Curiae submitted by the Electronic Privacy Information Center (EPIC) in *NASA v. Nelson*, Aug. 9, 2010, 7-10; EPIC, "NASA v. Nelson," http://epic.org/amicus/nasavnelson/ (accessed May 24, 2011).

99. Daniel J. Solove, "Why Privacy Matters Even if You Have 'Nothing to Hide'" *Chronicle of Higher Education*, May 15, 2011; Solove, *Nothing to Hide: The False Tradeoff Between Privacy and Security* (New Haven: Yale University Press, 2011). See also Helen Nissenbaum, *Privacy in Context: Technology, Policy and the Integrity of Social Life* (Sanford, CA: Stanford Law Books, 2010).

100. Solove, "Why Privacy Matters Even if You Have 'Nothing to Hide.'"

101. Daniel J. Solove, "Why 'Security' Keeps Winning Over Privacy," Salon.com May 31, 2011, http://www.salon.com/news/politics/war_room/2011/05/31/solove_privacy_security.

102. Julian Sanchez, *Leashing the Surveillance State: How to Reform Patriot Act Surveillance Authorities*, Cato Institute, May 16, 2011, 25.

103. "Justice Watchdog Looks Back on 10 Years in Post," *National Public Radio*, Jan. 28, 2011, http://www.npr.org/2011/01/28/133272339/justice-watchdog-looks-back-on-10-years-in-post.

104. "F.B.I. Spying Not Fueled by Politics, Report Says," *New York Times*, Sept. 20, 2010.

105. For a comparative study with a different conclusion, see Stuart Farson and Mark Phythian, eds., *Commissions of Inquiry and National Security* (Santa Barbara: Praeger, 2011).

106. Harry S. Truman Library and Museum, "The Buck Stops Here," http://www.trumanlibrary.org/buckstop.htm (accessed Feb. 3, 2011).

107. Coleen Rowley, "How Top Secret America Misfires," Huffington Post, Jan. 19, 2011, 5, http://www.huffingtonpost.com/coleen-rowley/how-top-secret-america-mi_b_811049.html.

108. These documents may be requested under the Freedom of Information Act. Kel McClanahan "FBI Policy and Procedure Library," FOIL posting (online), Aug. 13, 2011; FBI, "Policy and Guidance Library," March 8, 2011, 1-8, Policy and Guidance Library FBI file, http://www.nationalsecuritylaw.org/files/received/FBI/CPO_PGL_index.pdf

109. "FBI Illegally using Community Outreach to Gather Intelligence, ACLU says," *Washington Post*, Dec. 1, 2011.

110. For an uncritical treatment of Mueller, see Garrett M. Graff, *The Threat Matrix: The FBI at War in the Age of Global Terror* (New York: Little Brown and Co., 2011).

111. "Procrastinating on a New FBI Director," *Washington Post*, May 12, 2011; American Civil Liberties Union, "ACLU Opposes Extension of FBI Director Robert Mueller's Term," May 12, 2011.

112. Karen Greenberg, "Now That Bin Laden is Dead, Can We Have Our Freedoms Back?" AlterNet, May 3, 2011, http://www.alternet.org/world/150830/now_that_bin_laden_is_dead,_can_we_have_our_freedoms_back/.

113. David Bromwich, "Obama, Bush and the Patriot Act," Huffington Post, May 30, 2011, http://www.huffingtonpost.com/david-bromwich/patriot-act-obama-_b_868831.html?ref=fb&src=sp.

114. Barack Obama, "Remarks by the President on National Security," speech before the National Archives, Washington, D.C., May 21, 2009, http://www.whitehouse.gov/the_press_office/Remarks-by-the-President-On-National-Security-5-21-09/.

115. Tom Engelhardt, "Welcome to Post-Legal America," TomDispatch.com, May 30, 2011, http://www.tomdispatch.com/blog/175398/tomgram:_engelhardt,_welcome_to_post-legal_america.

116. About 90 percent of Obama hires had civil rights backgrounds, up from about 38 percent during the Bush Administration. "In Shift, Justice Department is Hiring Lawyers with Civil Rights Backgrounds," *New York Times*, May 31, 2011.

117. Congressional Research Service, "The Federal Bureau of Investigation and Terrorism Investigations," April 27, 2011, 11-12; "F.B.I. Focusing on Security over Ordinary Crime," *New York Times*, August 24, 2011.

118. "F.B.I. Agents Get Leeway to Push Privacy Bounds," *New York Times*, June 12, 2011.

119. Congressional Research Service, "The Federal Bureau of Investigation and Terrorism Investigations," 21-22.

120. Spencer Ackerman, "Bill Would Force Intel Chief To Renounce 'Secret Patriot Act,'" Wired.com, July 28, 2011, http://www.wired. com/dangerroom/2011/07/bill-would-force-intel-chief-to-rebuke-secret-patriot-act/; Ackerman, "There's a Secret Patriot Act, Senator Says," Wired.com, May 25, 2011, http://www.publiceye.org/magazine/v24n4/intelligence-fusion-centers.html

121. Dean McCullagh, "House Panel Approves Broadened ISP Snooping Bill," July 28, 2011, www.news.cnet.com/8301-31921_3-20084939-281/house-panel-approves-broadened-isp-snooping-bill/.

122. Senator Ron Wyden, "Legislation Provides Needed Clarity for Use of Geolocation Information," June 15, 2011, www.wyden.senate.gov.; "Lawmakers Propose Warrant Requirement for GPS Data," Wired.com, June 15, 2011, www.wired.com/threatlevel/2011/06/gps warrant-proposal/.

123. Jules Lobel, "The War on Terrorism and Civil Liberties," in Thomas E. Baker and John F. Stack, eds., *At War with Civil Rights and Civil Liberties* (Lanham: Rowman and Littlefield, 2005), 25-48.

124. Robert S. Mueller III, speech before the International Association of Chiefs of Police, San Diego, California, Nov. 10, 2008.

125. "The Federal Bureau of Investigation and Terrorism Investigations," 2; Graff, *The Threat Matrix*, 22.

126. "Obama's 2012 Budget," *Federal Times*, Feb. 15, 2011, http://www.federaltimes.com/article/20110215/AGENCY01/102150302/.

127. This agenda is advanced, for example, by former CIA official Ronald A. Marks in *Spying In America in the Post 9/11 World: Domestic Threat and the Need for Change* (Santa Barbara, CA: Praeger, 2010).

128. For a recent analysis of state violence elsewhere in the world, see David M. Crowe, ed. *Crimes of State Past and Present: Government-Sponsored Atrocities and International Legal Responses* (London: Routledge, 2011).

129. Quoted in Aryeh Neier, "Introduction," in Brown, ed., *Lost Liberties*, 8.

7

Postscript: The Tenth Anniversary of 9/11

The tenth anniversary of the September 11, 2001, terrorist attacks became a "big event": It gripped the nation as did few other anniversaries. The day arrived with both solemn remembrance and patriotic fanfare. As the nation collectively grieved, its leaders also offered expressions of nation-state hegemony. President Barack Obama's speech-making on the subject began two weeks prior to the anniversary. He called for the nation to rekindle the "spirit of unity" that followed the attacks. What type of unity? It was built on a sense of nationalistic victimhood and included large expressions of nativism and xenophobia. Obama conveniently forgot the hate crimes at home and military violence overseas remembering only American "generosity and compassion."[1]

Several million American Muslims and Arabs were not included in this unity. Several months before the anniversary, a major opinion poll found 50 percent were called offensive names or otherwise looked at with suspicion. They blamed Obama and the FBI. Overall, 52 percent said government anti-terror policies profiled them for increased monitoring and suspicion, and this problem was greater than at the end of the Bush administration.[2] Both Bush and Obama failed to build meaningful, trusting relationships with American Muslims. Since he became president, Obama had not visited a single mosque in the U.S.[3]

Threat-mongering by the FBI remained at a high level. Despite spending several billion dollars during the war on terrorism, the FBI said the threat of attack was *greater* than ever before. A top counterterrorism official indicated a few months before the anniversary that lethal "quick-hitting strikes" could be executed with "less funding, fewer operatives, less training" against a "wider array of terrorism targets."

> I do not think this nation has ever faced a more fluid, more dynamic, or more complex terrorism threat. We are seeing an increase in the sources of terrorism, a wider array of terrorism targets, a greater cooperation among terrorist groups, and an evolution in terrorist tactics and communication methodology. The long-term planning undertaken by senior core al Qaeda leaders which led to the 9/11 attacks is much more difficult for them to attain in today's environment. It is replaced with somewhat less sophisticated, quick-hitting strikes which can be just as lethal but which take less funding, fewer operatives, less training, and less timing to execute.[4]

It seemed the FBI wanted the population to live in fear of lethal attacks. A week before the anniversary, the bureau told the media to announce that the use of small airplanes as weapons remained a serious threat. But, predictably, FBI intelligence remained vague about time or place.[5] Three days before the September 11 anniversary the FBI issued a major scare announcement of a "credible but unconfirmed" threat involving a car bomb. Where? They said either in New York City or Washington, DC. As a result, bomb-sniffing dogs were set loose in Washington subways and vehicle searches on New York City bridges led to massive traffic jams. Again, if it is "unconfirmed" why make headline news?[6] The government framed the arrival of the anniversary with nervous tension to discipline the population.

A major media theme was "survivor" stories. More than 10,000 people had safely evacuated the Twin Towers before they fell. Along with emergency responders and the relatives of victims, they told their accounts in dozens of press articles and television news programs. The survivors felt very fortunate to be alive and grieved for those who did not make it out of the Towers. Relatives of victims shared their profound pain. Attention focused not only on the 2,983 people killed in the attacks but also the "demons" that allegedly haunted thousands of others, especially in Manhattan. At least 10,000 firefighters, police officers, and other emergency responders were determined to have developed post-traumatic stress disorder (PTSD) and many apparently had yet to recover. There are different ways to view psychological or mental illnesses related to terrorism, as opposed to those who developed physical ailments, such as breathing difficulties, at the rescue scene. New York City's health department also suggested that about 61,000 of the 409,000 people in the disaster area may have developed PTSD. Why did so many have symptoms such as nightmares, sleep problems, trouble concentrating, jitters, and feelings of helplessness, anxiety, and guilt?[7]

Americans are unaccustomed to warfare (as opposed to crime) in their homeland. It has not happened in a substantial way since the 1941 surprise attack on Pearl Harbor. The last direct attack on the American continent goes back to the 19th century—the brief Mexican-American war in 1848 in Texas and the War of 1812 along the eastern seaboard against the British.

The American empire has been so dominant in the modern period that its citizens cannot easily tolerate destruction due to a foreign war within its borders. The bombing of Manhattan was limited to only one place—the World Trade Center, which occupied 16 acres of land. The American psyche was so protected and—I hate to say it—"spoiled" by a century of victory in world affairs that it cracked very fast and easily when several airplanes served as weapons. This was not a mass bombing of a city so common, for example, in Europe during World War II. It did not involve the complete nuclear destruction of a city as the U.S. accomplished in Japan (Hiroshima and Nagasaki) in 1945. Of course, mass loss of life is a tragedy under any circumstance, but since when are most Americans pacifists?

Even more telling of the shock to the American sensibility, the nation used a simple series of numbers—"9/11"—to characterize the event. (Put aside the issue that these numbers also are the ones for national emergency telephone calls. It does not appear al Qaeda gave much importance to this coincidence.)[8] A single date—"September 11"—also became a type of slogan or justification for revenge and militarism. Nothing more needs to be said by the government than to evoke "September 11"—the date shut down debate and gave American power (including that of the FBI) a virtual blank check. Very few days in U.S. history have such importance. September 11 may stand alongside December 7 (the bombing of Pearl Harbor) and July 4 (the signing of the Declaration of Independence) for their symbolic significance. I hope it is not so.

My Escape from New York City

I lived in Manhattan on September 11, 2001, only a few miles from Ground Zero. While my residence on West 106 St. near Broadway was far enough away not to see, hear, or smell the destruction, my younger brother, Roger, lived in the disaster zone (near the South Street Seaport) and saw some of the attack from his window and terrace. Authorities forced his family to evacuate their apartment for several weeks. About a week after the attacks, he and I went back to his place to gather some clothes and other items. We put paper masks over our noses and mouths, showed identification to get past a police line, and walked the deserted streets which still had dust in the air and smelled very, very foul. The debris from the Twin Towers had not fully dissipated.

Almost a life-long New Yorker, I left the city about 7 months later for the west coast. My escape from New York was related to the changes brought about as a result of 9/11. Put simply, New York had become a terrible place to live. It was not so much the attack itself that was traumatic for me but the way local residents and official power responded to it.

First, there was so much hype and celebration surrounding Rudolf Giuliani—now labeled "America's Mayor." Giuliani's politics were very conservative. He was a Republican who profoundly alienated minority and progressive communities. He became a polarizing figure who relished the role to fight with those he opposed politically. His record on civil liberties was very poor, especially soft on police brutality. The phrase, "Giuliani Time," came to represent for many residents the way his police department acted in repressive ways to contain and put down the disadvantaged. (During a case of police brutality, officers allegedly repeated that phrase as they struck the victim with their batons.) Remember Haitian immigrant Abner Louima—officers savagely sodomized him. In the case of African immigrant Amadou Diallo, police shot him 41 times as he reached for his wallet. In a 1999 poll, more than two-thirds of black New Yorkers said that the policies of the Giuliani administration caused an increase in police violence.[9] The mayor had been one of the first to implement the zero tolerance, broken windows theory of crime control: Aggressively police small crime to create a law and order environment to reduce big crime. As a result, he directed the NYPD to harass and arrest panhandlers and the homeless who begged for a quarter. I told my colleagues and friends we should call the mayor "J. Edgar Giuliani"—a boss in the mold of the FBI's infamous director.

After 9/11, the mayor almost overnight became a popular hero for no legitimate reason. After all, he was an odd figure to lead collective grieving. More than a few people noted he was not a very empathetic figure. Could the overly combative mayor feel my pain? Yet, typical of the uncritical praise was this assessment by *Newsweek*'s Jonathan Alter just two weeks after the attacks: "No matter what happens now, Rudy Giuliani's legend is in place." Alter compared him to Winston Churchill and saw "a new global standard for crisis leadership: strong, sensitive, straightforward and seriously well-informed about every meaningful detail of the calamity."[10]

The mythmaking included being named *Time* magazine's "Person of the Year" in 2001. Yet, there is much fault to be found in his crisis leadership. His administration did not compel the thousands of rescue workers at Ground Zero to wear proper protective respiratory equipment. Many worked for days with no protection at all. As a result, firefighters, construction workers, and others subsequently became ill—many more than were killed in the attacks. A study of 27,449 rescue workers found nearly 28 percent developed asthma. Cancer rates also were much higher in this group than in the general population.[11]

The political messaging coming from Washington added to the sense of trauma and crisis. The president, the Justice Department, and the FBI issued weekly warnings about vague threats to apartment buildings, bridges, malls, airlines, nuclear power plants, and national monuments. The government told us to be alert for trouble. The FBI said another terrorist attack was certain to occur. President Bush said Americans should not criticize the "war on terror" because any criticism helped the enemy. State propaganda sustained a culture of fear demonizing dissent. The loss of liberty in New York seemed great. Was it okay to criticize the government? Were fellow residents listening to your political speech ready to call the police?

Bush incorporated the idea of citizen volunteerism into the war on terrorism by urging Neighborhood Watch groups to look for terrorist activity in addition to regular crime. Millions of Americans already worked with Watch groups, and their activity would be politicized in new ways. According to Attorney General John Ashcroft, "Through the Neighborhood Watch program, we will weave a seamless web of prevention of terrorism that brings together citizens and law enforcement." Citizen spying promoted conformity and silenced speech. The Bush administration's new 24-page "Citizens' Preparedness Guide" told Americans: "You know what is normal for your neighborhood, workplace and daily routines. If a behavior or event seems to be outside the norm or is frightening, let law enforcement authorities know."[12] What behavior is perceived as "outside the norm"? Reading books or marching in the street for social justice?

The New York City Metropolitan Transit Authority (MTA) began what was termed a "citizen education program" to alert riders to spy on others. The program promoted the slogan: "If You See Something, Say Something." What behavior should be reported to the authorities? The MTA listed five criteria.

Be alert to unattended packages.
Be wary of suspicious behavior

Take notice of people in bulky or inappropriate clothing.
Report exposed wiring or other irregularities.
Report anyone tampering with surveillance cameras or entering unauthorized areas.[13]

Was I supposed to notice the clothes that men and women wear?
That was a tall order that could generate paranoia. I hazard to
say that most people riding the subway or bus should keep their
eyes off other people. It was safer and less confrontational. A direct gaze can be interpreted the wrong way. Again, what people
deem "suspicious" is not obvious. Is there one standard of allegedly normal, non-suspicious behavior? Such public vigilance is a
dangerous thing when it was integrated into the state's surveillance control systems. A year before the 9/11 anniversary, the
Department of Homeland Security promoted the MTA's "Say
Something" program on a national basis.[14]

Right after 9/11 the NYPD raised their presence walking
the beat and parking their cars nearly everywhere in Manhattan looking for suspicious activity. They patrolled the subways
inspecting bags and eyeing people as potential terrorists. A little
sweat on your brow or your palm? The police might believe
you are carrying a dangerous package. New York City became
a "law enforcement mess." When terrorism occurs, it shows
that they are failing. The new police warnings kept the threat of
terrorist violence at the top of the public's mind in order to get
the public to support expanded police and military power. The
media refused to let dissidents or radicals speak to the public,
which is a form of censorship. Instead, the media celebrated police officers and firefighters as our newest heroes.

A significant portion of the Manhattan population also
seemed to respond to the attacks in ways I found hard to tolerate. For example, they raised American flags in thousands of
places. The flag's new mass presence in the windows of commercial establishments and private residences shaped a feeling
of patriotic suffering.[15] It felt as if the high-pitched mourning
was orchestrated by the government. Americans were victims
and they needed to stick together, focusing aggression on outsiders. It did not help that street vendors hawked their wares to

tourists and residents with law enforcement symbols littered on hats, shirts, and trinkets. The shameless selling of the 9/11 tragedy seemed just as offensive as the president's appeal two weeks after the attacks for the population to resume traveling. Where should they go? "Get down to Disney World in Florida. Take your families and enjoy life, the way we want it to be enjoyed."[16]

Living in New York City had become a daily burden. All the raw pain and raw patriotism expressed by people who uncharacteristically wore their emotions on their sleeves. As I sat in a diner with a friend and lamented the rise of hate crimes against innocent Arab Americans, someone nearby overheard me and ruminated that I support the terrorists. It was an easy choice to move away from Ground Zero.

Memorials and Commemorations

The official 9/11 Memorial at Ground Zero opened on the 10th anniversary. It occupied half of the site with 400 white oak trees at a main plaza and two square, below-ground reflecting pools with waterfalls where the original Towers stood. The reflecting pools were bordered by bronze panels containing the names of all those killed in the attacks. Architect Michael Arad envisioned a "stoic, defiant, and compassionate" design which he titled, "Reflecting Absence." Indeed, the below-ground pools provided a haunting reminder of the Towers and their absence now was clear. There was nothing in the space. One did reflect on what had been there: the structures themselves; the people inside; and how the Towers came down. Arad's design was selected in an open competition which drew 5,201 entries. That it took a decade to build at a cost of $700 million (including the museum) testified to the complexity of the project and competing interests, which fought over several issues such as the placement of victim names. Should official power—police and firefighters—be given special placement and have their insignias included? Were their lives more valuable than others? Was there a "hierarchy of loss"? Arad's initial plan listed the names randomly so "no attempt is made to impose order on the suffering." The final design, responding to complaints of victim families, listed the names according to their floor location in each Tower. Official emergency responders were grouped together without any special symbols.[17]

At the anniversary, the framing of which leaders got to be on the stage at Ground Zero and what they might say became a topic of great significance. New York Mayor Michael Bloomberg, who designed the ceremony, urged Presidents Obama and Bush, as well as other elected leaders including Giuliani, not to give political speeches but simply read quotations and poems to commemorate the day, as well as the names of 9/11 victims. "This cannot be political," Bloomberg said. "No speeches whatsoever. It's not an appropriate thing."[18] Did the leaders follow this advice? Yes. Obama read religious passages. Bush read a letter from President Abraham Lincoln during the Civil War.

The Obama administration also carefully orchestrated the conduct of federal officials around the nation. It issued special guidelines, "9/11 Anniversary Planning," to shape the tone and content of political expression. The administration promoted three themes. First, government officials should memorialize those who died in the attacks. Second, they should thank the intelligence and homeland security community (FBI, CIA, NSA, and DHS). Third, they should warn Americans to continue to be on alert for another attack. These themes supported the official narrative of a nation at war. The Obama administration also carefully controlled sentiment about the Islamic enemy by telling federal agency officials to "minimize references to al Qaeda."[19] U.S. statements about the terrorist organization would be left to the president and other top officials.

The Ground Zero site became one of the most surveilled public spaces in the nation with about 400 closed-circuit cameras projecting live feeds to a nearby NYPD command center. A computer system analyzed the video images to detect threats, such as unattended bags. Analytical software also scanned faces in the crowd to identify known terrorist or criminal subjects. In a related security/control development of an even more ominous dimension, the NYPD planned to install cameras, radiation detectors, and license-plate readers at all 16 bridges and four tunnels traversed by vehicles that enter lower Manhattan.[20] While this mass surveillance might help to deter terrorism, its wider impact on the civic and political environment seemed enormous. Who can really enjoy a city encased in what authorities called a "ring of steel"? Overall, the NYPD planted about 3,000 cameras in lower Manhattan.[21]

Tens of thousands of Americans took part in the federally recognized 9/11 Day of Observance and Remembrance on the anniversary making it one of the biggest community and charitable activity dates in U.S. history. The patriotic "good deeds" included corporate donations and an effort prior to the day to restore the specially designated "9/11 National Flag"—a 30' x 20' flag that stood at the Twin Towers site and was partly destroyed during the attacks. The Flag had made a journey across the nation to allow local "service heroes" in all 50 states to stitch the stripes as part of a restoration project. The fully restored flag became part of the permanent collection of the Ground Zero museum.[22]

How was Islam viewed at the anniversary? It would be simplistic to suggest it only was demonized. The *Washington Post* published a sympathetic treatment of Arab-Americans and Muslims in a series titled: "Under Suspicion." The editors wrote: "A decade after the Sept. 11 attacks, the Washington Post examines the struggle by Muslims to reconcile their American identity with their faith."[23] A month before the anniversary, Obama invited Muslim-American leaders to the White House for an *iftar* dinner to break the Ramadan fast. His speech to the group emphasized that Muslim-Americans also suffered/died as workers at the Twin Towers and as innocent passengers on the airplanes.[24]

There were a few a dissenting voices at the anniversary criticizing American hegemony. Not at Ground Zero itself, but a few miles away a large "Peace Story Quilt" went on display at the Metropolitan Museum of Art. Artist Faith Ringgold supervised young students making the quilt asking, "What will you do for peace?"[25] Meanwhile, more than a dozen progressive groups in New York City held community hearings ("Unheard Voices of 9/11") to discuss the impact of the attacks on Muslim,

Arab, Sikh, and South Asian communities. These groups told "stories of discrimination" as well as their experiences of being victimized by bullying and hate crimes.[26] The American Civil Liberties Union (ACLU) helped organize a rally with the theme, "Our Strength is Our Diversity," and a panel discussion on the "Meaning of 9/11": "What did it show us about who we are, and who we want to be? How can we best move forward with rebuilding, healing and revitalizing our city?"[27]

The city's large universities also participated in memoralization. At the Graduate Center of the City University of New York (CUNY), the American Social History Project oversaw the largest public digital archive of the attacks. By 2011, they collected more than 150,000 digital objects, including more than 40,000 first-hand stories and 15,000 images.[28] At Columbia University, the September 11 Oral History Narrative and Memory Project interviewed about 600 survivors to generate a "living memory." The Project collected some of these interviews into a book, *After the Fall*. The editors noted that they were less interested in the "national" narrative promoted by authorities, which included the slogan "America at War," than the narratives of local people who responded in relatively unconditioned ways.[29] The 10th anniversary also inspired more than a dozen books of reminiscences by New Yorkers.[30]

More broadly, the nation's cultural expression (both high and low) seemed obsessed with the event. The critic Edward Rothstein noted: "It seems as if every cultural institution, television network and book publisher feels duty-bound to produce some sort of Sept. 11 commemoration. Is there a precedent for this almost compulsive variety show about an attack on a nation's people? No examples suggest themselves."[31]

Asking the Wrong Questions

The leaders of the official 9/11 Commission issued a follow-up report at the anniversary asserting that the nation still was not safe. The American government had not made sufficient progress on about one-quarter of the Commission's original security recommendations.[32] This assessment became part of a popular discourse that asked many questions in remembering the attack. The most popular query—"Are we safer?"—was rooted in false scare politics. Overall, violence from terrorism was negligible. Few Americans suffered as a result of political violence, as opposed to other forms of violence and exploitation. We should be asking: How much of the American tradition of political freedom has been sacrificed? Instead of praising the government (and specifically the intelligence community) for preventing another terrorist attack, the population should be worried about the level of political spying imbedded in the society. Whose interests are being served by this spying? How far has the surveillance state progressed and where is it headed in the future?

In its original report, the 9/11 Commission recommended the establishment of a Civil Liberties Oversight Board as a check on the intelligence infrastructure. Should it come as a surprise that neither Bush nor Obama allowed it to function by making the requisite appointments?[33] This negligence was outstanding suggesting the executive branch under both Republican and Democratic leadership refused to provide effective oversight of government spying.

The second popular question became, "Did 9/11 change everything?" For many people, this was not a question but a slogan: They were certain "everything" in America had changed related to national security, accepting the official narrative of threats and safety. How shortsighted Americans seem to have become. They imbibed the popular refrain from 2001, "Nothing will ever be the same." This new view shaped popular understandings of politics with ominous implications for civil liberties and privacy. The society may never regain the already diminished level of civil liberties that existed prior to the September 11 attacks. Civil liberties usually are put under strain during wartime. Democratic and Republican leaders viewed the "war on terror" as a near permanent condition with no deadline or exit strategy. What were the limits of American power in this new environment?[34]

"To say the world changed on September 11, 2001, is both a tired cliché and an absolute truth," the editors of the *Atlantic* monthly magazine wrote in a special feature on the anniversary.[35] In a sense, the evaluation of "change" in society was unusual for popular discourse. It was an historical inquiry but the historical frame was limited. The society evaluated change over only a ten-year period (2001-2011). America seemed to forget the persistent insecurity created during the Cold War—now 20 years in the past. Indeed, the post-9/11 world was much safer in terms of facing the threat of total nuclear war. While President Bush in particular talked at length about the threat posed by Weapons of Mass Destruction (WMD), the danger to the homeland still did not rise to the level of a nuclear exchange in a hostile bipolar world. By contrast, President Obama seemed to downplay WMD. When asked about the prospect of future terrorist attacks, Obama could say that a single person—a "lone wolf"—acting alone was more likely to plan a small incident than a coordinated group intent on a major attack.[36]

There were some critical views. News commentator Rachel Maddow on MSNBC framed the discussion of the anniversary with the apt title: "Day of Destruction, Decade of War." What took place on a single day, without a follow-up, has had such a large impact. *Mother Jones* magazine published a special issue on the FBI's repressive investigatory practices. The cover copy read: "Exclusive! Terrorists for the FBI. Inside the secret network that surveils and entraps Americans. Ten terror plots directed by the feds. Anti-war agitator or FBI spy?"[37] *Los Angeles Times* columnist Ken Dilanian also referenced FBI (and NSA) domestic snooping. "In one of the biggest changes to American life since the 2001 terrorist attacks, the government now collects vast quantities of information about its citizens. . . . Thanks to new laws and technologies, authorities track and eavesdrop on Americans as they never could before, hauling in billions of bank records, travel receipts and other information."[38]

In the *Washington Post*, the liberal opinion writers E.J. Dionne Jr., Eugene Robinson, Kathleen Parker, and Michael Lind urged a change to the endless era of war. "The last decade was a detour that left our nation weaker, more divided and less certain of itself," Dionne noted. "In the flood of anniversary commentary, notice how often the term 'the lost decade' has been invoked."[39]

Robinson pointed to the wasting of resources—hundreds of billions of dollars poured into the "sinkhole of perpetual war."[40] Parker reflected on negative changes to the American psyche. The attacks "released a free-ranging hysteria that has contaminated our interactions ever since....The event was so cataclysmic and horrifying that it caused a sort of breakdown in the American constitution."[41] Of course, America's personality or soul is not a single composition but differs by race, ethnicity, class, and gender background. The idea of a single American character long has been contested in historical scholarship. Lind smartly posed a counterfactual question: What would America be like today if 9/11 never happened? One can speculate widely but at least one conclusion seemed certain: "Without the catalyst of the attacks, Congress would not have undertaken the greatest reorganization of the national security bureaucracy since the Truman years."[42]

During the "lost decade," government leaders falsely framed the so-called "trade-off" between liberty and security. That is, people were told they have to give up civil liberties to gain greater security from threats. The trade-off equation was misleading. To begin with, there was the efficacy question: Few studies evaluate the extent to which new surveillance systems are effective in maintaining security. Moreover, who sacrificed and for what purposes? Why did the mass population have to sacrifice their rights? Were there other ways to achieve both security and liberty? A very important issue rarely debated concerned whose interests benefit from new surveillance systems. It has been noted that the evolving technology industry for the surveillance society has become part of a neoliberal political framework generating vast private market profits for large firms. Here, as elsewhere, private profit helped to frame national security policies. What if popular democratic participation helped in the governance of surveillance systems? Lastly, the media rarely asked about the root causes of terrorism or the new types of inequality and segregation created by surveillance systems.[43]

A few people posed a big question, "What is the meaning of 9/11"? Unfortunately, a popular response too often was small-minded. Former New York governor George Pataki, who served in office in 2001, told *Fox News* television that people wanted to kill Americans and the nation needed aggressively to defend itself against enemies. Why the foreign anger at Americans? The U.S. has an "outspoken belief in freedom," Pataki said. "We were attacked because of American exceptionalism—because of what we stand for in the globe and we have to be aware of that as we defend our freedom."[44] *Atlantic* magazine correspondent Jeffrey Goldberg echoed this view in a more sophisticated way writing that the meaning of 9/11 was radical Islam's embrace of murder: "A compulsive need to murder one's way to glory." While al Qaeda hated America both because of its freedoms and its policies, behind all the reasons was the group's "sociopathic core" and "hatred of humanity."[45] There is no meaningful way to argue with that view except to note it was used by power elites to advance hegemonic interests. Of course, mass murder of civilians was intolerable on any level. But even if we equate al Qaeda with Islamo-Fascism, the U.S. is dealing with a rag-tag army of bandits on the run, not a sovereign nation state. The transformation of U.S. society during the last decade has not been proportionate to the threat it faced.[46]

Where are All the Terrorists?

The threat of Islamic terrorism has not been nearly as severe as many expected. There hardly has been of clash of civilizations between the West and Islam. Fewer people overseas or at home joined jihadist movements than either the Bush or Obama administrations would like to acknowledge. Even the intelligence community admitted there was no clear model to explain why a very small segment of American Muslims are radicalized toward violence. In 2010, the Congressional Research Service reported: "Homegrown violent jihadist activity since 9/11 defies easy categorization. No workable general profile of domestic violent jihadists exists."[47] Only four terrorist incidents took place since 9/11 and none was on a large-scale. All perpetrators were "lone wolves" operating without wider social movement connections. By contrast, an estimated 1,000 to 2,000 American

Muslims engaged in violent jihad overseas (Afghanistan, Bosnia, and Chechnya) during the 1990s. And during the 1970s, when the FBI first began to adopt the terrorism framework for domestic policing, as many as 60 to 70 terrorist incidents, most of them bombings, occurred in the U.S. every year.[48]

So the period after 9/11 had been relatively calm in terms of domestic political violence. How many Americans die due to terrorism? In 2010, about 15,000 Americans were murdered in crimes; none as a result of terrorism. The U.S. homicide rate remained the highest of any affluent democracy.[49]

It was not because the FBI foiled potential attacks. Agents provocateur cases should not be counted as foiled attacks. They usually were fabrications of the government to create sensational news stories in efforts to discipline the population.

The point is not to be relativistic about violence. Rather, it is to acknowledge the low level of the problem and the great distortion of the issue by U.S. leaders who have used the issue to pursue their own narrow political objectives. The sociologist Charles Kurzman has several recommendations for dealing with radical Islamic terrorism. First, Americans should "turn down the volume on the terrorism debates." The exaggerated language of threats and enemies misrepresented the problem. Americans also should "give credit to Muslims as the primary defense against Islamist revolutionaries" and treat Muslim nations as allies, not enemies. Moreover, policymakers and the public should better "accept uncertainty" about the possibility of attacks without overreacting and seeking total forms of social control. Leaders can not master change in society. Terrorists wanted the U.S. to overreact to their violence. It became their strategy to cause the population to panic.[50]

The attitudes of American Muslims toward extremism were documented recently by the Pew Research Center. It found that 64 percent expressed little or no support for Islamic radicalism. Only six percent said a great deal of support for extremism existed in the American Muslim community. This contrasted with polls that find about 40 percent of the American population believed extremism thrives among this ethnic/religious group.[51]

Elites also must recognize that new surveillance technologies were not as effective as they would like. Whether the issue was biometrics or wiretapping, the so-called "bad guys" will find ways to evade surveillance.[52] Policymakers and the general public should not embrace a facile technological determinism in which myths of surveillance's superpowers overwhelm any ability to consider alternatives, or resistance.[53]

There are ways that people in everyday life can appropriate these technologies for purposes that government and corporations do not anticipate. One example is use of social media to organize collective action and build protest movements. Another way is nonprofessional or amateur surveillance. With her eye on Europe, Hille Koskela notes four stages in the amateur approach that developed since the 1980s.

> First, there was *passive acceptance* of surveillance, character-
> ized by the naïve, optimistic, often expressed public attitude,
> 'I have nothing to hide.' Second, the *critical approach* arose,
> fostering public discussion, research projects in social studies,
> and surveillance-critical attention in the media, art circles and
> NGO's. Third, various *counter-surveillance* practices were de-
> veloped by vigilant individuals, NGO's and artists. Presently,
> the scale has reached the fourth phase, which I call *hijacking
> surveillance*. People use various items of surveillance equip-
> ment for producing visual material for their own purposes
> with different motivations. This does not necessarily form any
> critical or other statements.[54]

In the U.S., the public in all likelihood has begun to inhabit phase two in this four-phase scheme. It is beyond passive acceptance developing a critical approach. Perhaps we can look forward to counter-surveillance organizing from below and citizen hijacking of technology to live with it on their own terms.[55]

After the tenth anniversary, the nation needed to regroup and reckon with all the recent changes. At the top of any agenda for social change, Americans should demand reform of FBI political policing practices which have proved detrimental to a robust, public expressive culture. The people need to become "emergency responders" to rescue the rights of free speech and assembly threatened in the new surveillance society. The right to dissent in a democracy never should be endangered by the narrow objectives of official power.

Notes

1. "Obama Appeals to Americans to Rekindle Post-Sept. 11 Spirit of Unity, Seeks More Cooperation," *Washington Post*, Aug. 27, 2011.

2. Pew Research Center, "Muslim Americans: No Sign of Growth in Alienation or Support for Terrorism," Aug. 30, 2011, 2-3, www.people-press.org/2011/08/30/muslim-americans-no-signs-of-growth-in-alienation-or-support-for-extremism/?src=prc-headline.

3. "Obama's Outreach to Muslims is Limited at Home," *Washington Post*, Sept., 5, 2011.

4. Mark F. Giuliano, "The Post 9/11 FBI: The Bureau's Response to Evolving Threats," speech before the Washington Institute for Near East Policy Stein Program on Counterterrorism and Intelligence, April 14, 2011, http://www.fbi.gov/news/speeches/the-post-9-11-fbi-the-bureaus-response-to-evolving-threats.

5. ABC News Channel 8, Washington, DC, 5pm show, Sept. 4, 2011.

6. "Possible Al-Qaeda Plot against D.C., N.Y. Investigated," *Washington Post*, Sept. 8, 2011; "Hearing Rumors of a Plot, Cities Make Their Security Forces Seen," *New York Times*, Sept. 9, 2011.

7. "10 Years and a Diagnosis Later, 9/11 Demons Haunt Thousands," *New York Times*, Aug. 8. 2011. See also Karen M. Seeley, *Therapy After Terror: 9/11, Psychotherapists, and Mental Health* (New York: Cambridge University Press, 2008); Yuval Neria, Raz Gross, and Randall Marshall, *9/11: Mental Health in the Wake of Terrorist Attacks* (New York: Cambridge University Press, 2006); Paul R. Kimmel and Chris E. Stout, eds., *Collateral Damage: The Psychological Consequences of America's War on Terrorism* (Westport, CT: Praeger, 2006).

8. Robert Simpson, *9/11: The Culture of Commemoration* (Chicago: University of Chicago Press, 2006), 13-14.

9. "Poll in New York Finds Many Think Police are Biased," *New York Times*, March 16, 1999.

10. Quoted in Wayne Barrett and Dan Collins, *Grand Illusion: The Untold Story of Rudy Giuliani and 9/11* (New York: HarperCollins, 2006), 24.

11. Ibid., 250-258, 268-269; "Persistence of Multiple Illnesses in World Trade Center Rescue and Recovery Workers: A Cohort Study," *Lance*, 378 (September 1, 2011): 888-897.

12. "In the Crosshairs," *Village Voice*, Jan. 29, 2002; "Neighborhood Watch Enlisted in Terror War," *Washington Post*, March 7, 2002.

13. New York City Metropolitan Transit Authority, "If You See Something, Say Something," n.d., www.mta.info/mta/security/ (accessed Aug. 20, 2011).

14. "Citizen Involvement Key to Fighting Terrorism, says Napolitano," *Government Security News*, June 6, 2011, www.gsnmagazine. com/node/23542.

15. The chain store Walmart sold about 500,000 American flags within three days of 9/11. Daniel T. Rodgers, *Age of Fracture* (Cambridge: Belknap Press, 2011), 258.

16. Andrew J. Bacevich, "He Told Us to Go Shopping. Now the Bill is Due," *Washington Post*, Oct. 5, 2008.

17. "Architect and 9/11 Memorial Both Evolved Over the Years," *New York Times*, Sept. 1, 2011; "The Breaking of Michael Arad," *New York Magazine*, May 14, 2008; "Review: 9/11 Memorial in New York," *Washington Post*, Aug. 26, 2011.

18. "Obama and Bush to Visit New York for 9/11 Anniversary," *New York Times*, July 29, 2011.

19. "White House Issues Guidelines on Sept. 11 Observances," *New York Times*, Aug. 29, 2011.

20. "For 10th Anniversary of 9/11, Ground Zero will have Massive Police Presence, Stringent Security Measures," *Associated Press*, Aug. 7, 2011, www.masslive.com/news/index.ssf/2011/08/for_10th_anniversary_of_911_gr.html.

21. "Lower Manhattan 'Ring of Steel' to Have 3,000 Cameras by 9/11/11," CBSNewYork.com, July 29, 2011, www.newyork.cbslocal. com/2011/07/29/lower-manhattan-ring-of-steel-to-have-3000-cameras-by-91111/.

22. "For 10-Year Anniversary of 9/11, Plans for Largest Day of Charitable Activity in Nation's History Unveiled with Congressional Leaders at U.S. Capitol," Aug. 9, 2011, www.911dayofservice.org/ news_and_press/10-year-anniversary-911-plans-largest-day-charitable-activity-nation%E2%80%99s-history-unveil.

23. "Under Suspicion: Muslims in America," *Washington Post*, www. washingtonpost.com/muslims?hpid=z13, (accessed Aug. 20, 2011).

24. "Obama Hosts Muslim Leaders for Ramadan Iftar," *Washington Post*, Aug. 10, 2011.

25. "Remembering 9/11: 10th Anniversary Tributes and Memorials," *CityArts: New York's Review of Culture*, Aug. 2, 2011, 2, www. cityarts.info/2011/08/02/remembering-911-10th-anniversary-tributes-and-memorials/.

26. Emma Roderick, Bill of Rights Defense Committee, email to author, Aug. 19, 2011.

27. New York Civil Liberties Union to Ivan Greenberg, email, "Remembering Sept. 11," Aug. 22, 2011.

28. American Social History Project, September 11 Digital Archive, www./911digitalarchive.org/index.php (accessed Aug. 29, 2011).

29. Mary Marshall Clark, Peter Bearman, Catherine Ellis, and Stephan Drury Smith, eds., *After the Fall: New Yorkers Remember September 2001 and the Years that Followed* (New York: New Press, 2011), xv-xvi.

30. "Stories of 9/11 and Its Aftermath," *New York Times*, Aug. 28, 2011.

31. Edward Rothstein, "Amid the Memorials, Ambiguity and Ambivalence," *New York Times*, Sept. 2, 2011.

32. "9/11 Panel Says Action Plan Unfinished," *Wall Street Journal*, September 1, 2011.

33. "9/11 Privacy Board Fails to Meet," *Washington Times*, Aug. 30, 2011.

34. Andrew J. Bacevich, *The Limits of Power: The End of American Exceptionalism* (New York: Metropolitan Books, 2008).

35. "Ten Years Later, 9/11 and Its Aftermath," *Atlantic Monthly*, September 2011, http://www.theatlantic.com/special-report/9-11-ten -years-later/.

36. "Obama: 'Lone Wolf' Terror Attack More Likely than Major Coordinated Effort," HuffingtonPost, Aug. 17, 2011. http://www.huffingtonpost.com/2011/08/16/obama-lone-wolf-terror_n_928880.html.

37. "Terrorists for the FBI," *Mother Jones*, September/October 2011.

38. Ken Dilanian, "A Key Sept. 11 Legacy: More Domestic Surveillance," *Los Angeles Times*, Aug. 29, 2011.

39. E. J. Dionne, Jr., "Time to Leave 9/11 Behind," *Washington Post*, Sept. 7, 2011.

40. Eugene Robinson, "Post-9/11 Permanent State of War Should Have Ended Long Ago," *Washington Post*, Sept. 8, 2011.

41. Kathleen Parker, "An America That No Longer Knows Itself," *Washington Post*," Sept. 9, 2011.

42. Michael Lind, "A World Without 9/11: No President Obama, More China Trouble, Same Debt Crisis," *Washington Post*, Sept. 9, 2011.

43. Torin Monahan offers an excellent discussion of some of these issues. Monahan, "Questioning Surveillance and Security," in Monahan, ed., *Surveillance and Security: Technological Politics and Power in Everyday Life* (New York: Routledge, 2006), 1-26.

44. "George Pataki: This Administration Has Never Understood the Meaning of 9/11," *Fox News*, Aug. 31, 2011, www.foxnewsinsider.com/2011/08/31/george-pataki-this-administration-has-never-understood-the-meaning-of-911/.

45. Jeffrey Goldberg, "The Real Meaning of 9/11," *Atlantic*, Aug. 29, 2001, www.theatlantic.com/national/archive/2011/08/the-real-meaning-of-9-11/244120/.

46. For a wide-ranging analysis, see the special issue of *Radical History Review* 111 (Fall 2011), "Historicizing 9/11."

47. Congressional Research Service, "American Jihadist Terrorism: Combating a Complex Threat," Dec. 7, 2010, 2, www.fas.org/sgp/crs/terror/R41416.pdf.

48. Ibid., 7.

49. Jill Lepore, "Rap Sheet: Why is American History So Murderous?" *New Yorker*, Nov. 9, 2009; Charles Kurzman, "Muslim-American Terrorism since 9/11: An Accounting," Feb. 2, 2011, Triangle Center on Terrorism and Security, 3-4, www.sanford.duke.edu/centers/tcths/about/documents/Kurzman_Muslim-American_Terrorism_Since_911_An_Accounting.pdf.

50. Kurzman, *The Missing Martyrs: Why There are So Few Muslim Terrorists* (New York: Oxford University Press, 2011), 203-204. See also Mike German, *Thinking Like a Terrorist: Insights of a Former FBI Undercover Agent* (Dulles, VA: Potomac Books, 2007), 179-190; Gabriella Blum and Philip B. Heymann, *Laws, Outlaws, and Terrorists: Lessons from the War on Terrorism* (Cambridge: MIT Press, 2010).

51. Pew Research Center, "Muslim Americans," 1-3.

52. Kelly A. Gates: *Our Biometric Future: Facial Recognition Technology and the Culture of Surveillance* (New York: New York University Press, 2011); Susan Landau, *Surveillance or Security? The Risks Posed by New Wiretapping Technologies* (Baltimore: John Hopkins University Press, 2011).

53. Richard Maxwell, "Surveillance: Work, Myth, and Policy," *Social Text* 83 (Summer 2005): 9-13.

54. Hille Koskela, "Hijacking Surveillance: The New Moral Landscape of Amateur Photographing," in Katja Franko Aas, Helene Oppen Gundus, and Heidi Mork Lomell, eds., *Technologies of Insecurity: The Surveillance of Everyday Life* (New York: Routledge-Cavendish, 2009), 162.

55. Gary T. Marx provides some 11 suggestions for resisting surveillance in "A Tack in the Shoe: Neutralizing and Resisting the New Surveillance," *Journal of Social Issues* 59 May (2003): 369-390. See also Colin J. Bennett, *The Privacy Advocates: Resisting the Spread of Surveillance* (Cambridge: MIT Press, 2008).

Selected Bibliography

The Names of FBI Files Cited in the Book

William C. Sullivan
Donald E. Moore
W. Mark Felt
Alan Belmont
Robert G. Kunkel
*American Negro Labor Conference
New Left COINTELPRO
*"Stool Pigeons or Loyal Citizens?"
*"Pretexts and Cover Techniques"
*"Unusual Investigative Techniques"
Gerald R. Ford
*Communist Infiltration of the FBI
*Security of Telephone Services, 1952-1995
Clarence M. Kelley
*Confidential File Room 6527
*"Smear Campaign Against the FBI"
*"The Struggle Against Lawlessness"
Women's Trade Union League
*Sacco-Vanzetti
*Bonus Army (BEF)
'John L. Lewis
Plant Informant Program
Walter Cronkite

*Walter Winchell
Henry Steele Commager
*"The FBI in Our Open Society"
*Howard Zinn
*Art Buchwald
Book Review FBI File
Magazine Subscriptions FBI File
*The Nation
Dissent
*The Daily Worker
*Village Voice
*Ramparts
off our backs
Radical America
Journal of Negro History
*RIDS FOIA BUZZ
*William Albertson
Irving Howe
L. Patrick Gray
Samuel Eliot Morison
Richard Hofstadter
Alan Nevins
John Hope Franklin
C. Vann Woodward
Herbert G. Gutman
William Appleman Williams
Warren Susman
*Employee Suggestion
Socialist Scholars Conference
*Do Not Contact
*"Extremists Attack the Courts"
Watergate
John P. Mohr
October Plan
*Scott Crow
*Terrorist Photo Album
Note: Asterisk denotes files posted online. (See www.Governmentattic.
org. or www.fbi.gov./foia/.) Most other files are in the author's pos-
session.

Aas, Katja Franko, Helene Oppen Gundus, and Heidi Mork Lomell, eds. *Technologies of Insecurity: The Surveillance of Everyday Life*. New York: Routledge-Cavendish, 2009.

Abelove, Henry, et al. *Visions of History*. New York: Pantheon Books, 1983.

Abt, John J., with Michael Myerson. *Advocate and Activist: Memoirs of an American Communist Lawyer*. Urbana: University of Illinois Press, 1993.

Abramson, Albert. *The History of Television, 1942 to 2000*. Jefferson, NC: McFarland, 2007.

Alinsky, Saul. *John L. Lewis: An Unauthorized Biography*. New York: Vintage Books, 1970.

Alwood, Edward. *Dark Days in the Newsroom: McCarthyism Aimed at the Press*. Philadelphia: Temple University Press, 2007.

Andrews, Ernst, ed. *Legacies of Totalitarian Language in the Discourse Culture of the Post-Totalitarian Era*. Lanham: Lexington Books, 2011.

Andrews, Lori. *I Know Who You Are and Saw What You Did: Social Networks and the Death of Privacy*. New York: New Press, 2012.

Aronson, James. *The Press and the Cold War*. New York: Bobbs-Merrill, 1970.

Arsenault, Raymond, ed. *Crucible of Liberty: 200 Years of the Bill of Rights*. New York: New Press, 1991.

Aucoin, James L. *The Evolution of American Investigative Journalism*. Columbia: University of Missouri, 2005.

Austin, Curtis J. *Up Against the Wall: Violence in the Making and Unmaking of the Black Panther Party*. Fayetteville: University of Arkansas, 2006.

Babson, Steve, Dave Riddle, and David Elsila. *The Color of Law: Ernie Goodman, Detroit, and the Struggle for Labor and Civil Rights*. Michigan: Wayne State University Press, 2010.

Bacevich, Andrew J. *The Limits of Power: The End of American Exceptionalism*. New York: Metropolitan Books, 2008.

Ball, Howard. *Bush, the Detainees, and the Constitution: The Battle over Presidential Power in the War on Terror*. Lawrence: University Press of Kansas, 2007.

Ball, Kristie, and Frank Webster, eds. *The Intensification of Surveillance: Crime, Terrorism and Warfare in the Information Age*. Sterling, VA: Pluto Press, 2003.

Bamford, James. *The Shadow Factory: The Ultra-Secret NSA from 9/11 to the Eavesdropping on America*. New York: Doubleday, 2008.

Barber, Lucy G. *Marching on Washington: The Forging of an American Political Tradition.* Berkeley: University of California Press, 2002.

Barrett, Wayne, and Dan Collins. *Grand Illusion: The Untold Story of Rudy Giuliani and 9/11.* New York: HarperCollins, 2006.

Batvinis, Raymond J. *The Origins of FBI Counterintelligence.* Lawrence: University of Kansas Press, 2007.

Bennett, Colin J. *The Privacy Advocates: Resisting the Spread of Surveillance.* Cambridge: MIT Press, 2008.

Berger, Dan. *Outlaws of America: The Weather Underground and the Politics of Solidarity.* Oakland: AK Press, 2005.

Berman, Jerry J. "FBI Charter Legislation: The Case for Prohibiting Domestic Intelligence Investigations." *University of Detroit Journal of Urban Law* 55 (Summer 1977): 1041-1077.

Bernhard, Nancy. *Television News and Cold War Propaganda, 1947-1960.* Cambridge: Harvard University Press, 1999.

Bernstein, Irving. *The Lean Years: A History of the American Worker, 1920-1933.* New York: Houghton Mifflin, 1970.

Blum, Gabriella, and Philip B. Heymann. *Laws, Outlaws, and Terrorists: Lessons from the War on Terrorism.* Cambridge: MIT Press, 2010.

Boghosian, Heidi. *The Policing of Political Speech: Constraints on Mass Dissent in the U.S.* New York: National Lawyers Guild, 2010.

Bovard, James. *Terrorism and Tyranny: Trampling Freedom, Justice and Peace to Rid the World of Evil.* New York: Palgrave Macmillan, 2003.

Boykoff, Jules. *Beyond Bullets: The Suppression of Dissent in the United States.* Oakland: AK Press, 2007.

Bozell III, L. Brent. *Weapons of Mass Distortion: The Coming Meltdown of the Liberal Media.* New York: Crown Forum, 2004.

Brin, David. *The Transparent Society: Will Technology Force Us to Choose Between Privacy and Freedom?* New York: Basic Books, 1999.

Brown, Cynthia, ed. *Lost Liberties: Ashcroft and the Assault on Personal Freedom.* New York: New Press, 2003.

Brown, Julia. *I Testify: My Years as an Undercover Agent for the FBI.* Boston: Western Islands, 1966.

Brown, Nikki, and Barry Stentiford, eds. *The Jim Crow Encyclopedia.* Westport: Greenwood Press, 2008.

Buhle, Paul, ed. *History and the New Left: Madison, Wisconsin, 1950-1970.* Philadelphia: Temple University Press, 1989.

Buhle and Edward Rice-Maximin. *William Appleman Williams: The Tragedy of Empire.* New York: Routledge, 1995.

Buitrago, Ann Mari, and Leon Andrew Immerman. *Are You Now or Have You Ever Been in the FBI Files?* New York: Grove Press, 1981.

Campbell, Craig, and Fredrik Logevall. *America's Cold War: The Politics of Insecurity.* Cambridge, MA: Harvard University Press, 2009.

Carnevale, Nancy C. "No Italian Spoken for the Duration of the War": Language, Italian-American Identity, and Cultural Pluralism in the World War II Years," *Journal of American Ethnic History* 22 (Spring, 2003): 3-33.

Chang, Nancy. *Silencing Political Dissent.* New York: Seven Stories Press, 2002.

Charns, Alexander. *Cloak and Gavel: FBI Wiretaps, Bugs, Informers, and the Supreme Court.* Urbana: University of Illinois Press, 1992.

Chevigny, Paul. *Cops and Rebels: A Study of Provocation.* New York: Pantheon Books, 1972.

Chomsky, Noam, et al, *The Cold War and the University: Toward an Intellectual History of the Postwar Years.* New York: New Press, 1997.

Chomsky and Edward Herman. *The Washington Connection and Third World Fascism: The Political Economy of Human Rights.* Boston: South End Press, 1979.

Churchill, Ward, and Jim Vander Wall. *The COINTELPRO Papers: Documents From the FBI's Secret War Against Dissent in the United States.* Boston: South End Press, 1990.

———. *Agents of Repression: The FBI's Secret Wars Against the Black Panther Party and the American Indian Movement.* Boston: South End Press, 1988.

Churchill. "From the Pinkertons to the PATRIOT Act: The Trajectory of Political Policing in the United States, 1870 to the Present. " *CR: The New Centennial Review* 4 (Spring 2004): 1-72.

Clark, Mary Marshall, Peter Bearman, Catherine Ellis, and Stephan Drury Smith, eds. *After the Fall: New Yorkers Remember September 2001 and the Years that Followed.* New York: New Press, 2011

Cleaver, Kathleen, and George Katsiaficas, eds. *Liberation, Imagination, and the Black Panther Party.* New York: Routledge, 2001.

Cole, David, and Jules Lobel. *Less Safe, Less Free: Why America is Losing the War on Terror.* New York: The New Press, 2007.

Cook, Fred J. *Maverick: Fifty Years of Investigative Reporting.* New York: G. P. Putnam, 1984.

Coulson, Danny O., and Elaine Shannon. *No Heroes: Inside the FBI's Secret Counter-Terror Force.* New York: Pocket Books, 1999.

Crow, Scott. *Black Flags and Windmills: Hope, Anarchy, and the Common Ground Collective.* Oakland: PM Press, 2011.

Crowe, David M., ed. *Crimes of State Past and Present: Government-Sponsored Atrocities and International Legal Responses.* London: Routledge, 2011.

Cull, Nicholas J. *The Cold War and the United States Information Agency: American Propaganda and Public Diplomacy, 1945-1989.* New York: Cambridge University Press, 2009.

Culleton, Claire A. *Joyce and the G-Men: J. Edgar Hoover's Manipulation of Modernism.* New York: Palgrave Macmillan, 2004.

Culleton and Karen Leick, eds. *Modernism on File: Modern Writers, Artists, and the FBI 1920-1950.* New York: Palgrave Macmillan, 2008.

Cunningham, David. *There's Something Happening Here: The New Left, the Klan and FBI Counterintelligence.* Berkeley: University of California Press, 2004.

Davidson-Smith, G. *Combating Terrorism.* London: Routledge, 1990.

Davis, Darren W. *Negative Liberty: Public Opinion and the Terrorist Attacks on America.* New York: Russell Sage Foundation, 2007.

Davis, James Kirkpatrick. *Assault on the Left: The FBI and the Sixties Antiwar Movement.* Westport: Greenwood Press, 1997.

———. *Spying on Americans: The FBI's Domestic Counterintelligence Program.* New York: Praeger, 1999.

Dellums, Ronald V., and H.L. Halterman, *Lying Down with Lions: A Public Life from the Streets of Oakland to the Halls of Power.* New York: Random House, 2000.

Diamond, Sigmund. *Compromised Campus: The Collaboration of Universities with the Intelligence Community, 1945-1955.* New York: Oxford University Press, 1992.

Dickson, Paul, and Thomas B. Allen. *The Bonus Army: An American Epic.* New York: Walker and Co., 2004.

Diffie, Whitfield, and Susan Landau. *Privacy on the Line: The Politics of Wiretapping and Encryption.* Cambridge: MIT Press, 2007.

DiMaggio, Anthony R. *Mass Media, Mass Propaganda: Examining American News in the "War on Terror."* Lanham, MD: Lexington Books, 2008.

Donner, Frank J. *The Age of Surveillance: The Aims and Methods of America's Political Intelligence System.* New York: Random House, 1980.

———. *Protectors of Privilege: Red Squads and Police Repression in Urban America.* Berkeley: University of California Press, 1990.

Downey, Kirstin. *The Woman Behind the New Deal: The Life and Legacy of Frances Perkins.* New York: Anchor Books, 2010.

Drabble, John. "Fighting Black Power-New Left Coalitions: Covert FBI Campaigns and American Cultural Discourse." *European Journal of American Culture* 27 (July 2008): 65-91.

Dubofsky, Melvyn, and Warren R. Van Tine. *John L. Lewis: A Biography.* Urbana: University of Illinois Press, 1986.

Dudziak, Mary L., ed. *September 11 in History: A Watershed Moment?* Durham: Duke University Press, 2003.

Durr, Kenneth D. *Behind the Backlash: White Working-Class Politics in Baltimore, 1940-1980.* Chapel Hill: University of North Carolina Press, 2003.

Eisenback, David. *Gay Power: An American Revolution.* New York: Carroll and Graf, 2006.

Elliff, John T. *The Reform of FBI Intelligence Operations.* Princeton: Princeton University Press, 1979.

Emery, Fred. *Watergate: The Corruption of American Politics and the Fall of Richard Nixon.* New York: Touchstone Books, 1995.

Etzioni, Amitai. *The Limits of Privacy.* New York: Basic Books, 1999.

Fariello, Griffen. *Red Scare: Memories of the American Inquisition.* New York: Avon Books, 1995.

Farson, Stuart, and Mark Phythian, eds. *Commissions of Inquiry and National Security.* Santa Barbara: Praeger, 2011.

Feldstein, Mark. *Poisoning the Press: Richard Nixon, Jack Anderson, and the Rise Washington's Scandal Culture.* New York: Farrar, Straus and Giroux, 2010.

Fernandez, Luis A. *Policing Dissent: Social Control and the Anti-Globalization Movement.* Piscataway: Rutgers University Press, 2008.

Felt, W. Mark. *The FBI Pyramid From the Inside.* New York: Putnam, 1979.

Felt and John O'Connor. *A G-Man's Life: The FBI, Being 'Deep Throat,' and the Struggle for Honor in Washington.* Cambridge: Public Affairs, 2006.

Finnegan, Lisa. *No Questions Asked: News Coverage since 9/11.* Westport: Praeger, 2007.

Flaherty, David. *Protecting Privacy in Surveillance Societies.* Westport: Greenwood Press, 1989.

Fordham, Benjamin O. *Building the Cold War Consensus: The Political Economy of U.S. National Security Policy, 1945-1951.* Ann Arbor: University of Michigan Press, 1998.

Fox, Stephen. *Fear Itself: Inside the FBI Roundup of German Americans during World War II.* New York: iUniverse, 2007.

Frank, C. E. S., ed. *Dissent and the State.* Toronto: Oxford University Press, 1989.

Freeman, Alexia P. "Unscheduled Departures: The Circumvention of Just Sentencing for Police Brutality." *Hastings Law Journal* 47 (1996): 677-777.

Gage, Beverly. "Terrorism and the American Experience: A State of the Field," *Journal of American History* 98 (June 2011): 74-84.
———. *The Day Wall St. Exploded: A Story of America in its First Age of Terror.* New York: Oxford, 2009.
Gall, Gilbert J. *Pursuing Justice: Lee Pressman, the New Deal and the CIO.* Albany: SUNY Press, 1999.
Garfinkel, Simson. *Database Nation: The Death of Privacy in the 21st Century.* Cambridge: O'Reilly, 2000.
Garment, Leonard. *In Search of Deep Throat: The Greatest Political Mystery of Our Time.* New York: Basic Books, 2000.
Garrow, David. *The FBI and Martin Luther King, Jr: From "Solo" to Memphis.* New York: W.W. Norton, 1981.
———. *Bearing the Cross: Martin Luther King, Jr., and the Southern Christian Leadership Conference.* New York: HarperCollins, 1988.
———. "FBI Political Harassment and FBI Historiography: Analyzing Informants and Measuring Their Effects." *The Public Historian* 4 (Fall 1988): 5-18.
Gates, Kelly A. *Our Biometric Future: Facial Recognition Technology and the Culture of Surveillance.* New York: New York University Press, 2011.
Gentry, Curt. *J. Edgar Hoover: The Man and the Secrets.* New York: Norton, 1991.
German, Mike. *Thinking Like a Terrorist: Insights of a Former FBI Undercover Agent.* Dulles, VA: Potomac Books, 20007.
Ginger, Ann Fagan, and Eugene M. Tobin, eds. *The National Lawyers Guild: From Roosevelt through Reagan.* Philadelphia: Temple University Press, 1988.
Gitlin, Todd. *The Sixties: Years of Hope, Days of Rage.* New York: Bantam, 1993.
Glick, Brian. *War At Home: Covert Action Against U.S. Activists and What We Can Do About It.* Boston: South End Press, 1989.
Goldberg, Chad Alan. *Citizens and Paupers: Relief, Rights, and Race from the Freedmen's Bureau to Workfare.* Chicago: University of Chicago Press, 2007.
Goldsmith, Jack. *The Terror Presidency: Law and Judgment Inside the Bush Administration.* New York: W.W. Norton, 2007.
Goldstein, Robert Justin. *American Blacklist: The Attorney General's List of Subversive Organizations.* Lawrence: University of Kansas, 2008.
———. *Political Repression in Modern America: From 1870 to 1976.* Urbana: University of Illinois Press, 2001.

———. "The FBI and American Politics Textbooks." *PS: Political Science and Politics* 18 (Spring 1985): 237-246.

Graff, Garrett M. *The Threat Matrix: The FBI At War in the Age of Global Terror.* New York: Little Brown and Co., 2011.

Gray, L. Patrick, III, with Ed Gray. *In Nixon's Web: A Year in the Crosshairs of Watergate.* New York: Times Books, 2008..

Greenberg, Ivan. *The Dangers of Dissent: The FBI and Civil Liberties since 1965.* Lanham, MD: Lexington Books, 2010.

———. "The FBI and the Making of the Terrorist Threat," *Radical History Review* 111 (Fall 2011): 35-50.

———. "Reagan Revives FBI Spying." Pp. 43-63 in *The 1980s: A Critical and Transitional Decade.* eds. Kimberly R. Moffitt and Duncan Campbell. Lanham, MD: Lexington Books, 2010.

———. "Federal Bureau of Investigation." Pp. 294-298 in *The Jim Crow Encyclopedia,* eds. Nikki Brown and Barry Stentiford. Westport: Greenwood Press, 2008.

Gurr, Ted Robert, ed., *Violence in America: Protest, Rebellion, Reform.* Vol. 2, London: Sage Publications, 1989.

Gutman, Herbert G., and Ira Berlin, eds. *Power and Culture: Essays on the American Working Class.* New York: The New Press, 1987.

Guttenplan, D. D. *American Radical: The Life and Times of I. F. Stone.* New York: Macmillan, 2009.

Haggerty, Kevin D., and Richard V. Ericson, eds., *The New Politics of Surveillance and Visibility.* Toronto: University of Toronto Press, 2006.

Harris, Shane. *The Watchers: The Rise of America's Surveillance State.* New York: Penguin Press, 2010.

Hendershot, Cynthia. *Anti-Communism and Popular Culture in Mid-Century America.* Jefferson, NC: McFarland and Co., 2003.

Hentoff, Nat. *The War on the Bill of Rights and the Gathering Resistance.* New York: Steven Stories Press, 2003.

Hershberger, Mary. *Jane Fonda's War: A Political Biography of An Antiwar Icon.* New York: W.W. Norton, 2005.

Herman, Edward S. and Gerry O'Sullivan. *The Terrorism Industry: The Experts and Institutions that Shape Our View of Terror.* New York: Pantheon Books, 1989.

Herzberg, Bob. *The FBI and the Movies: A History of the Bureau on Screen and Behind the Scenes in Hollywood.* Jefferson, NC: McFarland, 2007.

Hill, Robert A. ed. *The FBI's RACON: Racial Conditions in the United States during World War II.* Boston: Northeastern University Press, 1995.

Hilliard, David. *Huey: Spirit of a Panther*. New York: Basic Books, 2005.

Hogue, James F., and Gideon Rose. *How Did This Happen? Terrorism and the New War*. New York: Public Affairs, 2001.

Hutchinson, Allan, and Patrick Monahan, eds. *The Rule of Law: Ideal or Ideology*. Carswell, 1987.

Isserman, Maurice, and Michael Kazin. *America Divided: The Civil War of the 1960s*. New York: Oxford University Press, 2000.

Jayko, Margaret, ed. *FBI on Trial: The Victory of the Socialist Workers Party Suit Against Government Spying*. New York: Pathfinder Press, 1988.

Jeffreys, Diarmuid. *The Bureau: Inside the Modern FBI*. New York: Houghton Mufflin, 1995.

Jeffrey-Jones, Rhodri. *The FBI: A History*. New Haven: Yale University Press, 2007.

Jerome, Fred. *The Einstein File: J. Edgar Hoover's Secret War Against the World's Most Famous Scientist*. New York: St. Martin's Press, 2002.

Jezer, Marty. *Abbie Hoffman: American Rebel*. New Brunswick: Rutgers University Press, 1993.

Johnson, Christopher H. *Maurice Sugar: Law, Labor and the Left in Detroit, 1912-1950*. Detroit: Wayne State University Press, 1988.

Johnson, David K. *The Lavender Scare: The Cold War Persecution of Gays and Lesbians in the Federal Government*. Chicago: University of Chicago Press, 2004.

Johnson, Loch K. *A Season of Inquiry: The Senate Intelligence Investigation*. Lexington: University Press of Kentucky, 1985.

Johnson, Marilyn S. *Street Justice: A History of Police Violence in New York City*. New York: Beacon Press, 2004.

Kazin, Michael. *American Dreamers: How the Left Changed a Nation*. New York: Alfred A. Knopf, 2011.

Keen, Mike Forrest. *Stalking the Sociological Imagination: J. Edgar Hoover's Surveillance of American Sociology*. Westport: Greenwood Press, 1999.

Kelley, Clarence M., with James Kirkpatrick Davis. *Kelley: The Story of an FBI Director*. Kansas City: Andrews, McMeel, and Parker, 1987.

Keller, William W. *The Liberals and J. Edgar Hoover: Rise and Fall of a Domestic Intelligence State*. Princeton: Princeton University Press, 1989.

Kessler, Ronald. *The FBI: Inside the World's Most Powerful Law Enforcement Agency*. New York: St. Martin's Press, 2003.

———. *The Secrets of the FBI*. New York: Crown Publishers, 2011.

Kimmel, Paul R., and Chris E. Stout, eds. *Collateral Damage: The Psychological Consequences of America's War on Terrorism*. Westport, CT: Praeger, 2006.

Kurzman, Charles. *The Missing Martyrs: Why There are So Few Muslim Terrorists*. New York: Oxford University Press, 2011.

Landau, Susan. *Surveillance or Security? The Risks Posed by New Wiretapping Technologies*. Baltimore: John Hopkins University Press, 2011.

Lapham, Lewis H. *Gag Rule: On the Suppression of Dissent and the Stifling of Democracy*. New York: Penguin Press, 2004.

Larabee, Ann. "Why Historians Should Exercise Caution When Using the Word 'Terrorism,'" *Journal of American History* 98 (June 2011): 106-110.

Leab, Daniel J. *I Was a Communist for the FBI: The Unhappy Life and Times of Matt Cvetic*. University Park, PA: Pennsylvania State University Press, 2000.

Levy, Guenter. *The Cause that Failed: Communism in American Political Life*. New York: Oxford University Press, 1990.

Leone, R.C., and Greg Anrig, eds. *Liberty Under Attack: The War on Our Freedoms in an Age of Terror*. New York: Public Affairs, 2007.

Lichtenstein, Nelson. *Walter Reuther: The Most Dangerous Man in Detroit*. New York: Basic Books, 1995.

Linden, A.A.A. Van Der, *A Revolt Against Liberalism: American Radical Historians, 1959-1976*. Amsterdam: Rodopi BV Editions, 1996.

Lobel, Jules. "The War on Terrorism and Civil Liberties." Pp. 25-48 in Thomas E. Baker and John F. Stack, eds. *At War with Civil Rights and Civil Liberties*. Lanham: Rowman and Littlefield, 2005.

Lopez, Ian F. Haney. *Racism on Trial: The Chicano Fight for Justice*. Cambridge: Harvard University Press, 2003.

Lorence, James J. *Organizing the Unemployed: Community and Union Activists in the Industrial Heartland*. Albany: SUNY Press, 1996.

Lowen, Rebecca S. *Creating the Cold War University: The Transformation of Stanford*. Berkeley: University of California Press, 1997.

Lyon, David. *Identifying Citizens: ID Cards as Surveillance*. Cambridge: Polity Press, 2009.

———. *Surveillance Studies: An Overview*. Cambridge: Polity Press, 2007.

———. *Surveillance After September 11*. Malden, MA: Blackwell Publishing, 2003.

———. *The Electronic Eye: The Rise of Surveillance Society*. Minneapolis: University of Minnesota Press, 1994.

Mackenzie, Angus. *Secrets: The CIA's War at Home*. Berkeley: University of California Press, 1997.

MacPherson, Myra. *All Governments Lie! The Life and Times of Rebel Journalist I. F. Stone*. New York: Scribner's, 2006.

Marks, Ronald. *Spying In America in the Post 9/11 World: Domestic Threat and the Need for Change*. Santa Barbara, CA: Praeger, 2010.

Marx, Gary T. *Undercover: Police Surveillance in America*. Berkeley: University of California Press, 1988.

——. "What's New About the 'New Surveillance'? Classifying for Change and Continuity," *Surveillance and Society* 1 (Late 2002): 9.

——. "A Tack in the Shoe: Neutralizing and Resisting the New Surveillance," *Journal of Social Issues* 59 May (2003): 369-390.

——. "Electric Eye in the Sky: Some Reflections on the New Surveillance and Popular Culture." Pp. 193-226 , in *Computers, Surveillance and Privacy*. David Lyon and Elia Zureik, eds. Minneapolis: University of Minnesota Press, 1996.

Matthiessen, Peter. *In the Spirit of Crazy Horse*. New York: Viking, 1991, 2nd ed.

Mattson, Kenin, *Intellectuals in Action: The Origins of the New Left and Radical Liberalism, 1945-1970*. Pennsylvania State University Press, 2002.

Matusow, Allen J. *The Unraveling of America: A History of Liberalism in the 1960s*. New York: Torchbooks, 1986.

McChesney, Robert W. *The Problem of the Media: U.S. Communication Politics in the 21st Century*. New York: Monthly Review Press, 2004.

McElvaine, Robert S. *The Great Depression: America, 1929-1941*. New York: Times Books, 1984.

McCormick, Charles H. *The Nest of Vipers: McCarthyism and Higher Education in the Mundel Affair, 1951-52*. Urbana: University of Illinois Press, 1989.

McKnight, Gerald D. *The Last Crusade: Martin Luther King, Jr., the FBI, and the Poor People's Campaign*. New York: Basic Books, 1998.

McMillian, John. *Smoking Typewriters: The Sixties Underground Press and the Rise of Alternative Media in America*. New York: Oxford University Press, 2011.

McMillian, John, and Paul Buhle, eds. *The New Left Revisited*. Philadelphia: Temple University Press, 2002.

Mitgang, Herbert. *Dangerous Dossiers: Exposing the Secret War against America's Greatest Authors*. New York: Donald I. Fine Books, 1988.

Monahan, Torin. *Surveillance in the Time of Insecurity*. New Brunswick, NJ: Rutgers University Press, 2010.

——. ed. *Surveillance and Security: Technological Politics and Power in Everyday Life*. New York: Routledge, 2006.

Morgan, Ted. *Reds: McCarthyism in Twentieth-Century America*. New York: Random House, 2004.

Nasaw, David. *The Chief: The Life of William Randolph Hearst*. Boston: Houghton Mifflin, 2000.

Nelson, Jill, ed. *Police Brutality: An Anthology*. New York: W.W. Norton, 2000.

Neria,Yuval, Raz Gross, and Randall Marshall. *9/11: Mental Health in the Wake of Terrorist Attacks*. New York: Cambridge University Press, 2006.

Nissenbaum, Helen. *Privacy in Context: Technology, Policy and the Integrity of Social Life*. Sanford, CA: Stanford Law Books, 2010.

Nacos, Brigitte L., Yaeli Bloch-Elkon, and Robert Y. Shapiro. *Selling Fear: Counterterrorism, the Media, and Public Opinion*. University of Chicago Press, 2011.

O'Harrow, Robert. *No Place to Hide*. New York: The Free Press, 2004.

Olmsted, Kathryn S. *Challenging the Secret Government: The Post-Watergate Investigations of the CIA and the FBI*. Chapel Hill: University of North Carolina Press, 1996.

O'Neill, William L. *A Bubble in Time: America During the Interwar Years, 1989-2001*. Chicago: Ivan R. Dee, 2009.

O'Reilly, Kenneth. *Hoover and the Un-Americans: The FBI, HUAC, and the Red Menace*. Philadelphia: Temple University Press, 1983.

———. *"Racial Matters": The FBI's Secret File on Black America, 1960-1972*. New York: The Free Press, 1989.

Pallitto, Robert M., and William G. Weaver. *Presidential Secrecy and the Law*. Baltimore: John Hopkins University Press, 2007.

Persico, Joseph E. *Edward R. Murrow: An American Original*. New York: McGraw-Hill, 1988.

Piven, Frances Fox, and Richard A. Cloward. *Poor People's Movements: How They Succeed, How They Fail*. New York: Vintage, 1979.

Polenberg, Richard. *Fighting Faiths: The Abrams Case, the Supreme Court and Free Speech*. New York: Viking, 1987.

Potter, Claire Bond. "Queer Hoover: Sex, Lies, and Political History," *Journal of the History of Sexuality* 15 (July 2006): 355-381.

Powers, Richard Gid. *Secrecy and Power: The Life of J. Edgar Hoover*. New York: The Free Press, 1987.

———. *Broken: The Troubled Past and Uncertain Future of the FBI*. New York: Simon and Schuster, 2004.

———. *G-Men: Hoover's FBI in American Popular Culture*. Carbondale: Southern Illinois University Press, 1983.

Pratt, William C. "Using FBI Records in Writing Regional Labor History." *Labor History* 33 (Fall 1992): 470-482.

Preston, William. *Aliens and Dissenters: The Federal Suppression of Radicals, 1903-1933*. Urbana: University of Illinois Press, 1994.

Price, David H. *Threatening Anthropology: McCarthyism and the FBI's Surveillance of Activist Anthropologists.* Durham: Duke University Press, 2004.

———. *Weaponizing Anthropology: Social Science in the Service of the Militarized State.* Oakland: AK Press, 2011.

Pulido, Laura. *Black, Brown, Yellow and Left: Radical Activism in Los Angeles.* Berkeley: University of California Press, 2006.

Rabinowitz, Victor. *Unrepentant Leftist: A Lawyer's Memoir.* Urbana: University of Illinois Press, 1996.

Reeves, Richard. *President Nixon: Alone in the White House.* New York: Simon and Schuster, 2001.

Revell, Oliver "Buck." *A G-Man's Journal.* New York: Pocket Books, 1998.

Richardson, Peter. *A Bomb in Every Issue: How the Short, Unruly Life of Ramparts Magazine Changed America.* New York: The New Press, 2009.

Ritchie, Donald A. *Reporting from Washington: The History of the Washington Press Corps.* New York: Oxford University Press, 2005.

Robins, Natalie. *Alien Ink: The FBI's War on Freedom of Expression.* New York: W. Morrow, 1992.

Rodgers, Daniel T. *Age of Fracture.* Cambridge: Belknap Press, 2011.

Rosen, Jeffrey. *The Unwanted Gaze: The Destruction of Privacy in America.* New York: Random House, 2000.

Rosen, Ruth. *The World Split Open: How the Modern Women's Movement Changed America.* New York: Penguin, 2001.

Rosswurm, Steve. *The FBI and the Catholic Church, 1935-1962.* Amherst: University of Massachusetts Press, 2009.

Rubin, Jerry. *Do It!* New York: Simon and Schuster, 1970.

Safire, William. *Before the Fall: An Inside View of the Pre-Watergate White House.* New York: Doubleday, 1974.

Sbardellati, John. "Brassbound G-Men and Celluloid Reds: The FBI's Search for Communist Propaganda in Wartime Hollywood," *Film History: An International Journal* 20 (2008): 412-436.

Schmidt, Regin. *Red Scare: FBI and the Origins of Anticommunism in the United States, 1919-1943.* Copenhagan: Museum Tusculanum Press, 2000.

Schorr, Daniel. *Come to Think of It: Notes on the Turn of the Millennium.* New York: Viking Press, 2007.

Schrecker, Ellen. *Many are the Crimes: McCarthyism in America.* Boston: Little Brown, 1998.

———. *No Ivory Tower: McCarthyism and the Universities.* New York: Oxford University Press, 1986.

Schultz, Bud, and Ruth Schultz. *The Price of Dissent: Testimonies to Political Repression in America.* Berkeley: University of California Press, 2001.

Shantz, Jeff, ed., *Law Against Liberty: The Criminalization of Dissent.* Lake Mary, FL: Vandeplas Publishing, 2011.

———, ed. *Protest and Punishment: The Repression of Resistance in the Era of Neoliberal Globalization.* Durham, NC: Carolina Academic Press, 2012.

Seale, Bobby. *Seize the Time: The Story of the Black Panther Party and Huey Newton.* Black Classic Press, 1970, 1995.

Seeley, Karen M. *Therapy After Terror: 9/11, Psychotherapists, and Mental Health.* New York: Cambridge University Press, 2008.

Shelden, Randall G. *Controlling the Dangerous Classes: A History of Criminal Justice in America.* Boston: Allyn and Bacon, 2007.

Shepard, Alicia C. *Woodward and Bernstein: Life in the Shadow of Watergate.* Hoboken: John Wiley and Sons, 2007.

Shipler, David K. *The Rights of the People: How Our Search for Safety Invades Our Liberties.* New York: Alfred A. Knopf, 2011.

Simpson, Christopher, ed. *Universities and Empire: Money and Politics in the Social Sciences During the Cold War.* New York: New Press, 1998.

Simpson, Robert. *9/11: The Culture of Commemoration.* Chicago: University of Chicago Press, 2006.

Skocpol, Theda, Peter B. Evans, and Dietrich Rueschemeyer, eds., *Bringing the State Back In.* New York: Cambridge University Press, 1985.

Solove, Daniel J. *Nothing to Hide: The False Tradeoff Between Privacy and Security.* New Haven: Yale University Press, 2011.

———. *The Digital Person: Technology and Privacy in the Information Age.* New York: New York University Press, 2004.

Sparrow, James T. *Warfare State: World War Two Americans and the Age of Big Government.* New York: Oxford University Press, 2011.

Stacks, John F. *Scotty: James B. Reston and the Rise and Fall of American Journalism.* Boston: Little, Brown and Co., 2003.

Staples, William G. *Everyday Surveillance: Vigilance and Visibility in Postmodern Life.* Lanham, MD: Rowman and Littlefield, 2000.

Staples, ed. *Encyclopedia of Privacy.* Westport, CT: Greenwood Press, 2007.

Streitmatter, Roger. *Voices of Revolution: The Dissident Press in America.* New York: Columbia University Press, 2001.

Stromquist, Shelton, ed. *Labor's Cold War: Local Politics in a Global Context.* Urbana: University of Illinois Press, 2008.

Sullivan, William C., with Bill Brown. *The Bureau: My Thirty Years in Hoover's FBI.* New York: W.W. Norton, 1979.

Sutzl, Wolfgang and Geoff Cox, eds. *Creating Insecurity: Art and Culture in the Age of Security.* Brooklyn, NY: Autonomedia, 2009.

Sykes, Charles J. *The End of Privacy: Personal Rights in the Surveillance Society.* New York: St. Martin's Press, 1999.

Theoharis, Athan G. *Abuse of Power: How Cold War Surveillance and Secrecy Policy Shaped the Response to 9/11.* Philadelphia: Temple University Press, 2011.

———. *The FBI and American Democracy: A Brief Critical History.* Lawrence: University of Kansas Press, 2004.

———, ed. *A Culture of Secrecy: The Government Versus the People's Right to Know.* Lawrence: University of Kansas Press, 1998.

———, ed. *From the Files of J. Edgar Hoover.* Chicago: Ivan R. Dee, 1991.

———, ed. *Beyond the Hiss Case: The FBI, Congress, and the Cold War.* Philadelphia: Temple University Press, 1982.

———, ed. *The FBI: A Comprehensive Reference Guide.* Phoenix: Oryx Press, 1999.

———, "Secrecy and Power: Unanticipated Problems in Researching FBI Files." *Political Science Quarterly* 119 (2004): 271-290.

Theoharis and John Stuart Cox. *The Boss: J. Edgar Hoover and the American Inquisition.* Philadelphia: Temple University Press, 1988.

Tuck, Jim. *McCarthyism and New York's Hearst Press: A Study of Roles in the Witch Hunt.* Lanham, MD: University Press of America, 1995.

Varon, Jeremy. *Bringing the War Home: The Weather Underground, the Red Army Faction, and Revolutionary Violence in the Sixties and Seventies.* Berkeley: University of California Press, 2004.

Walker, Samuel. *In Defense of American Liberties: A History of the ACLU.* New York: Oxford University Press, 1990.

Washburn, Patrick S. *A Question of Sedition: The Federal Government's Investigation of the Black Press during World War II.* New York: Oxford University Press, 1986.

Watters, Pat, and Stephan Gillers, eds. *Investigating the FBI.* Garden City, NY: Doubleday, 1973.

Weinstein, Allen. *Perjury: The Hiss-Chambers Case.* New York: Random House, 1978.

Welch, Michael. *Scapegoats of September 11: Hate Crimes and State Crimes in the War on Terror*. New Brunswick: Rutgers University Press, 2006.

Weiner, Jon. *Professors, Politics and Pop*. New York: Verso, 1994.

Weiner, Tim. *Enemies: A History of the FBI*. New York: Random House, 2012.

Whitaker, Reg. *The End of Privacy: How Total Surveillance is Becoming a Reality*. New York: The New Press, 2000.

Wilson, Richard Ashby, ed. *Human Rights in the "War on Terror."* New York: Cambridge University Press, 2005.

Winks, Robin W. *Cloak and Gown: Scholars in the Secret War, 1939-1961*. New York: William Morrow, 1987.

Zald, Mayer N., and John David McCarthy. eds. *The Dynamics of Social Movements*. Cambridge: Winthrop Publishers, 1979.

Zulaika, Joseba. *Terrorism: The Self-Fulfilling Prophecy*. Chicago: University of Chicago Press, 2009.

Zwerling, Philip, ed., *The CIA On Campus: Essays on Academic Freedom and the National Security State*. Jefferson, NC: McFarland, 2011.

Index